SAKHALIN

Sea of
Okhotsk

D1034772

Hokkaido

R I A

Harbin

Vladivostok

Changchun
xepingkai

ushun

Penchi

Pyong-
yang

38th PARALLEL

KOREA

Seoul

Chemulpo

Taegu

Hiroshima

Yellow
Sea

Nagasaki

gtao

Nagoya

Kyoto

Osaka

JAPAN

Tokyo

Yokohama

Sea of Japan

airen

hur

Shikoku

Kyushu

Pacific

Ocean

king-

Shanghai

East China
Sea

OKINAWA

HEKIANG

IEN

FORMOSA

outh China
Sea

ANTHONY SODARO & FRANK STOCKMAN

DANGER FROM THE EAST

Richard Lauterbach is a native New Yorker who has covered much of the globe since he joined the staff of *Life* in 1941. He was chief of the Moscow Bureau of *Time* and *Life* during 1943 and 1944 and visited Russia again in 1946. Out of these experiences came Mr. Lauterbach's first two widely-read books—*These Are the Russians* and *Through Russia's Back Door*. In 1945 and 1946, Mr. Lauterbach was Far East correspondent for *Life* and covered Japan, Korea and China. He wrote DANGER FROM THE EAST while on a Nieman Fellowship at Harvard and is now back at *Life*, reporting on the United States.

Books by

RICHARD E. LAUTERBACH

○

DANGER FROM THE EAST

THROUGH RUSSIA'S BACK DOOR

THESE ARE THE RUSSIANS

○

DANGER
FROM THE EAST

RICHARD E. LAUTERBACH

"If he fall in, good-night! or sink or swim:
Send danger from the east unto the west,
So honour cross it from the north to south,
And let them grapple: O! the blood more stirs
To rouse a lion than to start a hare."
—WILLIAM SHAKESPEARE
(*Henry IV, Part I*)

HARPER & BROTHERS PUBLISHERS
New York and London

11-7

DANGER FROM THE EAST

Copyright, 1946, 1947, by Richard E. Lauterbach
Printed in the United States of America

A-X

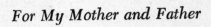

For My Mother and Father

ACKNOWLEDGMENTS

THE author is grateful to the Nieman Foundation for the Fellowship in Journalism at Harvard which made this project possible; to the Editors of *Life* for the Far Eastern assignment and for the leave of absence during which this book was written.

To Nancy Bean, the author owes a real debt for her considerable contribution in background research and in painstaking checking. Thanks are also due to Chinese, Korean and Japanese friends for their information and for their understanding translations; to the American correspondents in the Far East who are quoted in the text; to Frank Stockman for the jacket and to Frank Stockman and Anthony Sodaro for the end paper map; to Alice Weigel, particularly, and to Frances Holbrook for their assistance in preparation of the manuscript; and to the following for their many valued suggestions and corrections on all or parts of the manuscript: Edward C. Aswell, Nancy Bean, Simon M. Bessie, John K. Fairbank, Bettina Lauterbach, Jay Odell, Helen Staeuble, Armitage Watkins and Alice Weigel.

The views expressed in this book are only those of the author.

CONTENTS

INTRODUCTION

NOT LONG after V-J Day I flew across the Pacific to work as a correspondent in the Orient. Until then I had had very little contact with the Far East. My only previous travels in Asia were during the summer of 1944 when I visited the Central Asian Republics of the U.S.S.R. The bulk of my knowledge about Japan and China had been formed by unplanned reading added to the bits and scraps which a journalist, primarily concerned with European affairs, is likely to pick up. And like most Americans, I had the scantiest kind of information about Korea—and most of it turned out to be shockingly inaccurate.

My prejudices were probably as average as my knowledge. During the war I had been forced by circumstances to reside in the same Moscow hotel with Japanese correspondents. Although they walked down the dark corridors of the metropolis like anyone else, I thought they were sneaky and stealthy. On the other hand, the Chinese correspondents and officials whom I had met on a friendly basis appeared honest, decent and extremely likable.

These patriotic preconceptions were revised as the result of experiences in the Far East during the latter portion of 1945 and in 1946. As soon as you get to know a people, generalizations become worthless. It was more difficult for me to get to like the Japanese, but I met and talked with many whom I admired, from Ishi, the room boy at the Tokyo Correspondents' Club to old Admiral Nomura, who had been Japan's Ambassador in Washington at the time of Pearl Harbor. And other Americans soon felt a greater kinship with the Japanese than with any other Orientals.

In Korea and China I soon learned to discard one superficial standard of judgment: I did not necessarily like or trust people just because they said nice things about Americans and American policy.

Without a knowledge of their language, it is foolhardy to claim a thorough understanding of a foreign people. At best you begin to comprehend what makes them tick when it dawns on you that

ix

foreigners do not seem foreign to themselves and that they—despite their lack of books and shoes and flush toilets—probably have a sounder idea of what makes us tick.

I returned from the Far East with more questions than answers. I had a fairly good picture of what was happening, but I lacked sufficient background to evaluate it. I recalled the fate of earnest reporters who returned from Russia after a year, or even less, as "experts" on the Soviet Union and on the Russian people. Many of them then proceeded to paint colorful comparisons between the U. S. and the U.S.S.R., never realizing that the widely divergent cultural backgrounds of the two countries made the analogies fairly useless—and fairly dangerous. To further my knowledge of the Far East, I applied for a Nieman Fellowship at Harvard University. In Cambridge my work was concentrated in an intensive regional seminar program on China and related areas. The seminar turned out to be an unusual and invaluable course of studies with an integrated approach to the politics, history, geography, anthropology, sociology, art and philosophy of the region.

This happy combination of research and field investigation hardly endows me with the infallibility of an expert. But the year of applied study did help me to add up my experiences in the Far East with greater discernment. The end result of that adding up is this book. It is not pure reportage and it certainly is not history. It is an attempt to tell the story of how U. S. policy is affecting the daily lives and the futures of the peoples in Japan, Korea and China.

The title of the book is not merely a phrase to catch the eye. There is "danger from the East" for us and for all nations which fail, through inert ignorance or venal arrogance, to recognize that Asia is in revolution and to understand what that means. There is danger that some of our leaders will refuse to recognize the mass unpopularity of a system which has brought recurring hunger and war.

There is danger in our nonperceptive efforts to suppress, to channel or to guide the course of Asia's revolution. In China and Korea, and in Japan to a lesser degree, we are engaged in a struggle of ideas with the Soviet Union—our way of life against theirs. There is danger that we may lose the struggle of ideas through the short-sightedness of our policy-makers and the stupidity of some of our representatives charged with carrying out policy.

Perhaps in the long run these are not actual dangers but only danger signals. If so, these signs all point to one ultimate danger: in the event we suddenly discover that we are in peril of losing out in the struggle of ideas, we will risk the destruction of civilization by turning the ideological battle (where we are relatively unprepared) into a struggle of atomic arms (where we are fully prepared).

The Far Eastern assignment was welcome for many reasons: one was that I hoped people would stop asking me unanswerable general questions about Russia. But there was no escape in Japan, Korea or China: the questions about Russia went right on. In addition to the interest and concern about the Soviets, I found that there was great interest and concern about us. Even the people we were attempting to help feared our bigness and our power.

The Koreans told me that their fear of the U.S. and the U.S.S.R. was based on self-interest. "We have an old Korean saying," one of them remarked. "When whales fight the shrimp are eaten."

RICHARD E. LAUTERBACH

Cambridge, Massachusetts
June 1, 1947

PART ONE

MACARTHUR'S JAPAN

"A social revolution is under way in Japan. Every Japanese, even in the remotest farms and villages, is touched by this revolution. This new life for the downtrodden farmers, the rise of new parties and leaders, a press set free, participation in elections of recently enfranchised men and women, the new Constitution, the resurgence of the long oppressed labor movement—all these attest to progressive trends of incalculable significance."

> —Ambassador George Atcheson, Jr., chairman of the Allied Council for Japan and the United States political adviser to General Douglas MacArthur in Tokyo, in an NBC broadcast, February 22, 1947.

"We have changed the laws, standards and ideals of this country from the feudalistic ideals of the past into the concept of what is the greatest thing in life, next to spiritual beauty—dignity of man. . . . I don't mean to say that the thing called democracy has been accomplished. The process is one of continual flux."

> —General of the Army Douglas A. MacArthur in Tokyo, March 17, 1947.

CHAPTER I

KILROY WAS HERE: IMPACT AND FLUX

TOKYO is not the monument to the airman's prowess that is Berlin, nor to the foot soldier's persistence that is Stalingrad, nor to the scientist's progress that is Hiroshima. By statesman's strategy and bomber's design Tokyo's superstructure of authority—modern and medieval—remains. But as I first saw it in November 1945, it was a city with its muscles smashed, its guts burned out, its picture post card face scorched. Enough of the charming peacetime façade lingers intact so that the city's maimed condition evokes the wince of the tourist, who remembers the gay folders in the travel agencies.

It is easier to observe how the terror of explosion and fire changed the buildings than to discover what it did to the people. If the Japanese were merely as unpredictable as their streets, they would be difficult to understand. There are alleys for ox-carts, single file, and broad avenues built for town cars, six abreast. There is the wide boulevard lined with trees, with the old Japan on one side and the new on the other. On one side there is a bordering moat and behind that the low, cold palaces of the ancestral rulers. Across the street behind the white wall of concrete over steel are the modern offices of the conquering powers.

There is the narrow alley running away from the boulevard toward the Ginza area with the Hollywood night club where a rouged Japanese, fattened on G.I. food, whines:

> The chassis is smooth and smart.
> The G.I.'s have the art.
> Hello, hello, the jeep is racing.
> O the gay American soldiers,
> They open the throttle wide,
> And today again the jeeps are racing.

3

Beneath the street runs a subway, its dilapidated stations smelling of urinals. Patiently the crowds wait. A few blocks away are movie theaters and Shinto shrines, their gods and marquees rubbing elbows and competing for ten-yen contributions. (The official value of the yen was fifteen to the dollar, but unofficially a carton of U. S. cigarettes sold for several hundred yen.)

This is the scorched but still familiar face of the city, the Tokyo of the tourist hotels and the great Meiji Stadium, of Hibiya Park with its show of stunted trees, the Tokyo of charcoal-burning trucks and thousands of workers pedaling home on bicycles at twilight. Here are the jerry-built shops, their window panes still missing and their customers refastening their dirty, cloth nose-masks against dust and infection.

It is easier to observe these physical changes. But what of the ways and the thoughts of the eager shoddily dressed people who pedal their bikes or stroll on a Sunday in Hibiya Park or bow low three times before the moated palace—how are they changing? Day after day I watched them, talked with them, trying to determine whether or not the new Japan was merely exchanging, temporarily, Tojo for MacArthur, traditional *kagura* for jitterbug, or whether the seeds of perennial spiritual growth were really emplanted there.

A reporter in Japan, without the safer and sounder perspective of the historian, must inspect each promising bud, each treacherous weed and send back word. Will a Kansas sunflower take nourishment in a chrysanthemum bed? It is surely too early to tell for certain how the garden will grow.

But there are portents. Before examining each spore and shoot, here are some of the things a reporter sees and hears and notes in the new Japan. . . .

2

One day in Tokyo, early in 1946, a roar of mingled singing and shouting resounded along the street behind the Meiji Building. I walked over to observe what seemed, at first, to be gay holiday festivities. Hundreds of shabbily clad Japanese workers, festooned with red and green crepe paper, were energetically waving banners, flags, and signs to the staccato rhythm of their chants. Some of the posters, in English, proclaimed KNOCK DOWN FEUDALISM! and ELEC-TRIC WORKERS MUST HAVE EAT. The gathering was in front of the

Furakawa Electric Company, Ltd., and celebrants were office clerks who had gone on strike because the management refused to meet their demands for a 250 per cent wage increase.

As I watched and listened a youthful male demonstrator in a shiny, blue serge suit came up to me. "You American?" he asked. He pointed to himself, then waved grandly toward his fellow demonstrators and said rapidly in excited pidgin English: "We won war. Won war. One year ago no could do this. Now we can shout and sing and strike. *We* really win war. Yes?"

3

In Japan, the islands where almost 80 million people live compressed into an area no larger than California, the bold feet of America cross and crisscross the black earth from the southernmost tip of Kyushu to northern Hokkaido. The unmistakable imprint of the American way is everywhere.

General of the Army Douglas MacArthur touched his feet to the ground at Atsugi Airfield on August 28, 1945. Since then the Japanese body politic has rocked under the verbal blows of his velvet-fisted social revolution. Millions have been disarmed. Hundreds of thousands of undesirables have been debarred from public office. Civil liberties have been granted, monopolies attacked, free elections established, a liberal constitution bestowed and an Emperor humanized. Smirking devils have become smiling friends, and peace reigns.

Divine Wind, Greater East Asia Co-Prosperity Sphere, Asia for the Asiatics are thrown in the locker like last year's baseballs. Democracy is the shiny, new catchword. Suzuki-san (the Japanese John Doe) sits, thinly-clad, in the public stands munching his rice and trying to understand the new game with the aid of a simplified score card. He watches the postwar catchword being flung around the intellectual infield, batted into the air by strong-tongued politicos. And when Suzuki-san thinks he has caught on, he barges onto the field to demonstrate.

The score card he leaves behind on his seat is numbered with neat precision. Perhaps it is written: One World, Two-ocean Navy, Big Three, Four Freedoms, Five-Star General, Six-o'clock Chow, "Seven-Come-Eleven," Eighth Army, Nine-year Primary School, Ten Prophylactic Stations and 1,172 Directives.

The new democracy is all things to all Japanese. It is a tipped hat, a stick of chewing gum, a hopped-up jeep, a bold newspaper editorial, a four-letter epithet, a bag of flour, and the G.I. It is the imperfect impact of a stranger's way of life. It is most discernible in the dust of the big cities, in Tokyo, Osaka, Sendai, Hakkodate, Nagoya, and even in ancient, unscathed Kyoto. It pops up like a brassy new tune along the paths of ruin and rubble, in the flimsy new wood and plastic dance halls and resturants, in depleted shops and stuffed trains, in press and radio, in movies and theaters, in styles and manners, and in the small talk of the public bath-houses.

By example, more than directive, new designs are drawn over old cultural patterns. Womanhood is emancipated by laws which most Japanese men never read nor comprehend. But the gallant and sex-hungry G.I. sweeps the frightened female from the sub-servient to the sublime. Now the Japanese maiden walks, almost unabashed, side by side with her escort and not one respectful step behind. In jammed streetcars and busses Americans yank smug-bottomed men from their seats and make the ladies sit down.

The teen-agers scan slick American magazines or their Japanese imitators seeking out the latest New York skirt-length or Hollywood hair-do, insist on wearing brassieres for the first time and on learn-ing how to jitterbug. The shaved-head style for men which came in with Emperor Meiji has grown out with MacArthur. The bow is less low, the hiss less sibilant, the handshake less perfunctory. The marriage of two age-old Japanese characteristics, self-discipline and self-deception, is on trial as never before. But the impact of two atomic bombs and 200,000 Allied troops with blunt Western ways may not be sufficient to bring about a final divorcement in less than several generations.

4

We arrived in the prairie of devastation that is Hiroshima some four months after the atomic explosion. The pitiful survivors beat around the junk heap of their city for weeds and firewood. They tell about it when asked with almost the detachment of a veteran surgeon describing an operation that resulted in the patient's death. There seems to be little rancor, for resentment takes a strength and comprehension which they lack.

A little way out of the city in a modern building which appears untouched by the bombing, we meet the well-dressed, well-fed local officials. Pleasantly they furnish us with facts and figures about the destruction and about the difficulty of reconstruction. Then the interpreter says, "We shall have a 'close conversation,'" which apparently means an interview.

The Acting Governor of the Hiro Prefecture, Shigeru Kojo, is very intellectual-looking in his thick tortoise-shell glasses and his gold-capped teeth. He wears a brown pin-striped suit of fine quality, a Madras striped shirt, and an electric blue silk tie. From a prepared statement he reads: "A rebuilt Hiroshima will be an international symbol of humanity and peace. This city will be a center of intercourse between the United States and Japan. But we require American wisdom and advice. We will make the cradle of peace-loving, reconstructed Japan from this city, which is a symbol of militarism's downfall."

Mayor Schichiro Kihara, in a coal-black tweed suit, continues: "You look like messengers sent by God for the reconstruction of our once-beautiful city. We are helpless like babies. We cannot walk alone. The revival of the city depends on the articles you write in your papers. . . . Let us make a firm and eternal bridge over the Pacific that will not be destroyed by any bomb."

The Mayor is asked: "What do you want us to do to rebuild Hiroshima?" The Mayor replies: "We need supplies and materials for building: lumber, cement, iron. Also food, clothing and medicines."

"And automobiles? Would you like them?"

"Yes, yes," the Mayor quickly agrees. In the same sarcastic vein the correspondent inquires: "Would you like the American Army to supply the labor?"

The Mayor says that Japan can supply the labor if America supplies the materials.

I ask if it would be all right with the Mayor and the Governor if we first rebuild cities which the Japanese destroyed, like Manila and Nanking. The Mayor says: "This request comes from the people and they do not know about those cities."

"But you Hiroshima officials know about Manila and Nanking. Yet you ask American aid for Hiroshima. What do you think?"

I have to repeat the question in different ways several times before the interpreter conducts a whispered poll among the Jap-

anese officials who line one side of the long conference table facing
the Americans seated on the other side.

The interpreter finally reports: "We are all feeling very sorry
for those cities."

Everyone stands up. The Japanese bow. As we file out, the Mayor
hands each member of the press party a *presento*—a box containing a tablecloth and napkins marked: "A souvenir to the American
correspondents from the Mayor of Hiroshima city."

5

There is free talk in the tea shops and wonderful, new grumbling
at the rice distribution centers. There is hunger for food and for
knowledge and a sign on a Tokyo shrine reads: MY DEAR MR. G.I.
THANKS GIVING GRATITUDE FOR SAVING ONES LIFE. An overflow crowd
in Tokyo's Hibiya Park braves a Communist rally while elsewhere
tens of thousands submissively sign a petition pleading that a condemned militarist be pardoned.

Hollywood movies, banned for four years, return and attendance
records are smashed at the three largest Tokyo cinema emporiums.
The first imported film is "The Call of the Yukon," a decade old,
and a Japanese comments, "So cold in America, maybe your G.I.'s
stay here in mild Tokyo long time." A Japanese movie company
sends the American chief of Counter Intelligence a fat bankroll as
a New Year's gift; when it is refused and they are rebuked, the
Japanese are hurt and mystified, saying, "We always sent it to the
old secret police (*kempei tai*), why not the new?" The first Japanese movie with a kissing scene, *Hatachi no Seishun* ("Young
Hearts") is less popular and is severely criticized in Tokyo newspapers for violating not only taste and tradition but "health considerations."

The House of Peers abolishes itself and steel helmets are sold as
cooking pots on the Ginza along with trinkets made from half-
completed tanks. Prices inflate and wages tail behind. Radicals
walk out of jails and jingoists walk in. The cities and villages are
overcrowded. Tokyo's Ueno Station and old half-destroyed temples
become flea-ridden flophouses. The lack of housing is accentuated
by the return of five million disgruntled repatriates who are
promptly deloused and demilitarized, and then discouraged by the
cool reception accorded them in their native towns and villages.

Gang rule, beneath the surface, still dominates small business in the cities. No person can build or open a store without paying a whopping forfeit. The Neighborhood Associations still exist, quiet but firm. There is little or no consciousness of war guilt and the common man co-operates with the authorities now as always. The casual visitor, the barn-storming congressman, or the junketing newspaper publisher marvels at MacArthur and cannot comprehend how these same Japs once died as *kamikazes*. The discovery that there had been a well-organized plan to plant living mines called *furukyus* (Recumbent Dragons) along the coastal waters to greet the invading Americans with certain death makes scarcely a dent in the solid wall of approval.

6

Kohgo Takahashi, an ex-*furukyu*, is 5 feet 5 inches tall, thirty years old, and alive today because the war ended without an Allied invasion. He was born in the northern part of Honshu near Sendai, the second son of a smelter who was employed in the big steel works there. At the age of fifteen, having completed eight years of primary schooling, Kohgo was apprenticed by his father as a handy man and helper in a furniture manufacturing company. He worked there for four years, when he left to join the army.

"Why did you join the army?"

After a while Kohgo said: "I like soldiers." I repeated the question. Finally he said: "My pay as a helper was five yen a month with food. In the army I received six and a half yen a month with food and clothes."

In 1936 he was transferred to the marine corps to do woodwork on a new cruiser; then he was sent to a naval technical school for two years; then he was with the Japanese landing party at Amoy and stayed in China a year; then he joined the navy air force and became a warrant officer, lower grade; then he was appointed as an instructor at a navy woodworking school, where he taught for four years during the Pacific War.

Kohgo, in ten years with the armed forces, said he had never heard a shot fired in anger.

"Did you hate the Americans?"

No reply. Question repeated. "I hated my country's enemies."

Question repeated. "Only the enemies who sought to destroy my country."

In May 1945 he decided to kill himself by killing hundreds of Americans. He was not sure how it all came about or how he made the decision or even whether he ever consciously made it. "While in technical school I learned some diving, to examine ships' bottoms. I was asked to stop teaching woodworking and to teach diving. At some point I understood it was a special attack corps for underwater."

"You were drafted or did you volunteer?"

"I volunteered."

"Why?"

"My duty."

"To whom?"

Silence. Question repeated. Kohgo whispered to my interpreter. The interpreter said, "He does not know if he should say it now. The Emperor, of course."

The attack corps was made up half of volunteers, half of draftees. The volunteers were "anxious," the draftees "reluctant."

I repeated: "Why did you volunteer?"

This time, Kohgo did not know.

"Why did some others volunteer when they knew it was certain death?"

"One must die one time, why not now." There was no question in his voice.

The corps were treated with the same deference as *kamikazes*, given special pay, special rations. They were awarded ranks equivalent to "battleship," "cruiser," "destroyer," depending upon their capacity to remain under water.

In response to further questioning, Kohgo said it had first occurred to him that Japan might lose the war after the fall of Saipan. Allied forces were advancing and the Japanese planes and fleets were unable to go and meet them. "And then the bombing of the homeland," he recalled. Kohgo lost his mother, his sister-in-law, and his niece in a B-29 raid. He was willing to sacrifice his life in a losing cause because it might "delay the defeat." He said this as if he felt delaying the defeat was a moral victory.

"What do you think of the Emperor's statement that he is not divine?"

"It is a foregone conclusion that he is not divine," Kohgo responded without thought.

Kohgo is married to his first cousin and has a son, one year old. They live with his wife's family who, having no sons, adopted Kohgo. He is planning to go into the furniture business. Now he is living on savings and "by selling things." The new Diet, he hopes, will improve conditions.

"Whom will you vote for?"

"Anyone who will work for the common people. Any party except the Communists."

"Why not the Communists?"

For the first time, Kohgo looked pleased. "I do not know very much about politics," he began, "but since I was a child I was taught that Communism was not right and I still have that idea in the back of my mind."

"Do you think there will be war between Russia and America?"

"According to present happenings, war between Russia and America . . . " he broke off. "I do not know."

"Have you heard the radio series, 'Now It Can Be Told'? What did you think about it?"

"Yes, of course. But I did not find myself especially interested."

"Why?"

He shrugged off that and similar questions.

"Who do you think was responsible for the war?"

He thought before replying carefully: "If we are to blame anybody, it would be the leaders of the country at the time the war started."

"The Emperor included?"

"The subordinates of the Emperor."

"Is the Emperor responsible for the actions of his subordinates?"

"Yes, in a way."

"Is he then guilty?"

"That is too delicate a question for me to answer. But generally the Emperor cannot always know when he is deceived."

"How long should the American occupation last?"

"Two or three years from today."

"And then?"

"The Potsdam Declaration will be fulfilled; there will be a peace treaty. The Emperor can then rule without the advisers who deceived him."

7

Even in backward communities the accustomed pattern of life is slowly altering. The force of the American impact attenuates as it shudders into smaller towns and villages. There the directive prescribes change but outmoded institutions linger on, secure in their isolation from the garrulous broadcast, the gregarious G.I.'s, and the shacked-up colonels. There the Confucian family way is stronger than the American way. The Meiji Constitution of 1878 has not yet superseded the code of Confucius: "Parents must be obeyed during their lifetime; after their death, their son must do as they do." In weather-worn wood and paper-thatched houses it is still colder in winter, warmer in summer. Modern plumbing is a myth, sanitation is just around the corner, and the Allied occupation is something to be endured like death, taxes, and child-bearing. But the realities of peace are pleasing. The rice producers know they are allowed to keep 60 per cent of their crop instead of 30 per cent, as in the war years. Any surplus not eaten by the family can be sold for a handsome profit on the black market or to government collectors who offer shoes and smokes as bonuses.

The hollow-cheeked rabble in the remains of the big cities are closer, geographically, to the new ways of democracy. They can be viewed any day on the much-traversed road between Tokyo and Yokohama. Most of them are free to live in their twisted and rusted tin-covered huts, huddled together amid the burned acres. In the lumpy soil, enriched by crumpled plaster and decayed flesh, they manipulate their crannies of green vegetation. To raise money for bits of dried fish and other luxuries they troop to the Ginza to join the lines of shabby salesmen offering their cherished curios, their cheap lacquer boxes, cultivated pearls, and frayed kimonos to "Mr. Yank." Hopefully they exchange goods for currency in the vain effort to keep abreast of unchecked inflation. The newspapers tell them that living costs have soared 3,800 per cent since 1937, but the Japanese man-along-the-street counts it only as one less meal a day.

Living as they do within the shadow of the directive and its enforcement, they have breathed the air of freedom. Their appetites are more, not less. They are close enough to be moved by the liberated tongues of newspapers, union organizers and politicians. They can enjoy their physical poverty and spiritual riches without fear of the *kempei tai*. They can vote and worship as they please. They can, if they wish, ridicule the Emperor. "Best of all," one Japanese says, "we can talk to a policeman without bowing, showing reverence, and trembling."

The Japanese marvel at the Americans who buy up their old trinkets, these fabulously rich and handsome Americans whom they call "the carefree ones." They are baffled by the G.I.'s energy, warmed by his kindliness to children, astounded by his great capacities for eating, drinking, and aggressive love-making. With their short Oriental noses pressed against the windowpanes the men in their unpressed suits and the women in their ugly, pajama-like *mompei* study the clothing at the officers' store. Ex-servicemen, still wearing army handouts, eye the steady stream of soldiers eddying from the big Ginza PX, their khaki pockets bulging with candy bars, cigarettes, and contraceptives.

The middle class, in their worn white collars, listen attentively to the G.I. radio programs, especially the popular music. Religiously they tune out the educational programs, which they consider propaganda. "The Japanese will only be saddened by this," observes one of the new Diet's lady members, listening to a preview of a radio show emphasizing Japan's war guilt.

They are pleased, if surprised and a little suspicious, as a result of the fair trials given their former heroes. But the citizens of Yokohama do not follow the proceedings of the trials with much more interest than the citizens of Omaha, Nebraska.

8

In the Yokohama courtroom a voice booms: "The United States of America versus Tatsuo Tsuchiya. . . ." The first defendant in the war crime trials shivers in the cold, stucco courtroom. Two panes of glass are missing in the skylight. This is a small show for a small fish. If the legal bait works here, the line will be dressed up and used to hook the Tojos. The defendant does not seem to care that his place in history is assured. He is a skinny fellow, dressed in a seedy, gray civilian suit. His bent spectacles rest too far forward on his rabbit's nose, his face is pinched, his lips protruding. He follows the words from the booming voice on a Japanese translation: ". . . variously known as 'Little Glass Eye' did willfully and unlawfully commit brutal atrocities . . . in violation of the laws and customs of war." Tatsuo Tsuchiya betrays no emotion as the charges are enumerated, as the names and places and dates are reeled off as efficiently as trains are called.

During a recess I ask "Little Glass Eye" a question through his Japanese counsel's interpreter, but Tsuchiya only stares at my uniform blankly and shivers. The amiable interpreter answers for him. "Sir," he says with a slight hiss caressing a suspiciously Oxford accent, "slapping is not contrary to Japanese army customs." As he talks the interpreter makes an unconscious movement with his right hand and I jerk my head away without thinking. The interpreter blushes, overdoes his confusion. "Sir, I am in excruciating sorrow. It was only to demonstrate . . ." The hearings resume.

9

The new patterns and the old sometimes merge, more often clash. The postwar crazy quilt covers a multitude of sins. Divorces are becoming very popular and the homicide rate rises 250 per cent in one year. The number worshipping at the Grand (Shinto) Shrines declines 80 per cent. The American correspondent of a national weekly magazine receives a cabled request to write about why G.I.'s prefer Japanese women to the girls back home. In a Japanese women's magazine a lady author confesses gratefulness because a U.S. major taught her and her husband how to be demonstrative in public and not just in the privacy of their boudoir.

In the first year of defeat there are an estimated 90,000 unmarried Japanese mothers of concern to the occupying powers. On December 26, 1946, American officials release 1,322 tons of imported canned goods and 60.6 tons of candies to Japanese children under six. Generals and correspondents hunt duck on the Emperor's private preserve, and an American lady is imported to tutor the Crown Prince. A trashy novel about a hot romance between an American reporter and a Japanese girl becomes the peacetime best seller, and a G.I. runs amuck killing two Japanese bystanders.

Business readjusts slowly. Industry limps along at less than half of normal capacity. Fortunes are lost through legislation and remade on the black market. Tobacco, culled from discarded butts, is re-rolled into cigarets which are quickly sold to Japanese. National flags, hidden away in boxes buried in the ground when the invaders came, are sold to these same invaders as souvenirs.

The babble of democracy talked-about is deafening. College students and professors, miners and mill-owners, salesmen and silk growers, all speak of the foreign democracy. Some want to translate it into wages and hours, or freedom of the individual. Others want only to shout it from the housetops and then are satisfied to listen to the echo. School children jump up in the middle of a recitation period and begin bellowing their school song while the teacher looks on aghast at this new interpretation of democracy.

At an American officers' mess the Japanese waitresses band together to protest the head waitress's appointment from above and to demand the right of electing their own chief. On a streetcar an old conductor bawls out a bright-eyed student for smoking. "Can't you see the NO SMOKING sign?" the conductor demands. The student jabbers back. The conductor stops the car and insists. Other passengers reinforce the conductor's argument. The student removes the last inch of his cigarette from the tiny brass pipe and puts it out, pocketing the pipe and the butt. Turning to this writer he stammers in English, "You Americans say Japan have democracy. In democracy common people do what they want. Yes? Japan not yet democratic."

At a mass meeting a Japanese feminist complains that Americans are ruining the structure of Japanese classical society. Afterwards she says, more sharply, about some of the changes: "Factory girls are becoming prostitutes, prostitutes become waitresses, waitresses become so-called geishas, geishas become mistresses, mistresses move into the Imperial Hotel with your colonels."

A large new brothel near Tokyo is named "Willow Run" by the alert Japanese entrepreneur who is impressed by pictures of assembly line production in an American magazine. This is the new twist on the oldest profession which touches the American soldier: this and pearls and chopsticks and cheap incense are the new Japan he sees and buys and remembers.

10

The Japanese prostitutes think democracy and MacArthur are wonderful. "He has almost doubled my earning power," confides Kazuko Ogawa, a puffy-cheeked, slant-eyed minx clad in a rainbow-colored silk kimono. This generous praise is offered despite the fact that SCAP had no direct connection with the decision of the Tokyo Brothel Keepers' Association to abolish the system of licensed prostitution in Japan as of January 15, 1946. Brothel-keepers claim they "are moved by the spirit of democracy" to free their girls from slavery.

In the past, Japanese prostitutes were often sold to houses by their parents and were never again free until the entire debt was paid off. Repayment of the sale price took most of the girls' financially productive years, as the madames charged them high prices for room, board, clothes, doctors' bills and "training."

In the past, the girls were only paid 30 per cent of fees. Under the new "American-style" regulations, the girls and the house split 50–50.

With the abolition of the national licensed prostitution laws promulgated in 1889, the girls are officially classed as "entertainers." Pressed for an exact definition of this new status, the association's executive secretary hedges politely for ten minutes before boiling it down to: "The girls can now say 'no' to a customer if they want to say 'no.'"

The new law has not resulted in "freed" girls flocking from brothels to do business on their own. "There are enough street girls," one explains, "and besides, with the terrible housing shortage, we would rather stay here." The G.I. driver, overhearing the conversation, says: "She means she never had it so good."

He is right. Although the Yoshiwara District of Tokyo is now "off limits" to Allied personnel, business is booming. Before the Allied ban, about 90 per cent of the customers were foreigners. Now it is half and half. The houses of "entertainment" still close their doors daily at 8 P.M. and put out the sign "Standing Room Only."

The Yoshiwara has changed—not only financially. The district was almost entirely flattened by B-29 raids. Of 310 houses employing 2,000 girls before the war, only nine sturdy stone brothels with 120 girls are left. The houses jut up on the ravaged landscape like haunted houses on the jackets of mystery books. Their canary-yellow balconies and shocking-pink window shades make them almost as colorful as the nearby sign which says "Army PRO Station." Girls huddle over charcoal fires on the first floor, warming their hands until a customer strolls in.

Of the Yoshiwara's famous sixty theaters only a half-dozen still stand and only a few are open. Where high giggles once rent the air, vegetable gardens now split the frost-starched soil. Here and there ex-pimps work, putting up wooden shacks which eventually will hang out the welcome shingle. Over one hundred such sin shacks are in the process of building. When they are completed, the military police will call around and paint OFF LIMITS in white and then go away. If necessary, another PRO station will open to take care of increased business.

Editorially the Tokyo daily, *Yomiuri Hochi*, points out that prostitutes once came from the poverty-stricken farming areas of Hokkaido and Northern Honshu, but today the farmers' daughters are replaced by office workers, waitresses and housewives— "eloquent testimony to the reversed economic conditions of the farming and urban areas." The issue, says the *Yomiuri*, is not morals but food: Give the working girl enough food and shelter and she won't walk down the bombed-out garden path to the Yoshiwara.

11

Japanese admire American women for their dress and their erect carriage but doubt their "utility." They like American games, American expressions. They are beginning to want more fresh meat, more books, more indoor toilets, more perfumes. Those Japanese who realize how new enthusiasms are altering Japanese society are cheered by the old devotion to the Emperor. An obscure Japanese poet writes an ode to "August Fifteenth" to please the Americans, and a Japanese newspaper is pleased to publish it as a tribute to Hirohito:

Behold! There has taken place today
Japan's felicitous rebirth, leaves State of Democracy and Liberties,
Where Love and Peace hold full sway;
A country of the arts and poetry
Where flourish music, drama and peace-industries.
A country of everlasting neutrality;
Aye, we should endeavor to make our fatherland
The East Asia's Switzerland.
A free state where equality
Is enjoyed by both sexes in harmony
In politics and in the family.
A country where every cultured man writes poetry,

Whose themes are mostly natural beauties, blessed with beautiful
   Nature, wealth untold,
Japan is a peerless park in the world.
In sum, our Empire is a Utopia on earth,
It was indeed ignorant soldiery
Who ruined our sacred country;
So, in the bottomless pit
Let us militarism bury.
AH, BUT
GODS OF HEAVEN AND EARTH,
DO I PRAY YE, LET OUR IMPERIAL FAMILY
ENJOY EVERLASTING GLORY
AND ETERNAL PROSPERITY.

In Nagoya, taking advantage of the foreign democracy, a former
Buddhist priest, now a down-at-the-heels shopkeeper, claims the
Emperor's throne. Hiromichi Kumazawa, attempting to right a five-
hundred-year-old wrong, says: "I consider Hirohito a war criminal—
with an illegal member on the throne there can be no democracy,
nor can there be friendly relations with friendly nations." The bald
pretender writes a special poem to General MacArthur:

In the Land of Nippon
Dust and slime is piled up
—A messenger of heaven
Has descended
To sweep and cleanse.

But most Japanese worship their Emperor and they cannot admit
any fault in him, nor any in their savior, General MacArthur.

A few, perhaps, are shocked enough to turn completely on the
old ways. The demobilized soldier, not yet caught up in the all-
absorbing scramble for food, his old gods tottering if not destroyed,
ponders the past before facing the future. How did Japan get this
way? What is to be done?

At noon on January 15, 1946, a youth wearing the cap of the
Niigata Higher School and a shabby black cape, walks into Communist Party headquarters at Yoyogi, Tokyo. He gives his name as
Yoshitaro Nishioka, twenty-six, a former army captain and a *kami-
kaze* corps leader. After questioning by party officials for two hours
he is given a party card. A reporter inquires as to why Nishioka, a
member of the 56th graduating class at the Military Academy and
recipient of an Imperial prize, has turned Communist. Nishioka explains that it is due to his revulsion at the lies that marked the war

as well as the deception which forcibly brought war in the Emperor's name.

He says: "A number of men under my command died. They were dear to me and dear to their families. I felt a great personal responsibility for sending them to their deaths. In what way do you think I exhorted them and trained them? Did I not tell them it was for Emperor and country?

"At the war's end I found out how utterly false the war had been and how I had been deceived. I entered the Niigata Higher School in desperation, somehow to prop myself up, but what the School gave me was the same kind of education, minus the practical side, that I had at the Military Academy.

"Because I belonged to an air unit I flew extensively over East Asia, but Japanese policy toward the natives was not liberation for East Asia as orally professed. To even an amateur in politics it was pure aggression. But I did not even then question the war. However, today I cannot help but feel the great crime committed against East Asian races. I should like to concentrate the same kind of feeling of the *kamikazes* to saving the natives and rebuilding a new Japan.

"During my Army life I experienced time and again the evils of the Emperor system. For example, whenever the Air Unit Staff Office planned operations, and we were even the slightest degree critical, the operations were forced on us under the Emperor's name."

12

In two years the surface manifestations of change in Japan are great and obvious. If the farmer and the laborer, the student and the housewife, now have a vested interest in democracy, obviously they will resist any return to the old ways. But the obvious in Japan has often proven deceptive. As a Tokyo editor informs me, even the myths which the Japanese believed about themselves have been dissipated. Basing their attitudes on history, psychology and tradition, they were confident they would never surrender; that domestic strife would ensue if the government did surrender; that a strong underground resistance would operate after the surrender; that Japanese who were too friendly with the Americans would suffer retaliation by the diehards; that the Japanese people would not stand for the abolition of state Shinto; that the Japanese were law-abiding; that the Japanese were clean and aesthetic, polite and courteous. "But you see," he says, "we did surrender, there is peace, almost no underground resistance. It is an honor to know an American, we are indifferent to the changed status of Shinto, and we are not law-abiding. We have black markets, thefts, murders, robberies more than ever. We are not really clean unless forced to be—Tokyo is vulgarized and debased. We are polite when well-fed, but now we squabble for seats in cars, for places in queues, even for scraps of your bread."

Historically Japan has again and again been reshaped to challenge, later, the nations opposing her. Some say it is a conscious or unconscious national adaptation of judo, utilizing the tactic of seeming to yield completely at the proper moment only to throw an adversary by his own weight. Others say that the example is followed while the example is around. Miss Rachael A. Johnstone, of Bartlesville, Oklahoma, operates a school to train Japanese domestic help for the wives of American officers in Tokyo. She has a hard time getting the girls to serve ladies first. But her toughest teaching job is making the Japanese girls understand that American methods of dusting and dishwashing are to be followed even when she is not watching them. "Like many Japanese," Miss Johnstone remarks, "they would do things correctly by Western standards as long as an American was around. But the minute my back was turned they went back to doing things by their own methods."

This time Japan is being reshaped under the expert guidance of General of the Army Douglas A. MacArthur, an adversary with far greater skill than his many enemies credit him with having. A shrewd dialectician, his master plan for the new Japan is both negative and positive. Or, as the General has summed it up in his simplest Old Testament-style rhetoric, "Be kind to your enemy, you never know when you may need a friend."

CHAPTER II

HIROHITO: FROM GOD TO MAN

GENERAL MacArthur's utilization of Hirohito as the Charlie Mc-
Carthy of the Allied Occupation was in the best Japanese tradition.
For centuries before 1868 the Emperor had not been the real ruler
of Japan. The man behind the throne was called the *shogun*. After
the Meiji Restoration, the Emperor became in name the temporal
as well as spiritual ruler of Japan. Still he was manipulated from
behind the scenes by the fingers of first one clique and then another.

Hirohito, before the war, was no exception. He knew of the expansionist plans of his cabinet and of his army and navy. Whether
he approved them or not is almost, but not quite, academic. Could
he have stopped them? General MacArthur asked the Emperor that
question when Hirohito, silk top hat in hand, formally visited the
new "Yankee *Shogun*" shortly after the occupation commenced.
Hirohito replied that if he had opposed the war, "they"—meaning
Gumbatsu and *Zaibatsu*—would have got another Emperor. He
later explained to another American that he had to approve the war
because "the Japanese Emperor, being one with the state and nation, cannot refuse what it demands."

No matter what the official versions will say, Hirohito knew all
about the war plans and approved them. Whether or not he secretly
opposed them in his heart of hearts is as pointless as discussing
whether or not Hitler was sincere. The net effect in terms of lives
lost and in terms of the course of world history is what counts.

Incriminating documents secured for the War Crime Trials, but
never publicized, proved conclusively that Hirohito was in on the
war preparations step by step. Prince Konoye's memoirs, published
after his suicide, state that the militarists refused to disclose their
plans to his cabinet but the Emperor promised to keep him (Konoye) informed. Admiral Toyada, Commander-in-Chief of the

21

Combined Fleets and naval adviser to Hirohito, was asked: "Did the Emperor know in advance of the plan to attack Pearl Harbor?" Toyada replied: "Yes. All naval plans were submitted to him for his approval."

Throughout the war Hirohito held daily conferences with his commanders and was briefed on progress and strategy. His Grand Chamberlain said he was the best-informed man in Japan on the course of the war. When it became obvious to any sane man (and Hirohito is sane, although his father died insane) that the war was lost, Hirohito summoned a meeting of the Supreme War Council. This omnipotent group, which was composed of the Premier, the War, Navy, and Foreign Ministers, plus the Chief of the Imperial General Staff and the Chief of Naval Operations, was asked to decide whether to continue fighting or to end the war. After discussion, Konoye's memoirs reveal, three members voted for war, three for peace.

Hirohito then cast his decision not *for peace* but *against war*. According to Konoye, the Emperor stated that the continuation of the war did not promise a successful outcome, no matter from what angle the situation was considered. He told them: "Therefore I have decided to order the conclusion of the war, as I cannot endure the thought of having thousands, even hundreds of thousands, of my subjects killed, and moreover, of being called the disturber of the world peace. It is extremely difficult for me to have to turn over to the Allied authorities officers and men upon whom I have depended all this time as though they were part of my own body, but I have decided to endure what is unendurable and to accept the terms of the Potsdam Declaration." The Emperor made a recording of his surrender message and it was broadcast on the morning of August 15, 1945, despite attempts of some youthful militarists to capture and destroy the platter on its way to the studio. The sense of the call to surrender was that Japan had fought a just war in an unsuccessful attempt to free backward Asia. For instance, Hirohito expressed "the deepest regret to our allied nations in East Asia who have consistently co-operated with the Empire towards the emancipation of East Asia." This rescript, the last "free speech" by the Emperor, may someday come to mean much to a revived Japan. Skillfully used for propaganda, it might be especially meaningful to thousands of demobilized soldiers of the crack divisions stationed in Formosa, Korea, China, and Manchuria who were never conquered by the Americans and therefore feel no sense of military defeat.

2

The Japanese who have influenced power are never without a plan. Before the Americans landed they destroyed documents, shifted bureaucrats and secret police functionaries so they could avoid responsibility, secreted wealth, changed bank and corporation statistics. It was agreed that the basis, if any, for the "unendurable" defeat was the retention of the Emperor. The Potsdam Declaration fitted those plans. A new *shogun* would come and pull the royal strings, but *shoguns* do not last forever, nor do military occupations. One day the *shogun* would be gone, but—if their plan was to succeed—the Emperor must remain. Whether it was Hirohito or his son, Akihito, mattered little.

Granted this prime consideration, the Japanese were willing to accept almost anything. In the sixteenth century had not the *shogun* Ashigawa given lip service to the Ming Emperor of China and accepted the lowly title of "King of Japan" because it profited the oligarchy in Japan to play a humble role? At some future time— ten, twenty, thirty years—they could regain power, not in a revolt against the Emperor, but against his counselors. Was there not a pattern for this in 1877 when the Satsuma rebelled because the Emperor was badly advised? That was the long-term view. In the meanwhile the Tenno (Emperor) system would provide a bulwark against the hunger and anger of the people, against the possibility of violent change and social revolution.

The Allies kept Hirohito for a variety of valid reasons, among them: to save Allied lives, to maintain stability and to prevent his becoming a martyr. Taking this decision, we traded undeniable immediate gains against the danger of possible long-term losses. The logic was weak, the benefits great. On the one hand the Emperor was kept because his name and his command were so all-powerful and influential that he could put an end to armed opposition. On the other, he has been exonerated from war guilt because he had no real power or influence.

Hirohito will always be potentially powerful and, in the wrong hands, potentially dangerous unless the re-education of Japan is at once devastating in what it roots out and constructive in what it emplants. The evil of the Tenno system resides not in Hirohito himself but in the minds of the Japanese people. No matter how much Allied propaganda tears down the Tenno, the peasant still thinks of him as the head of the complicated Japanese family system. The Tenno remains the father of fathers, the symbol of the country. Five, ten, or fifteen years may not extirpate that ingrained concept.

In the second year of the occupation a great sign decorated a Tokyo street corner, sponsored by the "Society for International Friendship through Language." Two questions and answers, in Japanese and in English translation, are emblazoned on the billboard. The first, and therefore most important, inquires: WHO IS THE WORLD'S MOST AWESOME PERSONAGE? The reply: HIS IMPERIAL MAJESTY. The second: WHO IS THE WORLD'S MOST POWERFUL BEING? is answered by the words, ATOMIC BOMB. Something new has been added to the Japanese hierarchy, but the old remains.

The Yankee *Shogun* and his directives have had a hand in remaking the form of the flesh-and-blood Tenno. Hirohito must pay income taxes for the first time on his previously untold wealth. Since he is known to be extremely stingy, this will not please him. He must talk to visiting foreign journalists, educators, missionaries, and politicians. He must get along with the personnel of the Imperial Household cut from a wartime high of 8,900 retainers to a mere 1,400; this reduction, reported the Japanese press, represented "the barest essential to run the Imperial Family." The Family also will have to get along in 1947 on a third of its normal income—which is still considerably more than the sum appropriated to establish the means of enforcing the new constitution. Hirohito can still putter around with his laboratory and fiddle with experiments in marine biology, collect clocks, study Christianity, read Darwin and Lincoln, worship his ancestors, and write poetry. He can receive Roger Baldwin of the Civil Liberties Union, Father Flanagan of Boys' Town, see a soccer game, but not vote in the elections. Beneath it all he is still the same little man waving a false flag. He is ignorant and ignoble, abstemious and conservative, frightened and dangerous.

The Supreme Command for the Allied Powers (SCAP) has not been entirely unaware of the inherent dangers in the Emperor system. It has, therefore, been busy lifting the public face of the Emperor and of the system which he represents, changing a pompous little god into a shy little democrat.

Hirohito, SCAP suggested, must become more accessible to his people. "How can anyone believe him divine if they once see him?" an American colonel asked me. Reluctantly a timid start was made. In December 1945, the Imperial Household arranged Hirohito's first "press conference." In a corner of the Imperial Palace grounds six aged reporters who had been covering the Imperial Household for two decades (but had never had an audience) were talking to one of the Chamberlains by appointment. Suddenly along a garden path came the Minister of the Imperial Household and the Emperor. The Emperor, in surprise, greeted the pressmen like a startled faun. They bowed low. The Minister made introductions. The Emperor commented on the weather and the peace and then walked on.

The reporters, trembling, filed out. "Do not write about this," the Chamberlain warned.

That month was a worrisome one for the diminutive ruler. His generals and admirals and finally his friends and advisers began disappearing into Sugamo Prison to await trial for "crimes against humanity." Marquis Kido, a lifelong friend, Prince Konoye, and Prince Nashimoto—all close to the Imperial family—were taken into custody. The little Emperor again asked his advisers to sound out SCAP on his abdication. SCAP said no. Fear mounted that pressure from the Australians, New Zealanders and Russians would cause the naming of Hirohito as a war criminal. But MacArthur held out. He could always use it as a threat if "Charlie," as the G.I.'s called Hirohito, balked. "The Emperor eats out of my hand," MacArthur said. This recalled to mind an apt remark about the "Son of Heaven" made by Hugh Byas, former *New York Times* correspondent in Tokyo. "If Hirohito had been a little boy in America during the green decades," Byas once wrote, "he would have liked spinach after he had been told it was good for him."

In the Diet, aged Prime Minister Shidehara rose to defend the Tenno. It was all right for democracy in the United States to consist of government of, for, and by the people, he said, "but in Japan it must be run under the Emperor."

Old one-eyed Admiral Kichisaburo Nomura, who had been Japan's Ambassador in Washington at the moment of Pearl Harbor, grasped my arm when I told him I did not think Hirohito would be brought to trial. "I am very glad that you did not fire the Emperor," he said. "Having been personal tutor to the Emperor on naval affairs,

I feel anything that happens to him as if it were happening to myself." Nomura was not indicted as a war criminal, either.

3

On New Year's·Day, 1946, a greater step to revamp the Emperor was taken. Reading what sounded like a MacArthur handout, Hirohito proclaimed that he was not really divine. When first approached to humanize himself, the Emperor had sent word to MacArthur that it would be "a personal embarrassment" to him to divest himself of something he did not have. The reply came back that belief in the Emperor's continued divinity was bad for Japan's reputation abroad.

And so, the little man said:

We have . . . to proceed unflinchingly toward elimination of misguided practices of the past . . . The ties between us and our people . . . do not depend upon mere legends and myths. They are not predicated on the false conception that the Emperor is divine and that the Japanese are superior to other races and fated to rule the world. . . . The Emperor is not a living god.

The response to this negation of deity from the Japanese public was hardly revolutionary. The renunciation received a warmer press reception in the United States. On the Japanese it had no more visible effect than if John D. Rockefeller had suddenly announced to Americans that he was no longer the richest man in the world. Americans would still think of him as way out of their class. A year after the divinity rescript, W. K. Bunce, chief of SCAP's Religious Section, who had written the directive abolishing state Shinto, was to observe, rather glumly, "All we can do is tell the Japanese the Emperor is not divine, but they still regard him as a god."

Calmly the Nippon *Times* commented, tongue-in-cheek, that the rescript on divinity did not "represent an unprecedented innovation, as many foreigners think, but really represents a return to the true traditions of Japan after a period of temporary perversion. It can occasion no astonishment, therefore, but only a quiet and profound satisfaction."

Tokyo citizens whom I interviewed seemed to have suddenly discovered, in typical Japanese fashion, that they themselves did not really think the Emperor was divine. They admired the Em-

peror for his frankness and sincerity. Some indicated that they believed divinity changed with the times. Perhaps this move, too, was
a "temporary perversion" like the whole occupaion—a bad dream
from which everybody would be happy to wake up when the Americans departed.

The strangest comment, and a shrewd one, came from the Communists, who almost alone continued to attack the Imperial idea,
human or holy. "The statement of the Emperor's non-divinity shows
he was obliged to retreat because of the pressure of the international situation and the attacks of the people. . . . It is like an octopus
eating its own tentacles when hungry."

4

The divinity striptease gave me fresh hope that I could get a
story on Hirohito for *Life*. Like many others, I had been seeking an
audience for several months. As tribute, one reporter actually had
sent the Emperor, who does not smoke or drink, a weekly gift of
chocolates along with his request for an interview. In addition to
an audience, I wanted permission to have *Life's* photographer, Alfred Eisenstaedt, shoot an informal picture-story about the royal
family.

A member of the Imperial Household staff was enlisted in the
endeavor. He entertained, at considerable expense, higher-ups in
the palace staff and members of the Cabinet. Various arguments
were advanced against the "candid" picture-story. It would break
tradition. The Japanese people were unprepared for it. Others had
asked before me. One of Premier Shidehara's aides suggested that
the last objection could be met by raising my rank above that of an
ordinary Tokyo correspondent or bureau chief. *Life* obligingly elevated me to Chief Far Eastern Editor and Correspondent and Business Manager, *pro tem*.

I was invited to outline in writing for the Emperor the kind of
pictures desired. It was carefully explained to the Emperor's staff
that this was impossible to do accurately unless something was
known in advance about the ordinary activities of the Imperial
family. The aides were evidently unprepared or too embarrassed
to discuss this. In desperation I typed out a script which had the
Emperor reading the funnies with Crown Prince Akihito on his
knee, listening to his daughters play the piano, pushing his grand-

child in a perambulator, browsing in his library with a good book, and squinting over a microscope in his biological laboratory. A letter with the synopsis explained that this script represented the *Life* formula for great men and urged that a picture-story be permitted "to show the people of the world how the Emperor actually lives."

Eisenstaedt never got into the palace to take the pictures, much to his disappointment and mine. But one afternoon an urgent summons came from the director of Sun Photo, the largest Japanese picture agency. With shades drawn and doors closed, the director revealed that he had the greatest scoop in the history of journalism. It did no good to try to hasten his story. He unfolded it at great length between loud sips of tea. Finally he built up to the denouement: for the first time in history photographers had been allowed to photograph the private lives of Their Imperial Majesties. With much ceremony the prints were taken from a wall safe and unveiled before me.

There were about forty of them. My script, offered only as a sample, had been followed to the last detail. In fact, the Japanese had thought up certain telling details which had been omitted. In the library scene, for example, where Hirohito was shown reading the *New York Times*, a bronze bust of Abraham Lincoln was discernible in the corner of the room.

When I protested that the set was sensational and magnificent but undoubtedly untrue, the director was incensed. His own sons had been in the crew of photographers who snapped the pictures. He himself, dressed in frock coat and top hat, had supervised the entire production. They had worked a month of Sundays to obtain the pictures.

The Imperial Household was contacted. Would they verify authenticity of the pictures? Certainly, why should anyone doubt them? Were they not "exactly satisfactory"? I pointed out that the pictures followed my outline very closely. The Imperial Household man looked me straight in the eye and asked, "What outline?" He and his colleagues from that moment on stoutly maintained they had never seen any outline or suggested script. The pictures, they stated, represented the true way in which the Imperial Family lived. I think they believed it even if I did not.

The Imperial Household issued instructions that the pictures must not be released in Japan because they would "shock" the Japanese people. After *Life* published the best of the set, duplicates were released in Japan—with certain exceptions. The Imperial Household ruled that no Japanese publication could show the royal family eating lunch ("because of the food on the table") or in the living room ("because most Japanese do not have pianos"). I inquired, in conversation with a prominent Tokyo editor, if this censorship had been protested. "Oh, no," he said, "it is a praiseworthy censorship. The censors merely want to show the people that the Emperor does not live any better than his people. That is censorship in the name of democracy." Later I found out by talking with two of the photographers who worked on the story that the forty pictures which I received had been pre-censored. The Privy Council men had eliminated various shots showing Hirohito in uniform. The Americans must only see him as a harmless little man.

The photographers felt that they had reached the pinnacle of their careers. "Unless we photograph MacArthur," one said, "there is nothing left to do." When they began the palace assignment they found everyone "stiff and cold" because they had always posed for formal shots. But "the Emperor saw that all was not well and said, 'We will be natural so you be at ease, too.'" When the cameramen recovered from their shock at being addressed directly by the Emperor, they set to work. The Crown Prince asked his father, "What shall I do? How shall I pose?" His father replied, "As you do ordinarily."

The Emperor and his family live in an eight-room house which formerly sheltered the imperial archives. All but one section of the former Tokyo palace was destroyed by the B-29 raids. In October 1944 over 3,000 laborers, many of them Koreans, were sent to Matsushiro in Nagano Prefecture to build an underground redoubt for the royal family. Six of them died working on the mile-long tunnel which led to an air-conditioned hideaway, scheduled for completion by October 1945. Those who have seen both subterranean suites claim that Hirohito's would have surpassed Hitler's in magnificence if not utility. Hirohito never entered his. If he had, he probably would not have been pleased by the showy opulence, since he enjoys living in luxurious simplicity.

When the photographers saw the Imperial slippers, worn and frayed, on the floor outside the Imperial bedroom (which they could not enter) they broke down and cried. "We had no idea things were like that," they told me. "You see the Emperor makes sacrifices for his people."

On the following Sunday when they returned to the palace, the cameramen noticed that the slippers had been mended with tape. They wept again.

The pictures were sent off to *Life* with the warning that "Naturally this is all part of a galvanic public relations campaign to prove the Emperor is a good guy and lives very simply, therefore he is democratic and should be retained."

The campaign to humanize Hirohito was expanded into Japanese publications, too. "My Big Brother, The Emperor" was the headline on a precedent-breaking interview with Prince Takamatsu. He assured reporters that Hirohito "is extremely displeased when he sees something incorrect in the newspapers," and that he is fond of what is right above all. "If he had his way," Takamatsu said, "the people would be told the truth.

"In playing golf, my big brother sticks very close to the rules," Takamatsu gushed on, "and likewise his respect for international law is profound. And in all respects he strives for perfection where the ordinary person might cut corners." The Prince sighed, contemplating so much goodness in one individual. "When he once came down with a children's disease," the Emperor's younger brother reminisced, "he had to be isolated without his toys. Becoming bored in another suite [of rooms] he caught a lot of baby spiders and amused himself with them.

"He is exceedingly considerate of others. When I have a cold, he always asks after my health.

"He is a man of peace," the Prince concluded.

More than a year elapsed before the Emperor and the Empress gave their first joint interview to the Japanese press. The reporters began by making timid inquiries on the progress of the young rice plants being grown within the palace walls. "I know little about rice," Hirohito replied nervously, hoping to shut off any more specific questions on that subject. "Rice is grown within the palace grounds so that I may not forget the farmers' labors and pains in growing it."

Their Majesties then told the sympathetic reporters that they, too, suffered with the people; they could not order new suits or dresses, they ate substitutes for rice. "What food does the Emperor like best?" the reporters asked. "The Emperor eats anything," responded the Empress.

5

Sandwiched in between the new-style ballyhoo, the old guard saw to it that much of the "continuous custom" of the court went on unchanged. During the third week of January 1946, all members of the Imperial Household assembled in the cold, white-walled temporary audience hall of the Imperial Household Ministry for the annual Imperial poetry party. Formerly held in Phoenix Hall of the Palace, which is now destroyed, the party was presided over by the Emperor, who sat on a raised dais in front of a gold-leaf screen. Next to him was his mother. Everyone else in the old rose-bud-carpeted room was given a printed diagram showing exactly where each must stand during the ceremonial.

In the middle of the 80 by 40 foot hall stood the poetry participants, dressed in striped pants and morning coats. First the *koji* read the poems through slowly without incantation. Of five phrases in the poems, the first phrase was then sung by the *hass,* following which the chorus intoned the other four phrases.

Before the war, about 50,000 poems were submitted. In 1946 there were only 14,262. In addition to Hirohito's, five were selected for oral reading—one by a court chamberlain, one by a lady-in-waiting of the Empress Dowager, plus three by ordinary citizens. The five winners did not, of course, attend the party. The poems were read in reverse order of the author's importance—the Empress Dowager's lady-in-waiting's was next to the last and the Emperor's last.

Hirohito's poem was written in his own hand with a badger brush and black ink. It is customary for males to use a white, absorbent type of paper called "Otaka Danshi." Females use scarlet, lavender, or purple in a hard-finished heavy paper "for harmony in color" and according to the seasons. Poems sent into the contest in letters had been reinscribed on scrolls by expert calligraphers.

The party lasted an hour and a half, after which all the poems submitted were presented to Hirohito. "This is a very great honor and also a duty," explained the tall, aesthetic Secretary of the Imperial Poetry Bureau who had succeeded his father in this post and who told me he writes poetry standing up. "The people cannot send any presents to their Emperor except poems," he said, "that's why this event is so important to them."

Some emperors of Japan have written their poems as they would perform any traditional rite, with respectful boredom. But Hirohito since his ascension has each year approached his seventeen-syllable offering as a real labor of love. The Japanese people have come to look forward to his verse knowing that a subtle significance would be worked into the Imperial rendition of the selected theme. Before Pearl Harbor the Emperor extolled the concept of peace while his advisers (and captors) vigorously prepared for war.

In the first year of MacArthur the theme was "Snow on the Pines," and Hirohito's poem advised his people:

> Be like the manly pine
> Which does not change its color
> Though bearing the fallen snow.

The MacArthur men saw nothing strange or ominous in this simple little verse. But Japanese and students of Japanese culture saw much more. On the face of it this was an exhortation to the Japanese to bear up under adversity. But it could also suggest that the weight of defeat was temporary and that the Japanese should not change their ideals; perhaps the occupation forces might melt away, in the spring of their discontent, like the fallen snow—leaving the Imperial tradition still strong and verdant.

6

The next MacArthur-approved step in the democratization of the Emperor began about a month after the poetry contest and seven weeks after the renunciation of divinity. Since the war's end Hirohito had crossed his carp-filled moat only twice: once to pay his respects to General MacArthur, and once to entrain for Kyoto, where he informed his Imperial ancestors of the war's end. Since those peeks at the world outside Hirohito had shed his divinity. In the third week of February 1946, dressed in a fly-front, Oxford gray topcoat, a pearl-gray felt hat which looked as if it had been sat upon more frequently than worn, a dark business suit, blue shirt, white collar and somber, striped silk tie, the new Hirohito sallied forth to meet his public.

At 9 A.M., precisely as advertised, a big black Mercedes Benz spun sedately through the palace gates. The Emperor sat bolt upright in the back seat, looking neither to the right nor to the left. As his car turned right, forty other cars prepared to turn right—including two score black jeeps bulging with foreign reporters and photographers anxious for their first encounter with Japan's ruler.

The road from Tokyo to Yokohama cuts across a bomb-made wasteland. Through the ground glass of his thick lenses and the polished windows of the Mercedes, Hirohito's eyes focused on the magnitude of his country's devastation. Along the bumpy route he saw his people: shabby, shivering, shambling. They greeted their ruler's bizarre cavalcade with bewildered reverence.

Hirohito stepped stiffly from his car at the Kawasaki branch of the Showa Electrical Company near Yokohama. Although this once-great industrial city is only eighteen miles from Tokyo, it was Hirohito's first visit to the area in seventeen years. Plant officials and workers were standing at attention for the occasion, faces drawn up in Sunday smiles. With quick, mincing steps Hirohito's pointed tan shoes pattered toward a tentlike pavilion. He walked uncertainly—like a not-quite-recuperated invalid treading on a path of eggshells. He stood behind a table on which were arranged some flowers and two samples of nitrogen fertilizer in graceful glass vases. While the Emperor clasped his ungloved hands behind his back, the president of the company intoned a long report. The photographers inched closer. Hirohito blinked, squinted, twitched, nodded. The Mayor of Kawasaki succeeded the industrialist, and in his carefully creased morning-coat-voice read another report. The photographers were now almost as close to the Emperor as the vases of fertilizer. Hirohito wet his lips, shifted from foot to foot, sniffled, unclasped his hands, jerked his receding chin up and down.

Standing next to me, his high silk hat in his white-gloved hand, was the Governor of the Kanagawa Prefecture. "This will animate the people," he whispered in my ear. "It will be good for their morale."

The Mayor finished and backed away, bowing. Hirohito's lips moved. The reporters stepped closer. The Emperor said: "Ah so."

Then His Majesty wandered through a maze of wreckage in the plant which had been 75 per cent destroyed. Everywhere workers lined up to catch their first glimpse of their ruler. The Emperor kept his right hand on his hat, bobbed it off and on mechanically like a monkey on a string. Nervously he paused in front of a worker. Photographers and reporters shouldered through the Imperial aides.

"How long have you been working here?" the Emperor asked politely.

"Fifteen years."

"Ah so," said the Emperor.

"*Ah sodeska*," said the worker with finality.

Following chalk marks, Hirohito found his way to an aged woman. "Have you any relatives working in the plant?"

"A sister," she stammered, her eyes on the ground.

"Ah so," said the Emperor. "Are you working hard?" Her face was very dirty. "Yes, I'm doing my best." Hirohito sat his hat back on the top of his head, bowed stiffly, said: "*Ah sodeska*," and moved on.

One of the Emperor's uniformed aides, detailed to keep the tour on schedule, carried a printed program in one hand. In the other was a plexiglas box lined with cotton, containing a Waltham pocket watch. I asked him why he carried the watch that way. "To protect it against dust and shock while the Emperor is depending on it," he replied.

At his second stop Hirohito inspected a Nissan heavy industry factory filled with American machinery from Erie, Cincinnati, Pittsburgh, Toledo, Cleveland. The plant had been scrubbed down for three days to prepare for the royal visitation from Tokyo. The paths were spread with clean sand. Even as the pointed tan shoes timidly approached, the gardeners smoothed the surface like bakers glazing a cake's icing. If anyone dented the surface with a non-regal imprint, willing hands recoated the finish. When Hirohito walked back to his car, he found it surrounded by several hundred G.I.'s, most of them behind cameras. They kept their shutters tripping even after the harried little man had retreated into his 1936 Mercedes and his unsmiling chauffeur had slammed the gold-crested door. One of the G.I.'s turned to me and remarked, "I always called him 'Charlie' after Charlie McCarthy. Hell, he's an Oriental ringer for Chaplin—that *walk*. Jesus!"

After munching a box lunch of hard-boiled egg and cheese sandwiches brought from the palace, Hirohito started out again. He looked tired and unwell. At the Inaridai home for war sufferers he was visibly moved on several occasions as he trailed his guide from dingy room to dingy room. The poor people bowed and scraped, and some wept unashamed tears. In one dark, chilly room there was a demobilized soldier with a wooden leg. Hirohito's jaw sagged, his shoulders seemed more hunched than usual. He rested his battered hat on his chest and addressed the man's wife.

"Where did your husband get wounded?"

"The Philippines."

"Ah so. In the Philippines. Ah so. You have children? I'm very sorry. How long have you been here? This place is rather cold. But it will become warmer. I hope you will cheer up." It was Hirohito's longest speech of the day. The woman bawled. Hirohito darted out of the room.

On the roof of the Yokohama Reconstruction Office, Hirohito blinked as he peered out over the devastated city. Through binoculars he focused on the once busy harbor. American photographers surrounded him.

I saw Hirohito incline his head to his host and I started for the staircase. Somehow the Emperor got there at the same moment. I backed off. Hirohito backed off. I said, *"Dozo,"* which means "please." Hirohito buttoned his coat. He appeared sleepy—the epicanthic eyefold always made him seem that way to non-Orientals. After a second we both started for the top of the stairs again, and then checked. At this crisis a worried aide came forward. "Please," he bowed to me and extended his gloved hand toward the stairs. "No, I cannot go in front of the Emperor. It is better if I follow," said I, glancing at Hirohito. The Emperor shifted his weight; his face remained expressionless.

"If you please, it is preferable if you go first, sir," insisted the aide after exchanging a black look with His Majesty. Hirohito bobbed his head. Slowly I descended four steps in front of the Son of Heaven. At the bottom of the steps he passed me. "Thank you," he said in perfect English.

Seven hours after he had crossed the moat, Hirohito returned. He had seen more people on the streets that day than ever before and more people had seen him. Previously when the Emperor traveled, his car had spun along the high crest of the road and all shades had been drawn so that no mortal could look down upon the Son of Heaven.

With my interpreter I had talked to many Japanese during the trip, and they were nearly all pleased with the Emperor's new tactics. One or two said they thought he had "lost face." If so, he more than made up for it in the affection he gained. Hirohito knew what he was doing. The Potsdam Declaration stated that the Japanese people would choose their own form of government. Hirohito was making sure of their votes.

He had frankly commenced his campaign to run for retention as Emperor on MacArthur's ticket. Shortly afterward, in one of his periodic reports, MacArthur announced that the Emperor's junkets had been well received by the Japanese people. They were continued. In the villages there was great awe and love added to curiosity and pity.

Only the Communists protested. They realized that the Emperor's tours were influencing the coming Diet elections against them, the only anti-Imperial party, and they made an official protest to SCAP. It was, of course, laughed off.

The Emperor ventured farther and farther. In a railway carriage on the way to the much-bombed town of Mito, he wrote this verse for the 1947 Imperial poetry contest:

> The day dawns hopefully upon the
> town of Mito;
> The sound of the hammer is heard clearly.

Students of Japanese joyfully seized on this as a sign that the Emperor was making up for his 1946 lapse and "giving Imperial sanction to the forces that are working for a new, democratic nation." "The sound of the hammer" was undoubtedly meant to symbolize Japan's reconstruction. The democrats read into it "peaceful democratic reconstruction." Those who hoped for the restoration of the old order read into it "the reconstruction of the old order."

Hirohito, the public figure, has not always been a complete success. During the rice planting season last spring he suddenly appeared in a farming village. Superstitious peasants were deeply moved, believing the visitation augured well for the future crops. Some wept with mingled love and pity for the Emperor who stood, huddled in his ill-fitting coat, waiting to be told where to walk. But a disillusioned peasant, noting his indecision, was heard to remark, "The Tenno does not recognize rice."

That fall he was happier celebrating Kannamesai, the traditional Japanese thanksgiving day, in the old way. The Emperor donned his gaudy ceremonial robes, cleansed his hands with holy water, and reported to the Imperial ancestors on the new crop. Then he respectfully placed samples of the harvest on the Shinto altar: a small box of new rice, some fruits and greens, and a bottle of *sake*.

When he spoke on the radio during the 1946 food crisis because MacArthur was worried about mounting dissatisfaction, Hirohito asked the people to "share with each other during the time of poverty." *Asahi*, Japan's most widely circulated newspaper, commented editorially: "The broadcast failed to move the people greatly. . . . His Majesty is the personification of all the tragedies in Japan's history." The editorial writer was quietly rebuked for his temerity and Hirohito was so aggrieved that he was moved to write another poem, this one on the theme of "a pain rising to my breast."

7

By the end of his first year, MacArthur could say, "The Emperor eats out of my hand," and be accurate, at least figuratively. On the surface, things were going well. MacArthur had most of the important editorials and press clippings from American newspapers sent to the Palace after the divinity statement. The Emperor was as delighted with his notices as an ingenue's understudy who suddenly stepped into a too-big role on opening night and got by somehow. Associates let it be known that Hirohito had had misgivings about the advisability of the statement on divinity; now the doubts were dispelled by the fulsome praise from far-off pundits. He sent MacArthur a message admitting that the New Year's declaration had been a fine idea.

Hirohito began to lean more and more on MacArthur for advice and less and less on the remnants of the old palace gang or Privy Council. In the words of one American observer who knew the Imperial family well during the period, they had developed "an intense, devout gratitude to General MacArthur," whom they considered their "savior, protector, champion and, almost, colleague."

In his turn, MacArthur waxed more and more enthusiastic about Hirohito, describing him variously as a "perfect little gentleman" or "the kind of chap you'd be proud to have in your golf club" or "a harmless idealist" or "the most liberal man in the Jap government." The General perhaps began to feel that Hirohito had been born anew, full sprung from MacArthur's brain. When it became propitious for the promulgation of Japan's new MacArthur-inspired constitution, the General saw to it that the show's spotlight centered on the Emperor. In giving his approval for the celebration which would hail the new basic document, MacArthur practically let the Emperor write his own ticket. Later SCAP was to regret this magnanimity. Left to his own devices, the frightened little fellow called in some of his old counselors. They did not lose this opportunity to arrange the setting in the time-honored style which bespoke the old Japan.

The date for the promulgation was fixed so that it fell on the holiday marking the anniversary of the birthday of the Emperor Meiji, whose name is associated with the last Japanese Constitution. This, the group around the Emperor believed, was a shrewd psychological move. Next, they received SCAP's permission for the public display of the Japanese flag, hitherto restricted. Third, they embellished the day with as many Shinto trappings as possible. Early on the morning of November 3, 1946, the little Emperor donned ceremonial robes and, according to Tokyo accounts, formally reported the promulgation of the new Constitution "to the three Imperial sanctuaries within the palace grounds where the souls of the Imperial ancestors are enshrined." This function was attended by Premier Shigeru Yoshida and other high government officials. All this went on despite the fact that the MacArthur directive ordering the abolition of Shinto as a *state* religion specifically forbade Japanese government employees from taking part in official Shinto ceremonies.

Two hours later the Emperor, wearing the dark-blue Imperial uniform, white gloves, and the sixteen-petal insignia of the Grand Order of the Chrysanthemum sing-songed the one-hundred-forty-five-word Imperial rescript proclaiming the promulgation to the Diet. During the brief ceremony which lasted seven minutes, members of the Diet bowed thirty-six times. In the afternoon, at precisely 2:15, six hundred pigeons were released from within the Imperial grounds, the band played the national anthem, and a holiday crowd of 100,000 waited motionless as Their Imperial Majesties arrived outside the palace gates in an open carriage drawn by two chestnut horses. To shouts of *"Banzai!"* the Emperor and Empress mounted the bunting-draped platform and acknowledged the frenzied acclaim of the crowd and the deep bows of the diplomats. They had come, according to the official announcement, to "share with the people the happiness of the new constitution."

Hirohito was pleased and so were his intimate friends. The Cabinet was pleased, too, until they received a sharp warning from MacArthur. The War Department had deferentially called SCAP's attention to the fact that the press stories on the promulgation of the constitution had clearly indicated that the fuss made over Shinto shenanigans and the furor caused by the Emperor had well camouflaged the original significance of the ceremonies. SCAP sent a note to Premier Yoshida and told him to guard against permitting "irresponsible elements again to win influence over the Emperor." The misguided Emperor was sorely grieved over MacArthur's displeasure; he consoled himself that SCAP did not consider the fault was his but rather that of his advisers.

8

The eventual price society may have to pay for the retention of the Tenno system is impossible to foretell. Hirohito's casting aside of divinity and being fitted with a cloak of constitutional monarchy seemed revolutionary not so many months ago.

A scholarly authority on Japan, Dr. Willis Church Lamott, who was a Presbyterian missionary in Japan for twenty years, has since pointed out that "The shift of the Emperor from being successor to the progenitress of the cosmos to being a mere symbol of state was no more revolutionary than his elevation as the moral center of the nation in 1868." Count Makino, who impressed prewar United States Ambassador to Japan, Joseph C. Grew, as "a really great gentleman," was asked how the new constitution affected the Emperor. "Not at all," replied Makino, former Lord Keeper of the Privy Seal, "he has always been a constitutional emperor." A responsible SCAP official cautioned a correspondent, "Let's face the facts," he said, referring to any rumors of change in the relation between the people and the Emperor, "they still worship him."

The Japanese, long trained in the recognition of force and rank, have been tremendously impressed by the symbol of the American occupation. It is not the American flag. They note with satisfaction that the victorious armies are also ruled under a rigid hierarchal system, that in all Japan there is only one five-star celestial body, and that nobody talks back to him. In their eyes the economic strength, the military might, the moral prestige of all the Allied powers is given form and substance in the frame of a tall authoritarian in khaki. Today and tomorrow their submission to MacArthur makes the path of the occupation smoother, just as yesterday their blind submission to the Emperor made easier the roads to war and to surrender.

One day last year in Tokyo I asked a former Japanese Army private named Ishigawa what would happen in Japan when MacArthur departed.

The youth's expression was one of intense concern. He respected MacArthur greatly.

"He go back now, soon?" he asked.

I explained I did not think MacArthur would be recalled, but there was always the chance, since the General was well advanced in years, that he might retire or he might even die.

"Die? Die?" the Japanese shook his head dejectedly. "What happen then, please?"

I did not know. After a moment's silence the Japanese smiled cheerfully.

"If maybe not die soon," he said, "maybe Maccassar son take his place, Japanese people very happy."

CHAPTER III

MacARTHUR: FROM MAN TO GOD

On November 28, 1946, Tokyo's largest stadium was filled with thousands of school children celebrating Thanksgiving Day. They heard Japanese speakers express thanks to America for its kindnesses, for its guidance, and most particularly for General Douglas MacArthur. The Supreme Commander, said a member of the Yoshida Cabinet, "always shines before us, as the morning star which throws its glorious beams upon this earth."

There seems little doubt that MacArthur has caught the Japanese imagination more completely than any American has since George Herman ("Babe") Ruth last visited Japan in 1934. Hundreds of fans line up daily outside American headquarters at the Dai Ichi Building just to watch for the dramatic moment when MacArthur appears in the doorway, hesitates a long second, touches his jaunty military hat, and then strides majestically to his polished Cadillac limousine.

Since the Americans arrived, thousands of MacArthur's Japanese subjects have written him every month. These expressions of unsolicited opinion, better than any newspaper editorials, indicate the feelings of the Japanese man-in-the-street toward the new *shogun*.

Letters come from Japanese in all walks of life: university professors who write him volumes suggesting shifts in the nation's economy, war criminals admitting their guilt, self-appointed spies, prostitutes, farmers, small business men, school children.

Although almost convinced that MacArthur is human, they take no chances of offending his vanity. Salutations usually err on the side of the gods. The General is addressed as "Your Highness," "To the Highest Commander of Them All," and very frequently "Marshal MacArthur." Most letters are quick to say something complimentary about the new ruler in the first sentence or two.

41

One correspondent stated categorically that MacArthur is "the greatest man in the world," another urged him to "bring your family to Japan and become our President." A Japanese Christian minister wrote from prison, "We believe that our Lord has dispatched you to save us from the dark miserable world."

The most popular subject in MacArthur's mail, and for the General himself, is the occupation. Opinions are nearly all favorable. One MacArthur partisan requested SCAP to make Japan pro-American and pledged, "When America fight with any other country every young people of Japan naturally stand and join American Army as volunteers." Another pro-American urged a permanent occupation by the United States, while another advocated that Japan become an American territory like Hawaii. A deaf and dumb boy was so stricken with admiration for all things American and for MacArthur, too, that he beseeched the General's help in getting to the States so he could become an American citizen. "I have absolute no Japanese spirit," he assured the General. "I am yankeefied."

When scribes compare their own temporal leaders with Mac-Arthur it is much to the General's favor. The chief reason his correspondents are impressed is because MacArthur "works late at night" and "goes about without bodyguard." There are several triggermen around the General always, but compared to Hirohito's Imperial retinue it seems scarcely worth mentioning.

MacArthur never issued a directive requiring the Japanese to write to him. But when letters started dropping through his slot he permitted stories in the Japanese press to hint strongly that he was not displeased. Approximately two-thirds of MacArthur's mail is in English. The other third, which is more serious and lengthy, keeps a special staff of translators busy. It is a common occurrence for letters in Japanese to arrive in heavy paper scrolls which, when unwound, measure ten yards. Translators, all Nisei, put everything into English. Once they translated an entire religious play about Christ before someone realized it was not meant to be an ode to MacArthur.

The General personally likes to keep up with this fan mail. Each morning his aide puts a two- or three-line English summary of each letter on the General's desk. MacArthur believes this helps him sense the trend of people's thinking on the occupation. At first he ruled that the Supreme Commander should not personally answer any communications from the Japanese. Later he relented and wrote to a few small-boy admirers.

Most letters are shuttled around to the various headquarters sections which might be especially interested in the subject matter. Letters which require answering then receive polite formal replies from junior officers.

As the occupation progressed, more and more writers offered personal favors to MacArthur and sought them from him. He was invited to attend a mushroom hunt, *samo* games, or to undergo a course in Japanese Buddhist culture at Kyoto. Small gifts often arrive with the letters: fruits, nuts, silks, handkerchiefs, ceremonial cakes, handmade wooden trays. One letter informed MacArthur that he would find a wild boar at the railroad station which the writer had sent as a present. The boar was so huge it filled an army truck. The General graciously dispatched the truck and the boar to an enlisted men's mess. Most frequent offerings are specially composed poems and colorful prints. A sixth-grade student "as appreciation" enclosed in his note to the General his drawings of MacArthur, Henry Ford, President Truman, and a jeep.

But favors asked are far more numerous than favors bestowed. Three French teachers wanted MacArthur to use his "influence" to obtain for them a room in a Tokyo hotel. A hunter pled for permission to retain his ancient rifle for rabbit hunting. An author begged official blessing for his projected historical novel.

In accordance with Japan's new-found free speech, MacArthur's mail is now spiced with warnings, suggestions, and even criticisms. A man signing himself only "a journalist of Japan Times" flexed his pen before MacArthur with this charge: "I have the honor to inform you that Ichero Tokutami (old journalist, his pen name Soho) is the terrible criminal of the war. He has always the extreme antipathy for the American peoples. He is the worst leader of abominable Japanese militarism. I believe he shall be punishable most quickly."

Aside from over-all approval of the occupation and of MacArthur, the most frequent subject touched on by the letters has been the prosecution of war criminals. Occasionally a special pleader will protest the innocence of the royal family or of Marquis Kido. But the overwhelming majority approve the trials. Inevitable topics for complaint are food and rations (they want more), Japanese bureaucracy (they want less), bringing relatives back home from

Siberia or prison camps overseas, revision of election and education laws, and charges against Japanese police. Non-complainers have very varied suggestions: abolish prostitution and birth control; use parachutes for making G.I. souvenirs; make baseball and rugby available everywhere; withdraw freedom of speech because Japan is not ready for it; change from left- to right-hand driving; investigate the Government's announced plans to build wider roads because it is only "a blind for another war."

The men who handle MacArthur's mail pay special attention to letters from women. To them it is an indication that the Japanese are taking seriously the directive which equalizes the status of the female sex. They are amazed at the number of woman who suggest that the General sire a Japanese-American baby. One self-styled lady correspondent says she prays for MacArthur's health, and continues, "Due to propaganda the writer had thought that American soldiers were barbarous, but on the contrary found that they were well-behaved. She sincerely appreciates this and requests that the Americans stay as long as possible."

Another lady letter-writer confesses:

General MacArthur,
I had no man to appeal to till now. If I had written to the War Minister in Japan he would not cast a glance over my letter and it is in vain. The Emperor must have pity upon us; but he is too high and unapproachable for us. My letter to him will never be read by him; his vassals will break it and throw it away under the reason of being too awfully, I know.
Before closing my letter, I am very glad to support you and your work in Japan heartily. You are doing very nicely and now you are getting the confidence of all Japanese people, not only men but also women. I want to send my hearty encouragement to you. 'Spare the rod and you will spoil child'; now Japan is just a little baby in democratic life, you see.
Hoping you may keep a complete health, and sending my best love to Mrs. MacArthur. Sincerely yours, Kazuko Karasawa.

2

After more than a year of adoration and adulation typified in these letters a few Japanese intellectuals began to have worries. The MacArthur myth was becoming so strong that, at least in the cities and towns, it was rivaling the Emperor myth. A popular biography idealizing MacArthur and written by Journalist Kazuyoshi Yamzaki, sold almost a million copies. The author was besieged by letters thanking him for the "glorious" book; the letters called MacArthur "a living god" and "the reincarnation of Emperor Jimmu."

On October 3, 1946, an editor of the *Jiji Shimpo*, a Tokyo newspaper, wrote an editorial warning the Japanese people against believing that MacArthur was a living god. The editorial, after a week's delay, was passed by the SCAP censorship office and the article was published on October 11. The *Nippon Times*, the English language newspaper controlled by the Japanese Foreign Office and now read mainly by occupation forces, approved the sentiments in the *Jiji* editorial and prepared to reprint it with appropriate comment. The editorial page was dispatched to the censors and came back approved. After the presses had started to run, occupation officials rushed to the plant and confiscated all the papers.

The paragraphs in *Nippon Times* which MacArthur's men had decided to suppress were:

Now a few Japanese must once have esteemed Hitler as a person greater than Napoleon. More wished that a Hitler might emerge from among the Japanese. It may be assumed that today many Japanese are wishing for General MacArthur to take the leadership of the nation.

It must be emphasized that unless and until the Japanese are cleansed of this servile concept, democracy in Japan will make no progress. Only a nation with enough guts to carve a destiny for itself will be able to establish a democratic government and operate it successfully. The first step in the process of democratization must be to rid the nation of the habit of hero worship which has imbued [Japanese] minds for the past twenty centuries.

Junior officers found nothing "dangerous" in this warning to the Japanese people, but General Charles A. Willoughby, in charge of SCAP's intelligence outfits as well as its censorship division, did not like it. With a squad of M.P.'s he rushed to the ramshackle *Nippon Times* plant, stopped the presses, and sent men to remove already printed copies from outgoing trains and trucks. "Occupation authorities," said Willoughby sternly, "must be protected against correspondents. The article was not in good taste." Willoughby has been chief of MacArthur's G-2 since Bataan.

The infallibility of great men is one of the rigid precepts upon which the MacArthur occupation rests. It also leans heavily on the codified dogma of democracy. When the two come into conflict

it is often found that democracy is more susceptible to interpretation and pliability than the rights and privileges of great men.
In May 1946, during the food crisis, an irate Japanese named
Matsutaro Matsushima, who believed what he had heard about
freedom of expression, caricatured Hirohito on a placard. It
depicted the Emperor eating while other Japanese starved. Matsushima was arrested on charges of lèse majesté.

This action did not sit well with the Dai Ichi brain trust,
especially since the press had heard about the arrest. If Hirohito
were a democratic Emperor, there should be no such thing as lèse
majesté. MacArthur lawyers conferred with Japanese judges.
Matsushima was sentenced to eight months' imprisonment on a
charge of "defamation." This penalty seems unduly severe; some
of the chief Domei directors who "defamed" Americans daily for
years were wandering freely around Tokyo not many months after
the occupation commenced. But "authority" had to be protected.
Later Hirohito pardoned Matsushima. But the new precedent had
been established in Japanese minds. "The Americans do not call
it lèse majesté," they observed, "it is only libel." (Japan never
had a law of libel.)

A year later the Japanese again were baffled by a SCAP action
in defense of authority. Earlier in the occupation G.I.'s had performed the Gilbert and Sullivan operetta, "The Mikado," which
had previously been banned in Japan. But in June 1947, when a
Japanese company was preparing to present the musical satire for
the first time, SCAP interceded and prohibited the show out of
deference to Hirohito and the Imperial Family.

MacArthur's censors have given the American working press the
same rough treatment accorded the Japanese. Two men were removed from the Tokyo edition of Stars and Stripes for a "negative
loyalty check" which showed one had fought for the Loyalists in
Spain and the other had edited a C.I.O. newspaper. The G.I. daily
was not allowed to publish a letter from forty-four soldiers griping
about the food. In fact the newspaper was not permitted to print
reports on the occupation by its own staff; it had to use copies of
wire service stories being filed out of Japan.

Although a free press is to be the goal in Japan, few would be
willing to allow Japanese newspapers unrestricted liberties to
attack the occupation. Censorship had to be established for reasons
of morale and security. But the record indicates that MacArthur,

through his censors, has used his power over the Japanese press
for reasons other than the progress of the occupation. At times these
reasons have partisan political significance and on other occasions
they seem to represent only personal prejudices.

There are numerous examples of this kind of interference in
news originating in the United States as well as Japan. Henry
Wallace's letter to President Truman about foreign policy and his
subsequent speech were held up by the censors in Tokyo for
forty-eight hours. When they were finally released they were so
sliced into ribbons that only an "interpretive" article and not a news
story could be written by bewildered Japanese journalists.

For New Year's Day, 1947, President Philip Murray of the C.I.O.
sent a greeting to Japanese labor which SCAP censored for reasons
of its own. Here is the Murray message with the censored portions
bracketed in italics:

I am happy to send a message from the American C.I.O. to Japanese
labor. Laborers of the world have many things in common and all
(*opposed to dictatorship in the black days before the war*) seeking peace,
safety and jobs. The C.I.O. believes in world peace and depends on the
collaboration of the laborers of the whole world. This collaboration has
been possible through the World Federation of Trade Unions. (*I
earnestly hope the day will come soon when Japanese labor will send
delegates to this fighting organization of democratic labor unions. There
are American C.I.O. members in the American Occupation's labor division, and others of our members helped reform the Japanese educational
system. These men praise the Japanese masses who are longing for
democracy.*)

Burton Crane of the *New York Times* examined sixty stories
censored by SCAP and found that "only two or three seemed direct
violations of the press code" which was promulgated on September
18, 1945. This code required the processing of news in truthful
and uncolored manner and banned anything likely to upset public
tranquillity, or that criticized the Allies, or invited "mistrust or
resentment" against occupation forces.

Owing to its abuses, censorship has almost become a greater
evil than unrestricted license. The Japanese people are not to
know how great a hand SCAP has had in shaping their future; they
are not to know the cost of the occupation; they are not to know
the ultimate plans for reparations. Such ignorance of facts breeds
rumor, which is often more "likely to upset public tranquillity"

than straight reporting. It also begins to dry the powder for future Japanese explosions against the Allies; it will surely supply ammunition for future fanatics to "expose" to the Japanese people how they have been taken in.

3

MacArthur has the double misfortune of being the world's most and worst press-agented General. The stories of his troubles with the press during the long Pacific campaign are well known. His communiques kept up the myth of small casualties, they kept MacArthur's name in the papers, they kept the censors busy cutting out any references which reflected on the verity of MacArthur's releases or his generalship. Much of this could be excused as wartime necessity, but the abuses did not end with the war. On the day of the United States victory in the Pacific, his press relations officers barred all Navy broadcasts on the grounds that "this is the Commander-in-Chief's day." They refused permission for a recorded speech by Admiral Thomas C. Kinkaid to go on the air. "Nothing shall be said or done this day to detract from the personal publicity or glorification of the Commander-in-Chief," was the explanation.

As reward for their services, thirty-seven of MacArthur's forty censors and press-relations men received decorations. Brigadier General A. LeGrande Diller, the chief MacArthur PRO for most of the war, told his staff, "Thank you for helping me attain my goal of seeing that General MacArthur got the credit for everything in the Pacific and making sure that he was appointed Supreme Commander."

When Diller left Japan early in the occupation, his role as chief tub-thumper for the MacArthur troupe was taken over by roly-poly Brigadier General Frayne Baker, a genial National Guardsman from North Dakota. Correspondents felt that press conditions would be better under Baker. They were—so long as reporters rewrote the daily releases from headquarters. When persevering journalists began digging into the untold stories of the occupation, when they found out that there was often a glaring discrepancy between directive and implementation, Baker hurriedly erected MacArthur's defenses. Section heads suddenly refused to talk to reporters without clearance from GHQ. A conclave of American and British correspondents protested to Baker. He appeared not to know what all the fuss was about.

The busy, big PRO office kept itself and MacArthur well-informed on which correspondents were saying nice things about the Old Man and the occupation, and which were being critical. A file of stories and a comment "plus" or "minus" was cabled daily by the War Department in Washington to Tokyo. When a correspondent with a "minus" rating left Japan for a trip to China or a vacation home, he often found it difficult to get back into Japan.

On December 3, 1946, Drew Pearson broke the story of a MacArthur cable to the War Department announcing that he did not welcome representatives of certain newspapers which had been unfavorable to his occupation. The War Department had tactfully suggested a press tour such as had been carried out in Germany. According to Pearson, MacArthur cabled back:

While continuing my doubts as to the advisability of the contemplated trip, in view of the insistence of the War Department, I will withdraw my objection. I would like to have an opportunity to pass upon those contemplated for selection before their invitation is accomplished.

I believe the list should not include actual writers but should be limited to publishers and editors and should not include those connected with papers of known hostility to the occupation.

Such papers as the *Christian Science Monitor, Herald Tribune*, Chicago *Sun*, San Francisco *Chronicle, PM, Daily Worker*, and others of this stamp whose articles and editorials have not only been slanted but have approached downright quackery and dishonesty.

Those familiar with the conservative, Republican policies of the *Monitor*, the New York *Herald Tribune* and the *Chronicle* may be amazed at this outburst. By strange coincidence some of the most capable, fearless, and independent correspondents in MacArthur's theater since the end of the war have been the representatives of these newspapers. Frank Kelley, a reporter for the *Herald Tribune*, brilliantly detailed the abuses of censorship under MacArthur; Gordon Walker of the *Monitor* sent a keenly analytical series of dispatches on the good and bad points of the occupation. When he tried to return to Japan from another country, his visa was held up by MacArthur. His only sin had been "a lack of patriotism" in writing about the bad as well as the good.

When important editors and publishers are ushered in to meet MacArthur during their junkets to Japan, the General always assures them there is complete press freedom for Allied reporters in Japan. Many American and British correspondents do not believe this to be true and if MacArthur believes it, then he is being "shielded" by his staff from the facts of the case.

In the spring of 1947 Robert P. Martin of the New York *Post* went back to Japan to care for the effects of Correspondent Dixie Tighe who died in Tokyo. Martin, who is one of the keenest reporters in the Far East, naturally filed stories to his paper. After he had been sending dispatches for five weeks, SCAP suddenly gave him 26 hours to board a plane for Shanghai on the technical grounds that he had not entered Japan as a correspondent. The other newsmen in Tokyo unanimously protested to MacArthur's headquarters and at the last moment Martin's status was changed and he was allowed to remain. The correspondents had threatened to make a big issue of "freedom of the press," and SCAP backed down, although an earlier cable from the War Department directing that Martin be duly accredited as a correspondent had been ignored.

Writing of this incident, Martin was convinced the attempt had been made against him because he had filed critical stories about certain phases of the occupation. He also reported that SCAP had warned Japanese officials not to talk with Allied reporters, that five correspondents had been threatened with court-martial if they filed a certain story, and still another was told he would be tried under the articles of war if he did not divulge his sources of information.

On several occasions SCAP's Public Relations officers have interfered with press freedom by cabling to home offices urging that a correspondent's dispatch not be published or suggesting that the offending reporter be withdrawn from the theater. The great issue at stake, according to Martin, is no longer the personal glory of Douglas MacArthur. The issue is a more important one for the American people. "SCAP's public relations policy at present," Martin cabled after he had been reinstated, "is to convince America that the democratization of Japan has achieved unprecedented success and that the Japanese government has furthered this process voluntarily. The first premise is debatable and the second is contrary to fact."

Not long after the "Martin Affair," SCAP did expel another correspondent. David Conde was chief of SCAP's Motion Picture Division while I was in Japan, working hard to help the Japanese develop democratic themes in their movies. Later he went to work as a correspondent and for nine months filed stories for International News Service and the British agency, Reuters. Early in 1947 he had a by-line article in the St. Louis *Post-Dispatch* critical of the way SCAP was censoring the Japanese press; in the *Far Eastern Survey* he published an exposé of the way the Yoshida government was mismanaging the problem of the Korean minority in Japan. Although he had applied for a correspondent's accreditation in July 1946, he was suddenly notified in March 1947 that he must leave. The members of the Tokyo Correspondents' Club again protested, but even their demand that Conde be permitted to remain in Tokyo until he had appealed to the State Department was denied.

If they could get away with it, MacArthur's top public relations officials would never settle for anything less than complete approval of the occupation and deification of the "chief."

When Dennis McEvoy was starting the Japanese edition of the *Reader's Digest*, it was decided that it would be good business and good politics to include a profile of MacArthur in the first issue. A copy of the article, which originally appeared in *Collier's*, was sent to General Baker. When he had read the copy, Baker called in McEvoy. The normally placid General was slightly apoplectic. He said the article was a disgrace, an insult to MacArthur. McEvoy insisted that the over-all content of the story was favorable to the Supreme Commander.

After they had argued for a while, it became apparent that Baker objected to any criticism of MacArthur which the article cited but did not necessarily condone. "You think it should be 100 per cent favorable?" McEvoy asked. Baker agreed.

Like his chief, Baker believes that any unflattering reference to the Old Man is "playing the Russians' game." Therefore, such reporting of the state of the occupation is unpatriotic, disloyal, and in effect, treasonable.

This writer had a similar experience. After a long period of waiting I was informed by Baker that "certain high officers around the Old Man" had advised against the granting of permission for a *Life* story on MacArthur. Baker explained that *Time* and *Life* had been critical of the General and therefore he could see no reason for doing a favor for the Luce publications. I drafted a cable to this effect for the New York office and submitted it to Baker for his approval. He changed a few words to tone it down slightly. In New York a comprehensive check was made in both magazines and practically nothing which could be considered "critical" or unfavorable about the General was found. When General Baker was apprised of this he suggested that the "Old Man" was extremely fond of Henry and Clare Luce, and that perhaps the best step was for one of them to send MacArthur a personal cable asking the *Life* story as a favor. To my knowledge, this was never done.

Before I left Japan General Baker told me that he had a camera and he might be able to get the needed pictures for *Life* all by himself. His kind offer was rejected. On that occasion I asked whether or not he could arrange for me an interview with Mac-Arthur before my departure. Baker replied that the Old Man was probably too busy but that he would let me know. Baker never arranged the interview. The day before I was scheduled to leave for Korea, Guthrie Janssen of the National Broadcasting Company and I requested and got an interview through the intercession of MacArthur's aide, Colonel H. B. Wheeler.

4

MacArthur's office on the sixth floor of the Dai Ichi Building bears no inscription on the door. We walked past the lone G.I. guard through a small anteroom with a table and coat-racks and into a really spacious, air-conditioned, walnut-paneled office, decorated in tones of brown. General MacArthur was pacing up and down behind his neat, polished desk. He was taller and thinner than I had expected, and he had less hair. His dress was casually correct. As Colonel Wheeler introduced us the General strode forward, shook hands, and said, "I am *very* glad to meet *you*."

Indicating that we should sit on the brown leather sofa, Mac-Arthur dropped into a big, overstuffed, leather armchair and Wheeler left the room. The General seemed tired. There was a strange tenseness in his face despite the waxworks smoothness of his skin. He did not look his sixty-seven years. While he talked he continually worked his hands, and sometimes the well-manicured fingers which held his familiar corncob pipe trembled. The nervous tension never ceased. It kept building up. Emphasizing a point he would spring out of his chair, reach his desk in two giant steps, pick up a box of matches, and rattle them over his head like a saber. He seized on our questions as if they were the most important things in the world. He would eagerly catch the question, no matter how casually asked, and then he would lean back and play with it. His tension was that of a coil tightly wound around a resilient core. With head reared back and chin jutting out, he would begin answering and the words rolled forth as if they were heaven's final dictum on the subject. For emphasis MacArthur employed a sort of breathless eloquence, almost whispering a word here, drawing out a word there, then clipping one very short. It was effective, at least partially. Comparing our impressions later we found that we had both thought MacArthur sounded more like an educator than a militarist. MacArthur reminded Janssen of a university president who was excited about the poetry of Horace, while I kept thinking of him as headmaster of an Episcopalian prep school.

It was more of an interview than we had anticipated. Most sessions with the General, we had heard, turned into fascinating monologues. We had been forewarned that the only time for asking questions was when the General stopped to light his pipe. But on this occasion the General was in fine fettle despite his nervousness. He talked about the Soviet Union as "The Russian Bear" and about China as "The Chinaman." He reserved his greatest eloquence for Japan and the bringing of democracy to Japan. There were evangelical overtones as he talked of his mission; there was an Aimee Semple McPherson look in his eye. It was almost inconceivable that this same thin-lipped man had said, looking down upon some dead Japanese at Los Negros, "This is the way I like to see them." MacArthur, the civil administrator, was now against the "kick-'em-in-the-face" boys. The man who had once been a symbol of last-ditch opposition to the Japanese was now their ardent defender. He seemed to believe completely in the sincerity of their humility.

We gathered nothing from this interview that MacArthur has not since told others. He was not pleased by the creation of the Far Eastern Commission, but he was glad they had come to Japan because he thought he had something pretty good to show them. Time and again he has told visitors that Japan is a great spiritual and economic vacuum which offers an unparalleled opportunity to those who believe in Christian democracy and the Christian Church. He likes to divide his own mission into distinct stages: first, the formulation of policies and second, their execution. The first phase was completed with the framing of the new constitution. MacArthur recognized that America had a stupendous selling job ahead of it. To win Japanese acceptance of the "democratic ideal" was important, but even more vital was selling the Japanese the idea of peace. "War," the General admitted, "is a failure. We should renounce it and at the same time hold on to the atom bomb." At another time he observed, "There must not be a next war. If there is, the loser is not the only loser—the victor loses, too."

MacArthur has projected his thinking to the not far distant day when Japan will re-enter the family of nations as a friend and ally of the United States. Since we decided not to wipe out the Japanese, even though we had the means to do it at a relatively low cost, the General is convinced we must help the Japanese to live. Consequently Japan should import food as well as ideas from the United States and must be allowed to export raw materials and some finished products. He has come to rate the Japanese high on ability as well as sincerity and he is not likely to favor any program or peace treaty which will retard their progress.

In conversations MacArthur often refers to the period of military occupation as "from three to five years." He recognizes that the controlling factor on the length of the military control will be America's relations with Russia. The General likes to talk of vacuums and he foresees one in Japan if we leave too soon, because then "the Russian will move in." While on the topic of Russia the General will freely admit he is sorry the Soviets entered the war against Japan. They should have come in at the time of Bataan, he believes, or not at all.

Although he rarely exhibits in public any grave forebodings about the success of the occupation, there is one concern which nags at MacArthur. It has nothing to do with the Soviet Union or with worry about Britain "playing the Muscovite game." He has a strong hunch that underneath the surface calm the Japanese are burning over their defeat and that one day they will turn against their leaders and their institutions, even against the Emperor "unless I democratize him." In line with this hunch he has a feeling that there comes a point at which an occupation force loses its usefulness. It may become the scapegoat for this deep-seated Japanese "burning." MacArthur recognizes, too, that men placed in a foreign country as overlords become corrupt or tempted by corruption after a while. He knows that he and the "Bataan crowd" are above this, but he has doubts about the G.I.

These were some of the things that Douglas MacArthur had in the back of his mind when he surprised everyone, including the United States Department of State, by suggesting in his talk at the Tokyo Correspondents' Club on March 17, 1947, that he was anxious to have a peace treaty concluded with Japan "as soon as possible" and to have non-military control by the United Nations substituted for occupation by Allied armed forces.

5

By education and experience, Douglas MacArthur appears to be eminently suited for his exalted status as Japan's *shogun*. From the very beginning his career has been illuminated by the spotlight of success. He graduated from West Point in 1903 with the highest marks in the history of that institution. In World War I he became the youngest divisional commander in the annals of the U. S. Army. Subsequently he was also the youngest superintendent of West Point and the youngest Chief of Staff of the United States Army. While occupying the latter post he was in charge of routing the veterans' bonus army and burning their temporary camps in Washington. In 1935 on his return to the Far East, where he had first journeyed with his father three decades earlier, MacArthur was appointed Field Marshal of the Philippine Army. At Manila he began molding a closely integrated, intensely loyal staff of officers, many of whom have served with him ever since. Since the epic defense against superior Japanese forces, this group has come to be known as the "Bataan crowd."

MacArthur's conduct of the war in the Pacific will be a debatable topic for generations to come. In the final analysis his strategy and tactics proved successful, although not as superhuman as his press-agents and his communiques would lead one to believe. In fairness to MacArthur, history will almost certainly show that he was maligned by rumor almost as much as he was deified by idolaters. His extreme vanity, his photogenic profile, his flair for distinctive uniforms and his gift of phrase made him an obvious target for vicious caricature and violent vituperation. While he could do no wrong in the words of Hearst, McCormick, and Patterson editorialists, he could do no right in the eyes of many G.I.'s whom he commanded and of the Marines whose command had eluded him. The Pacific jungles buzzed with satiric song and verse about the great MacArthur. One Guadalcanal Marine, annoyed by Mac-Arthur's flamboyant utterances, wrote this jingle:

> And while it's possibly rumor now,
> Some day it will be fact
> That the Lord will hear a deep voice say:
> "Move over, God, it's Mac."

Today in Japan, stories and rumors about MacArthur are still swapped by soldiers after lights are out.

They tell how during the first cold spell of the occupation MacArthur sent for the aging Premier Shidehara. Shidehara tried to speak but MacArthur interrupted and told him that his government had better get coal from the closed mines and get it fast. Shidehara kept attempting to say something through an interpreter but MacArthur never gave him an opening until he stood up as a signal for Shidehara to leave. Finally Shidehara asked the interpreter to apologize to the General because he, Shidehara, was dressed only in an informal sack suit, and to explain that he did not have many clothes left. MacArthur barked at the interpreter, "Get this! Tell him he is damn lucky to have any clothes left."

They tell how later MacArthur relented and when Shidehara was sick, the General sent him penicillin and doctors.

They tell how the Emperor's Grand Chamberlain asked a liaison officer if it were true that one of MacArthur's grandmothers had been Japanese. When informed that this was not so, the Grand Chamberlain shook his head sadly and said, "We in the palace wondered because only someone with Japanese blood could have such a fine attitude towards the Imperial family."

They tell how it was planned for the Russians to send a token occupation force to Japan like Britain and other Allied countries. But when the Russians asked to land on Hokkaido, the northernmost island, the Old Man bellowed: "Nothing doing. If the damn Reds want to come in, we want to have troops between them and their home bases in case of war!" And, they tell, that is why the Russians didn't come in.

They tell that when the wind whips from the Dai Ichi Building across the moat toward the Palace, MacArthur can walk out the window of his sixth-floor office and walk across the water of the moat.

They tell how MacArthur gave an audience to the women elected to the first postwar Diet and charmed them all with a pretty speech and a warm handshake. On another occasion they tell, some Japanese women who brought him flowers knelt low before him and he bade them rise, saying unto them, "In a democracy we bow to no one."

They tell how MacArthur has ordered that the M.P.'s who guard him must be specially selected for their good looks and fine physiques, so as to impress the Japanese.

They tell how SCAP is the most powerful and influential American alive because even the Secretary of Interior flew to Tokyo to ask Mac's views on the administration of the Pacific Islands, ignoring MacArthur's superior, the Secretary of War.

They tell how, at one time or another, MacArthur has told the Far Eastern Commission, the Secretary of War, the Secretary of State, and even the President what they could do with their instructions.

They tell how General Eisenhower, when asked at a press conference if he knew MacArthur, said that he had spent four years studying dramatics under him in the Philippines.

Rarely do they speak with affection for their chief. Their affection is reserved for "Ike"—Lieut.-General Robert Eichelberger, the big, bluff, friendly commander of the Eighth Army in Japan.

Most of the replacements, who never served under MacArthur during the war, do not share the cynicism of combat troops about the Commander-in-Chief. Very few of them have not at some time or other joined the eager throng of Japanese who daily wait outside the Dai Ichi Building to catch a glimpse of the General. Some of them resent his aloofness, his apparent unconcern for G.I. welfare, and the fact that he lives in comparative luxury. But this is no more than the usual feelings of a factory worker for the head of his corporation. Many army men believe MacArthur's manner and mode of living is psychologically valuable to the occupation.

6

With his quiet, pretty wife and their frail, ten-year-old son, Arthur, the Supreme Commander resides in the United States Embassy atop Renanzaka Hill. This is a compound of four rambling, many-roomed structures, built at great expense in 1930 to impress the Japanese with the grandeur of the United States. It is surrounded by a high, white concrete wall and the iron gates of the entrance are under a clock-around watch by stalwart M.P.'s.

The General spends most of his time at home. He makes two daily trips to his office, remaining there from 11 A.M. to 2:30 P.M., and from 5 P.M. to 8 P.M. in the afternoon. He almost never attends diplomatic parties, preferring to spend his leisure playing with his young son or reading to him from the classics of literature. He has never appeared at a Japanese public function. Only once has he been out of Tokyo since his arrival; on that occasion he drove to Atsugi Airfield to fly to Manila for the celebration of Philippine independence. He has appeared, to most Japanese, as haughty and aloof as Hirohito was before the war.

Mrs. MacArthur is a delicate foil for her husband's leading role. When there are guests, she is a charming conversationalist until her husband appears. Then she speaks infrequently except to draw him out—which is rarely necessary. "She is a Bess Truman rather than an Eleanor Roosevelt," an American diplomat after staying with the MacArthurs explained to me. "She blends rather than adds, if you know what I mean."

In the past year Mrs. MacArthur has devoted some of her energies to the redecoration of the Embassy, returning the pieces which former Ambassador Joseph Grew and his wife had left behind. Over the fireplace in the spacious MacArthur drawing room is a brilliantly colored wall decoration, conceived by Mrs. MacArthur, and made from a Japanese *obi*. She has learned a good deal about the Japanese art of flower decoration and spends a half-hour each day arranging bouquets sent by admirers.

The MacArthurs seldom entertain formally but even a visitor invited casually for luncheon or dinner is impressed by the dignified pomp and harmonious circumstance which always accompany a meal at the MacArthurs. "Say, this *is* Oriental splendor," is what the touring Congressman says after he has padded along half a city block of plush carpet from the iron grilled gateway to the drawing room. Then Mrs. MacArthur politely reminds him that the Embassy was built while Hoover was President.

In the long and stately dining room lit by tapering candles, eight perfectly trained Japanese serve food which has been called "interesting and substantial but not fancy." The Japanese wear black kimonos with the seal of the United States emblazoned in white. The General frequently appears at the table after everybody else has been seated and his wife explains he has been "resting." The General is careful not to overeat. He does not get much exercise, but his health has been good. His physician, Lieutenant Colonel D. B. Kendrick, gives him a regular check-up and finds that despite MacArthur's sixty-seven years "his reflexes and appearance are those of a man of fifty." In May 1947 scoffing at rumors that the General might retire due to ill health, Kendrick declared, "The General is in robust health and seems almost indestructible physically. He looks younger and better now than at any time during the occupation, in spite of his seven-days-a-week, ten-hours-a-day schedule."

In his undramatic home life there seem to be a few clues as to what makes Douglas MacArthur such a paradoxical combination of the sublime and the ridiculous. Studying his past statements and achievements, his shortcomings and his successes, one is tempted to compare him with two other famous figures in recent American history. From time to time MacArthur has exhibited a mixture of the political thinking of Theodore Roosevelt and the political flare of Franklin Roosevelt. Like both Roosevelts, MacArthur has inspired passionate devotion and fanatical enmity. He has displayed their genius for making all battles, even verbal ones, seem dramatic. He is an earnest and fearless nationalist, as rampantly pro-American as T.R. was. He sees nations as pawns in a fascinating game of power politics. He labels and often libels whole peoples with an over-emphasized racial characteristic. He thinks of himself as an "enlightened conservative"—not wanting to revolutionize government but to rid it of abuses. And again like T.R., his personal bravery, his certainty of his own right, have helped to win him the respect of men he has led.

Franklin Roosevelt's friends would be the first (and MacArthur's friends would be the second) to deny it, but the General nevertheless has traces of some good and bad characteristics of the late great President. The jaunty manner is reminiscent of Roosevelt. So is that rare ability to make a listener feel that he or she is getting a *special* conversational effort. Both men maintained intense personal loyalty to old friends and associates, even to the point of retaining them in high places when they no longer pulled their own weight. Above all else MacArthur, like Roosevelt, has the innate ability to play things by ear; the master's sense of timing, of public presence, of coining the ringing phrase for the right occasion. MacArthur's historic "I have returned . . ." will echo down the pages of history not far behind Roosevelt's memorable, "I hate war. . . ."

MacArthur's friends believe him to be a real humanitarian and there is nothing in his record as SCAP that would taint this claim. On the big issues he has demonstrated the fairness of a man above petty recriminations. There is also no denying his tremendous intellect, his ability to synthesize a welter of conflicting opinions and research and arrive at a decision. Once he reaches his decision he has the weakness of other great men; he often sticks to it far too long. In his handling of the Japanese Government under Premier Yoshida, for example, SCAP made the decision to let Yoshida sink or swim in his attempts to revive the nation's economy without exercising stringent controls. No amount of persuasion by subordinates in Tokyo or Washington could persuade MacArthur to shift his stand until practically the eleventh hour.

He admires great men even if he does not agree with their principles. In addition to the Bible he frequently refers to such diverse sources as John L. Lewis, Confucius, Alexander the Great, Napoleon, and Kipling. He is silent on Generals Marshall and Eisenhower. He was not sympathetic to the social and economic program of President Roosevelt, but he has "more sympathy" for Harry Truman. Incidentally the President on more than one occasion invited MacArthur to return home for a "hero's welcome," but the General preferred to stay on the job until his part in it could be considered "accomplished." He has said, however, that when he does go back to the United States he will live in Milwaukee where he spent part of his childhood.

Although a "MacArthur-for-President Club" was again incorporated in Wisconsin during the spring of 1947, MacArthur no longer has White House aspirations—if he ever had them. His advanced age is one reason. For another even his closest associates admit that he could never stand the slings and arrows of a campaign. The General has been in high places in the army for so long that he does not react favorably to criticism, even if deserved.

MacArthur has a vision and he has determination. For a while he thought out loud about becoming the first "Supreme Commander for the Defense," a position several notches above the top army and navy commanders. Then he talked of remaining on in Japan as first

"United Nations Governor." But lately he has, like Winston Churchill, looked forward to the day when he can partially retire and write his memoirs. After all, there are few jobs in the world that rate higher than that of Supreme Commander for the Allied Powers and even fewer with more complete authority. "This task is," MacArthur once observed, "Mars' last gift to an old warrior."

Most of the officers and high-ranking civilians who held ideas in any way at variance with those of MacArthur, have long since departed or have been shifted to unimportant posts. They left for various reasons, some because they were not promoted, some because they were "busted" to a lower rank, others because they felt they could not do an honest job.

Today under MacArthur as Supreme Commander for the Allied Powers (SCAP) there are three main special sections which "suggest" to the Japanese Government how Japan should be run. The top men in each of these sections have taken the places of experts who were better suited by experience for their functions. The head of the Government Section, Brigadier General Courtney Whitney, succeeded Brigadier General William E. Crist. This able officer, previously on the War Department General Staff, had been trained to take over the administration of Military Government in Japan and had, in fact, performed that job on Okinawa. After the occupation began MacArthur decided that the standard Military Government set-up as employed in other occupied countries, and as planned for Japan by the War Department, would not mesh smoothly with his ideas of personal leadership. General Crist, it became known around headquarters, was not a "team man"— which meant not a MacArthur man. He had also not been on Bataan.

Courtney Whitney, a thin-lipped, round-faced precise man with a reddish-brown moustache, knew MacArthur before the war in Manila where Whitney was a lawyer. At the time of Pearl Harbor he was in the United States. He was commissioned and sent to Australia where he joined MacArthur as the trusted head of GHQ's Philippine Section. Now his swank office is right next to MacArthur's on the sixth floor of the former insurance company building which is the nerve center of GHQ and SCAP in Tokyo.

The original head of the important Economic and Scientific Section was Colonel Raymond C. Kramer. This large, far-reaching section looks after labor, finance, monopoly, scientific research, and a dozen other problems. A keen analyst and a successful businessman with a practical knowledge of economics, Kramer started on the job of breaking up Japan's monopolies and revising the nation's economic and commercial structure. The reason he departed shortly after Crist was probably not his tremendous initiative and energy, but the fact that he was not a regular Army officer or a member of the inner circle. Nominated for the rank of general several times, Kramer somehow never made it and returned to private life long before his assignment was completed. He was succeeded by Major General William F. Marquat, a jolly, stocky man who sported a moustache and a riding crop and had been MacArthur's anti-aircraft expert on Bataan. In his favor it could be said that he is thoroughly honest and has made no pretense to any knowledge of economics. Under him have worked some talented officers and civilians.

During the first half-year of the occupation the Information and Education Section was ably guided by Brigadier General Ken R. Dyke, a well-educated advertising and radio executive. This section, located in the Radio Tokyo Building a few blocks from SCAP, handles the Japanese press, radio, and movies, as well as schools, arts, and religions. When Dyke returned home to become a vice-president of the National Broadcasting Company, the Bataan crowd was glad to see him go. Dyke's insistence that left-wing publications should have the same claim to news and newsprint sources as the more conservative press, made him a radical in the eyes of MacArthur's men. The chief of another section let it be known around headquarters that Dyke was considered "pink" and that his staff had been infiltrated by Reds. As soon as Dyke was succeeded by one of his former assistants, Marine Lieut. Colonel Donald R. Nugent, the section was purged of many liberals as well as any real Reds who may have been around. Nugent carries out orders brilliantly, rarely suggests or initiates.

At least a half-dozen other important and able officials have been weeded out or allowed to go home. MacArthur now has his machine so well oiled and so well meshed that the visiting publisher, congressman, educator or clergyman cannot but be impressed by the smooth efficiency which unanimity often brings. To say that SCAP officials are all "yes men" would be an exaggeration. But none of them have the temerity to argue very long with MacArthur on a major issue. He does not like disagreement. When an important decision must be made he will ask a section chief to submit one or more opinions. On occasion MacArthur has called in the officers who have prepared briefs with opposing viewpoints. After listening to them he makes the final decision. This kind of teamwork keeps everybody happy except perhaps the man who has drafted a directive which is issued in MacArthur's name. However, no one has to quarrel with The Boss, and subordinates optimistically feel that by weighting the briefs in favor of what they feel to be right, MacArthur can be influenced.

Not all the important documents are finally put together in this manner, and not all of them bear MacArthur's name. Much of the best basic thinking on Japan has been done in the State Department. But Allied implementation is firmly under SCAP and so are the important public papers issued by the Japanese Government. The one of which the General is most proud is supposedly, and for the record, a grass-roots inspired creation of the Japanese, a glowing testimonial to their quick conversion to democratic thought if not action. That document is the Japanese Constitution which went into effect on May 3, 1947, embodying the nation's renunciation of war as a means for settling international disputes.

"That," said MacArthur at the conclusion of our conversation with him, "is an epic idea, and, gentlemen, you cannot stop the power of an idea. You can stop any war machine, any army. But you cannot stop the power of an idea once it snowballs. Peace, gentlemen, is such an idea."

CHAPTER IV

THE NEW CONSTITUTION:
WE, THE PEOPLE

On October 11, 1945, General MacArthur ordered a revision of the
Meiji Constitution which had lent itself so well to military despotism.
This constitution, under which Japan had been ruled since 1889,
included the doctrine of a divine emperor with full sovereignty; it
guaranteed no human rights, sharply curtailed the Diet's powers
and prerogatives, gave the army and navy chiefs direct access to the
Emperor, and made the Cabinet solely responsible to the throne and
not to the legislative body.

The Emperor and the Privy Council, his close advisers, requested
Prince Fumimaro Konoye to study the problem of a new constitution
and to make a report. In the same period the Shidehara cabinet invited the eminent constitutional lawyer, Joji Matsumoto, to do the
same. One of the cardinal points of concern in any revision was the
position and power of the Emperor. Konoye, a prewar premier and
friend of the Emperor's, turned in his draft at the palace and a
week later was named as a war criminal with certain members of
the Privy Council. The Prince committed suicide before he could
be arrested, and that ended the usefulness of his proposals on the
new constitution. The Emperor, and particularly MacArthur, were
at great pains to make it apparent that they had not cleared the
selection of Konoye for this assignment, although it was known
that Konoye had been in contact with MacArthur's office and was
held in high regard by SCAP. His being listed for the war crimes
trial was largely the result of newspaper pressure in the United
States.

Japanese intellectuals and politicians discussed the constitutional
problem for months. In the main those given the assignment were
evasive and unwilling to put forward any serious changes. Early in
December 1945 I attended a session of the Diet's Lower House

64

with an interpreter. I had been informed that debate on the new constitution would come up during the session. It did. This is the way the double-talk went.

Isaji Tanaka, a wiry, weazened-faced member of the Independents' Club got up and said in a thin, cracking voice: "The revision of the Constitution should be made in accordance with the initiative of the Emperor. Is it the State Ministers who have the responsibilities to give their advice to the Emperor, or the Lord Keeper of the Privy Seal who asks the throne to take the initiative?"

STATE MINISTER JOJI MATSUMOTO: "Responsibilities to assist the Emperor, of course, are the duties of the State Ministers and not that of the Lord Keeper."

TANAKA: "Who asked the Throne to take the initiative on the revision of the constitution?"

MATSUMOTO: "No person has ever asked the Throne to take this initiative."

TANAKA: "Was the initiative of the Emperor on revision of the Constitution taken by the Emperor himself?"

MATSUMOTO: "His Majesty did not reveal his intentions of revising the Constitution. However, the Emperor might in some way or other have revealed his intention to the office of the Lord Keeper."

TANAKA: "In the Imperial Court, Prince Konoye, who is adviser to the office of the Lord Keeper, is making preparations for constitutional revision. Is that a fact?"

MATSUMOTO: "I do not deny the fact that investigations for the possible revision have been made for the office of the Lord Keeper. However, to ask the Throne to take the initiative on the revision should be made only after the Government has made deliberations on the revision plan on its own responsibility. It may be said in advance that the Government may shortly ask the Throne to take the initiative on the revision, though the Lord Keeper might make some preparation for it. But I did not think that the Lord Keeper participated in state affairs."

TANAKA: "Why are the Lord Keeper and the Government making separate studies?"

MATSUMOTO: "The study of revision by the office of the Lord Keeper appears as though it has already been completed. I was unable to co-operate with that office in reference to this study though I desired to do so. The result of that office's study will, I hear, be available to the Government as reference."

TANAKA: "I think the revision should be made in a democratic way and that steps to that effect be made public."

MATSUMOTO: "Since this matter is so important I will make it clear that every member received Imperial advice to study the revision of the Constitution on the basis of the plan made by the office of the Lord Keeper. We are carrying out our investigations and study freely on our own responsibility and without any restrictions from outside."

TANAKA: "Is the Government restricted by the draft of the plan made by the office of the Lord Keeper or will the Government revise the Constitution from its own standpoint?"

MATSUMOTO: "Of course, the Government will consider the draft of the plan as a reference but will not be restricted by it."

TANAKA: "Prince Fumimaro Konoye has made statements several times on the possible abdication of the Emperor and even referred to the time of the occasion. An announcement of a possible abdication, if it were to be made, should be made by the Government, not by an adviser to the office of the Lord Keeper. What is the opinion of the Government on this problem?"

Matsumoto made a long, rambling reply which, if Tanaka understood, it was not evident from his next question.

TANAKA: "The abdication of the Emperor is not to be made from a legislative viewpoint. In view of the nation's belief, the Emperor has no responsibility. News that the Emperor will abdicate to fulfill provisions of the Potsdam Declaration, I believe is unfounded. What is the Government opinion on this matter?"

MATSUMOTO: "I also believe that such a matter will never happen. I think it is very exceptional for certain Japanese to have ideas contrary to ours."

Tanaka sat down on one of the Diet's baby-blue plush chairs and scratched his head, while Matsumoto went back to dreaming of the war criminals list.

This took place the day before Konoye was named on the list.

2

Another month dragged on. MacArthur was getting impatient. Finally, in February 1946 the job was taken away from Matsumoto and given to Brigadier General Courtney Whitney, head of SCAP's Government Section. The word went out to his colonels and majors: dig up something democratic on all the constitutions of the world which will satisfy the Old Man. For three weeks, behind closed doors, the section read and wrote with all the secrecy of atomic workers at Oak Ridge. MacArthur had laid down only two major precepts: the new document must renounce war for all time and it must give sovereignty to the people.

Many Japanese were under the impression that the work was being carried out directly by the Emperor or under his close supervision, and little appeared to discourage this myth. Whitney saw to it that picked Japanese were consulted and reference was, of course, made to preliminary articles drawn up by Konoye and Matsumoto. In the end, MacArthur was able to say, "The Government draft is a Japanese document"; later, Secretary of State James F. Byrnes categorically denied it was an American doctrine.

It was obvious, however, when the draft was made public that much of its inspiration, if not the actual wording, had come from the Dai Ichi Building boys and the Supreme Commander himself. Whitney and his top assistants were so steamed up they thought their handicraft would mark "the greatest event in the world since Pearl Harbor." On March 6 the sixteen-page text was published and MacArthur placed the power and glory of the occupation and the Allies squarely behind it when he said, "It is with a sense of deep satisfaction that I am able today to announce a decision of the Emperor and the Government of Japan to submit to the Japanese people a new and enlightened constitution which has my full approval. This instrument has been drafted after painstaking investigation and frequent conferences between members of the Japanese Government and this headquarters following my initial direction to the Cabinet five months ago."

The "instrument" played lovingly on concepts and phrases culled from MacArthur rhetoric, the Declaration of Independence, the Atlantic Charter, and the Gettysburg Address. The inevitable joke among Japanese newspapermen of my acquaintance went like this:

Fuji: "Have you read the new Constitution yet, Yoshi?"

Yoshi: "No, has it been translated into Japanese?"

Nevertheless, Japanese newspapers were forbidden by SCAP to publish the fact that the draft had been put together in English and then translated into Japanese. The Shidehara Government had been wary up to the last at accepting the MacArthur version. Finally SCAP was forced to tell Shidehara bluntly that if the Government did not sponsor the MacArthur draft it would be published anyhow and left up to the people for approval.

The people were largely apathetic. Their newspapers seemed to like the new Constitution, but if they had violently opposed any of its provisions the censors would have stepped in, swishing scissors.

Asahi did observe, in respect to the "no war" clause, that "world peace cannot be maintained by the unilateral action of Japan alone." The old leaders were pleased about only one thing. The Emperor had been tied into the Constitution and this appeared to give him Allied approval even before the electorate had a chance to decide on his retention as provided for in the Potsdam Declaration. While the Emperor was termed only "a symbol of state," he nevertheless still had the power to promote constitutional amendments, laws and treaties, to convoke the Diet, and dissolve the House of Representatives. By the same token, Tokyo election officials ruled that the Emperor did not have the right to vote. As "symbol of state" he was above the petty politics of democracy.

Shidehara assigned the delicate task of making the official translation of the text to Minister without Portfolio Kanamori who frankly believed that "The new Constitution is not to remain fixed for good but is full of flexibilities to respond to the requirement of new times as they come in the future." It was obvious that "the future" referred to the end of the occupation. Diligently Kanamori set to work to "stretch" the terms of the draft by using expressions in Japanese which held slightly different meanings semantically. He went so far that he actually lifted sovereignty from the people and restored it to the Emperor. This blatant change was caught by democratic proponents of the draft in the Diet. They brought it up in debate some two dozen times before SCAP stepped in and warned Kanamori to adhere to the original English text.

Shigeru Yoshida, then Foreign Minister, was not enthusiastic about the new Constitution which he thought was inconsistent with Japanese traditions; he also said that there was nothing wrong with the Meiji Constitution which was "immutable for all ages." After weighing alternatives, Yoshida and other canny conservative leaders decided that a new MacArthur Constitution was preferable in the long run to meddling with the old Meiji Constitution.

The debate on the draft continued fruitlessly for months. When

Shigeru Yoshida became Prime Minister in May 1946, MacArthur told him frankly to stop the double-talk, which was not only delaying the Constitution but was also having the effect of a filibuster on urgently needed legislation affecting Japan's economy. An undeclared agreement was reached. Yoshida promised to push through the Constitution if SCAP held back on its pressure for economic and agrarian reforms. On August 24, 1946, the Constitution was finally adopted by the House of Representatives, 421 to 8. Of the opposition, six were Communist deputies who held that the document failed to "represent faithfully the will of the people."

The House of Peers then went to work on the draft. They made some word substitutions and three specific changes, the most significant of which applied to Article 66 concerning the make-up of the cabinet. The additional sentence says: "The Prime Minister and other ministers of state must be civilians." Since the following article requires that the Prime Minister must be drawn from the membership of the Diet, it would seem to guarantee that future heads of government will be popularly elected.

3

On November 3, 1946, the birthday of Emperor Meiji, the new Constitution was promulgated. The day, already a Japanese holiday, was widely celebrated. Many Japanese objected that this "doubling-up" deprived them of an additional holiday. As previously reported, they were more affected by the holiday spirit and the sight of the Emperor than they were by the new democratic credo.

To celebrate the day the Constitution became legal, MacArthur restored the Rising Sun flag as a symbolic gift on May 3, 1947. This is the flag which irreverent G.I.'s call "one meat ball." In a letter to Premier Yoshida, the General said the new Constitution would inaugurate a government elected on democratic principles by a free expression of the popular will. . . . SCAP also took precautions that Hirohito would not be able to repeat his stunning performance on "Promulgation Day." He was given the role of a mere spectator at the formal ceremonies. It was a non-speaking part; he could not even issue an imperial rescript, which tradition would have demanded.

Nevertheless, the Emperor proved to be the star attraction for the five thousand Japanese who braved the rain to attend the rally.

Yoshida led the crowd in giving three *Banzais* for the ruler as a Japanese band played "Stars and Stripes Forever."

Most of the Tokyo press hailed the new document. *Mimpo,* a left-of-center newspaper, felt that it should have "guaranteed against unemployment and insecurity of livelihood," and admitted "we are doubtful of the propriety of its hasty enforcement because less than two years have elapsed since the surrender, and the democratic revolution has not started yet."

One little thing which occurred on the holiday indicated how difficult it would be to translate democratic ideas into egalitarian actions. To celebrate the occasion the government declared a special ration of ten cigarettes and an extra amount of *sake.* Women, supposedly raised to co-equal status, received three cigarettes and no *sake.*

Mrs. Yoshiyo Oichi, one of the first women elected to the Diet, denounced this "feudalistic favoritism." In her unsuccessful campaign for Mayor of Kyoto she had popularized the slogan: "Equal *sake* and tobacco rations for the women of Kyoto." But the men had voted overwhelmingly against her, fearful that the new equality would lower their own ration of tobacco and *sake.*

Thus the Constitution went into effect May 3, 1947. Few could guess how long it would be before the spirit and letter of the document took effect. A program was begun to publicize it by means of simply written pamphlets, radio broadcasts, and lectures in the universities. MacArthur was certain that the Constitution marked the beginning of a new era for Japan and the world, but others were more wary. W. McMahon Ball, the brilliant British member of the Allied Council for Japan, had candidly pointed out months before, "No one can foretell today whether this promulgation will be merely a notable event of the occupation period or whether it will mark the emergence of a new Japan."

Within the framework of the eleven "chapters" and one hundred articles there was plenty of room for the evolution of Japanese democracy. They embodied some of the best statutes of American and British constitutional law. The preamble to the new constitution begins:

We, the Japanese people, acting through our duly elected representatives in the National Diet . . . do proclaim the sovereignty of the people's will. . . .

Article I states that:

The Emperor shall be the symbol of the state and of the unity of the people, deriving his position from the sovereign will of the people.

These phrases represent a distinct change from the Meiji Constitution which stated:

The Tenno stands at the head of the Empire combining in Himself the rights of sovereignty. . . .

At times, as in Article XII, the instrument sounds like a manifesto. This proclaims, in terms which hark back to 1776:

All of the people shall be respected as individuals, and their right to life, liberty, and the pursuit of happiness shall, within the limits of the public welfare, be the supreme consideration in legislation and in governmental affairs.

Deep breaks with Japanese custom, which can probably never be changed by legislation, are decreed. For example, Article XXII says:

Marriage shall be based only on the mutual consent of both sexes and it shall be maintained through mutual cooperation, with the equal rights of husband and wife as a basis. Laws shall be enacted concerning choice of spouse, property rights, inheritance, choice of domicile, divorce and other matters pertaining to marriage and the family from the standpoint of individual dignity and the essential equality of the sexes.

The most unusual and dramatic passage in the Constitution, and one which unmistakably bears the MacArthur stamp is the short Chapter Two. Called "Renunciation of War" it emphatically states:

War, as a sovereign right of the nation and the threat or use of force, is forever renounced as a means of settling disputes with other nations. The maintenance of land, sea, and air forces, as well as other war potential, will never be authorized. The right of belligerency of the state will not be recognized.

Addressing the first session of the Allied Council for Japan a month after the draft was published, MacArthur hailed this particular article as "one further step in the evolution of mankind." But Japanese leaders in the Diet had subdued loud opposition to this clause by private assurances that disarmament was "only temporary."

Less heralded but more basic for the development of a democratic tradition in Japan are Articles LXXXVIII-XCI, which provide for local administrative self-government. The principle of "local autonomy" is adopted and deliberative assemblies are to be elected along with local officials "by direct popular vote." Dr. David Nelson Rowe, associate professor of international relations at Yale, has pointed out that this group of Articles, if carried out, "lays the foundation for the local development of political parties, and will make it possible for a national party system in Japan to be rooted in the localities and thus to be not merely the servant of powerful vested interests with influence in the national government." Local autonomy can, potentially, destroy the once all-pervading influence of the Ministry of Home Affairs and make certain that the police are locally controlled and not under the thumb of the central government.

4

Despite all the cribbing from past examples of the singing phrase, the new Japanese Constitution is, at least on paper, a praiseworthy one. It guarantees freedom of all forms of expression including those of religion, press, speech, and association. It sanctions collective bargaining, free universal elementary education, trial by jury, and almost everything a theoretically perfect constitution should endorse. It is technically a compromise between the British system with its constitutional monarchy and our own ideas on government. As in England, the lower house of the Diet will wield the real power. There is, however, a provision for a Supreme Court similar to that in the United States Constitution. The strength and influence of this judicial organ will only be determined as a body of decisions are established, just as there was doubt in America about the Supreme Court's scope and power until Chief Justice John Marshall wrote his famous decision in the case of Marbury versus Madison.

The Far Eastern Commission in Washington (the eleven-nation, policy-making body for Japan) had watched the progress of the Constitution's gestation with some misgivings. Some of the more outspoken anti-MacArthur members were afraid that SCAP had interfered too much and might later be open to the charge of having "forced the bloody thing down Japanese throats." After much wrangling, the Far Eastern Commission voted to send Mac-Arthur a directive stating that the Constitution would be subject to review and revision within two years so that valid Japanese criticisms might be included. MacArthur was furious, and reportedly made charges that the FEC was bent on sabotaging his work. Although the FEC decision was taken in October 1946, it was March 27, 1947, before its terms were publicly announced:

In order that the Japanese people may have an opportunity, after the new Constitution goes into effect, to reconsider it in the light of the experience of its working, and in order that the Far Eastern Commission may satisfy itself that the Constitution fulfills the terms of the Potsdam Declaration and other controlling documents, the Commission decides as a matter of policy that, not sooner than one year and not later than two years after it goes into effect, the situation with respect to the new Constitution should be reviewed by the Diet.

Without prejudice to the continuing jurisdiction of the Far Eastern Commission at any time, the commission shall also review the Constitution within this same period. The Far Eastern Commission, in determining whether the Japanese Constitution is an expression of the free will of the Japanese people, may require a referendum or some other appropriate procedure for ascertaining Japanese opinion with respect to the Constitution.

One of the earliest, and to my mind valid, criticisms of the document came from Japan's Dr. Tetsukichi Minobe, the constitutional authority who ran into trouble with the militarists in 1934 because of his view that the Emperor should function under a limited monarchy. Minobe did not think the Emperor should be described in the new Constitution "as a state symbol" believing that this could later be refitted into the old Shinto shibboleths. He felt, too, that the failure to place sufficient checks and provide sufficient balances to the power of the House of Representatives might lead to "runaway legislation."

Another cautionary voice amid the general self-praise in Japan was that of Yukio Ozaki, patriarch of Japanese liberals. He pointed out that the new charter would not mean much unless the Japanese first radically altered their moral code, which he claimed was based on "murder and falsehood." Ozaki felt that a minimum of three generations of education would be required before the Japanese could make the new Constitution effective. The man who had been reform mayor of Tokyo for nine years said simply, "Their heads are filled with the sawdust of many years of bad education."

CHAPTER V

RESHAPING THE JAPANESE MIND

FROM the long viewpoint one of the greatest problems remaining to be solved by the new masters of Japan is education. Old-time liberals like Yukio Ozaki frankly declare it is *the* greatest problem, more basic than economic reforms. For the hope of a truly democratic Japan in the future depends on how successfully the next generation of school children learn to interpret the precepts of democracy.

The paradox of education in Japan has been a powerful hidden weapon in the hands of its old masters. During the Meiji Restoration in 1872 Japan adopted the theory of universal education and established a free public school system. Rigidly controlled by centralized authorities in Tokyo, the youth in Japan were trained "to offer themselves courageously to the State." There was little danger that widespread learning would bring with it widespread demand for individual freedom. Paradoxically, Japan was a nation with compulsory education and almost compulsory illiteracy.

During the first year of MacArthur, the program for the re-education of the Japanese was under the supervision of Brigadier General Ken R. Dyke who understood the scope and the significance of his assignment. He recognized that Japanese education had to be given "a fresh start and a new kind of hope," and that the reorganization of the school system was certain to be a long and difficult problem. Dyke began his work realistically with an attempt to reform and to revitalize the media of mass education—the press, radio and movies. Early in the occupation "Now It Can Be Told," a radio series styled after the "March of Time," was broadcast to the Japanese people dramatizing the true history of Japanese aggression. Movie scripts were prepared showing the real nature of Japanese aggression. Other scenarios emphasized the role of Japanese pacifists in the struggle against militarism. Newspapers were

74

urged to print fact rather than rumor, news rather than opinion.

Not being a Japanese "specialist," I thought that the Civilian Information and Education Service was doing a brilliant job. Later as I moved around the countryside and questioned the Japanese public, I found that Dyke's high-pressure propaganda was not having the desired effect. I'm sure he was keen enough to realize it as a result of the opinion polls that were made.

"Our psychology is different," a thin, sharp newspaper man named Yamamoto explained to me in Kyoto. "What is good theater to Americans can be bad theater to Japanese. Our tempo of life is different. Your pace is too fast. That radio series on the truth about war guilt was too confusing. Voices kept coming in from all sides. Music beginning and ending. We are not tuned to that in our listening. Things must be said over and over again, very simply."

"But your people flock to American-made movies," I protested.

"Which ones?" he countered. "Escape movies. Things that have nothing to do with reality. Musical movies. Adventure movies. Or even movies about life in America—that is escape. I do not think your movie people if they are like your radio people would do so well if they made movies about things that were real to us."

He was later proven correct. Leading Tokyo movie houses boycotted the SCAP-instigated and approved "Tragedy of Japan," a film version of the years of aggression. The film was "temporarily" withdrawn from circulation.

Yamamoto and others thought we did better with our cartoons and posters depicting the rights and privileges of democracy. "But even so," Yamamoto persisted, "the people are more impressed by the poster campaign on VD—which is for your troops—than they are by propaganda on how to be a good citizen, politically."

Although they 'hesitated to say so in public, Japanese resented Allied censorship because censorship had always been associated in their minds with totalitarianism and thought control. It was almost impossible to explain to them why it was necessary to destroy hundreds of movie films, ban traditional *Kabuki* dramas, and forbid newspapers to criticize the Allies or the occupation.

2

At first the approach to a revision of the education system had to be negative, too. Textbooks on history, geography, and morals were thrown out and the teaching of these subjects temporarily forbidden. Ballistics problems were even dropped from mathematics courses. The Ministry of Education in Tokyo was directed to purge officials and teachers too closely allied with the militarists. This was an assignment of stupendous proportions. Again and again during the period since 1931 teachers had been victims of reaction; they had been spied upon and terrorized. Those with progressive views, those who opposed aggression, those who in any way strayed from the official line, were all ruthlessly weeded out.

The screening of Japan's 500,000 schoolteachers went very slowly. In the first place there was difficulty in setting standards for the selection of the screening committees themselves. The Ministry of Education, which ran the "purge," was under the direction (for nine months) of Timon Maeda, who had been director of Japan Institute, the pro-war propaganda organization in New York before Pearl Harbor. By the end of MacArthur's first year only 331 out of the first 16,000 teachers interviewed were dropped for militaristic or jingoistic beliefs. Since these same teachers had previously been screened many times for anti-militarist beliefs, it was difficult to believe that so many of them had so quickly and effectively changed their minds. The Japanese investigators were apprised of Allied suspicions, and in the next four months almost 20 per cent of those educators questioned were removed as unfit. Many of these, however, merely packed their trunks and moved to a distant prefecture where they were quickly rehired. This is one more costly example of how the Japanese bureaucracy, if left pretty much to its own devices, will bend every effort to maintain the status quo.

The Japanese and SCAP postponed the re-education of the country's "acceptable" teachers. This would seem an indispensable beginning to the education of the nation's 19 million school children. New decrees and new textbooks can change the basic information which will be imparted. But they will not enable teachers, who have never learned themselves, to help individuals in thinking independently. The deeply imbedded tradition of Japan's educational system, and of Japan itself, is the acceptance of form rather than content, of authority and rank rather than ability. Until the groundwork is laid for undermining and eventually overcoming this tradition, bad leaders will always have a potential, blindly obedient following just as MacArthur has now.

Under General Dyke, orders were issued for the revision of

Japanese histories; the selection of many books in the higher schools was given to local authorities rather than Tokyo; the metric system was adopted; the study of Russian and Chinese was added to the curriculum of higher schools; educational opportunities for women were expanded and the study of politics and science opened to them for the first time; archery, judo, jujitsu, fencing, and other martial sports were outlawed.

3

The first new Japanese history books revised under the SCAP directive became available early in 1947. "The new textbooks represent the first objective treatment of Japanese history for school use," SCAP's headquarters proudly announced. "The texts will furnish the children of Japan with a story of their people that is honest and straightforward. They will play an important part in training the children of a nation that is striving to achieve democracy."

Kuni-no-Ayumi (*Progress of the Country*) was written under the supervision of the Ministry of Education. Instead of the traditional myth about Hirohito's ancestry dating back for more than 2,600 years to Amaterasu, the Sun Goddess, the textbook simply states, "It was a very, very long time ago that our ancestors settled to live in this land. Although we cannot tell for certain how long ago it was, it must be scores of thousands of years ago."

Despite the substitution of much fact for fable, the new textbook is an excellent illustration of the wide gap between the content of the directive and the end results. The new histories were supposed to clarify for the Japanese the development of militarism and fascism without any of the sugared rationalizations sprinkled through former texts. And yet *Progress of the Country* has this to say about the Meiji Constitution under which militarism and fascism developed in Japan:

In the civilized countries of the world, each had had its respective constitution made and established a parliamentary régime to enable its people to conduct state affairs. Therefore it went without saying that our country had to enact a constitution, too.

In the Constitution the matters of the Imperial Diet were defined in detail, by which the first members of parliament were elected from the people in the following twenty-third year of Meiji (1890), and the first session of the Imperial Diet was convoked in December. Thereafter the government came to administer the affairs of state in co-ordination with the Diet. It had been a form of government by military men in the olden time, and by officials at the beginning of the Meiji Era, but it has been a constitutional government ever since.

Further on in the history a completely "objective" account of Japan's Manchurian conquest is presented. The opening of the war with China in 1937 is explained in these polite terms:

At first the then Japanese government strove to bring the matter to the earliest possible settlement and conclude peace with China, but the war extended too far to do so. . . . Under those circumstances, the government declared the war to have as its object the creation of a new order in the Far East. Also it went so far as to proclaim that Japan would not take the Minkuo (Chinese) government seriously. When things came to this, Japan became clearly dissentient from the United States and Britain on the Chinese problem.

The subsequent description of how the Pacific war occurred in 1941 is strikingly different from the "Now It Can Be Told" broadcasts written by Americans. The radio series left no doubt as to Japan's highly developed plans and unswerving motives dating back long before the breakdown of peace negotiations. A baffled Japanese student, searching for a true account of how and why it all happened, would probably not be able to understand the justice of the Tokyo War Crime Trials after reading this in *Progress of the Country*:

About that time in Japan the pacifists lost their influence and the government enforced the reconstruction of all administration, economics and culture in accordance with the need of consolidating the internal condition of the country on account of the war (Chinese war). Japan, however, negotiated with the United States in many ways, but as the arrangements went on, the government and the military party came to disagreement. Consequently Fumimaro Konoye resigned from his premiership, being succeeded by Minister of the Army Hideki Tojo.

Thus the negotiations with America finally came to a standstill. On the morning of December 8, the Japanese Navy suddenly made a surprise attack on the Pearl Harbor of Hawaii, and then proclaimed war on both the United States and Great Britain.

When Hessell Tiltman, the British journalist who cabled the above quotations from the new textbook to the *New Republic*, discussed the history with a MacArthur official, he was reminded that *Progress of the Country* was "only the bare bones" which would be "clothed" by the teachers themselves. Mr. Tiltman found little satisfaction in this thought, since "Japanese children are still being taught by teachers who would in many cases be eliminated as dangerous under General MacArthur's purge directives had anyone got around to carrying them out. . . . The Japanese Ministry of Education—notoriously the world's most prolific producer of robots—has pulled a fast one and got away with it. It has effectively stalemated the reformation of Japan's feudalistic educational system and has produced a 'history' which is as quaint and dangerous as many other things in Japan."

4

Early in 1946 MacArthur repeated his request of October 1945 for an advisory committee on education. The commission of twenty-seven Americans selected by the State Department was headed by Dr. George D. Stoddard, then Commissioner of Education of New York State, and now President of the University of Illinois. After a month's conducted tour beginning on March 5, 1946, the commission returned and submitted its recommendations and criticisms to SCAP. The following from the introduction to their official report is worth noting:

We do not come in the spirit of conquerors, but as experienced educators who believe that there is an unmeasured potential for freedom and for individual and social growth in every human being. . . .

In these, as in other matters of basic policy, negative measures will be effective only as they embody the will of the liberal Japanese. Eventually, an education that is administered from the top down must give way to education conceived as a responsibility and a privilege at every level of society. Others may help in saving a nation from its war lords, as the Allies have helped the Japanese, but in the long run a nation must free itself. Freedom comes only from the practice of freedom. . . .

We believe in the power of every race and every nation to create from its own cultural resources something good for itself and for the whole world. This is the liberal creed. We are not devoted to uniformity; as educators we are constantly alert to deviation, originality and spontaneity. That is the spirit of democracy. We are not flattered by any superficial imitation of our own institutions. Believing in progress and social evolution, we welcome cultural variety all over the world as a source of hope and refreshment. . . . No nation is without some elements of the democratic way of life, and no nation has them all. The sportsman, who plays the game for the love of it, but according to the rules, is an exemplar of this way of life. And more conspicuously for Japan, the artist furnishes an example. He works for the joy of the working, learning his discipline not from external authority but from the limitations of his medium. Through many centuries, Japan has been developing a culture touched to its very core with a sense of beauty.

Equality of rights and of duties may be come at from wherever a nation is. Some nations have found their way to equal justice by starting with liberty, saving it from license by letting rights compete with one another until a middle course emerges. Japan, which has made an art of social relations in a cohesive family system, may come at equality from fraternity.

Whatever the approach, the nation that achieves unity through democratic virtues will build for itself a new spiritual life, a dynamic synthesis of art and science, of all its traditions and values. To this end, the various religions in Japan have contributed and will contribute in so far as they are good; have detracted and will detract in so far as they are bad. Negatively, Japan's new spiritual life has been already furthered by denying ultra-nationalism the right to operate under the guise of religion. Positively, the guarantee of freedom of religious thought and practice will now enable the Japanese to judge their several religions and to embrace those forms which give the highest meaning to their culture.

We believe that the Japanese themselves, under the vital impact of both events and ideas, are moving in the direction of a fuller meaning of the worth of the individual—that they, too, desire a more humane approach to the problems of the day. The fulfillment of this desire would give Japan a new life, spiritual in its import, guaranteeing equal opportunity to all religions and appropriating the contributions of each.

In education these new directions will yield a freedom of teaching and learning at all levels. An equality of opportunity will create a new structure of education, open to all youth, alike to both sexes. Every student and every teacher, we feel, will be encouraged by this prospect to look within himself and about him, and not only above, in order to discover what to do or what to think or what to be. In this regard the schools will be simply sharing, as schools ought, in a nationwide enterprise, and indeed contributing notably to its success. They will join as an effective partner the great struggle against obscurantism, feudalism, and militarism.

Dr. Stoddard's group made six major recommendations: (1) an improvement in the aims and content of the Japanese educational system along democratic lines; (2) the introduction of Romaji in some form (roman letters instead of Japanese characters); (3) the transfer of authority from the Ministry of Education to local administrators elected by popular vote; (4) the training of teachers "more as people than as parrots"; (5) the fostering of adult education, extension courses, and organizations like Parent-Teachers Associations; (6) increasing and broadening the opportunities for higher education and, in that connection, sponsoring the exchange of scholars and scholarships among Japan, the United States, and other nations.

The most significant of these proposals was the suggested adoption of Romaji, a reform which Japanese liberals have sought to bring about for decades. Until such language reform is introduced, little can be done to reduce the high rate of illiteracy in Japan.

5

Widespread illiteracy among supposedly educated people has been one of Japan's best-kept secrets. American authorities were amazed to discover that many Japanese had not understood the language of the Emperor's broadcast about the surrender. In fact, at Karuizawa, just a few hours from Tokyo, the citizenry staged a victory parade. An hour or so after Hirohito's broadcast his words were translated into colloquial Japanese and the parade ended. Similarly the Emperor's message to the first postwar Diet was understood by less than half the members of that august body.

Allied investigations indicate that during the first six years of Japanese primary education more than one-half the students' time is devoted to learning how to read and write the highly complex ideographs of Chinese origin supplemented by the elaborate Kana syllabary. The average primary school graduate, exposed to 1,400 Kanji ideographs (of a total over 56,000) remembers only about 600. And yet 2,400 are needed to read a newspaper fully, and 8,000 to 10,000 characters are required to read a college textbook.

The hopelessness of fundamental educational reform without drastic simplification of the Japanese written language has now been established. Nevertheless scholars and other traditionalists argue that Japan would suffer "great cultural losses." This argument is about as valid as the claim that Italians have lost their cultural heritage because they no longer read, write, and speak Latin. Kanji has long been used by authoritarians as a barrier to keep culture and knowledge from the common people. After 1938 Japanese who advocated the adoption of Romaji were imprisoned for the crime of lèse majesté. The campaign of the reactionaries to stabilize illiteracy succeeded so well that today in Tokyo only one out of every ten Japanese can even read the names of the Japanese war criminals on trial.

On the basis of such statistics John Ashmead, Jr., wrote in the *Atlantic Monthly* (January 1947) that "We may be able, by using the radio, to democratize Japan to a limited extent. But much of our present effort to re-educate the Japanese is just money down the drain."

Dr. Harold Benjamin, Director of the International Educational Relations Division of the U.S. Office of Education, reported after his visit to Japan with Dr. Stoddard's group that "Romaji or some equally phonetic alphabet should be adopted for the writing of Japanese and [that] this reform will have to be carried out decisively under national control." Tests conducted by the Japanese themselves since the occupation strongly indicate the value and practicality of such reform. In two weeks spent studying phonetic Japanese, fifty thousand primary school children reached a level of literacy achieved after six years studying Kanji. But nevertheless conservative Japanese prevailed upon SCAP. The Old Guard claimed that the large number of homonyms in the language would lead to ambiguity. And so millions of new textbooks were ordered in the old-style calligraphy. It was a victory for the traditionalists.

6

For many months the only concrete result of the educators' mission was to help the Imperial family find a compromise solution for Japan's No. 1 individual problem in education: the training of Crown Prince Akihito.

In December 1945 Cornelius Ryan of the London *Daily Telegraph* and I were having a talk with General Dyke about re-educating the Japanese. When I inquired what plans had been made for Akihito's education, Dyke was taken by surprise. If it had occurred to SCAP that this was their headache, they evidently had done nothing about it except talk. Dyke promised he'd look into it.

The subject came up for discussion again a few months later when the Stoddard commission had a standing interview with Hirohito. While they shifted from foot to foot in the chairless reception hall, Hirohito broached the question of an American tutor for Akihito. Could the commission think of a likely person? They could. Later Stoddard asked Terasaki, the Imperial Household's master of ceremonies, whether a man or a woman was desired. Terasaki went to sound out the Emperor, returned with the precedent-breaking reply: a woman.

Mrs. Elizabeth Grey Vining of Philadelphia, Pa., was selected for the unusual assignment. A widow in her early forties, Mrs. Vining had written many successful books for teen-agers and had some experience teaching English. When she accepted the post she had no prior knowledge of the country to which she was going nor of the boy whom she was going to tutor.

Unless the Japanese people turn against the Tenno system, the next Emperor of Japan will be Hirohito's eldest son, Akihito. Mrs. Vining began tutoring this passive, obedient, chubby thirteen-year-old schoolboy on October 15, 1946. At the Kogane Peers' School, dressed in his dark-blue wool uniform with the metal cherry blossoms on each side of the collar, he seemed almost indistinguishable from the other boys. Mrs. Vining found Akihito living in the stoic simplicity which can best be afforded by little princes who someday will inherit untold millions and a scepter from their sires. Perhaps the theatrical contrast was not entirely lost on her. From her warm ten-room home in Tokyo, replete with servants and secretary, she was chauffeur-driven sixteen miles to a bleak, cold classroom. There the humble prince sat waiting to be taught "democracy" as he would learn the art of Chinese calligraphy, a necessary flourish for his new role.

Mrs. Vining brought to her job an American's sincere belief in the power of education and a Quaker's convictions on the urgency of peace. She was too realistic to hope for successes such as Anna Leonowens had with the King of Siam. Her mission could be termed fulfilled if her charge learned the rudiments of good English and was able to understand the content as well as the form of Carl Sandburg's Abraham Lincoln Grows Up.

But there was much in Akihito's past which would inevitably show up in the shape of his future. His was a heritage difficult to undo in one hour a week.

Akihito is the only heir-apparent in the world who was two years old eight days after his birth. This neat trick was not done with Hirohito's sacred mirror. In Japan every infant is one year old when born. Like race horses in America, Japanese then become a year older every New Year's irrespective of actual birth date. Thus, little

Akihito was two on January 1, 1934, although he first opened his owlish, brown eyes on December 23, 1933.

Akihito's arrival ended a lengthy period of intense suspense for the entire Japanese nation as well as for his mother, the Empress Nagako. The Japanese newspapers for months had daily reported on the Empress's condition. During the final months of pregnancy they printed detailed accounts of how she donned the sacred, twelve-foot-long, silk maternity girdle presented to her by the Chief of the Imperial Staff who had been designated "Honorable Girdle Parent." Thus began an unending series of ceremonials which will follow Akihito as long as he is slated to be the 125th Mikado.

As soon as the doctors pronounced the baby alive, Emperor Hirohito presented him with the sacred sword which is the symbol of the life force. Seven days after Akihito's birth a national holiday was declared. On this day he was doused with a ceremonial bath as three costumed archers twanged their bowstrings to ward off evil spirits, and two honored doctors of literature intoned from ancient Shinto scriptures. Bathed and dressed in a white silk kimono the Crown Prince was ready to receive his name. Emperor Hirohito inscribed *Tsugo-no-miya* ("The Prince who will ascend the Throne of Enlightened Benevolence") on a scroll which he handed to his Grand Chamberlain who bowed thrice and informed the Empress officially, then bowed thrice more and placed the scroll beside Akihito's pillow.

At this signal the Japanese Navy boomed a twenty-one gun salute, stock market prices soared to ecstatic heights, political prisoners received an amnesty, and Ginza hawkers sold an estimated three million Rising Sun flags and flimsy paper lanterns for the honorable holiday.

While still at the breast of his wet nurse, Akihito's training for the throne began. He was addressed only in court language, called *Kotoba*—supposedly the tongue of the natives who founded Japan. At three months his father made him a gift of a personal seal, the characters of which stand for "Mister Prosperity." At three years Akihito was given his own household complete with palace, chamberlains, guards, valets, gardeners, cooks and teachers. At five he was granted a Mongolian pony and his first formal audience with his father. For the first time he was permitted to meet boys of his own age, all carefully selected sons of the nobility. At six Akihito entered the Peers' School. A special building was erected within walking distance of his palace. Here the Crown Prince memorized the ritual which all Japanese school children have had to learn. When the teacher asked, "What do you love best in the World?" Akihito replied: "The Emperor, of course." "Better than your father and mother?" Seriously Akihito recited: "Yes, he is the Lord of Heaven, the father of my mother and father." "What will you give the Emperor?" His son answered: "All my best toys and my life when he wants it."

At eight—the year the Pacific war began—Akihito "showed keen interest in the progress of the Greater East Asia war," according to Domei, the official news agency. "Recently he visited the Meiji and Yasukuni shrines to pray for an early Japanese victory and restoration of world peace." They did not add that Akihito was being briefed by tutors Admiral Togo and General Nogi. During the later war years Akihito lived at the shrine city of Nikko, ninety miles from Tokyo where, conveniently, the Peers' School was also transferred. This was fortunate as the great B-29 raid on May 25, 1945, destroyed Akihito's Tokyo bomb shelter.

Like most Japanese, Akihito discovered the war was over at noon, August 15, 1945, when he heard his father broadcast the Imperial rescript. Akihito wept. When he had recovered from his "profound grief," he asked Baron Hozumi, his gentle and cultured Grand Chamberlain: "Why did we not win?"

Hozumi meditated before explaining: "The principal reason for defeat is after all the wide difference of real ability between Japan and America and our ignorance of that difference." This seemed to satisfy his pupil. He was politely advised not to refer to this embarrassing matter in the presence of the Emperor.

When the American occupation became a reality, half-hearted attempts were made at introducing simplicity and democracy, but bandy-legged Akihito still led a regimented prince's life for almost a year. With his eleven-year-old brother, Prince Masahito, and sixty servants he rattled around in the bleak, barren confines of Akasaka Palace, where Emperor Meiji lived (1872–1888) and where the Duke of Windsor slept in 1922. When I visited Akihito at Akasaka last year, Baron Hozumi explained that the task of unlacing the confining customs which corset the Crown Prince was a delicate one. He had begun by apprising Akihito of SCAP directives in general terms. With this slight bow to the presence of aliens on Japanese soil, Akihito's elders went right on preparing him for the throne as his ancestors were prepared before him. It did not seem strange to Baron Hozumi or the other chamberlains that outside the thick stone walls of the Akasaka compound Japan was seething with social revolution while within the Palace a small boy, who until recently believed he was divine, was learning how to become an anachronism.

This, then, was Akihito's routine when I saw him. He was up and dressed with the help of three valets by seven o'clock. The first thing in the morning and the last at night he entered his private shrine room to worship the spirit of the Sun Goddess and his Imperial ancestors. He also bowed low to photographs of his mother, father and grandmother. Devotion over, he was allowed to romp in his garden, feed his chickens, and do Danish-style (German-style before Hitler's defeat) calisthenics until his breakfast of toast, milk, and fried eggs at eight. Tin lunch-box in hand, he walked along a well-guarded path to school where at ten began the schedule of lessons in reading, composition, arithmetic, painting, manual training, singing, and gymnastics. The teaching of morals, history, and geography had been temporarily banned by SCAP. Where Akihito stood in relation to the other little nobles in his class was not made clear. Grades were not permitted then as it would have been lèse majesté for another pupil to be rated above Akihito. Akihito modestly admitted to being excellent in singing (like his mother) and in biology (like his father).

With lessons over at one, Akihito munched his beans, rice and fish with the other boys and then trotted home. Within the palace compound, weather permitting, Akihito rode on his bike or his pony, or perhaps punted on his private pond until three. Chosen members of his class were allowed to come and play after being cautioned that they must not excel their host in games. The Prince studied until four-thirty, when he was given a European bath in a full-length foreign tub. At five he supped—his favorite dish is curried rice—and then he played cards, read, or watched newsreel movies until bedtime at eight.

In the months just prior to Mrs. Vining's arrival, Japanese myths were put aside for translations of *Uncle Tom's Cabin, Peter Pan, The Prince and the Pauper, Tom Sawyer, The Count of Monte Cristo,* and *Little Lord Fauntleroy.* Akihito had heard so little in his previous years about the non-Japanese world that he found these books more wondrous by far than traditional Japanese tales. Last winter he gawked at Shirley Temple in "Kiss and Tell," the first Hollywood feature he has been able to see since the war. He liked it, but not as well as "Mickey Mouse" because he could not understand the English dialogue. In preparation for Mrs. Vining, Akihito learned to write our alphabet in seven hours, to sing "Twinkle, Twinkle, Little Star," and to read the comics in the Pacific edition of *Stars and Stripes*.

Every Saturday Akihito is examined by two court doctors. He is taller, a good deal heavier and healthier than most Japanese boys of his age. In March 1946, in a move which the domineering Imperial Household Ministry considered "extremely revolutionary," Akihito was sent to the Middle School at Kogane where Mrs. Vining now tutors him. Court tradition had established as precedent that upon completion of primary studies the mind of a Crown Prince should be exposed only to private tutors. It was decided that Akihito should learn practical subjects publicly and theoretical subjects privately.

Baron Hozumi, in charge of the theoretical side, told me that democracy was one of the subjects which he and Akihito discussed on Sundays before the boy left for his weekly visit with his Imperial parents. Akihito's definition of this elusive concept was "Democracy means governing the people according to their own wishes and for the happiness of all peoples." This notion was both pleasing and surprising to the Crown Prince because he believed that his father had ruled according to the people's wishes since "How could they have wishes other than the Tenno's?"

Akihito said, in effect, the same thing that Tojo's chief counsel said to the International War Crimes Tribunal in Tokyo on February 24, 1947. Dr. Ichiro Kiyose, after months of prosecution testimony to the contrary, told the tribunal that: "There is no fundamental difference between the [Japanese] Imperial way and [American] democracy."

To make the meaning of American democracy concrete, Baron Hozumi told his pupil the story of the *Mayflower's* voyage and of the signing of the Declaration of Independence. The Baron also talked with Akihito about the difference between individualism and egotism, about cabinet changes, liberalism, shortages of food and housing in Japan, and the positions of China and the United States in world affairs. Akihito was not able to understand the internecine strife in China but his sympathies were with the Government.

While some Allied authorities have privately discussed the prospect of sending Akihito abroad to college in four or five years, the Crown Prince's intimate attendants shudder at the thought. "You cannot rewrite more than two thousand years of tradition with such rapidity," one of "Mr. Prosperity's" guardians whispered to this reporter last year before Mrs. Vining arrived. "His Imperial Majesty, the Crown Prince, has not yet officially met an American and he has never even *seen* a Russian."

7

Casting aside a correspondent's cynicism for a moment, it appears obvious that even if Mrs. Vining instills a feeling for democracy in the future Emperor he may grow up to find his people unprepared for it. Sovereignty, the new Constitution says, resides in the people. Unless they know what to do with that MacArthur-given blessing, Mrs. Vining's visits with Akihito are as much window-dressing for the eyes of the Western world as Hirohito's visits to his people.

After her first six months Mrs. Vining said in an interview, "I don't know how much good I'm doing, or will be able to do. All one can do is to plant a seed and hope that it will grow." When and if the Crown Prince asks her, "What is democracy?" she said she expected to reply with William Penn's definition: "That country is free where the law rules, and the people are a party to the laws."

I remember one occasion in Tokyo, during a visit to one of the best institutions of higher learning in the country, when I had an opportunity to ask a Japanese student about *his* definition of "democracy."

It was a bitterly cold day in February 1946, when a projected trip to the country and my regular translator had not materialized. I had been to the Meiji University once before to witness a students' anti-Communist rally. Meiji is not one of the six government-supported Imperial Universities in Japan, such as Tokyo Imperial; rather it is privately endowed. Its campus—or the remains of it—was the strangest I had ever seen. Half the buildings were little more than rubble piles and only makeshift paths had been cleared through the wreckage of broken stone and rusted steel fragments.

I walked into the likeliest-looking building, a rather large, three-story, stone structure. A few feet inside the door a policeman, who was sitting on a box behind a pine table, hurriedly jumped to his feet and saluted. Only at that moment I realized I was wearing a uniform and regretted it. The policeman spoke no English and I found it impossible to explain to him that I was not an authority but a reporter and I wanted to listen in on a class. Our mutual bewilderment resolved itself only when he withdrew with what sounded like ten thousand apologies and returned with a small, bald-headed man who blew on his clenched fists the whole time he talked to me.

"My name is Shinsuki Mori," said the bald man. "I am in charge of liaison." I judged him to be about forty and later discovered he was in his middle twenties. He had lost his youthful appearance and his hair after surviving a tropical disease in the Solomons. He wore a tight-fitting frock coat over what might have been an old pair of naval officer's trousers. Mori remained at my side all morning as a translator and when I complimented him on his fluency he said, "I translated in our prisons. For your prisoners, that is. I learned much from them, more than at school."

While I waited outside, Mori entered a classroom to consult the instructor. Presently he reappeared and introduced a tall, haggle-toothed professor, who also spoke English. I was given a formal invitation to observe the class.

There were about two dozen men in a cold, rather dark, barren room about fifteen feet square. The windows in the room were so smudged with grime that very little light penetrated and there were no bulbs in the lamp sockets. The students, who were sitting cross-legged on the wooden floor, scrambled up when I entered, and Mori, at my request, quickly told them to sit again. Later Mori assured me that the seats and benches had been removed during the January cold spell "to make firewood in that iron cooker." He pointed to the black stove in the rear of the room. There was no fire in it.

At the opposite end there was a raised dais and a blackboard. The professor had a plain wooden chair and a low desk that looked unfinished. Mori whispered: "This is upper class in English grammar." The professor asked me to take his chair, which I refused.

I sat down against the wall facing the windows. I could feel the cold from the floor and the wall right through my heavy military coat. I wondered why the thin professor and the students did not keep their coats on. There was a pile of them in the back near the stove. Most of them were dressed in worn, dark-blue university uniforms with brass buttons, but three or four were in army uniforms without epaulets or insignia of any kind. Later I learned that it was impolite to keep your coat on in a classroom, but I didn't much care.

Mori and I stayed in the room for about twenty minutes. It was a weird experience. The class was conducted in Japanese; since it was an advanced section in English I had expected it would all be in English. The procedure was rather formal. The professor would call out a name. The student would get to his feet, not at rigid attention, but standing erect and motionless. Then the professor would ask him a series of rapid questions in a deep, raspy voice. The Japanese flow in both questions and answers was punctuated by English words like "gerundive" and "substantive."

Mori translated and from what I could recall of "advanced grammatical construction," the students all seemed letter-perfect. At the conclusion of the class the students rose, bowed, and then were dismissed. I told Mori that I would like to talk to one or two of the students, if they had time.

The professor came over and thanked me for coming to his class. I thanked him for allowing me to come. He hesitated and then said, "I have been to San Francisco."

"What did you think of it?" I asked.

"Oh, that was long time ago in 1913," he said, smiling. We shook hands and he excused himself. The students, I noticed, had all filed out except one youthful looking boy who remained behind chatting with Mori. The students had paid no particular attention to me, acting almost as if my visit was an everyday occurrence. Watching the recitation, I had sensed almost no flicker of real comprehension or interest. I remembered that John Morris, now a correspondent for the British Broadcasting Company, had been a guest lecturer in Tokyo just before the war and found it very difficult to discover what was going on in his students' minds. As Morris tells the story, the ice was finally broken one morning when he entered his classroom and found the following note written on the blackboard: "Sir, today we do not wish lecture on T. S. Eliot.

We wish to practice hearing King's English and hope for intimate lecture on details of your love-life. Have you visited Japanese gay quarters?"

Mori introduced the student and at the same time announced that he was twenty-three years old, born near Kyoto, had served in the Army air force, and wanted to enter government service near his home when he was graduated.

The student's name was Bunji Suzuki. I asked him if he was related to the old Japanese labor leader by the same name. He said he wasn't.

Suzuki was letting his hair grow. There was a half-inch bristle on his head and a dirty stubble around his chin. Addressing the question to him and to Mori, I inquired why the class was conducted in Japanese and not in English and if this were true in all language classes. Suzuki appeared embarrassed and looked at Mori.

"I was hoping for you not to ask that," Mori said apologetically. "The professor was afraid that his English would offend your ears and that his students would sound badly to you. Today it was in Japanese." Mori paused and watched as I scribbled in my notebook. "There is no intent to deceive," he whispered as though Suzuki should not hear him, "because I was with you to translate. Do you understand?"

"Was English taught during the war years?"

Mori again replied. "Certainly, although there was much opposition to it. But Tojo himself—General Tojo was also Minister of Education—wanted English taught. He spoke of the large numbers of English-speakers we would need in conquered territories."

"Where?"

"Australia," Suzuki said, casually.

"What else do you study?" I asked the student.

"Civics, law, literature, formerly history. . . ." Mori answered. I told Mori to let Suzuki speak.

"Civics, law, literature—Japanese and Chinese," said Suzuki.

"Do you live and eat here at the university?"

"In Japan we only study at the university," said Mori. "I am sorry. You say." He waited for Suzuki. When Suzuki did not reply immediately, Mori said something in Japanese.

"What did you say, please?"

Mori said he had translated my question.

"I live nearby this place," Suzuki began in slow English. Then he switched to Japanese. "He resides in lodgings with two other classmates in room of one private family near here," Mori went on. "He eats breakfast with them and brings his small lunch to eat here. There is—there are places to make tea. At night he goes to restaurants when he has money."

"How much is tuition?"

Suzuki replied and Mori translated, "The government pays on scholarship plan. For spending money to eat and clothes he has money from his army service." Suzuki added something. "But with inflation this is not much."

"Have the schools changed since the occupation?"

"Yes. There is now no military training. That is best change. They are colder, that is worst change."

"Academically, I mean. Is what you are taught any better?"

The two Japanese conferred. Finally Mori said, "He says they teach fewer things which are hard to believe."

"For example?"

"That your Christ was born in Japan. That Japanese invented radio, big fast guns, battleships and airplanes."

"How does he know they did not invent them?"

"Surely you know," Mori looked puzzled.

"Ask him, please."

They talked a minute. Mori grinned and reported, "He says because America has won the war."

"What is a democracy?"

Suzuki replied without waiting for a translation, "America is a democracy." He was pleased with that answer.

"What does that mean to you?"

Mori kept silent. Suzuki thought a minute or two and then said, "Democracy has president who comes from people and not from one family or class."

I told him, briefly, that it meant a little more than that. Mori translated and then said, "All this will appear in new books, I think."

"What should the Japanese people do about the Emperor and the Tenno system?"

Suzuki did not look as if he understood even when I had repeated the question. Mori blew on his hands mightily. When he did translate, at my suggestion, Suzuki answered in Japanese: "That is for General MacArthur to decide. We have lost the war."

"What about the British and Dutch and Russians? Should they have a voice in deciding Japan's future, too?"

Suzuki answered, in Japanese, "Not in my opinion. America defeated us. Early in war we defeated Dutch and British. Russians came late."

Suzuki then made a move to excuse himself. I asked him, before he left, if he would answer two more questions—what did he think of the atomic bomb and did he like the Americans?

There was a prolonged discussion about this in Japanese and then Mori replied, "He says he has not given any thought to atomic bombs but they are full of power. About Americans he is full of respect."

"Why?"

"They fight excellent and when fight is over they shake hands."

I shook hands with Suzuki. Mori walked with me down the cold, dirty corridor to the door. "Was Suzuki typical of the upper classmen?"

"Indeed no," said Mori, trying in vain to button his morning coat. "I picked him very special for you because he is more bright than others." I offered Mori a cigarette and he asked to take two. I presented him with the package and thanked him. As I left, Mori called after me, "He is also my wife's cousin."

8

In the second year of MacArthur, too, little had been accomplished on educational reform. MacArthur, who accepted the Education Mission's Report "in principle," balked on ordering the compulsory adoption of Romaji and the Yoshida Cabinet would not willingly accept this "basic change in tradition." In February 1947 the new Minister of Education, Dr. Seiichiro Takahasi, admitted that the recommendations of the Stoddard commission (almost a year before) "had not yet been applied to Japanese schools generally." He promised to do something about the slowness in adopting the American report. But he was talking for publication. He still had to work with the same underpaid, badly trained teachers, insufficient textbooks and a shortsighted budget which made it almost impossible even to check up on provincial school performance or standards. He did manage to place the study of Romaji in the elementary schools beginning April 1, 1947, but only as an elective to be taken *in addition* to the old language courses on characters.

Dr. Takahasi, an economics professor, had other problems beside the development of socio-civic consciousness in the school system. As an economist he knew that the schools must train skills for peace production as they had once trained wills for war destruction. A vocational program, however, had to wait the final decisions on the future path of Japan's economy. Meanwhile he wrestled with these stubborn statistics: more than three-quarters of the Japanese were not going beyond primary school; only one out of every three hundred secondary school graduates was entering college compared to thirty-five of every three hundred in the United States.

In an article published after his return from Tokyo, Dr. Benjamin underscored this deficiency in the Japanese school apparatus. "The Japanese must first of all expand secondary schools and enrich their curriculum," he wrote. "They should have at least five times as many pupils of ages thirteen to eighteen in the secondary schools as are now enrolled. Manpower is one of the most plentiful commodities in Japan. The country can find no better employment of its adolescent boys and girls than universal secondary education. The new Japanese secondary school . . . must discover and develop every scientific, artistic, vocational, and personal trait which its pupils can use for their own good and for the welfare of their country."

Limited by budget and personnel, the Americans tried raiding schools here and there to find out what was going on. At first this was chiefly a military rather than an intellectual assignment for the occupation forces, since the schools, along with certain shrines, had been turned into secret arsenals by Japanese diehards. An American correspondent who went on seventeen of these surprise visits reported that only four schools had fully complied with SCAP directives. In many instances the failure to comply was not visible to the eye; it was more subtle than the retention of old armaments or ancient rites.

In one girls' school between Tokyo and Yokohama I had watched the students begin their day with a military formation, then a bow and a prayer for the Emperor, followed by a snappy marching drill. The school was ice-cold; bombed-out windows had not been replaced. The rough wood floors were coated with dust. The individual classrooms had no real walls, only waist-high partitions between them. In the classroom the instructor was a minor despot whom the children feared. She had to shout to be heard above the din of passing traffic. Unsolicited questions were ruled out. The meek children were still learning by rote. They were marked on their conduct, not for their work, and nobody was put back. "It would bring too much shame," the teacher had explained.

9

The picture of the Emperor which once graced a special alcove in every one of Japan's forty thousand schools and colleges is gone—by SCAP's order. But what the picture represents lingers in the mind of young Japan.

Other correspondents making inspections in other sections of the country found that aggressive young teachers who encouraged free discussion, who made the teaching of democracy vital, were often labeled as "Communists" and "trouble-makers." In 1947 in Japan the prevalent reply to the nagging question of "Why democracy?" was, in most cases, simply "Because Japan has lost the war."

There were few encouraging signs as the students registered for the spring term in April. The new constitution (Article XXIV) pledged that "All people shall have the right to receive an equal education corresponding to his ability, as provided by law." Teachers were organizing into unions, even though there were charges that the most militant of them were Communist-led or dominated. In some schools boys and girls, formerly in complete segregation, were going to school together as equals. The compulsory period for attending school had been lengthened from six to nine years. An effort was being made to bring more females into the universities (in 1944 there were only 226 women in Japanese universities compared with 64,000 men).

But misinformation and hunger were still working against the flowering of democratic thinking. The new history textbook for grade-school children still referred to Japan's aggression against Korea this way: "Our country annexed Korea after negotiations in which we made the Japan-Korea treaty." Teachers and students found it hard to concentrate on anything but getting enough to eat, despite free school lunches bought by American donations. A twenty-year-old former soldier, quoted in *Time*, summed up the bewilderment of thousands of other students:

We students talk and talk, but cannot find the answers. How do you figure values between the former education and the present? If one is better than the other, we must understand it. But we have no one who can tell us. In Japan today there are many restrictions which MacArthur has placed upon the people which are not the will of the people. Where is the difference between democracy and what we had before the war?

I don't know. There are too many things about democracy which we students have not had time to study. All of us here walk three kilometers a day to get a meal of a little rice and radish. It is difficult to contemplate the philosophy of government under such circumstances.

No matter how well the reform policies sprout on paper or in the Diet, it will be years before they actually take root in the Japanese educational system. The soil is hardened with the rock of tradition, and many of the hands that water it now are still controlled by the brains who starved it before.

CHAPTER VI

POLITICS AND POLITICIANS

LONG before the promulgation of the new Constitution, long before the re-education program could be much of an influence, MacArthur called for the first free elections in Japan. The Far Eastern Commission in Washington politely raised objections that it might be too soon to expect a "fully instructed, intelligent and authoritative expression of the views of the Japanese people on their political future" and that "members are not without the apprehension that the holding of the election at such an early date may well give a decisive advantage to the reactionary parties. . . ." But MacArthur grandly waved aside all doubts.

"Political activity is now widespread," the General replied. More than sixty new parties had been formed where there were none. (Prince Konoye's Imperial Rule Assistance Association had replaced the usual multi-party structure in 1940.) "Should the results of the election prove disadvantageous to the purposes of the occupation," SCAP continued in his reply to the FEC, "the remedy is always in my power to require the dissolution of the Diet and the holding of a new election under such provisions as are deemed necessary."

Both before and after the elections there were mob outbursts against Premier Shidehara. Just three days prior to the balloting a large and disorderly crowd threw rocks through the windows of his home and injured eight policemen in a demonstration. But on April 10, 1946, 27 million Japanese went to the polls peacefully and cast their votes for some 3,000 candidates, most of whom they had never heard about before. The political directive of January 4, which the Japanese called the "MacArthur Typhoon," had left only about fifty members of the former Diet eligible to run for office. Military candidates were barred. All the leading parties, except the Communists, were severely affected.

To many Japanese a new face is a suspicious face. Despite the editorials in the newspapers and the radio lectures to which they were exposed, they preferred to vote for the old names and, if there were no old names, then those backed by the old names. Of the 466 seats in the lower house, the Liberal Party won 139; the progressives, 93; the Social Democrats, 92; the Co-operative Party, 14; the Communists, 6; to the minor parties went 38 seats, and to men listed as "independents," 82. The independents were almost all extremely conservative, and later most of them joined forces with the Liberals and Progressives.

The Liberal Party, most powerful in the first peacetime Diet, was composed of remnants of the disbanded and disbarred Great Japan Political Society and was headed by Ichiro Hatoyama. It was about as liberal as Senator Bilbo. The Progressive Party, later led by Baron Shidehara, was also misnamed. If anything, it represented more conservative interests than the Liberals.

The Social Democratic Party, really two parties, was culled together from members and followers of the prewar Social Masses Party, the labor unions and surviving supporters of the radical popular-front movement of the early thirties. Dominated by a right-wing faction which consistently opposed working with the Communists, the Social Democrats advanced a program of reform less far-reaching than that of the present British Labor Party. The Party's leader is sixty-year-old Tetsu Katayama, a Christian and a former Tokyo labor lawyer who served in the prewar Diet. Katayama is a Fabian socialist, known for his sincerity and simplicity. The left wing of this party, made up of intellectuals and trade unionists, believed that all working-class parties should co-operate on broad issues; they favored a temporary alliance with the Communists although they did not publicly back the extremists on the abolition of the Imperial system. The two factions were somehow welded together by Suehiro Nishio, a former steelworker, who became the behind-the-scenes party boss.

The man who received the greatest number of votes in this first postwar election was the president of the Liberal Party, Ichiro Hatoyama. As Minister of Education in 1932 he had suppressed progressive student movements and hounded professors for their "dangerous thoughts." During the war he had evidently refused to join the Imperial Rule Assistance Association and thus acquired the reputation of an anti-militarist. At the time of the campaign

I talked with him at his party headquarters across the street from the Tokyo Press Club. He was a tall man in his early sixties, well-dressed and carefully manicured, with alert eyes and an agile tongue. After an hour spent amiably discussing his personal credo and that of his party, I came away with the feeling that either Hatoyama did not know what he was talking about or he did not want me to know what he was talking about. In the entire interview he had allowed himself to be pinned down on only three specific points: he liked MacArthur and the *New York Times,* and he did not think that Japan's Pacific war was "really a war of aggression." To Japanese reporters he protested against free speech for the Communists and urged prosecution of anybody who did not believe in the Emperor.

Some weeks later at the Press Club a large group of Allied correspondents led by Mark Gayn of the Chicago *Sun* and Frank Robertson of International News Service challenged Hatoyama's "liberalism" by quoting from his book, *The Face of the World.* In this volume, which he wrote in 1937 after a trip to Europe, Hatoyama had been unstinting in his praise of Hitler and Mussolini and their methods.

As a result of this session at the Press Club, Hatoyama and his past record received widespread publicity. During the election campaign in Tokyo's First District only his Communist opponents had been tactless enough to assail Hatoyama's previous fondness for fascism. The candidates of other parties and the unfettered Tokyo press refrained from exposing the Liberal Party leader because he had not been declared ineligible by SCAP. Only after election returns had come in and the unfavorable publicity had gone forth did SCAP move to have Hatoyama disbarred. They had known of his record all along; MacArthur had reassured the Far Eastern Commission that all Diet candidates had been carefully screened before they were accepted as candidates.

In the month following the elections the Liberals and Progressives argued and bickered over the choice of a new premier. Finally, Shigeru Yoshida took the job. He is sixty-eight, a pudgy, gruff man who wears pince-nez glasses and smokes big cigars. He had held his first important political post as far back as 1928, when he served as Vice-Minister of Foreign Affairs under the late Baron Giichi Tanaka, author of the infamous Tanaka Memorial and spokesman for an aggressive imperialist policy. Two years later, as Am-

bassador to Italy, Yoshida had obtained preliminary pledges of
support from Mussolini for Japan's plans in Asia. Transferred to
the Court of St. James as Hirohito's envoy, Yoshida defended
Japanese aggression in Manchuria. In 1936 his signature adhered
Japan to the Anti-Comintern Pact. When asked how this fitted
into his supposed "liberal" views, Yoshida said that "Liberalism
may not be rejected altogether, but its evil aspects should be
corrected."

During the optimistic years of the Pacific war, Yoshida did not
speak out. Early in 1945, believing that Japan could not win, he
counseled the Cabinet to seek a negotiated peace. For this heresy
he was taken into custody by the *kempei tai* and confined to a
Tokyo cell for a couple of months. This prison record made him
eminently acceptable to SCAP despite his previous career. During
the first months of the occupation he was frequently mentioned
as a candidate for the premiership but was shrewd enough to
sidestep this responsibility until he was certain that collaboration
with the Americans would not spell political suicide. Under pressure
he did accept the role of Foreign Minister in the Cabinet of his old
friend, Baron Shidehara.

When Hatoyama was disqualified, Yoshida joined the Liberal
Party and was named its second President. At ceremonies some
time later marking his formal installation as party chief, Yoshida
warmly praised his purged "friend." His remarks to the party elite
had a ring of "There but for the grace of MacArthur go I. . . ."

Although he had not even been elected a member of the new
Diet, Yoshida was given the premiership. He formed a Cabinet
composed of five Liberals, four Progressives, and four members
of the moribund House of Peers. This very conservative coalition
met with immediate criticism from the Japanese press. In an
editorial describing the new Cabinet unfavorably, *Asahi* lamented
"The conservative Liberal and Progressive Parties have demonstrated that they are closely tied to the reactionary bureaucracy."
Mainichi, a more moderate Tokyo daily, stated: "It may be supposed that the new conservative Cabinet will be but a bad second
to the outgoing Shidehara Cabinet . . . and will probably attempt
to patch up the situation without damaging the interest of big
business and other privileged classes. Without doubt this kind of
government is incapable of solving the present crisis."

The Co-operatives, a new party of the center, drew its candidates and support from members of the Agricultural Co-operative Society, middle-class landowners and small entrepreneurs. Its busiest organizer was Takeo Miko, thirty-nine, a businessman who had once studied in the United States.

The party of the extreme left, the Communists, legalized for the first time under MacArthur, actively campaigned with a program veering sharply away from the status quo and the platforms of the other parties. They favored working with the occupation authorities but had urged a postponement of the elections and of the decision to draft the new Constitution immediately. In addition to condemning the Imperial system and demanding a republican form of government, the Communists proposed immediate nationalization of basic industries. Although it had only a small party membership and limited campaign funds, the Communists received two million votes, largely from the industrial centers.

2

Historically, the significance of this election was not the political composition of the new Diet, which differed only moderately from the previous one. There had been few clear-cut issues and a profusion of confusion. The size and the result of the vote were unusual but not unexpected. Japanese were used to being told to go to the polls; 75 per cent of those eligible had voted in 1937 and 82 per cent in 1942. The 74 per cent who voted in 1946 did so chiefly because the ward heelers, MacArthur, and the Americans had told them it was their duty and the habit of obedience is strong. They elected thirty-nine out of eighty-two female candidates—not because they believed them more able, but because SCAP informed them that this was how it was done in MacArthur's home country. More than half the registered electorate were women, given suffrage for the first time in Japan, and they tended to vote for their sex. The feminine representatives ranged in age from twenty-seven to sixty-one, in experience and background from typists to college professors.

MacArthur was as happy as a football coach whose underdog team has just won its first game. "Democracy has thus demonstrated a healthy forward advance," he proclaimed. He quoted Lincoln's maxim, "The people are wiser than their rulers," which is almost the exact opposite of the Japanese adage, "Respect for officials, contempt for the people."

To this observer the most impressive factors in the campaign were the role of the women and the wide latitude given the extreme right and the extreme left. The work of one WAC attached to SCAP, Lieutenant Ethel Weed, in organizing what amounted to a Japanese League of Women Voters, was tremendous. If there had been ten WACs with her qualifications assigned to the task of explaining "the democratic way" to the women of Japan, the job could have been done with even greater thoroughness and effect.

The status of women in Japan began changing during the war from the old feudal basis of the arranged marriage and the single morality standard, of the household drudge and extra worker in the fields. The desperate need for a bigger labor force drew the Japanese housewife into the economic orbit of the nation. Women who had never ventured farther than the nearest shrine journeyed to factories in Yokohama, Kobe and Osaka. By February 1944 even the prostitutes of Tokyo's Yoshiwara district were ordered into more productive fields. At the war's end it was estimated that half of Japan's labor force was female. This social dislocation gave women the first glimmerings of new social responsibilities and securities. They were far more emancipated than either their Chinese or Korean sisters. In Japan, at least, the woman traditionally has carried the family purse and has done the shopping for the household.

Under MacArthur, women received political equality. For the first time a Japan Women's Party was formed. But it will be a long, hard fight before they achieve social and economic equality from their own men. They are still discriminated against in wage scales and very few unions are fighting for their equal rights. Slowly the women are learning to act for themselves. During the coal strike in Hokkaido the wives of miners were shepherded to a meeting and were urged not to remain spectators but to "do something." A thousand of them then marched to the company offices and demanded that the officials bargain with the strikers.

When the women members in the Diet were rather coolly received by their male colleagues, they banded together and formed a "Feminine Association" regardless of their political differences. Their prestige rose considerably when General MacArthur sent for them, spoke to them, and then shook hands with each woman individually.

During the campaigning I attended the first mass meeting in

Tokyo for women candidates. It was organized by the daily paper *Mainichi,* and was attended by over 3,000 Japanese, at least half of them women, many with babies on their backs. Candidates from various parties spoke and the audience enjoyed the forum immensely. But *Mainichi* did not, at that time, think that the women's meeting which it had sponsored merited a story in the next day's paper.

Commenting on this to Japanese friends that night at dinner, I asked Chiro Watanabe if he had discussed with his wife the new part women were playing in Japan. "No, sir," he said in his precise English, "we have not a great amount of time to worry about this matter. Usually we discuss what our new son will have to eat and to wear."

I then asked Mrs. Watanabe what she thought of rallies like the one *Mainichi* had just held. "I do not know about such matters," she said almost in a whisper, keeping her glance on the table.

Watanabe was a former newspaperman for *Domei* who considered himself a liberal and an internationalist. But he could not see that the political freedoms granted to women were particularly important.

"You undoubtedly understand these things much better than we do," he said, "but it is quite difficult for us to become greatly excited about political freedom for women when they must spend their day raising children, cleaning house and fighting for foodstuffs on the black market in order to survive. To make an example, if you do not mind, I may give my six-months-old son freedom to go to the movies. That is potentially valuable, we will admit. But for some months to come it is meaningless since he cannot walk so he cannot get to the movies. If he could walk, he would not yet be ready to understand the movie."

3

One of the phenomena of the pre-election period was the warm and widespread welcome accorded to Sanzo Nosaka. This fifty-five-year-old Communist had led the Japanese People's Emancipation League in Yenan where he was known as Susumu Okano. When he returned to Tokyo early in 1946 he was greeted as something of a hero by widely diverse segments of Japanese public opinion.

The English-language *Nippon Times*, traditionally controlled by the Japanese Foreign Office, wrote editorially:

The homecoming of Sanzo Nosaka from Yenan has created a great sensation in Japanese political circles, even in these days of surprises. Rarely has an individual received so much attention of the newspapers. His homecoming was like the triumphal return of a victorious general. A democratic revolution is proceeding apace and he is a portent to anyone who can read the signs of the times.

The public is heartily sick of the cowardly bureaucrats who acted as convenient instruments of the militarists. Under the domination of the militarists and the repressive measures of the bureaucrats, the political sense of the people suffered an atrophy, but they still retain a strong horse sense.

Here we are not concerned with the merits or demerits of the Communist program, but Sanzo Nosaka, who has come into the limelight, has certain attributes behooving a new leader. This is what has attracted the people, and in giving him much prominence, the newspapers are echoing the popular demand for a new leader.

It is a significant fact that there are more men of a similar type in Leftist than in Rightist circles. New wine must be put into a new skin. The future belongs to the parties and leaders who can win the heart of the people. The politician of the old type, whose personal strength consisted in personal affiliations or the bulge of his purse, has become an anachronism. Let it be repeated that Sanzo Nosaka is a portent to any who can read the writing on the walls.

Variations on this theme appeared in other Tokyo editorial columns. Representatives of left-wing parties and trade unions staged a small celebration for Nosaka at a local restaurant and the same day these groups combined with the Communists to call a public rally. U. S. Counter-Intelligence agents estimated the crowd which flocked to Hibiya Park in Tokyo as about ten thousand. It was the first big outdoor political mass meeting. There were very few women and most of the men appeared to be demobilized soldiers, many still wearing parts of their uniforms. After a band number, a soprano sang the "Internationale" in Japanese. Then seven or eight speakers failed to rouse the cold and silent gathering until Nosaka spoke. He is a small, slight man with a nose like a rabbit. His oratorical form, even when his content became emotional and explosive, was exceptionally mild. Nevertheless the standing thousands responded to him with instantaneous sympathy. He began by saying that he had thought of his native land every day during his long exile. Now he had returned to help the construction of a democratic Japan. The present method of democratizing Japan was, he charged, the "cart before the horse technique." He recommended that the Shidehara Cabinet should resign, that a democratic-front government be formed and that a democratic constitution be promulgated. Only then, he felt, could a truly democratic election be held. This was the climax of his speech and the crowd cheered him enthusiastically.

When the meeting broke up, a spontaneous parade marched along the bank of the Imperial moat. The demonstrators carried their flags and banners aloft as if they hoped the Emperor might catch sight of them.

During the long meeting I talked with the Colonel who had charge of the score of the Counter-Intelligence Corps men scattered around the park. I asked him why his men were there. He replied that it was to forestall any possible attempt by a rightist group to break up the meeting.

"How does SCAP feel about the vigorous campaign which the Communists are putting on?" I asked.

The Colonel smiled and said, "Why, very good. You see there are certain questions of basic reforms which must be put before the public. The Communists and their followers appear to be the only ones with enough nerve to bring these issues before the population. So right now our instructions are to let them blow off steam because we think it will encourage free discussion, work up interest in the elections and eventually create an opposition."

"Opposition to what, the occupation?"

"Hell no," he said, "to the Communists."

Japanese newspaper editors explained that the return of Nosaka might actually make possible a working agreement between the Communists and the Social Democrats. They believed that despite his sixteen-year-exile Nosaka, a former economics instructor at Keo University in Tokyo, knew more about conditions in Japan than the other top leaders of his party. Earlier in the occupation I had met and talked with Kyuichi Tokuda, General Secretary of the Communists, and Yoshio Shiga, editor of the newspaper, Red Flag. I found that they still had a tendency to talk in the slogans of a previous decade. Shiga, a big, burly man with gold teeth and a flat nose, had been a sociologist at Tokyo Imperial University, when he was arrested in 1928 for political activity. He had remained in solitary confinement until released under the political amnesty of October 10, 1945. Tokuda, Shiga and Nosaka were among the six Communists elected to the House of Representatives.

Before Nosaka's return the Communists had wanted to do everything at once: punish all adults in the Imperial family as war criminals, indict all members of the Progressive Party and most of the Social Democrats as war criminals, redistribute the lands of "parasitical landowners" without charge to the peasants, abolish the Tenno system, and nationalize industry.

Later some of these demands were modified—particularly those involving the Imperial family—and Nosaka made considerable headway in bringing about a rapprochement with the Social Democrats. But after several heated sessions at which the question of a popular front badly split the Socialist Party, the right wing won out and collaboration with the Communists was barred.

When he returned to Japan the Communists had only 1,200 dues-paying members, but Nosaka was hopeful about the future. "The people are not so depressed as I expected to find them," Nosaka told me. "They are looking for a new Japan, a new leadership. The Communist Party is going to give the people what they are looking for—political democracy and at the same time economic democracy." Nosaka denied that he had had any contact with Moscow during his long stay in Yenan and he was equally emphatic in stating that Japan must work to establish a liberal "bourgeois" democracy on the pattern of the United States.

4

A few weeks after the Hibiya Park rally for Nosaka the Tokyo newspapers announced "the first anti-Communist" demonstration. In a driving snow, several hundred blue-clad, brass-buttoned students huddled in the ruins of Meiji University's burned-out campus to listen to the speakers. I was the only Allied reporter on hand and after a while I was wishing I had remained in the Press Club bar.

The meeting had been called by a spirited group calling themselves the "League of Former Cheer Leaders of the Six Major Universities in Tokyo," ostensibly in protest against the "Itabashi Incident." The Communists had helped in the unscheduled distribution of food from a Japanese Government warehouse in Tokyo's Itabashi Ward. This humane but illegal action had won for them a popular following in that ward.

Signs, posted on two gaunt stone pillars in front of the audience, proclaimed: "Down with Red Gangsters" and "Itabashi Food Riot— Communist Party Downfall." Speakers repeated these slogans and then went on to paint the imminent dangers of world-wide Communism. Sadao Kubo, Director of the Alumni Association of the Big Six Universities, a short, balding man with horn-rimmed glasses, who seemed to be the key figure in activities, predicted: "This is only the first rally to awaken people to the fact that the Communist Party has no place in making the new Japan."

Yutaka Suzuki, who called himself "President of the Constitutional New Politics Association," orated in the style of Mississippi's John Rankin. "You—You," he harangued the freezing students, "You are the new leaders in Japan, not the Communists. You must take action!" But for all his arm-waving, neither Suzuki nor the other declamators, including student Tomoichi Murayama or Giichi Hira, member of the Independent Socialist Party and of the Kojimachi Ward Assembly, actually said what they wanted done with the Communists.

Murayama, wearing a black, turtle-neck sweater under a student's tunic, won the loudest cheers of "*Soda!*" ("That's right!") when he charged that the Communists should have given food to everybody and not just to a small group. With Japanese-born Trevor Gauntlett, *Time's* efficient translator, I tried to poll student opinion. Most of them gave the impression they did not know why they were at the rally. "But if it's O.K. with General MacArthur, it's O.K. with us," one youth told me in good Union Square English.

During the proceedings, which lasted about an hour, two bored, white-helmeted American M.P.'s drove up. They listened in perfect blankness for a minute, asked to see the meeting's permit, shook the snow from their noses, sniffed and departed with the friendly observation to me: "Them Commies is at it again."

More significant diehard groups openly campaigned on a platform demanding that Korea, Formosa, and Manchuria become Japanese mandates. SCAP was carefully tolerant. The big conservative parties talked in generalities, spent a good deal of money, and felt confident.

5

On election day the farmers dropped their hand plows in the spring furrows and hastened in to the village hall to vote. Their wives, trying hard not to forget the name or names their husbands had told them to remember, trotted behind. Often they brought. the whole family with them, the youngest child on the mother's back. Some of the women, and the men, too, forgot the names and voted for the village headman. Others with more imagination responded to the exhortation "to vote for their choice" by scrawling on the ballot the characters for the Tenno or for General MacArthur, himself.

In the cities and larger towns Military Government teams watched the elections but did not interfere. There was little of the enthusiasm which marks an American election, even after the results were tabulated. The Japanese voters, in the mass, were glad that SCAP seemed pleased and wondered if the new Government would be so pleasing to SCAP that they would get more to eat.

While the first postwar elections had changed quite a few faces, they had not turned up any new national leaders. In the current honeymoon-with-MacArthur mood of the Japanese people a Nosaka could expand his following only if tolerated by the new voice of authority, SCAP. The new Prime Minister, Cabinet, and Diet had no more of a positive peacetime program than the old ones. The big plus in the situation was that this time the opposition were free to speak loud and long against those in power, safe in their belief that SCAP would protect minority rights.

They did speak. Mrs. Shidzue Kato, the former Baroness Ishimoto (the Japanese "Margaret Sanger"), one of the ablest Social Democrats elected to the House of Representatives, called the Diet "untrustworthy" and charged that "a majority of its members come from the feudal forces within Japan." Mosaburo Suzuki, the Social Democrats' financial expert, disgusted at Yoshida's failure to combat inflation, even called for a dissolution of the Diet. He predicted economic chaos for Japan by March 1947 because of "the vicious inflation which is strangling our industries as well as the living standard of our workers while the Government remains optimistic and heedless of the danger."

Before the next national elections were to take place a year later there were to be many superficial changes in Japan and a basic change in SCAP's attitude toward the democratization process. In the intervening months popular support for the party of Mrs. Kato and Mosaburo Suzuki was to grow stronger and that for Yoshida's party weaker. It would be a year of indecision for the Japanese and a year of decision for American policy.

CHAPTER VII

OCCUPATION THEORY VS. PRACTICE

UNDER this first freely elected Diet, laws had to be considered and passed which could possibly change basic patterns in Japan. The Constitution had to be implemented by translating it into workable codes. The *Zaibatsu* had to be broken up, inflation curbed, industry reconverted, agrarian reform promoted, and new statutes written concerning the rights and responsibilities of labor and management. The Diet, however, acted like most diets. It waited for the Government to push bills at them. The Government, in turn, waited for SCAP to send them directives.

For almost a year and a half SCAP carefully avoided taking any direct responsibility for the basic economy of Japan. In an exceptional instance, food was imported to prevent unrest. Sweeping directives in various fields were drawn up and heaped upon the Japanese Government. Occasionally pressure would be exerted or criticism offered to make certain that a needed reform was acted upon. But MacArthur wanted the blame for any failures to fall upon the Government in power and not on the occupation. When the Government in power turned out to be one which SCAP trusted and wanted to succeed, it was given great amounts of expert advice and even help in the drafting of bills.

MacArthur was no economist and although economic experts and missions were sent to his theater from time to time, often over his objections, he paid them little heed. In fact, more than one mission submitted a report full of recommendations about improving the functioning of the Japanese economy which MacArthur did not see until he was asked about it by a visiting dignitary. The "Bataan crowd" protected him and themselves by pigeonholing these reports. "We don't like to worry the Old Man with a lot of technical stuff," a "Bataan" general explained to a visiting newspaper publisher who had asked about MacArthur's reaction to a report.

Thus from the beginning MacArthur was content to rely on the Japanese to rebuild their own economic structure once he had eliminated the "war clique." The rest, he felt, were all right. MacArthur understood from Japanese history that in a few short centuries they had constructed the greatest industrial empire in the Far East. They certainly had the technical know-how and there was no reason to doubt that, with a little watching here and a little prodding there, they could not revive under their own initiative and planning. In fact, they should do better because with the new MacArthur-given liberties the common man would be more cooperative and would work harder than ever.

SCAP hoped that this fostering of free enterprise would discourage any postwar trend toward communism or socialism in Japan. It was a beautiful theory but it did not work out. The uncontrolled, laissez faire approach produced such economic chaos before the second year of the occupation was over that MacArthur became, for the first time, uneasy about his job. It also produced the opposite effect: it made social democracy appear like a way out to the workers and the middle class caught in the economic squeeze.

But at the outset MacArthur had no such worries. The job somehow seemed fairly easy. The press reaction in the United States was good when SCAP announced he could get along with a smaller occupation force. No immediate drive was started to bring experts to Japan. "Let Mac do it alone," busy officials in Washington said, "he seems to be making out all right."

This logic stemmed from the naive assumption that American directives resulted in Japanese actions. SCAP, for a long time, acted as if such were the case. Demobilization proceeded merrily. More and more responsibility was given to the Japanese authorities. Newspaper correspondents wrote glowingly of SCAP directives, rarely ventured into the field to check on their ultimate application.

Outside of the Tokyo area, SCAP checked on Japanese compliance with directives through forty-five Military Government "teams," one for each political prefecture. These men were supposed to perform almost Herculean tasks, requiring specialized knowledge of economics, education, public health, rationing, agriculture, local politics, grain collecting, and trade unionism. In short, each "team" should have been sufficiently well rounded to inspect and interpret the results of millions of lines of directives and memoranda which rolled out of SCAP's sections (Economic and

Scientific, Civil Information and Education, Natural Resources, Public Health and Welfare, Government, Legal, International Prosecution, Civil Communications, Statistical and Reports, Counter Intelligence, Civil Intelligence and Diplomatic).

In all, SCAP's understaffed Military Government personnel shook down to about 2,500 officers and men. Their capabilities varied tremendously and very few of them found it possible to do a first-class job. In 1946 the rate of turnover was approximately 90 per cent so that no sooner had a man learned about his area than he was bound for home or another assignment. Beginning in 1947 the men placed in Military Government posts were signed up for a minimum of two years.

2

During the first winter of the MacArthur régime this writer went on a tour of southern Honshu and Kyushu with a group of correspondents. We had our eyes opened. The United States had the remnants of a great fighting force scattered throughout Japan looking for ammunition hidden in caves and learning the tea ceremony. But we were conspicuously lacking in the experts needed to check on ultra-nationalistic organizations, on schools, on textbooks, on civil liberties, on reconversion, or on any SCAP orders. The gap between theory and practice was enormous. Some Military Government officials in the field never even saw MacArthur directives until they read them in the *Nippon Times* three or four days after they were issued. They felt that the chain of command between them and the sixth floor of the Dai Ichi Building was too long and too loose.

As an example, let us take the reconversion problem in the city of Osaka, which was the largest and most important industrial center in Japan. In Osaka we began learning facts about the Japanese economy which were not publicly discussed in Tokyo, and which never appeared in the SCAP publicity releases or in any of the SCAP-censored newspapers. Under Allied supervision, Japan's economy was still regimented from the top by the Control Associations. These non-governmental organizations were formed by the *Zaibatsu* during the war as necessary appendages of the super-trusts. They consisted of representatives from the biggest companies in a particular field who assumed the power to manage, finance, fix prices and create trade pools in their own field. At Osaka, and throughout Japan, they were still setting the prices of raw materials and of finished products, squeezing as much as the traffic would bear to benefit the few rather than the many. The Associations' stranglehold on the economy effectively stymied the enforcement of any wide system of priorities.

(On August 6, 1946, SCAP got around to issuing an order that they be dissolved. But they lingered on for months in a manner which will be discussed more fully at the conclusion of this chapter.)

Superimposing SCAP on the red-tape bound Japanese structure only served to remove the source of authority several steps further away from local officials. Japanese bureaucrats in the prefectures excused themselves, saying they had no authority now and never had had any. They dared not make a move until it was authorized from Tokyo.

Orders or "suggestions" went from SCAP through the Central Liaison Office to the Imperial Government and then to the proper ministry and finally to the prefectures. This process took weeks and sometimes months. Purges had left gaps in the bureaucracy and many officeholders were demoralized or unwilling to help recovery for other reasons. When general instructions from Tokyo did reach the local officials, it was frequently found that they did not specifically apply to the situation on the spot. The Osaka Japanese said they were powerless to change the original instructions and they did not think it wise to protest. As a result, nothing happened in many instances.

Our chief guide in the Osaka region was a tall, handsome, and harried U.S. Army major who had charge of the zone's military government activities. AMG, the major informed us, was almost as powerless in the local situation as the Japanese officials. In theory he and his men were committed to a policy of supervision, although in actual practice individual officers were much tempted to speed up matters by taking a hand in implementation. But too often their attempts to lend a helping hand failed, even in purely humanitarian efforts. During the first bitterly cold months of the occupation part of the Japanese in the Osaka region suffered severely from the shortage of food and clothing. The major's men knew that the U.S. Army had seized huge stockpiles of Japanese army and navy supplies and turned them over to the Government for distribution. Despite the emergency the food and clothing were not given to the needy, and because of the cumbersome chain of authority Osaka AMG could do little more than bang a few desks.

"There's not much we can do about this starvation," said the major. "Even if we could prod the Japs sufficiently there are only eight of us for a city of three and a half million."

This overworked AMG team, which supposedly had time to supervise the implementation of all democratizing directives, was badly handicapped in its efforts to stimulate reconversion. They had to inspect factories several times, give advice to Japanese on what to make and how to make it, tell them how to fill out forms and applications, inspect the applications and then inspect the factories to make sure they were producing what they were licensed to produce. During the winter of 1945-46 AMG had received two hundred and fifty reconversion applications from the estimated one thousand plants in the Osaka district which presumably could resume work.

Among other things, these Japanese were planning to manufacture *suki yaki* dishes and pans from steel shell bottoms, bicycle frames from machine-gun bases, lipstick holders from cartridge clips, platters and soup plates from steel helmets, electric "reflector" heaters from brass shells, fishing boats from assault landing barges. But because of a limited investigating corps, the major and his men only had an opportunity to approve one hundred and twenty of the applications.

We visited several of the plants which had had their licenses for reconversion granted. At the largest one, there were no signs of activity. Noebehara, head of the Takahara Farming and Fishing Implement Company, told us he had made naval air weapons during the war and hoped to produce suction pumps and irrigation machinery in peacetime. He had not yet started his plant in operation, because "We are afraid that we shall be confronted with much difficulty for getting materials from the Control Association concerned. I do not know them nor they do not know me for this is new work for our manufacturing."

We asked him what could be done to help. Noebehara shrugged his shoulders and looked mournfully at the major. The major grimaced and led us out of the Takahara Company.

"Other plants won't budge until we decide on what equipment will be removed for reparations," the major said. We asked if Ambassador Edwin Pauley, the President's representative on reparations, had visited Osaka and if he had consulted him. "He was here," the major said, "and got a flock of Japanese statistics."

Headquarters in Tokyo, according to the major, were using ridiculous standards. "They ask us on our reports to ascertain whether or not a plant can be utilized for war purposes. This shows how little they know about machinery. Any machine that can convert from bullet cases to lipsticks can convert back again. Machines which ground gunpowder and will grind wheat into flour can naturally revert."

The major was typical of the best officers who had come to Japan from civilian ranks "to do a job." In St. Paul he had headed a big firm of his own. He was familiar with textile equipment and machinery of all kinds. In Japan he was submitting reports to superior officers who did not know the first thing about machinery. The regular army officers, including the West Pointers, the major claimed, were getting the rank, so it "is not worth it for me to remain in Japan when I could be back making $1,700 a month in St. Paul."

He knew that his AMG force in Osaka was insufficient to cope with the Japanese and the Japanese knew it, too. "In our preliminary investigations the Japanese gave us one set of figures. When we give them the go-ahead on reconversion they submit production plans for 1946-47 and cite an entirely different bunch of figures. The Japanese know we haven't either the time or men to run around and count them ourselves."

The major was bitter that neither SCAP nor the Japanese Government did anything about the "continued confusion in the Home Ministry" and the stranglehold of the Control Associations or the tradition of graft in business. "We once, just for fun, traced one hundred cases of apples from the grower to the consumer. By the time they reached the ultimate market only seventy-five cases were left. The officials and the Control Association grabbed off their shares on the way. We called this to the attention of the Japanese but they didn't see anything wrong in the operation. It's usual."

In another instance a Japanese factory manager had an order for wire rope but could not obtain the steel wire needed in the process from the Control Association. He appealed to the major, who located eight hundred tons of wire in a deserted Japanese army warehouse and informed the Control Association, through the

Home Ministry. "That was two months ago," he said, "and the factory still hasn't received the wire."

On a rare occasion this kind of slowdown drove him to extraordinary acts. A Japanese came to him and secured his permission to purchase a powder arsenal for conversion to a flour mill. He assented and took the matter to the Home Ministry. For a month the Ministry's bureaucrats held up taking any action until the major barged in one morning and yelled, "If you don't complete this sale immediately I will condemn that arsenal and blow it up. I still have that power."

The power of blowing up "dangerous targets" was frequently abused. "Young second lieutenants," the major told me, "who didn't know any more about machines than I know about hothouse orchids, were given these 'targets.' It was much simpler to demolish the machine and cross it off the list than to find out about its potential capacities in peacetime production. Oh, what beautiful lathes they've smashed to bits. Some of them made in Cincinnati, too. It's not the machine's fault that it was employed for war purposes, is it?"

After many months of dealing with the Japanese on an operations level, the major thought he had them pegged.

"Years mean nothing to these people," he said. "They may have lost for now. But in fifty, a hundred, or five hundred years they'll be back. You won't see the scheme building up directly. They do everything, even straight business, by indirection. That's something we Americans cannot understand. We haven't the patience to learn their ways and they know it. They know, too, that sooner or later we will leave."

The major had a theory about the Emperor, too. "Let's make him the head of this religion of theirs and give him a fine office with trappings in Kyoto. He's not so all-powerful. Take the big executives and bankers I meet here. When they are making money the Emperor's wonderful. When times are hard, well . . . it's like politics any place."

Questions of war guilt did not bother the major. "I will say this," he said. "The Japanese people are far less guilty than the Germans. The people here are more isolated from the world and certainly less well-educated. Lots of them didn't know what was going on. You know most of them were convinced they had bombed Seattle, San Francisco and Los Angeles? Can you beat that?"

3

Two fundamental reforms to which SCAP was committed under the terms of the broad directive of September 6, 1945, were the dissolution of the *Zaibatsu* and the break-up of large estates. Any detailed, final evaluation of the success or failure of these important changes in Japan's economic framework must await the collection of more evidence than is now available. However, on the basis of preliminary surveys it is possible to make at least an interim report.

Zaibatsu, the Japanese word for "moneyed clique," generally refers to the powerful families which controlled the nation's economy through their octopus-like holding companies. The State Department called them combines and cartels "comparable to the Nazis' world-girdling I.G. Farben Industrie." The biggest and best-known in Japan were the Big Four—Mitsui, Mitsubishi, Sumitomo, and Yasuda, who controlled 40 per cent of the total national wealth. They dominated the industrial, financial and commercial life of Japan so much that it was evident that Japan could not be democratized until the Big Four, and other similar combines, were dissolved and the wealth of the country redistributed in a more judicious and equitable manner. President Truman's occupation policy statement of September 6, 1945, ordered MacArthur to "favor" such a program.

The role of the *Zaibatsu* in aiding and abetting Japanese aggressions has been recounted frequently. (One of the best accounts appears in *Dilemma in Japan* by Andrew Roth.) Some of them were outright partners of the militarists; others contributed large sums to the secret jingoist and terrorist groups. In four successive wars of conquest big business reaped huge profits. In the past war they co-operated actively, lured by the promise of fabulous spoils in Manchuria, China, Dutch East Indies, Burma, and eventually Siberia and India. They were active in Japan's last two wartime cabinets. When their policies clashed with those of the military, as T. A. Bisson, the author of *Japan's War Economy*, has proved, "They succeeded in enforcing their program virtually *in toto*."

But as soon as the war was over, they exchanged their helmets for high silk hats, their steel bayonets for gold toothpicks. Allied officers and correspondents were wooed with steak dinners, *presentos* (gifts), geisha parties, and honeyed words. "We had no voice. We took orders," said Kyoshi Miyazaki, president of a Mitsui

company. "We didn't dare to speak. We were afraid to death," said
Ryozo Asano, president of the Japan Steel Tube Company and a
half-dozen other giant industrial firms. Asano, a Harvard man,
asked after his classmate, the late Robert Benchley, and wondered
how the last Yale game had turned out.

Neither Asano nor Miyazaki suddenly stopped being tempted
by profit or nationalist motives, but they put on an awfully good act.
On the whole the Army men were more impressed than the newspapermen. Asano was worried about the destruction, the difficulties
of reconstruction, the growing hunger and unemployment. "We are
alarmed," he told me in the exact words he had used in an earlier
interview, "because so much unemployment may lead to dangerous
thoughts, such as socialism."

At about this time Shigeru Yoshida also expressed an opinion on
the trusts. In an interview he assured Americans that the "old"
Zaibatsu were "good," and only the aggressive *nouveau riche*
Zaibatsu were "bad."

Miyazaki and his colleague, Yuijo Nagashima, were impressed
by the "bad name" the word *"Zaibatsu"* had become in the American lexicon. This moved the Mitsuis to convene in a star-chambered
session where plans were made for retrenching and waiting for
better days. "People in Japan and all over the world think of
Mitsui as some great, bad giant," Nagashima stated later. "I know
Mitsui is really not bad at all, but others will never believe this.
I think it is best that the House of Mitsui disappear."

The Mitsuis, headed by the old Baron, were harder to see or
interview than the Imperial Family. They were a world of their
own, a separate island in the universe of Japan. They had their
own family seal, their own constitution, their own laws of succes-
sion, their own rites. Each male Mitsui on coming of age had to
swear Shinto oaths to uphold the Mitsui constitution, and further
family interest. In July 1946, when the old Baron had died, the
Mitsuis recognized SCAP's law as higher than their own—at least
temporarily. In a secret family conclave they abolished their constitution and arranged to liquidate their holdings.

They had not made as much from the war as their leading rivals,
the Iwasaki family, who owned Mitsubishi. The Mitsuis in 1941
were largely in financial and commercial enterprises; but they
gradually expanded into chemicals, steel, electric products and
mining. When the Philippines fell, their mining subsidiary received

the rich Lepunto copper mines. When Hong Kong fell, their ship-building branch took over all the best British holdings on the island. Tojo also cut them in on the exploitation of Manchuria.

Before any measures had been taken by the Japanese Government to break up the *Zaibatsu*, the Yasuda family presented a plan, in October 1945 for the redistribution of their holdings. They proposed that they, and other families, sell their shares in all companies in which they had a dominant interest to a public Japanese liquidation Control Commission. In exchange, the families would receive government bonds non-negotiable and non-transferable for ten years. The Commission would then resell the families' shares to employees of the various companies and to the general public.

This scheme, coupled with a directive barring all members of the *Zaibatsu* families from jobs in their companies, was accepted by MacArthur. Despite its obvious weakness the plan involved a minimum of effort by SCAP's understaffed experts. And SCAP was not nearly as interested in this trust-busting as the State Department. Nevertheless, the Yasuda Plan was supplemented on November 25 by SCAP ordering the Japanese Government to impose a retroactive 100 per cent war profits tax on all war industries plus graduated personal and corporation income taxes up to 100 per cent. SCAP also insisted that the Yasuda Plan be backed by the wiping out of *Zaibatsu* claims of 40 billion yen in war losses. At first the Japanese Cabinet rejected the stiff taxes, but under pressure from Colonel Kramer's Section they prepared a bill for the Diet.

Corwin Edwards, chief of the Mission on Japanese Combines, visited Tokyo while I was there in 1946 and disapproved of the Yasuda Plan. He found it "obviously insufficient to destroy the power of the great Japanese combines." He stated further that "It does not adequately provide for the dissolution of the existing combines and destruction of the power of the great families, nor for elimination of the preferences which the *Zaibatsu* enjoy in finance and in relations with the government. It does not attempt to determine what form of industrial control shall replace that of the *Zaibatsu* nor what measures shall be taken to prevent the rise of new *Zaibatsu*-like organizations."

The Edwards Mission was far less sympathetic to the *Zaibatsu* than certain SCAP officials. It recognized that MacArthur had not really prepared anything but a superficial juggling of the Japanese economic set-up, preferring to leave any basic changes to a Japanese Government which itself was not basically altered. It pointed out that reform must go much deeper than the top holding companies; in fact, it should start with a revision of inheritance laws which encouraged leaving entire fortunes to the eldest son; it should be predicated on an increase of income and inheritance taxes for the very wealthy; it should demand revisions in the corporation law so that independent investors could determine what was happening and could exercise some control.

Edwards, himself, warned that without proper restrictions the *Zaibatsu* could be back in a decade, exercising control through relatives or persons loyal to them. The scheme to have the general public and employees buy stocks was good—but where would they obtain the necessary capital? From *Zaibatsu* banks? The savings of the middle class had been greatly diminished by inflation and taxes.

Not until November 1946 were the major interlocking corporations and holding companies dissolved. In February 1947 the Japanese Government ordered that the personal fortunes of fifty-six Japanese, totaling eighty million dollars, be liquidated. But the long delay in the implementation of directives led to the suspicion that the *Zaibatsu* were given an opportunity to maneuver their holdings or to store some away. It was known, for example, that certain of them put their cash into ancient and valuable Chinese bronzes which, in times of inflation, were better than currency. Observers felt, too, that the nine-man commission was much too favorable to the representatives of big business.

Correspondent Mark Gayn reported in *Collier's* that the dissolution law "has put the fate of the *Zaibatsu* in the loving hands of a committee of Japanese bankers. And it has not prevented *Zaibatsu* from muscling in on the new financial organizations or from sabotaging reconversion to gain the lusher profits of speculation." Many of these were later caught in a purge of all persons holding key positions in firms with capital investments over one million yen, or on the boards of such concerns. In all, SCAP's order affected about fifteen thousand individuals in industry, finance and publishing. They will be allowed to keep their stock if it does not exceed 10 per cent of the total.

Whether or not the huge trusts were successfully liquidated, the very attempt to do so presented at least two deeper questions than the threat of the reviving *Zaibatsu*. First, was the chipping down of *Zaibatsu* fortunes actually redistributing the top-heavy wealth in the country, thus enabling the middle class to buy a share in industry? Secondly, U. S. economists wondered if the retention of large-scale industry was essential in the effort to make Japan more self-sufficient. If this large-scale industry was not to be owned and operated by the trusts, then by whom?

Anxious to escape responsibility for any radical realignments in Japan's economy, SCAP avoided constructive suggestions on how the nation's highly centralized, highly integrated industry should be run. MacArthur was not in favor of nationalization and the Shidehara and Yoshida cabinets were opposed to building up the co-operatives. Under these conservative régimes "nationalization" would have been little more than the continuance of big-business monopoly. For a period many of the *Zaibatsu* themselves favored nationalization, believing it would save their industrial holdings from the long arm of reparations.

During Yoshida's year as head of the Government, the *Zaibatsu* felt they had a friend in court. For example, in February 1947, the month that their personal fortunes were ostensibly liquidated, the government agreed to lend 3,133,170,000 yen to seventeen "restricted" firms including Mitsui and Mitsubishi. Since the money was going to build up the chemical fertilizer industry, SCAP approved the plan. This was only the first of a series of SCAP-approved loans which the Yoshida Cabinet put through to aid in the reconstruction of "old and established firms."

CHAPTER VIII

PEASANTS IN THE PADDY FIELDS

"EIGHTY MILLION people need twenty million tons of food (annually). Seventeen million tons are produced here. . . . There is no way I can see within the appreciable future that these people can get enough food from indigenous products." In these words General MacArthur defended his views that Japan be permitted to resume foreign trade; he was also defending the land-reform program of the Yoshida government and his own decision to import U. S. foodstuffs. In 1946 SCAP had requested 3.3 million tons. This seemingly preferential treatment of Japan created such violent opposition in the Far Eastern Commission that Japan received only 800,000 tons.

This, however, proved enough to save the Japanese from widespread famine during critical months of MacArthur's first two years. While our allies in China and India were unable to obtain enough calories, SCAP saw to it that the Japanese were tided over. This was justified not only on the "love thy enemy" basis but also to promote stability and by the same token prevent serious rioting. "You can't expect these people to learn democracy on an empty stomach," MacArthur has said.

From the outset SCAP realized that the hope of helping overpopulated Japan to become more self-supporting was inextricably rooted in the complicated agrarian problem. Birth control and mass emigration were impractical. As in many other instances, however, SCAP had neither the thinkers nor the planners to cope with such a major reform. At first the Natural Resources Section was instructed to draft a general directive on agriculture. That agency, busily counting rivers and rocks, had never given any thought to agrarian reform and ingeniously ducked the assignment. The big Economic and Scientific Section, which had become a catch-all department issuing everything from banknotes to labor injunctions, was also unprepared. In the shuffle the request for land reform directive wound up on the desk of a young captain in the Civil Information and Education Section.

This officer, a former newspaper reporter, had been trained to write about anything. Enlisting the aid of a lieutenant, formerly a script-writer for radio, he conscientiously set about giving himself the proper background in a few short weeks. The facts and figures they gathered from Japanese agricultural experts have long been available in modern commentaries on Japan.

Before the war approximately half of all Japanese who worked for a living were engaged in agriculture. Adequate postwar statistics were not available but it seemed fair to assume that the proportion had not decreased. With the exception of large tracts owned by the Imperial Household and various religious sects, hardly a square foot of fertile land was uncultivated. Three-quarters of Japan's farmers had less than two and a half acres apiece. Extensive use of fertilizer, double cropping, and the back-breaking labor of men, women, and children were not enough to keep farm families out of debt. The cost of monopoly-priced fertilizer, in addition to the heavy taxes, prevented rural self-sufficiency and led to ever-increasing farm tenancy and share-cropping. The small farmer sold or rented a little bit of land or sold a younger daughter to a brothel in order to pay the interest on the village usurer's loan. Seven of every ten Japanese farmers rented at least a part of the plots they tilled. Land ownership had become highly concentrated through the age-old credit and foreclosure system. As a result, in recent years 10 per cent of the landlords owned 50 per cent of all the cultivated areas in Japan.

In spite of periodic rice riots and minor peasant revolts, the Tokyo oligarchy had been content to maintain this semi-feudal system. In times past they encouraged the trend towards small landholding, aware that it led inevitably to share-cropping and tenancy. The dispossessed, uneducated, and undernourished peasants provided the industrialists with a self-refilling reservoir of cheap and obedient labor. This same source was easily tapped by the Army and Navy which found little difficulty in making martial life more attractive to men already scraping on a level below subsistence.

The broad SCAP directive (December 10, 1945) on agrarian reform, issued in MacArthur's name, was written into a draft bill by the Japanese Ministry of Agriculture and Forestry. Among the chief proposals were these: that landholdings be limited to seven and a half acres except in sparsely settled northern Hokkaido where 30 acres could be retained; that absentee landlords would be required to sell estates over two and a half acres (ten acres in Hokkaido); that landlords be compensated for their expropriated land with government bonds and that new owners be permitted to pay for their plots in annual installments with low interest rates over a thirty-year period. In addition it was suggested that the government requisition and resell in small lots about 4 million acres of previously uncultivated "marginal" land in an effort to increase food production. The Diet displayed no more interest in coming to grips with realities of land reform than had MacArthur's Natural Resources Section. Ten months were required to enact necessary legislation. Then the Diet failed to appropriate an adequate budget for administering and enforcing the reforms properly and there was even some doubt that there would be sufficient funds for making needed surveys. No time limit was set for completing the redistribution although a Japanese government spokesman, when pressed for an opinion, said he thought "ethically" it should be carried out in two years.

Neither the Shidehara nor the Yoshida governments advanced the land-reform program very far during their year and a half in power under MacArthur. By June 1, 1947, only about 350,000 acres (of a total above 5,000,000 acres) had been purchased by the Government for redistribution. And up to this date, not one acre had been transferred to a tenant farmer. SCAP officials rationalized this slow progress by pointing out that it took the Soviets eleven years to complete their land-redistribution program in Russia.

Months before the directive became a bill—and, in fact, before the directive itself had been announced—wealthy landowners were evading the potential breakup of their estates by re-registering portions of their lands under the names of relatives and friends. In January 1946 a colonel in Military Government reported a typical case to this writer. Ryzo Yamagata, who lived in Tokyo, owned several hundred acres near Sagata in the northern Honshu rice-producing area. Estates of this size in Japan are equivalent to thousands of acres in the United States. When Yamagata heard of the pending reform, he traveled to Sagata for the first time in many years and evicted his tenant farmers. Then he offered to hire them back as farm laborers at a low wage. They refused and went to the local constabulary for help. The rural police have for generations been well paid to keep the peasants in their place and they still earn more money from the gratuities of wealthy landlords than from their meager salaries. The Sagata police shrugged their shoulders and did nothing in this case. At the end of a week Yamagata's former tenants, hungry and cold, returned and submissively took jobs as hired hands. Thus in the prefectural record, when and if the land reform is ever enforced, Yamagata would be registered as the manager of his own farm and not as an absentee landlord.

Under the present bill Yamagata's cultivation could be considered "reasonable" and his farm would not be touched although it is many times larger than the proposed seven and a half acre limit. "If a farmer has enough energy and ability to cultivate more than seven and a half acres of land, all power to him," said Hirowo Wada, Yoshida's Minister of Agriculture and Forestry.

This reversion to laissez faire effectively pulled the teeth from the SCAP directive. Contrary to earlier recommendations of the Allied Council, the bill put no limit on the acreage any one owner may possess; nor did it force a large landowner to sell farms in excess of seven and a half acres "if he has a good record in producing crops." A man, if he had the money, could actually repurchase from the Government more land than he could personally cultivate and then rent it. This, Minister Wada believed, "would be a violation of the spirit of the bill." But it would not be against the law.

Any notion that Japan's 3.7 million farmers are less happy under the Americans than they were previously should be discarded. Not only has their immediate living standard been appreciably bettered, due to black-market rice prices, but the possibilities for long-term change and improvement have been established. With education, those possibilities will expand. But the change will surely be ox-slow.

John K. Emmerson, Special Assistant to the Chief of the Division of Japanese Affairs in the State Department, recently cited what had happened to a big estate in northern Japan which had been owned by one family for twenty-eight generations. "In recent years," Mr. Emmerson recalls, "the family has been benevolent toward the tenants and they have been well treated. But the estate was a feudal manor and the tenants were the wards of the landlord. Now they can own their own little plots of land, and among them is a surge of exhilaration at this new-found free status in life."

2

I hope by this time that tens of thousands of Japanese do feel that "surge of exhilaration." My contact with the Japanese on the land indicated that they were so schooled in inertia it would be many years before the effects of the occupation shifted the course of their lives. They have been relying on human hands and backs for so long that there is scarcely even the vision of the machine age on the tiny Japanese farm. Even so they appeared better off than peasants in the wartime Ukraine, in Korea, China, or Poland.

In Chiba Prefecture near Tokyo I visited a farmer named Toshio Sakai. Inquiries among the villagers had revealed that Sakai was considered the best farmer in the community. He was not a leader in the political sense but his neighbors seemed to respect his judgment and to point with pride at his hillside farm.

When we walked up a steep incline to the little three-acre domain a small, wiry man with a stringy white beard emerged from an unpainted pine frame house to greet us. Sakai, in nondescript trousers rolled up to his calves and a torn padded cotton jacket, sucked in his breath and bowed almost to the ground. My translator, a girl named Yoko, explained at some length that I was a reporter and not officially connected with the armies of occupation. Sakai straightened up and said, "You are the first American that has honored us by coming here. I have seen them fly past on the roads and I did not know they were so tall."

My host paused in the narrow doorway to scuff off his heavy wooden clogs. When I bent down to remove my boots Sakai told the translator that his home was simple and very cold and that I should keep on my shoes. His house was a good one by peasant standards: it had two rooms. The rough wooden floor had no covering, there were no chairs and no tables. Most Japanese homes have floors covered by mats. A single electric light bulb dangled by a black wire from the center of the ceiling. On one wall was a framed picture of Hirohito in his plumed hat and in a corner was a *kamidana* or godshelf, complete with two *dharma* dolls for good fortune.

Sakai went into the other room and reappeared with two pillows. He dropped these on the floor and invited us to sit on them. Then he dragged in a heavy, rusted bin which he fitted into a hole in the center of the floor. From a wall cupboard he produced a small black bag and from the bag he drew a few sticks, some dried tangerine peels, and one or two chunks of charcoal. He placed these all together in the bottom of the metal container and asked the translator if I had a match. I dug out my cigarette lighter and flicked the wheel. When the flame sprung from the wick Sakai sucked in his breath excitedly. I blew out the flame and handed it to him. He held the case gingerly, then slowly drew it to his small, flat nose and sniffed.

"Light it yourself," I urged. When this was translated, he smiled. Two front teeth were gone and the others appeared to overlap each other in a completely unordered array. Sakai shook his head.

"I am not a military man," he said. "I gave two sons to the army but I have never held a gun. I do not know how to use such instruments as this and I do not want to know." He handed it to the translator who lit the fire. Sakai said something which Yoko did not acknowledge or translate. Later I asked her what he had said. "Oh," she said, "he's very old in his ways. He was mumbling something about women not touching such machines, but it was more of an old saying than a scolding."

Sakai then apologized for not bringing us any tea. His wife and daughter were at the next village looking after a sick aunt. We all squatted down as close to the fire as possible.

I began the interview by asking Sakai his opinion on the agrarian reform directive. He had never heard of it. We tried to explain it to him, but he obviously made no effort to understand.

"The land is poor," he said, "but it belongs to us and we know how to use it. We pay our taxes and do not ask that we be given our neighbor's land or the landlord's land."

From my notebook I quoted figures to Sakai indicating that he, with his three-acre farm, was practically a plutocrat. The average area tilled, per family, was 2.67 acres; but 70 per cent of Japanese farms were below the average size and 34 per cent were smaller than one and a quarter acres. It would help, wouldn't it, if the poorer farmers received some of the larger estates?

My argument and my statistics failed to move him. Covering his beard with his hand, he took a cigarette and bent over to light it in the feeble fire which was giving off a little smoke and a little warmth. "Americans should not worry about poor farmers," he said. "We do not worry. If their farms are small, their fathers and their fathers before them were lazy and their wives failed to yield stout sons."

I told Sakai that I couldn't follow his reasoning. "The more sons," I said, "the more the family land must be divided up. Isn't that right?"

"Sons are good," he said, bowing his head. "I have given two to the Imperial army."

I asked the translator to repeat my question.

"If my sons were here they would live with me and work with me and I would not worry about dividing the land," he said, finally.

Then I asked a series of questions to find out exactly what Sakai did. He was primarily a rice raiser, but before the war when his sons were at home they also tended mulberry trees belonging to Ashida, the man who owned one of the three acres of Sakai's farm. He paid for that acre by exchanging the labor of his sons for certain periods during the year. His wife, Sakai said, was expert at preparing the soil for the rice plants. He indicated with his dirty brown hands that she kneaded it, as an American housewife prepares baking dough. His daughter, thirty-two years old, was strong —almost as strong as another boy. She was good at polishing the rice, pounding it in a hollow log. The processes in between—setting out the plants, transplanting, harvesting, hanging the sheaves on bamboo racks to dry, separating the top of the rice from the stalk by drawing it through a "comb"—these tasks the whole family performed.

I asked Sakai if he had a specialty. He said that his was the art of every Japanese farmer who was smart enough and worked hard enough to get the most from his land. He built the mud containing walls to keep the terraces irrigated. "My father told me how to save the bark of trees and how to cure it. Worthless people burn bark here." He spat into the smoldering fire. "But in this family and in this village where we have always lived, we know how to use bark to strengthen the corners of irrigation walls."

Sakai accepted another cigarette. I asked if they had enough food and what and how often they ate. "During the war the rice was severely requisitioned. We had to eat carrots and sweet potatoes and buckwheat. Now it is all right and we have two good meals. Early in the morning, at dawn when we rise, we have rice and bean curd soup. In the evening when we have labored we have rice, dried fish which we get from nearby in exchange for rice, soup, and sometimes we have grasshoppers."

The translator asked a few more questions and then she turned to me and said, "They also eat twice more during the day in the field but he does not consider that a formal meal."

Somewhere I had read that Japan's caloric shortage could be overcome if farmers would plant sweet potatoes or grains with a higher protein content in place of rice. I had Yoko explain this to Sakai. He first looked very mad and Yoko hastened to make sure that he understood this was just somebody's idea and not a potential American edict. Then Sakai laughed, a long, high-pitched guffaw which sounded more like a bird hooting.

The two Japanese began chattering in quick, short bursts. Yoko indicated that I should not interrupt. After five minutes of this cross-talk she turned to me and said, "You have just been given a wonderful lecture on the ignorance of laborers, city dwellers and foreigners in general. Briefly, Sakai said you do not take the trouble to understand the meaning of a rice economy. Rice is not only food, it is everything. The pillow you sit on is stuffed with rice chaff. The thatched roof over this house comes from the rice plant. So do the sacks for transplanting and storing the rice. Sakai's overcoat is made from rice. The bed mats in the cupboards over there are made from stalks. Baskets and hats and even rugs are manufactured right here by his family from rice chaff and stalks."

Sakai interrupted. Yoko translated: "He says you probably know about *sake*, rice wine. But you probably don't know that even the dust from the skin of the grain—in the polishing process—is used for pickling vegetables. Onions, I guess."

I wrote down the list of usages. "Tell him I'm convinced," I said.

"Oh, yes," the translator went on. "Grasshoppers are a great delicacy. They are attracted by the rice."

"We have grasshoppers with only grass and no rice," I said. "I can't count that."

Yoko translated. Sakai shook his head. "He doesn't believe it," she said.

"Do you ever eat bread?" I asked.

The translator laughed, "Of course not. He probably will not know the word for bread. Rice cakes, perhaps." But she asked him. He said he did know the word for bread and that he had even tasted bread but that they did not eat it. "One son worked one winter at the harbor near Tokyo. He became a bread eater and brought some home once." He spat again. "It does not taste good. It is rough and dirty and it makes your mouth dry and thirsty."

Sakai did not want to talk about the war or the Emperor. He had heard of the directive abolishing state Shinto but he neither approved nor disapproved. He had his own gods and so long as they were not interfered with, he would be content. I inquired about inflation. "Paper money," he said, spitting, "is not as good as tree bark. Tree bark is good for many things. It is good this season and next and the one after that."

The village, Sakai said, had a co-operative to guard against the dangers of paper money. They marketed their surplus rice together and bought products, usually chemicals for fertilizing, from the city in bulk. "It is better to give rice and get a new spade or a new hoe than to get paper money. If everyone did that," Sakai said, "there would be no trouble with inflation. Inflation comes from printing paper money."

"Are the co-operatives used politically? I mean will you back a candidate for village headman or for the Diet together?"

Sakai shook his head. "My family has always voted for the Ashida family for headman. There is no need to change."

A year after my talk with Sakai I was not surprised to read an Associated Press dispatch from Tokyo about the "apathy" to social change in the rural areas. "Elections were held recently throughout the country districts for farm land committees, which will administer the break-up of the large estates for sale to tenant farmers. . . . [They] aroused such little popular interest that many must be repeated for lack of candidates or voters." This dispatch, as it appeared in the *Christian Science Monitor,* then concluded with one of those slight editorial notes which blend in with current news reporting: "It is plain that Japan cannot become democratic while the old atmosphere of feudalism persists in the rural districts, yet agrarian reform has been perhaps the most stubbornly opposed innovation of the occupation."

3

Only education will help the peasants to comprehend the benefits of reform; only supervision will compel landlords to abide by its provisions. American officials have frequently received information on landlords' chicanery, but they rarely had either the time or the forces to do anything but pass a complaint along, through channels, to the Japanese Government. The colonel who cited the Yamagata case, when asked for a solution, predicted that agrarian reform would never become a reality until the Japanese farmers were organized strongly and solidly enough to engage in effective political activity. The colonel vanished from MacArthur's Government Section during the May 1946 purge for advancing such "foreign" ideas. Months later, the relatively conservative Japanese Farmers' Union, with 600,000 members led by the right wing of the Social Democrats, denounced the loopholes in the land bill. Claiming that the bill sought "to perpetuate a semi-feudal land economy," they pointed out that its implementation was in control of those opposed to bettering the conditions of tenant farmers. They felt the land commissions of five landlords and five tenants would be dominated by the landlords. This was called to the attention of Minister Wada who said, "Then it is the responsibility of the Farmers' Union to educate tenants so they won't be dominated."

As is frequently the case, the immediate reaction to the directive and the bill was favorable. MacArthur commended it. Conservative and progressive leaders, both in America and in Japan, applauded. When experts had time to study all the implications of the bill, which Minister Wada made public in September 1946, a certain amount of sniping was directed against individual provisions. SCAP, itself, suggested that various loopholes be tightened. The Soviet member of the Allied Council for Japan, General Kuzma Derevyanko, charged that the price of the land was too high for the peasantry, that the proposed government subsidies to landlords for their expropriated acreage were too high and that the local agricultural land commissions which would eventually administer the program had been formed with "the interest of the landowners obviously in the foreground."

Similar objections were voiced by many Japanese radicals, none of whom cared or dared to attack the central concept of the reform. As they had done previously in Poland and Korea, the Russians and the local Communists supported land redistribution because such a policy fulfilled "the natural aspirations of the peasantry." It was also likely to pay short-term political dividends even if cruel experience in the Soviet Union had demonstrated that small plot farming on an individual basis was not economically sound. In

Japan there is obviously not enough land to distribute and in the long run millions would feel that the system of distribution has been unfair. At least a million peasants will not get any land at all. Expropriation and redistribution had been attempted in the early thirties by the young Chinese Soviet Republic, not once but several times, and on each occasion there was bitterness and dissatisfaction among those who received parcels.

Historically, it could be argued that the breakup of the big estates was a forward step. But to raise the general standard of living in Japan and to increase the country's food supply, planned agriculture on some kind of co-operative basis was obviously and urgently required. And yet few voices in Japan raised this issue at the time. Harold Strauss, who served a year in SCAP's Civil Information and Education Section, draws this logical conclusion from his keen analysis of MacArthur's land-reform program. "While it [SCAP] is denouncing the old militarists," Mr. Strauss writes, "it is fertilizing the soil in which a new spirit of militarism will thrive. While it is setting up a fine-sounding new constitution, it is fostering in rural areas the spirit that will evade its provisions. 'Forty acres and a mule' may have a grand sound to American ears, but the application of this slogan, born in a spacious land, can only bring disaster in narrow Japan. The only acceptable farm policy is one that will simultaneously raise both the standard of living of the Japanese peasants and their productivity. Lack of such a policy must have one of two results: either Japan will remain permanently an expensive ward of the United States, or it will be obliged to resume the drive for export markets, based on sweated labor and backed by rural militarism, which led to war."

The other alternative, which Mr. Strauss does not mention, is widespread adoption of birth control measures throughout Japan to cut down the increasing number of mouths to be fed. In the first two years under SCAP, besides the normal increase of population, over five million Japanese servicemen and civilians were repatriated to the home islands. At the present rate, Japan adds a million in population per year and the stress on public health services under the occupation might conceivably boost that figure.

But birth control is not popular in Japan and at least one Catholic missionary has advised SCAP that American backing for birth control education would be sharply opposed by the Church. A few

Japanese leaders understand the importance of such education, but even the Social Democrats' Mrs. Kato, long an advocate of birth control, could not induce her party to make it a national issue after they had gained power in the Diet. "For my people," she said sadly, "the choice is birth control or starvation."

If the failure to solve the agrarian problem leads to encouragement of Japan's export trade, as now seems likely, there will be at least one important fresh factor in the picture. This factor is trade unionism which today in Japan is rapidly becoming a guarantee against the "sweated labor" that permitted Japan to undercut prices and dump products throughout the world.

CHAPTER IX

LABOR GROWS STRONG

FROM the outset of the occupation the common man in the cities has been much quicker to grasp the significance of democratic processes than his tradition-bound brothers on the land. Of all the revitalized forces in MacArthur's Japan, the labor movement may become the staunchest guardian of democracy and may offer the firmest resistance against any return to the reactionary thirties. The movement's immaturity, its excesses and abuses are natural enough. In the United States where trade unionism has a longer democratic tradition, the perfect formula for industrial peace remains elusive. It would be naive to expect or to insist that the Japanese attain such a utopia in a relatively short period.

The amazing growth and political development of Japanese labor is worth close analysis. For in less than two years under SCAP it was able to exert considerable influence on MacArthur at a time when some of his superiors in Washington were still afraid to cross him.

2

Dating back to the nineties, Japan has had a small but militant trade union movement. Despite restrictive laws, labor fought actively against the increasing influence of the war-makers. Many working-class leaders were beaten, tortured, and imprisoned for expressing their views during the thirties. When Tojo embarked on his Pacific adventure, the organized resistance of the independent unions was completely crushed by the Government. The working day was lengthened to twelve, fourteen and in some cases even sixteen hours. With large reservoirs of cheap labor in rural areas and in conquered territories, wages were kept low. In an effort to satisfy the workers' demands for representation, the Government set up, under its control, the Great Japan Industrial Labor Patriotic Association.

Nevertheless in 1937, the year of the China Incident, there were 2,126 labor disputes in Japan involving 113,642 strikers. The next year 1,030 disputes occurred with 55,565 strikers. The year following Pearl Harbor there were only 238 disputes and only 14,372 went on strike. Labor agitation was outlawed and strikers were branded as "traitors." Despite the stringent penalties, the number of strikes increased in 1943 to 417 and rose even higher in 1944.

The policy of the United States was to favor the creation of strong, democratic trade unions at the very start of the occupation. Reiterating the basic Post-Surrender Policy directive (see Appendix F), Secretary of State James F. Byrnes declared on September 1, 1945, that "We shall take such steps as may be necessary to encourage democratic reforms among the submerged classes, the peasants and the industrial workers, so that they may have a voice in their Government."

SCAP faithfully implemented this policy for a year. The wartime "front"—the Great Japan Industrial Labor Patriotic Association was dissolved, anti-labor laws were removed from the statutes, and on October 11, 1945, a directive officially blessed development of trade unions. The Diet on December 21 passed a basic Labor Union Law under which trade unions could function.

Into the new Constitution were written suitable guarantees of labor's rights. Article XXV declares that: "All people have the right to work. Standards for working conditions, wages and hours shall be fixed by law. The exploitation of children shall be prohibited." The ensuing Article continues: "The right of workers to organize and to bargain and act collectively is guaranteed."

First to organize on a nationwide scale after the war ended was the Japan Federation of Labor (JFL), a revival of the old right-wing National Federation of Labor Unions (NFLU), led by Komakichi Matsuoka. They held a national convention in the first week of August 1946 and voted to support Matsuoka. A holdover from prewar labor struggles, the fifty-nine-year-old Matsuoka is a soft-spoken Christian who is dogmatically anti-Communist. Often dubbed "Japan's William Green," Matsuoka comes from a middle-class merchant family. He is a member of the Social Democratic Party's right-wing and was elected to the Diet in April 1946. When the Social Democrats became the largest party in the House of

Representatives a year later, Matsuoka was elected the first Socialist speaker of the House. The JFL majority reflects Matsuoka's mild views and its relation to the Social Democratic Party is about the same as that of British trade unions to the British Labor Party.

The left-wing, superficially following U.S. patterns, banded together a group of twenty-one strong, independent unions and on August 19, 1946, formed the National Congress of Industrial Unions (CIU). Its moving spirit and chairman is Katsumi Kikunami, a former London correspondent for *Asahi*. Educated in a Methodist Mission School in Kobe, Kikunami learned to work a lathe, gave up Christianity, embraced Marxism. He is forty-three years old, physically plump, mentally sharp, and temperamentally hot-headed. With Communist backing (which he accepted but did not endorse) Kikunami first founded the All-Japan Newspaper and Radio Workers Union. His ideas found immediate acceptance among white-collar workers, and the strength of the CIU is still largely among teachers, communications workers. The Communists in the organization are numerically weak, ideologically strong—especially among the young schoolteachers.

The response of Japanese workers, their living standard ebbing below the subsistence level, was immediate and overwhelming. Unions were part of the new American democracy; they promised higher wages, full employment, better housing, sanitary conditions. Why not join? By December 1945 there were 375 unions with a membership of 330,000. A year later there were 15,172 unions with 4.1 million members, and one out of every four was a woman. Incidentally, both national federations are predominantly industry-wide and organized horizontally. The primary difference between them is political. They have parallel unions among teachers, government employees, heavy industry workers. The more conservative JFL is especially strong in the textile industries.

3

My own limited contact with the Japanese labor movement occurred during the second week of February 1946. While writing about the number of labor disputes and their causes in a purely academic way, I heard that a strike was threatened at the Dai Nippon Printing Company, the second largest publishing house in Japan. In addition to printing new yen as fast as its presses would roll, Dai

Nippon published the Tokyo edition of *Time*. The magazine's representative having left for Manila or Shanghai, I accompanied Trevor Gauntlett of our office out to the plant.

The managing director, a smooth businessman in a dark, well-cut, double-breasted suit, was named Kitajima. In his cold private office heated only by two charcoal braziers, he poured out the sad tale of his labor troubles. His fifteen hundred workers, through their union leadership, were demanding a 300 per cent wage increase, a "winter bonus," and new minimum wages. That meant bankruptcy, he claimed.

"Living costs must have gone up that much," I said.

"They have gone up a lot," said Kitajima, "but that is not our fault. We granted the union a 50 per cent wage increase in December and another 50 per cent increase in January. This is too much."

"What's a 'winter bonus'?"

"They want 2,000 yen for the winter—for clothes and food and firewood. Then they want 200 yen additional for every member of their families."

The wage structure system in Japan is quite a bit different than in the United States. Traditionally, management is far more paternalistic. This leads to their paying a worker not on the basis of his particular ability but depending on his age, the number of years he has served the company, and the number of his dependents. In a sense it attempts to fulfill at least the latter half of the Marxist maxim, "From each according to his ability, to each according to his need."

I asked Kitajima what he was doing about the threatened strike.

"I called in the union leaders," he said. "The whole shop is unionized except for myself and the president. I pointed out to them the following: our monthly business amounts to 1.7 million yen. If the 300 per cent raise were granted it would bring our monthly payroll up to 1.45 million yen; with materials added on we would have a monthly net loss of 720,000 yen."

"What did they say?"

Kitajima shrugged. "What do they always say? It's a matter of life or death, that's what they say. Communists always talk that way."

"Is your union all Communist?"

"No, but the radicals lead them around by the nose. Workers who have been with us for years are willing to endanger their future because of lack of will power and a habit of following any outspoken leadership. Thus they easily shift from the extreme right to the extreme left."

I inquired what compromise Dai Nippon was offering. "I can give them another raise of 100 per cent. That is all or we will be bankrupt."

"You can always raise your printing rates," I suggested with a wink at Gauntlett. Mr. Kitajima thought that was very funny coming from the representative of a client. "We abide by our contracts," he said.

On the way out I asked Mr. Kitajima's secretary to let me know how the negotiations ended. That evening, to my surprise, I received a visit at the Press Club from a young girl and her elder brother who said they were members of the executive committee of the printing union local at Dai Nippon. The girl, who was about eighteen and quite pretty, spoke English and did most of the talking. They both wore Western-style clothes except for shoes. She had on wooden-bottomed *getas* and his big feet were shod in straw sandals.

"We learned you came to the plant today and heard the management's part of the dispute. You did not come to talk with us. Is that democracy?" she asked.

I felt very guilty and said so. "My only defense," I assured her, lamely, "is that I came on behalf of a client and not as an investigator or reporter." At best this was a half-truth.

"You told the secretary of Mr. Kitajima that you were interested further, so we have come. The dispute is concluded."

"You signed a contract?"

The brother, who looked about twenty-five and was big-boned, thin, and extremely nervous, responded in Japanese and his sister translated. "It is not possible for us to sign a contract with honor. That is because we would have to break this contract if the cost of rice and other food keeps climbing up. Many of us must go into debt now because of not having the 300 per cent wage increase."

I asked about the settlement.

"To keep the plant open we have given in very much," the girl said. "The increase is only 100 per cent and the winter bonus is only one thousand yen. Five hundred yen for those without families. The minimums are lower, too."

She gave me the figures: 650 yen a month for married men, 450 for single men, 200 for minors. The union had demanded 750, 600 and 350 in the three categories.

"My brother and I have no family. We live in a suburb of Tokyo on the top of a garage. We could pay our rent, our carfare, our union dues and our food every month all right if we could get enough to eat at ration prices. But sometimes there is no regular ration for days and we have to buy on the black market. At black market prices food alone would cost almost one thousand yen a month during the winter."

"When did you join the union?"

"We helped to organize it when we read the announcement about free trade unions in the newspaper," the girl said.

"Do Communists run the union?"

They shook their heads. I asked if they were Communists or pro-Communist. "We believe all workers' parties should be allowed," the girl said quickly, as if she had answered that many times before.

"What are you?"

"We are democrats," she said. "We are from the island of Shikoku but we will never go back until we have built a new democratic Japan under the Emperor. The reason we have no family is our father was a general. We have disowned them."

4

Agitation for economic gains began quickly and took many unique forms. In the first six months of the occupation, at least one strike occurred in every prefecture of Japan. The bulk of the disputes were in mining, manufacturing and public utilities. From the outset labor leaders were uncertain about MacArthur's attitude, particularly since they were advised that anything which could be construed as a "strike against the occupation" would be summarily dealt with. Violence was avoided and leaders were careful not to interfere with establishments serving Americans. They were also unwilling to alienate a goods-hungry public.

Some Japanese capitalists, faced with labor's growing demands, closed their plants. They claimed raises would force them into bankruptcy. Unions countered this by strikes *without* work stoppages. The 2,500 workers of the Keisei Electric Railroad, which runs between Tokyo and Narita, "struck" for a 500 per cent wage increase. They kept operating the trains but refused to charge the public any fares. When this form of protest did not win raises and their meager savings were eaten up, they shifted tactics. In their demands to the company they had suggested that fares be raised to take care of higher wages. In the second phase of their strike the union charged fares at the suggested higher rate and deducted their own wages at the week's end, placing the remainder of the income in escrow for management. During the strike period the workers also increased their efficiency. Service was speeded up. The company repair shops, under union management, overhauled fifteen cars daily compared to the previous rate of one and a half cars per day. The company met the union demands.

In Hokkaido, during a five-day strike, coal miners worked in the pits but barred management personnel. They raised production almost 250 per cent. At the end of the month when SCAP looked into the Japanese Government report on coal production there were no totals entered for the five days of the strike. Questioned, a Japanese official said that the company could not count the coal produced by the strikers "because that would recognize the validity of the strike." The strike was won.

In instance after instance, workers, taking over production, managed to increase output and thus demonstrate that management could afford pay increases. This reached its zenith in July 1946 when employees of the Tokyo Municipal Government assumed control of the city. They ran it so efficiently for eleven days that the top officials, dreading the obvious comparison, met the wage demands.

SCAP became increasingly alarmed by the spread of this technique which they called "production control." It was used in newspapers, mines, hospitals, and steel plants, as well as Government offices. To SCAP conservatives the method smelled of socialism; it violated the sacred right of private property. Reports to the War Department began stressing that perhaps Japan's infant labor movement was growing too fast, yelling too lustily. After the "Liberal" Cabinet of Yoshida took office in May 1946 the Premier, having quietly ascertained SCAP opinion, firmly opposed production control. On May 20 MacArthur publicly sounded off against the Japanese labor movement for the first time. He used the occasion of a rowdy hunger demonstration before the Imperial Palace gates to warn labor that boisterous demonstrations would not be permitted.

The left-wing unions opposed Yoshida's economic and labor policies immediately, still uncertain as to whether they were also MacArthur's views. That question was vocally answered in mid-July. At the ninth session of the Allied Council for Japan, General Derevyanko submitted twenty-two proposals for labor legislation. The Soviet delegate included a recommendation that workers be permitted to assume control of any enterprise which had closed down without awarding severance pay to its employees. Replying to the Soviet suggestions, the late George Atcheson, Jr., MacArthur's representative, was sharply caustic about Derevyanko's support of production control. The SCAP attitude was that "This measure of pre-emption and practical confiscation of property without due recompense violates the law of property rights providing for due compensation for seizure of property. So far as is known, no such provision exists in any nation of the world. Even in the Soviet Union it is believed most doubtful that such measures are provided for or permitted."

5

The following month the national trade union federations were formed and in September, Kikunami of the CIU called the first industry-wide strike in Japan since before the war. It occurred on September 14, lasted twenty-four hours and a half-million workers took part.

The background, briefly, was this: as an economy measure, the Government had announced its plans to cut down by 100,000 the number of employees in the transportation system which it controlled. The railway workers union tried a "shriek strike." Promptly at one o'clock each afternoon the employees screamed; every train, tram and station, every repair plant clanged, whistled, sirened.

A sympathetic walkout of CIU maritime workers at Sasebo halted the sailing of five ships which were to bring back repatriates. MacArthur directed the Japanese Government to man and operate the ships and take steps to prevent further walkouts. SCAP officially declared: "Strikes, walkouts or other work stoppages which are inimical to the objective of the military occupation are prohibited." Taking its cue from MacArthur, the conservative-controlled Diet then (September 20, 1946) passed a Labor Relations Readjustment Act prohibiting "strikes against the government."

From then on, all but the old-line Japanese union leaders considered that SCAP was anything but neutral in Yoshida's attempts to check the rapid strides of labor. A few weeks later, Kikunami's Newspaper and Radio Workers' Union claimed that a SCAP officer interfered in their plans for a walkout during a visit to one of the newspaper plants a few days before the strike vote. When the strike did come off, American M.P.'s co-operated with the Japanese police in dispersing a demonstration by radio workers.

In the fall of 1946 SCAP issued two educational pamphlets in Japanese for labor. One, on collective bargaining procedures, and the other on the development of union contracts with employees, contained warnings. Recognizing that both management and labor were unskilled in peaceful negotiation, SCAP cautioned against name-calling, and against violence in picketing. Strikes for political ends were termed "an inappropriate and dangerous waste of union strength and resources."

In October, labor undertook a concerted offensive to raise wages and at the same time to agitate against policies of the Yoshida Government. The more militant CIU called a series of industry-wide walkouts. These strikes had popular support primarily because prices had risen approximately four times as much as wages. In less than a month, CIU won salary increases in two dozen important contracts. Yoshida counterattacked. Under the Premier's urging, the Diet had passed a bill requiring compulsory arbitration of labor disputes in the utilities field. In a widely publicized statement on October 12, Yoshida declared that the wave of strikes was "a movement by small minorities aiming at the establishment of dictatorial government."

Labor spokesmen were infuriated by Yoshida's charge. They demanded the resignation of his "do-nothing" Cabinet and especially of Finance Minister Tanzan Ishibashi. The Government was blamed for its failure to control prices, its inability to increase production and its refusal to ration or regulate fairly or effectively the distribution of scarce commodities. Some employers co-operated with the government by firing the most militant of the trade unionists. Other industrialists, rather than bargain with the unions, actually found it preferable and more profitable to close down their plants. They then speculated with their stocks of scarce raw materials on the black market. These men were the heavy financial backers of Yoshida, Ishibashi, and the Liberal Party.

The Government's chief strategy was to coddle favor with SCAP and U.S. public opinion by charging that the unions and the strikes were Communist-fomented and Communist-led. Local police were directed to break up labor demonstrations. In case after case they did so under the guise of protecting Japan against the Communists. A year previously such tactics might have been disapproved by SCAP. But the Japanese Cabinet members were not novices at understanding the world balance of power. They felt, correctly, that they could go pretty far in their anti-union campaign by claiming it was only anti-Communist. The effort to discredit labor was made easier by the persistence, especially in unorganized trades, of the vicious "boss" system under which racketeering labor contractors kept feudalistic control over gangs of workers.

Unemployment increased and so did inflation. Popular pressure from its membership moved the more timid leaders of the conservative JFL to undertake a campaign for higher wages in November. The official price of rationed rice was fifteen times higher than in 1937; even so, a worker could not get enough on his ration to feed himself and his family. He was forced to buy almost half his daily food on the black market where rice sold at 1,500 yen a bushel as compared to the controlled price of 100 yen. Clothing was almost entirely unobtainable except on the black market. Postwar housing, as in most countries, was a wonderful racket for profiteers. The Government put no obstacles in the way of contractors lining their pockets; there was no control of prices or of allocations on lumber, cement and steel.

At the end of 1946 unemployment had soared over the 5 million mark, 8 million were on the relief rolls, food in the cities was scarce (the Government had collected only 140 of the 280 million-bushel rice crop) and charcoal and wood for the second winter of peace was being held off the market by profiteers. On December 17 an angry labor demonstration in front of the Imperial Palace demanded a new election. Two weeks later, on New Year's Day, Yoshida again spoke against labor, referring to union leaders as "lawless elements." The same day General MacArthur released a message to the Japanese people urging them to implement the reforms passed in 1946 and praising "the great majority of Japan's leaders" for their "exemplary approach." To the public this meant a benediction for Yoshida.

The unrest in labor's ranks reached a peak when 2.6 million Government and public workers in both the JFL and CIU decided to strike for a living wage early in 1947. They set up a Joint Struggle Committee to represent them. Their walkout would have paralyzed transportation of coal, food and mail, closed down business for lack of power and water, and in general thrown Japan into complete chaos. Negotiations for settling the dispute were half-hearted on the Government's side. As a result, sympathizers were ready to walk out in protest: coal miners, iron, steel and chemical workers, and pressmen.

In the week prior to February 1, 1947, the date for the beginning of the strike, SCAP had informally told labor leaders that such a walkout would not be tolerated by the occupying powers. The more moderate leaders were willing to call it off, but the more militant, including the Communists, insisted on a showdown. They wanted to prove to any doubters among the rank-and-file and to conservative leaders in the JFL that SCAP was not on their side and not neutral. They wanted to put MacArthur on record.

MacArthur was not anxious to issue a direct order. The day before the strike, Brigadier General Marquat of SCAP's Economic and Scientific Section held a conference with the union chiefs and instructed them to continue negotiations. They remained adamant about carrying out their plans. Ten hours before the deadline MacArthur, in a written order, forbade the strike. He said, in a statement to the public, "I have informed the labor leaders . . . that I will not permit the use of so deadly a social weapon in the present impoverished and emaciated condition of Japan." The General explained further that "I have taken this action in a dire emergency and do not intend otherwise to restrict the freedom of action heretofore given labor in achievement of its legitimate objectives.

"Nor do I intend in any way to compromise or influence the basic social issues involved. There are matters of evolution which time and circumstance may well orient without disaster as Japan gradually emerges from the present distress."

MacArthur said the plan for a general strike involved only a minority of the Japanese people, "yet this minority might well plunge the great masses into a disaster not unlike that produced in the immediate past by the minority which led Japan into the destruction of war.

"This, in turn," he said, "would impose upon the Allies an unhappy decision: whether to leave the Japanese people to the fate thus recklessly imposed by the minority, or to cover the consequences by pouring into Japan, at the expense of their own meager resources, infinitely greater quantities of food . . . than would otherwise be required."

The immediate popular reactions to MacArthur's order was to accept it and recognize that the strike could not have been permitted. The conservative Tokyo daily, *Mainichi*, summed up moderate opinion in an editorial which regretted the MacArthur order "since both the Government and the unions are equally responsible." The order gave *Izvestia* a chance to claim that SCAP's action was "gross violation of the democratic rights of the Japanese laboring masses and contrary to the principles of Potsdam." But many labor supporters and non-Communists, conceded for the first time that SCAP was not much more liberal than Yoshida. The wording of the MacArthur statement which compared the leaders of labor to the leaders of the militarists was, to their way of thinking, an insult and contrary to all that they thought they had learned about the workings of democracy. The MacArthur statement had evidently been prepared hurriedly, and the next day cooler heads in SCAP wished that its tone and emphasis had been different. New York *Post* Correspondent Robert P. Martin reported from Tokyo that "In many sections of SCAP there is a feeling that Americans were forced to crack down on a progressive and democratic group merely because we had failed to curb the excesses of a reactionary Government."

While the MacArthur order restored temporary quiet, it was evident that labor was not going to remain docile. On the day after the strike, leaders appealed to SCAP to "compel" the Government to grant its workers a 300 per cent wage increase. They also tried to take labor's case to the Allied Council. Two days later union heads asked the Far Eastern Committee in Washington to take action. It was the first time that Japanese labor had dared to go over SCAP's head.

One result of the general strike scare and the amount of public support for the workers' demands was a new recognition of labor's role. One week after the strike was called off, an "Economic Reconstruction Conference" was held, at which labor and capital representatives sat down to discuss ways and means of stepping up production. Although nothing much was accomplished, it marked the first time that organized trade unions had met with management on a national scale in an effort to plan a mutually beneficial program.

MacArthur, too, seemed to feel that perhaps he had made a tactical blunder in the wording of his strike ban. On February 7 he asked the Japanese Government, through "Dear Mr. Prime Minister," to call a new general election for April 25. The trade unions were quick to appreciate the opportunity; they had lost their immediate economic demands, but one of their political objectives—an election—was gained. Since the mass strike had been outlawed, their job was to elect a new Diet which would work for a labor program.

The consciousness of labor's great political task and the need of a common front led to a significant forward step in the Japanese trade union movement. The MacArthur ban on major strikes induced anti-Communists and pro-Communists in labor's ranks to get together. Despite their differences the CIU, the JFL and a middle-of-the-road group called the Japanese Congress of Labor, formed a Council of Labor Unions on March 10, 1947, to act as a liaison body. It represented thirty-eight unions with 5,837,000 members. The Council outlined a program of political action which included raising funds to support labor and pro-labor candidates (most of them Social Democrats), setting up a speakers' bureau to "educate" unionists and other voters, and screening candidates on their views about civil liberties and the control of inflation.

6

Rising prices had pushed up living costs, high living costs had impelled labor to militancy, labor's militancy had jogged MacArthur out of his complacency over Japan's economy. The difficult thing to understand about this familiar circle was that it seemed to take so long in getting around to MacArthur. Actually it didn't. MacArthur was aware of inflationary dangers early in the occupation. He just failed to connect them with political administration.

Between February 1945 and February 1946 Tokyo retail prices went up about 300 per cent. In that same period the note issue of the Bank of Japan increased from 18 billion yen to 62 billion. In the first three weeks of the occupation alone, 13 million yen in new currency went into circulation. In February 1946 SCAP first "suggested" to the Japanese Government that steps be taken to curb inflation. With advice from SCAP, the Japanese Ministry of Finance worked out a plan for recalling the old yen and issuing a new, limited currency. Between February 25 and March 2 all Japanese were ordered to turn in their old currency in denominations of five yen and over. In return, heads of families received up to 300 new yen and each member of the family up to 100, while the rest was frozen in bank accounts. Subsequent withdrawals were restricted to the same 300–100 monthly schedule. Salaries and wages were also frozen at a 500-yen top; anything in excess of that had to be kept in banks.

The theory was to reduce the amount of currency in the hands of consumers thereby forcing down black market prices. The amount of yen in circulation was cut from the high of 62 billion to slightly more than 15 billion by mid-March. The plan failed basically because it was not accompanied by a program for the increase of foodstuffs and consumer goods released to the public through a fair rationing system. It also failed, like so many SCAP directives, because the Japanese knew about it long before it was put into effect. They found dozens of ways of evading it, the chief one being to reward G.I.'s for converting old yen to new for them. G.I.'s were not limited in the amounts they could exchange. Within a month the amount of yen in circulation almost doubled and its trend was steadily upwards in subsequent months. From mid-March 1946 to mid-March 1947 the total increased by almost 100 billion yen, reaching a new all-time record high.

This runaway inflation was coupled with a poorly controlled, poorly operated food rationing system which forced people to buy on the black market in order to live. Staples cost ten times as much on the black market as their "official" prices.

Japanese politicians, including Yoshida, blamed this sorry state of affairs on demands of labor led by the Communists, on the inevitable disruption of economic life after a destructive war, on the moral letdown, on the exhaustion of stockpiles, on the blockade of essential raw materials, on the failure of industry to revive due to the threat of reparations removals. MacArthur tried to help them on several scores. He spoke up against disruptive left-wing elements and the trade blockade, demanded an end to the delay in reparations removals and talked to Yoshida about imbuing the Japanese people with "new spirit." But he failed to do anything about the slow sabotage from within the Yoshida group itself.

This is best illustrated by the case history of the Control Associations which I had found very active in bottlenecking recovery in the Osaka area. SCAP took no direct action against them until August 6, 1946, when the Japanese Government was ordered to get rid of them by November 1. Their functions in allocating and distributing supplies, raw materials and finished products was to be assumed by the new Economic Stabilization Board (created May 17, 1946). When the Yoshida Government stalled on carrying out the SCAP order, the deadline for dissolving the Associations was advanced to April 1, 1947. The ESB never really functioned properly and its duties were still largely left in the hands of old Control Association personnel which thought more of profit than people. In the winter of 1946-47 a SCAP official found in the Osaka area that more than 1.5 million tons of coal had been diverted into the black market. This farce of life-after-death by the Association was legalized under an act passed by the Diet, with SCAP approval, authorizing the head of ESB to designate certain existing control bodies to handle "temporarily" the activities of ESB.

Such obstructionism sharpened MacArthur's many-horned dilemma. He could not himself abolish the Control Associations unless SCAP or the Japanese were ready to step in with something else. "It would be chaos," SCAP's advisers warned. Also MacArthur hesitated to embarrass the Yoshida Government, fearing that it would be defeated in an election. Yet if the blundering and conservative Cabinet continued in office without controls, the radicals might benefit.

7

Labor's solidarity around the issue of electing candidates who would oppose Yoshida's laissez faire policies on inflation and economic reconstruction spurred SCAP to action. On March 22 MacArthur wrote Yoshida (this time "Mr. Prime Minister" instead of "Dear") pointing out that as far back as September 2, 1945, he had made the Japanese Government responsible for controlling wages and prices and for maintaining a strict rationing program to insure fair distribution of goods. The General did not say that SCAP had willingly ignored these instructions, as had the Japanese, for over a year and a half. MacArthur now wrote that "It is imperative that the Japanese Government carry out this responsibility to the Japanese people. . . . Unless determined measures are undertaken at once by the Japanese Government, the inflationary condition of the economy, together with the attendant maldistribution of food and other necessities, will become increasingly serious, industrial recovery will be further retarded and achievement of the social and political objectives toward which the Japanese people made such an encouraging start will be endangered." This was the first time that SCAP had publicly admitted any interdependence between economic conditions and political and social objectives.

In addition, MacArthur warned Yoshida that unless Japan helped herself the United States would not continue to give Japan food and credits. He specifically underlined the fact that the food collection program had failed, that the black market had been allowed to flourish, and he ordered that Yoshida take "early and vigorous steps" to control the country's economy.

Yoshida, faced with an election just a month away, promised to take "necessary measures with expedition and efficiency" and went so far as to say that force would be used, if necessary, to collect the food supply. Force, of course, was not used. Yoshida was far too good a politician. He had already figured out a compromise which would bring in more rice and more votes at the same time. The Government made a payment of a half-billion yen to more than a million farmers as a retroactive price increase for silk cocoons produced in 1946. Although SCAP's Economic Section was strongly against this measure as inflationary, MacArthur had supported Yoshida. He also refused to veto the Prime Minister's "expedient" plan to distribute two billion yen in bonuses to peasants who delivered their rice quotas promptly and who overfulfilled their quotas.

The sudden realization of the sad state of economic affairs in Japan deeply worried MacArthur. Within the fortnight after his critical letter to Yoshida, the General sent up his trial balloon on UN control for Japan, indicating a willingness to surrender a position which might become increasingly untenable for himself and costly for the United States. He also instructed his chief diplomatic aide, George Atcheson, Jr., to serve the occupation's hottest potatoes (including the stabilization problem) to the Allied Council for Japan, an organization for which MacArthur previously had little constructive use.

CHAPTER X

THE ALLIES SNAP THE CURTAIN

As EARLY as January 1946 Dr. K. K. Kawai, a Japanese who formerly taught at the University of California at Los Angeles and who is now an editorial writer on Tokyo's *Nippon Times*, politely asked: "Is U. S. policy to make Japan a peaceful, democratic country or is it a means to further U. S. foreign policy in the Far East?" Dr. Kawai indicated that the Japanese people would be willing to support the former, but "if we are being made to be the advance guard for U. S. interests in the Far East, then we are not so pleased."

MacArthur's men and officers were so thinly spread throughout Japan that the "Red scare" was pressed into use as replacement for an extra division. During the first serious coal strikes in Hokkaido, SCAP representatives warned the employers and employees: "If you don't behave for us, we'll get the Russians in here and they will make you behave."

Some Japanese quietly welcomed the possibility of conflict between the U. S. and the U. S. S. R. Many of them naively believed that a Greater Japan would re-emerge from the ashes of such a world struggle for power. Others, more impressed by radioactivity than by dialectics, realized that it was unlikely that any country—and certainly not strategic Japan—could survive a third World War. But all the people of Japan, regardless of their ultimate aims, watched and waited for the deliberations of the Allied Council for Japan. They watched, knowing that peace now depended less on the more spectacular war crime trials than on American-Soviet co-operation which was on trial in the Allied Council.

Thus far the record of this co-operation has been a non-spectacular failure. The impression made upon the Japanese has not been the desired one. Lindsay Parrott reported in the *New York Times*:

The Japanese have witnessed sniping between the two great Pacific powers as they argued generally trivial issues before the Allied Council.

It has done neither of these powers any good. If it indicates anything to the orderly Japanese mind, it is that an imperial system which at least knew where it was going, would be better than two systems which fail to agree either on ideologies—or even the fate of their victim.

The Allied Council for Japan was created by the Foreign Ministers' conference in Moscow on December 27, 1945. It, and the eleven-nation Far Eastern Commission, were sops thrown to the other nations by the U. S. State Department to quiet their howls about MacArthur's unilateral actions in Japan. At the Council's very first session the following April, General MacArthur clearly indicated that he did not like the whole idea. He had told the State Department exactly that when the sop was proposed, but he promised to try and make the new set-up work "whatever the merits or demerits." After informing the Council members that they would give advice only if and when he asked for it, the General calmly asked for "good will, mutual understanding, and broad tolerance."

The Council continued to receive instruction on what it could not do but not on what it could do. The Big Three Foreign Ministers had set it up "for the purpose of consulting with and advising the Supreme Commander in regard to the implementation of the terms of surrender, the occupation and control of Japan, and of the directives supplementary thereto; and for the purpose of exercising the control authority herein granted." At its second meeting SCAP's Brigadier General Whitney informed them that "The Council is not set up for the purpose of prying into the affairs of the Supreme Commander of the Allied Powers, attempting to find some weak point in SCAP armor, probing for something by which to create national sensationalism. The Council is here for the purpose of constructive assistance only. . . ."

In a sense the wrangling of the Allied Council has been merely a refrain of the louder and larger international cacophony which has been played and replayed by the Foreign Ministers in London, Paris, New York, and Moscow. There is this one important difference: most of the discordant notes in the Foreign Ministers' conclaves arose from arguments concerning world areas where the Big Three had joint responsibilities (Germany, Austria, or Trieste) or where Britain and the United States were sounding loud protests about something which Russia considered her primary responsibility (Bulgaria or Rumania). But in Japan the United States was really the big noise. MacArthur wrote the orchestrations, conducted, and beat the drum. Only occasionally were minor solo parts played by representatives from China (General Chu Shih-ming), the British Commonwealth of Nations (W. McMahon Ball), and the Soviet Union (Lieutenant General Kuzma Derevyanko).

Temperamentally, as well as politically, this cast of personalities has not harmonized very well. The Council has usually been chaired by the American representative. George Atcheson, Jr., who succeeded General Marquat as MacArthur's man in the Council, was a veteran career diplomat who was scheduled to become Minister to Siam at the end of the war. Prior to his assignment as chief of SCAP's diplomatic section, he was known as a China expert. The fact that he had the reputation of being "liberal" made him doubly valuable to MacArthur when he proved to be exceedingly sympathetic to SCAP's views. Atcheson had done well in previous posts, but on the Allied Council he proved the proverbial square peg. He was a high-strung man with a low boiling point, a nervous facial tic, and a drooping mouth. On August 17, 1947, an Army bomber, en route from Tokyo to Washington, crashed near Hawaii and Atcheson was reported killed. He was returning to the United States for consultation on the preliminary Japanese peace treaty conference.

William McMahon Ball, who represented jointly the United Kingdom, Australia, New Zealand, and India, is a lanky, forty-five-year-old former professor of political science at the University of Melbourne. Before he arrived in Tokyo he had appeared on the international diplomatic scene as an adviser to the Australian delegation at the United Nations Conference in San Francisco and as his country's representative in Java after the war.

China's Major General Chu Shih-ming had spent many years in the United States. He was graduated from M.I.T. and Norwich Academy Military School and the General Staff College at Fort Leavenworth. During the war he returned to the U. S. as military attaché of the Chinese Embassy. In 1947 his place on the Council was taken by General Shang Chen (also known as Yorkson T. Chen), a short, stout man with whiskers who looks like a Japanese. Chen had been a Kuomintang provincial governor, a longtime member of its top military councils and head of the military mission in the U. S. Both Chinese delegates speak English.

Russia was also represented by a military man who understands, although rarely speaks, English. General Kuzma Derevyanko, forty-five, is built like a football player, with broad heavy shoulders and a massive chest. He fought on the Soviet's western front from the Volga to the Danube where he met the late General George Patton. After V-E Day he was sent to the Philippines as liaison officer between the Soviet Far Eastern command and MacArthur, and he signed the surrender document aboard the *Missouri* for the U. S. S. R. He is an extrovert compared to many Russian represent-atives in foreign countries and a great party-goer. At the Empire Day celebration held by the British in Tokyo last summer Derev-yanko, feeling very fine after innumerable toasts, proposed to SCAP's General Whitney that they drink "to international friendship."

Glasses were filled and raised.

Said Whitney, in a voice loud enough to be overheard around the ballroom: "General, I drink to friendship or a fight."

Derevyanko hesitated and remarked that he had not said a word about fighting.

"Well," Whitney snapped, "that's what our country stands for. We'll fight you if that's necessary."

Derevyanko flushed from his square chin to the roots of his crew-cropped brown hair. "We too know how to fight," he said. "But let us drink. Bottoms up."

2

For more than a year now these four men or their alternates have met almost weekly around a highly glossed table in an oak-paneled, flag-draped, low-ceilinged room at Tokyo's Meiji Building, just across the moat from the Imperial Palace. With Derevyanko's assistance, Atcheson turned the Council into a forum for Soviet-American ideological battles, name-calling, and mutual recrimina-tion. The result has been to demonstrate how, in an area where the United States is in control, we can hamstring an allied group more neatly and more effectively than the Russians and with less unfavor-able publicity.

During the first months SCAP managed this by avoiding the discussion of any basic issues in the Council, using the filibuster in the worst tradition of the U. S. Senate. Then, for the record, SCAP invited advice on such relatively non-controversial issues as the future development of fishing and transport; plans for the development of tourist trade and for the exchange of students with other nations; patent and copyright practices; the dissolution of the Japanese Lumber Company; and minor measures concerned with the quarantining of small vessels.

One Allied observer called this tactic "loving the Council to death." MacArthur, through Atcheson, asked for so much advice and in such detail that the Council could not possibly give it in the time required. Then Atcheson blamed the members for not cooperating properly. For example, he requested advice on what kind of port regulations to institute in Japan. The only reply that Council members could give on the spur of the moment was to suggest they be made to conform with standard practice in Western nations. MacArthur then asked for advice on venereal disease control and even called for proposals on the most effective VD tests. On another occasion the Americans demanded that the Council consider whether or not Japanese public health doctors should use ether or alcohol for disinfecting the arms of patients before giving injections. Tall, unsmiling Chinese General Chu, in one of his rare retorts, said that if SCAP did not have sufficient technical men on his staff to guide him on such details the Chinese Government would be pleased to lend him some technicians.

SCAP's other method of "containing" the Council was a requirement that all requests for information to branches of GHQ be submitted in writing and through proper channels. Normally this procedure took weeks before an answer was forthcoming. Since the branch or section heads had been instructed to consult the highest echelon of authority before giving out anything but unimportant facts and figures, it took even longer. And yet Atcheson expected complete answers to his questions from the other powers within a matter of forty-eight hours.

The first major unpleasantness in the Council was related to the enormous and turbulent 1946 May Day celebration in Tokyo. The parade, which directed its slogans against the Yoshida Cabinet, became so unruly that the authorities had to intervene. Before that, a manifesto was read charging SCAP with failure to prevent food hoarding and with allowing former Japanese Army men to hide illegal weapons. General Derevyanko asked the Council for an investigation "of the truth" in the manifesto. At a Council meeting Atcheson said the manifesto, backed by the demonstrators, bore signs of having been translated from a foreign language. Since he obviously meant "from the Russian," this charge did not go very well with General Derevyanko. He protested loud and long.

Atcheson replied to Derevyanko's complaints and objected to the Soviet member's reference to claims contained in the manifesto as facts. Derevyanko withdrew from the debate but Atcheson went on: "I do not need to tell you that the United States does not favor Communism in the United States or Japan although it has been allowed in Japan to have the same rights as other political parties." Ball, the British delegate, tried to end the debate by protesting, "*I* didn't write the letter [manifesto]."

The non-American delegates asked for more advance notice of directives, otherwise they felt they could not even "advise." Atcheson refused to discuss the matter: "It is not intended that the Allied Council should become part of the headquarters organization," he snapped.

A few days later MacArthur issued his statement against "the growing tendency toward mass violence" and backed it up with the warning that "If minor elements in Japan's society are unable to exercise such self-restraint as the situation requires, I shall be forced to take necessary steps to remedy such a deplorable situation." Everyone understood that MacArthur meant the Communists, and if the Soviet delegate had any personal doubts he had only to read the press reports. Many Americans felt that this sharp delineation of American policy would put the quietus on Derevyanko's outbursts in the Council.

The Soviet delegate did not sit on his hands for long. At the May 14 meeting he charged that General MacArthur, by informing the Council only after important actions had been initiated, was violating the Moscow agreement and robbing the Council of even its advisory capacity. In this he was seconded by Ball who said he could see no need for the Council unless it could consult and advise with SCAP before major steps were taken.

When the other three members attempted to offer serious constructive criticism, Atcheson frequently ruled them out of order or sharply attacked their suggestions. One of Atcheson's methods was to accuse anyone who supported a Soviet suggestion of backing Russian policies in general. This tactic seemed to annoy Ball more than it did the thick-skinned Derevyanko who probably had not expected much more from MacArthur's disciple. At the Council's twelfth session, one of the numerous occasions when he was not in complete agreement with Atcheson, Ball said very frankly that he still found it rather difficult "to envisage that kind of work the Council is supposed to do. . . ."

Gradually Atcheson placed himself, MacArthur and the United States Government in the frequently embarrassing position of defending the status quo. This was in seeming contradiction to the post-surrender statement by the United States which said, "The policy is to use the existing form of government in Japan, not to support it."

Strangely enough a good share of the Atcheson-Derevyanko disagreements were not over sharply divided ideological issues, although the American tried to make them sound that way. In July General Derevyanko submitted twenty-two recommendations for labor statutes. Most were based not on Soviet trade union laws but on successful United States and British Commonwealth practices. Atcheson, however, threw them out without careful examination and stated that "In the light of all the circumstances surrounding them, these recommendations have a color which we have seen before. I regret to have to say it, but there is readily discernible here the familiar signmarks of propaganda. I very much regret that any issue involving Communism or Communistic influence in Japan has again risen before us." Ball objected that he had difficulty in reading signs of Communist propaganda in the Soviet recommendations and that to him they seemed quite conservative. For this indelicacy the British member received both a public and a private reproach from Atcheson. The incident became more ludicrous a short time later when it was announced that many of Derevyanko's suggestions had already been proposed to the Japanese Government by SCAP's new labor division. This division under young Theodore Cohen was established in the Economic and Scientific Section after Japan's labor problems proved too much for General Marquat.

Atcheson maintained such a defensive attitude in the face of Derevyanko's constant charges and demands for information that the Council frequently became a shouting contest between the two men. The Soviet member at the weekly session on July 24 strongly espoused his recommendation that all fascist, militarist and anti-Allied publications in Japan be confiscated. He wanted MacArthur to order the Japanese Government to collect all such material within two months, turn it into pulp, and punish any persons hiding such "seditious" literature. In reply, Atcheson said that MacArthur would have no part in "what might be called a book-burning campaign similar to those indulged in by the Nazis or Japanese themselves."

Atcheson went on to say that the Japanese had been granted the fundamental rights of freedom of thought and speech and therefore "to employ Nazi-like methods of suppression for the sake of destroying a few stray copies of *Mein Kampf* or other published works would be to vitiate those rights and to sacrifice a matter of principle for no practical gain."

Derevyanko was furious. "I think it is inadmissible," he roared, "this really monstrous comparison of the fascist practice of burning the best creations of human thought and culture on bonfires with the confiscation of the man-hating publications of fascism and militarism. I think the pseudo-democratic slant taken by Mr. Atcheson is as far from democracy as heaven is from earth." When he had calmed down, the General advanced the argument that a similar suggestion had been adopted by the Allied Council for Austria, of which the United States is a member, and that he did not think American principles on this question were different in Japan from those in Europe.

The other members thought Derevyanko had scored a point. General Chu, in his quiet, dignified way said: "I am not so optimistic as to think all fascist people have disappeared from Japan." Ball got to the core of the argument quickly. "I do not agree with the specific recommendations of General Derevyanko," he stated, "but his note of warning is serious. In actual practice, we cannot have complete intellectual freedom at this stage. As a matter of fact, we are censoring newspapers and the radio, and purging teachers from the educational system. We must employ common sense."

At a council meeting on October 2, 1946, General Derevyanko said that Japanese demobilization boards should be investigated, and added, "I cannot but express apprehension over the fact that the Japanese Government, as it seems to me, abuses the trust of the Supreme Commander [MacArthur] and creates the opportunity for legalized military activity by the officers of the former Japanese General Staff." The Soviet member's allegations were vehemently denied by Atcheson who found them "fantastic." He completely rejected concrete proposals suggested by Derevyanko for remedying the situation.

The very next day the New York *Herald Tribune* in a dispatch by Margaret Parton, reported that:

Local Japanese demobilization agencies, which the Soviet Union suggested yesterday might be serving in a liaison capacity between the Japanese Government and former army and navy officers, already are under investigation by American Military Government teams and intelligence officers, it was learned today.

Miss Parton then went on to quote one Headquarters officer as admitting that "We have been aware of this situation for a long time, but we cannot always reveal what we know or what we are doing."

Two weeks later Derevyanko suggested that in forthcoming elections the Japanese Government should be instructed to remedy the reported irregularities of the previous polling. This proposal brought forth from Atcheson the amazing statement that "The time has come when Japanese aims have become virtually identical with Allied aims." He accused the other members of making "continued allegations and charges" against the Japanese Government.

The British delegate objected. "I would like to go on record," said Ball, "as saying that I would not, without very careful further consideration, be able to identify myself with your expressions of cordiality and confidence toward the present Japanese Government." Later, in response to Atcheson's reply that he only had made "a plea for recognition where merit exists," Ball went on: "I have noticed in the last few months that when any member of this Council has raised questions which might be possibly construed as criticism of the Japanese Government, the United States member has been very quick and eager to defend the work of the Japanese Government."

As a result of this tiff Ball was advised rather strongly that he was "playing the Russian game." It was said around Tokyo that Ball's views were New Zealand's and Australia's rather than the United Kingdom's. In subsequent meetings he spoke less and rarely introduced new questions. The Chinese member almost never put anything on the agenda and seldom spoke except to support Atcheson. This left it squarely up to the Soviet delegate to supply both the questions for discussion and almost half of the discussion itself.

At the November 13 meeting General Derevyanko charged that the Japanese Government had failed to execute properly Mac-

Arthur's political purge directive and that seventeen members of the new Diet should have been dropped under the order. Atcheson's reaction was that this was merely another Soviet attack on the conduct of the occupation. Assuming that Derevyanko's charges were unsubstantiated, he challenged the Russian to produce evidence. Correspondent Burton Crane cabled the *New York Times* that "This reply puzzled Japanese who had been asking since February why some persons who seemed to fall within the purge provision were allowed to continue in office."

Gradually the Allied Council ran out of topics for its agenda. The British and Chinese members, not anxious to make any political hay, remained in the shade. Their Governments were in no position to antagonize the United States. Derevyanko only brought up issues which would, by Atcheson's handling, indicate that SCAP had something to cover up.

In the words of Guthrie E. Janssen, formerly the National Broadcasting Company's representative in Tokyo, "The main function of the Allied Council today is to act as a sounding board for General MacArthur's hostility toward Russia. Practically every meeting is full of innuendos or even open denunciations of the Soviet system or the aims and purposes of the Russian delegate. And most of these that I have witnessed were entirely irrelevant to the subject under discussion, and entirely *unprovoked* [Janssen's italics] by the Soviet members."

3

Opportunist Japanese political leaders, quick to sense and exploit any differences among the Allies, gained cockiness as the result of the Council's failure. They sized up American hysteria on the "Red" issue and they used it as their opposite numbers in China and Korea also used it to resist change. When pressed too hard on the question of reforms they have pointed out that the alternative would be dealing with the Communists or their sympathizers. It has been to their advantage to multiply, at least verbally, the Communist strength and influence among their opposition. They reason that the stronger it is, or they can make it out to be, the stronger will be SCAP's support for them. In the twenties the oligarchy had capitalized on a "Red" scare and later turned it into a scapegoat for the discontent of the thirties. Thus Premier Yoshida's drive on the labor unions at home and his clear references to the menace of the U.S.S.R. abroad won SCAP's favor.

Yoshida was quick to approve the "Truman Doctrine." He remarked, "We are having our battles with the Communists, too, and we have a very dangerous enemy to the north." In an election throughout Japan two weeks later, the Communists received only 1 per cent of the vote.

This did not deter members of the Japanese Foreign Office, who were preparing Japan's "case" against the day when the peace treaty would be argued. Writing a memorandum on Japanese claims, they suggested a plea be made for the return of the Kuril Island chain from Russia. At first they had founded their case on the fact that the Kurils were needed as fishing bases, but later they decided to emphasize the danger of Soviet infiltration through the islands. They also recommended that the Japanese representatives make an effort to get back Okinawa from the United States. Failing to secure outright return of these former possessions, the Foreign Office planners suggested that a request for U.N. trusteeship would be better than having the U.S.S.R. as such a close neighbor.

Those Japanese people who have most to gain from democracy are bewildered by the bickering in the Council. But the tendency had been for the rich—the landlords and the managers—to support the American position while the trade unionists, small farmers and students identify themselves with many of Derevyanko's views. This unfortunate truth cannot be explained away by "Communist propaganda." The Japanese have learned of the Council disputes from their newspapers and their newspapers are under SCAP-supervised censorship.

A student from the country north of Tokyo commented, when the Council was less than six months old, that "From the papers it seems that Atcheson, a wishful thinker, is painting a better picture of Japan than it really exists, while Derevyanko seems to understand conditions in Japan better. Would Atcheson say these things if the Russians weren't there?"

The answer is that Atcheson probably would not have said the same things. In adopting what seems to be an unswerving anti-Soviet, negative, defensive attitude, Atcheson surrendered the United States' enviable position as the force which had brought freedom and revolutionary democracy to Japan. To block Soviet suggestions, good or bad, SCAP had shielded itself with strange inconsistencies. A demobilized Japanese soldier told an American correspondent, "Atcheson said that the general elections were far better than anything held in Japanese history; he also said that the basis of labor was not democratic because people still don't understand democracy and voted for anyone they thought of, whatever his party, just because they thought voting would please the Americans. Perhaps it was because the results of the general elections were pleasing to SCAP while the results of elections for union officials were not?"

In the spring of 1946, following the attempted general strike, conditions in Japan began to live up to the advance warnings of those who had said that Yoshida's lack of policy would hasten economic disaster. MacArthur not only called for a new election but he tacitly admitted for the first time that the Government which SCAP had been defending was a failure. Unwilling to share the early glory of what junketing Congressmen called "a wonderful job in Japan," MacArthur was more than willing to share the immediate dilemmas. Early in April Atcheson, just returned from Washington where he took a bow for the "successful occupation," went to the Allied Council and asked for advice on the problem of stabilization. SCAP's staff had prepared a study of Japan's economic plight for the Council which Ball called "disquieting." He summed it up as a record of "continuous failure for eighteen months" on the part of the Japanese Government. He went on to make the inevitable tie-up between the economic situation and the political question, establishing an identity which SCAP had previously advised Japanese trade unionists was dangerous. In a talk which could have been given by Yoshida's left-wing opposition, Ball declared the real problem was to "find Japanese authorities who have the will and the capacity to establish a controlled economy."

During this discussion Dr. Sherwood M. Fine, an economic adviser to the Economic and Scientific Section, admitted that the failure was due to "unsatisfactory or partial implementation of the occupation's policies" and "administrative disorganization and a somewhat less than satisfactory level of administrative competence."

In an editorial on the important questions raised by the sudden confession of a muddle in Tokyo, the New York *Herald Tribune* commented wryly: "Perhaps answers would be more readily available if the General and his staff had placed less reliance on such men as Premier Yoshida and had made a real effort to identify and support more desirable Japanese leaders."

The only immediate "answer" appeared to be a change of governments and a change in SCAP's attitude. Somehow, either with Japanese consent or without, the emasculated Board of Economic Stabilization had to be given power to function much as the War Production Board did in the United States. Under the scrutiny of qualified SCAP or Allied Council experts, the BES could control the allocation and distribution of raw materials in such a way that production might be stepped up. A revision of the taxation system with higher levies on surplus profits would reduce excess purchasing power. Inflation could be held down by price controls and rationing backed up by strict enforcement.

Six weeks after Atcheson asked the Council for its advice on economic matters, Derevyanko presented a full-dress critique of SCAP's policy. "Since the surrender almost no serious measures have been taken to solve the huge economic problems of today," he charged. "Even the half-way measures taken have not been carried out."

The other Allies did not deny many of Derevyanko's allegations, but they resented his implication that SCAP had made no effort to correct the situation. SCAP's Dr. Fine challenged the Russian on his facts in several instances and Ball praised Fine's "adequate reply." But, observed Ball, "We do not improve the economic situation by giving adequate replies."

The economic picture in Japan, however, was not far from matching the angry sketch of the situation presented by Derevyanko. The Russian argued that the discussion of the wage-price structure could not be divorced from Japan's general economic situation. In perhaps exaggerated terms he claimed that the *Zaibatsus* were not effectively dissolved, that individuals were sabotaging industrial production, that the land reform was "unsatisfactory," that there had been "no struggle against inflation, no price control, no control of distribution, no measures against the black market, no move against unnecessary budget expenditures." He urged that "strong measures must be taken or the situation cannot improve."

4

In Washington, with headquarters in the former Japanese Embassy, sits another multi-nation body with which MacArthur has had frequent disagreements. This is the Far Eastern Commission composed of the representatives of the United States, United

Kingdom, the Soviet Union, China, France, India, the Philippines, New Zealand, Australia, Canada, and the Netherlands. The functions of this body, as outlined by the Big Three Foreign Ministers, are threefold: "to formulate the policies, principles, and standards in conformity with which the fulfillment by Japan of its obligations under the Terms of Surrender may be accomplished; to review, on the request of any member, any directive issued to the Supreme Commander for the Allied Powers or any action taken by the Supreme Commander involving policy decisions within the jurisdiction of the Commission; to consider such other matters as may be assigned to it by agreement among the participating Governments reached in accordance with the voting procedure provided for in Article V-2 hereunder."

This voting procedure required that all decisions must be passed by seven of the powers including the Big Four. In general the attitude of this body has been to go slow on embracing the new Japan as a member of the family of nations. It has tried to moderate some of MacArthur's fine enthusiasm for his charge.

In January 1946 the members of the Commission and their staffs sailed out to Japan for a three-weeks' inventory. In Tokyo, General MacArthur turned on his royal charm and many of the members succumbed. Daily reports on SCAP progress in various fields were read to them by bright young officers from SCAP's headquarters and they received an impressively heavy pile of mimeographed memoranda to carry back to Washington. The Commission issued no official report on its fact-finding expedition. They had not even been able to agree on the meaning of the "terms of reference" under which they supposedly functioned.

The most outspoken member of the group, Sir Carl Berendsen of New Zealand, said he had only one major worry after listening to the glowing SCAP summaries. "The occupation might be too good," Berendsen warned. "These Japs are busy beavers who can recover quickly from catastrophe as they have in the past. This time with the benefit of American ingenuity, direction, and guidance in the revision of their political, economic, and social structure, they may be better off than ever before. My main concern is to see that they are not better off than some of the liberated countries which Japan ravished and which do not have the benefit of American planning and push."

Since that time the FEC has publicly disagreed with SCAP on

a number of issues including the timing of elections, importation of food, the rights of labor unions to political activity, the scope of educational reform, and the handling of the new Constitution. Individual FEC members have become privately nauseated when MacArthur smacks his lips over "Japanese democracy." Berendsen, for example, took exception to SCAP's smug satisfaction with the 1946 elections in Tokyo. He labeled Yoshida and the first postwar Diet "as liberal as a smelly piece of cheese." Other members have had tart things to say about MacArthur's handling of the general strike threat and his chumminess with the Emperor. In most instances MacArthur has ignored their strictures.

The FEC has occasionally looked upon Japan as a piece in the Asiatic jigsaw puzzle and not just as a self-contained laboratory experiment where success was demanded. For example, on February 27, 1947, the Commission adopted a policy requiring controls over Japan's economy which would help relieve world shortages. They therefore directed MacArthur to limit severely domestic consumption of textiles and other goods in Japan so that nations which the Japanese invaded could be supplied.

The other powers offered little unified or consistent opposition to U. S. plans. It would not have availed them much if they had done so. By invoking "emergency powers" the American delegate could by-pass any FEC objections to "urgent matters," even if the dissent were backed by a majority of the nations. The first instance of this was the United States order to MacArthur (April 3, 1947) to begin sending industrial reparations from Japan to nations which had suffered from her aggressions. Half of these first reparations—iron, steel, machine tool and aviation equipment—were to go to China, with the rest divided among the Philippines, Netherlands East Indies, Burma, and Malaya. According to "an authoritative source" quoted in the New York *Herald Tribune*, France, India, Australia, and the U.S.S.R. had been among those objecting to the proposal. The U. S. delegate, General Frank McCoy, explained that the recipients were "in extreme need of industrial equipment for the immediate relief of their economies" and that delay was causing deterioration of the machinery and impeding SCAP's occupation program.

All of these reasons put forth by McCoy were accurate. The year-and-a-half debate on reparations had been ludicrous, the only possible gainer being the U.S.S.R. which had already seized an estimated two billion dollars' worth of equipment from Japanese industrial developments in Manchuria as "war booty." The victors spent so much time arguing over the division of the spoils that the spoils were not worth carting away by the time they were distributed.

Two American commissions had gone to the Far East to inspect and tally Japanese industrial assets. The first, headed by Edwin A. Pauley, returned early in 1946 and the second, a year later, was led by Clifford S. Strike, president of the New York engineering and construction firm of F. H. McGraw & Company. The first inventory, made for Pauley, was astonishingly slipshod. Due to lack of trained personnel, SCAP was forced to accept most Japanese estimates. The only precaution taken was to warn the Japanese Government that "If the statistics are wrong, the errors will be eventually found out." In several cases errors were found, much to the surprise of the Japanese. An Army checking team uncovered a quantity of silver bars beneath piles of steel plate. When asked why the silver had not been reported, the Japanese grinned and said, "We thought you refer to quicksilver." Over a billion in gold bullion was recovered from Tokyo Bay.

While the FEC quarrelled over whether Russia had seized "reparations" or "war booty" in stripping Manchuria, the uncared-for Japanese equipment rusted and rotted. Army engineers estimated that in one year after the war the equipment had depreciated at least 30 per cent and that by the time it was uprooted and transported and reassembled most of it would have been reduced in real value by 70 to 80 per cent. The long delay in earmarking which factories would be dismantled, supplied Japanese capitalists with a strong argument against risking reconversion.

The Pauley Plan, although not so drastic as the Morgenthau Plan for Germany, was the toughest reparations proposal for Japan made by the U. S. Its simple goals were to punish Japan and deprive her of war potential and at the same time utilize reparations in the reconstruction of Japan's victims. The Pauley proposals were fairly well thrown overboard before MacArthur even began implementing them. The Supreme Commander by the summer of 1946 had urged on Washington a "softer" approach to Japanese reparations.

The Far Eastern Commission then worked out an "Interim Program" which had MacArthur's strong support. It veered away from the Pauley formula and toward SCAP's view that a drastic reduction of Japan's war potential would remove the underpinnings of the country's basic industrial structure leading to social unrest. SCAP convinced the FEC that the military danger could be averted by scrupulous control of imported raw materials and frequent policing of a few key factors such as oil and steel.

Although the FEC generally agreed on the "Interim Program" it could not agree on carrying it out. For months they debated: who should get what and how much and in what order? The United States itself had no special desire for the equipment, which is obsolete in comparison to our own. But China and the U.S.S.R. needed it badly, and we were anxious that our deserving protege, the Philippines, receive fair share. Of course the United States had already first claims on Japanese gold, precious stones and manufactured goods against the cost of supplies furnished to Japan during the occupation.

In the fall of 1946 SCAP designated certain plants as primary targets for reparations removals. The Japanese Government was instructed to isolate these plants from industrial output as soon as possible. This year when SCAP agents went back to begin removals it was found that many of the earmarked plants had not been abandoned. In fact, production at them had miraculously stepped up from 20 per cent of normal to 70 per cent. The Japanese did this with the knowledge that SCAP, now preaching moderation and stability, would probably hesitate to dismantle a factory which was making a real contribution in a sick economy.

The Strike Plan, based on our world position a year after the Pauley Plan, also aimed at reducing the cost of Japan's economy to the U. S. taxpayer. (In 1946 it took $187,000,000 from the War Department's budget to finance the Japanese foreign trade deficit.) Strike favored expansion of chemical and fertilizer industries and the exemption of light metal plants from reparations. These proposals were therefore considerably milder and "more realistic." They would permit Japan gradually to re-enter competition for world markets and perhaps even to carry her own goods in Japanese ships, originally slated for the scrap heap.

According to an estimate by Brigadier General P. H. Tansey, SCAP's Civil Property Custodian, reparations claims against Japan might exceed a trillion dollars. He said that Japan's external assets in Sakhalin Island, the Kurils, Formosa, and the mainland of China totaled about 40 billion. These assets, he predicted, would be kept by Russia and China as their share of reparations.

The Strike suggestions on Japanese industry were gradually accepted as a procedural basis. But from the long-term point of view SCAP, the Allied Council and the larger Far Eastern Commission still had to decide on how and when and to what extent Japan's foreign trade could be resumed. MacArthur was on record as favoring resumption of foreign trading as soon as possible. But some of the Allied powers, with a weather eye on Pacific markets, were not in a hurry to approve. They were not only afraid that Japan's exports might menace their business; they were also anxious lest Japan turn into a U. S. economic "colony."

During a Parliamentary debate in London on this topic in the spring of 1947 a Conservative Member, W. W. Fletcher, observed: "A rubber curtain has been drawn over Japan. Nothing so regal or unmannerly as an iron curtain. You can lift one corner of a rubber curtain, but in a very few minutes it snaps back and you only get a glimpse of what is behind."

At a session of China's Political Consultative Conference in May 1947 Kuomintang delegates and scholars arose and expressed grave concern over the reactionary trend in Japan which was "supported by the U. S." and asked that China's Government do something about it. The Chinese spoke with the kind of urgency bred by propinquity which has characterized Russian fears of Germany. They demanded facts and figures about Japan's industrial capacity, about her future outlook. They were concerned by the report of the Chinese delegate who accompanied representatives from the United States, Great Britain, Australia, Canada, France, the Netherlands, and the Philippines on a six-thousand-mile tour of inquiry through Japan. He had sent in a memorandum charging that despite SCAP's assurances to the contrary Japanese were still hiding a great deal of rich war plunder. Even Foreign Minister Wang Shih-chieh, although he tried to remain calm, was patently troubled by the threat of reviving Japanese trade which his economic advisers reported.

During 1946 trade with Japan had been on a government-to-government basis. But it was on a scale far greater than generally assumed. Jiji News Agency in Tokyo reported that from the time of the surrender to September 1946, the value of Japanese exports and imports was around four billion yen, or almost half of the prewar volume. Before the war the United States's share of Japan's general overseas business was only 25 per cent; in the postwar period it has averaged 70 per cent. In the field of agricultural exports, including raw silk and tea, 89 per cent went to the United States during 1946. These facts, introduced into the House of Commons early in 1947, caused distinctly unfavorable comments about "U. S. imperialism." Minister of State Hector McNeil, under questioning, revealed that the United Kingdom was still attempting to restore British trade, while American businessmen already were privileged by SCAP to resume contracts in Japan.

This was evident even though SCAP and the U. S. State Department had seemingly made it difficult for American Dodsworths to visit Japan on private business. With its usual ingenuity, American industry found army officers and correspondents on the spot in Tokyo who could and would act for them. Military and civilian employees who left the army in Japan were finding lucrative commissions as agents for domestic concerns. In fact the *Wall Street Journal* proudly reported that "Military Government rapidly is becoming a training ground for Americans who plan to go into business in Japan."

Assuming that Japan is still the greatest industrial amalgam east of the Urals and, more important, that it has Asia's greatest reservoir of skilled workers and managerial personnel, the dilemma is what to do with it. The raw materials, the plants and the industrial savvy are not in themselves dangerous. They could be used as effectively for peaceful production as for war.

The resulting paradox of the U. S. program has been its desire to step up Japan's economy without arousing fears among the other FEC powers that Japan's war potential was also being expanded. It has also had to heed the insistence of Japan's economic rivals in the United States that their position be considered. Oil companies with interests in the Dutch East Indies want Japanese refineries curtailed; textile industries in the United States and China are lobbying for a limitation of cotton spindles in Japan.

Despite these pressures, SCAP has gone ahead with its plan to permit the rebuilding of Japan to a certain level. The FEC set that level as one which would give the Japanese a standard of living "substantially" equivalent to that of Japan in 1930 and 1934. This approach has kindled suspicion in other parts of Asia. Some fear the economic trend, some fear the political trend.

The *Straits Times,* a Singapore daily newspaper which represents influential British colonial opinion, flatly stated in an editorial on March 19, 1947, that it doubted whether MacArthur's social and political reforms would remain permanent. The newspaper expressed concern for the Malayas if Japan should quickly regain its prewar position as the Far East's dominant industrial nation.

Except in the meetings of the Allied Council, the most consistently outspoken criticism of MacArthur's "soft policy" toward Japan has come from China, not from the Soviet Union. The General's appeal for an early peace treaty with Japan and removal of troops brought forth this editorial in the big Kuomintang-owned paper in Shanghai, the *Hsin Wen Pao*:

We dare not be so optimistic as to believe, as General MacArthur says, that the Japanese have gone through a spiritual revolution, that their hidden fighting power has been entirely destroyed, that their old-fashioned legends and feudalistic traditions have disappeared, and that they are inclined towards personal freedom. Around the time of the Japanese surrender, the Japanese Emperor and the important military and political leaders held many meetings. They have long ago decided upon a set of policies with which they should deal with their new rulers. . . . Though the committees in charge of Japan include the delegates of China, U.S.A., Britain and U.S.S.R., the actual power is in the hands of General MacArthur. The Japanese know that if they wish to resurrect, they must first of all wheedle the Americans so that the Americans would be well turned towards them. The Japanese have never hesitated at any measures to attain their ends. When necessary, they can be most fawning and humble, and most sweet of tongue. They are well versed in this technique. In the last year and more, all from the Japanese Emperor down to the common Japanese have been respectful and compliant with the Americans. The Americans themselves have also been satisfied and feel that their power to convert others is great indeed. . . . But history tells us that there are previous examples in which the Japanese used measures of humble complaisance to deceive their enemies and seek revenge. . . . If the Americans have forgotten the deceit practiced by the Japanese before Pearl Harbor, the Japanese have not forgotten their national shame in the surrender ceremony on the *Missouri*. On March 19 the Japanese Premier made a statement to the Associated Press correspondents and did his utmost to praise MacArthur's speech [at the Tokyo Press Club], saying that MacArthur "entirely understands present conditions in Japan and the Japanese people," and that "the U.S. Army should stay permanently in Japan to maintain world peace," and that he would "prefer U.S.A. rather than U.N. to protect Japan." Ever since the beginning of their history, the Japanese have been cruel, aggressive and fond of fighting. And now, after not even two years of being conquered, they actually say that their conquerors are welcome to stay everlastingly in Japan. Only Japan could say such a thing which is altogether contrary to human nature. . . . We must warn our American friends who are too naive.

On that same day a statement by Senator Owen Brewster of Maine proposing that MacArthur's authority be "extended to China" drew a front-page blast from China's most influential newspaper, the *Ta Kung Pao*, which represents the opinions of the more liberal and outspoken statesmen in the Kuomintang Party. The *Ta Kung Pao* was irate. "Such outrageous talk actually comes out of the mouth of an American Senator. Is this because the Americans are too arrogant, or is it because we Chinese are too submissive? . . . How can our hearts help turning cold."

The same newspaper was bitter about the decision of the FEC, setting the Japanese industrial level as that of 1930–1934 and by MacArthur's report on the state of the occupation which stressed the need for increasing Japanese production. Its editorial, one of a series expressing the same fears about a revived Japan, said in part:

. . . We feel that a new Gospel has made its appearance in the world, and it will be possible for a defeated nation to become paradise. Jesus said, "Love your enemies." This is within the realm of religion, and is the highest virtue of mankind. These words of Jesus' can be applied to U.S.A.'s treatment of Japan, but of Japan alone. Our impression is that Hideki Tojo and Japanese imperialism have done a great service to Japan. Japan is now God's new favorite son. America is planning to reconstruct Japan into a paradise. . . . The Japanese paradise which the United States is prepared to create will be exclusively for the conservatives and reactionaries in Japan. The industrial level which the Far Eastern Commission has decided that Japan should be allowed to maintain is designed to preserve for Japan a firm foundation for her national regeneration. That industrial level was the one attained during 1930–1934. 1930 was one year before the Mukden incident, and 1934 three years before the Lukouchiao incident of July 7, 1937. . . . Japan, in this way, will remain the foremost industrialized nation in the Far East, a nation which will continue to be able to invade other countries in East Asia and to control the Far Eastern market through dumping her cheap goods. Some people may say, "Japan will have no armament." But this standard of industrialization is armament. . . . Some people may argue, "The new constitution of Japan provides that Japan should abandon war." But this standard of industrialization means she won't have to abandon war. . . . Japan used to be ruled by mad men. The Japanese ruling classes continue to be mad men. Should we give them the sword—the wartime industrial level—with which they used to kill people? . . . Japan's enormous trade schedule is sufficient to reflood Asia with Japanese goods and squash China's national industry. The Japanese predict that by 1950, the volume of Japan's trade will be 80 per cent larger than what it was in 1930, and that by then, her exports will equal that of the year after the beginning of the Sino-Japanese war in 1937, namely: 1938. The fact that the U.S. is so positive in helping Japan and that Japan harbors such inordinate ambitions has caused us amazement mixed with indignation. . . . . To tell the truth, the U.S.'s interest in Japanese politics and industry is designed solely to fulfill the requirements of U.S. strategy necessitated by the difference between U.S.A. and U.S.S.R. It is a pity that mankind's destiny is in the hands of these two powers. We urge that they spare us by drowning their differences. That would be the real Gospel, for only then can there be paradise on earth.

The Soviet press also cried out that Japan was being rebuilt by the U. S. with a military purpose. But both Russian and Chinese spokesmen ignored the fact that on June 21, 1946, the State Department had announced its proposal for a four-power treaty against Japanese militarism. This draft treaty, similar to the one proposed for Germany, would bind the U. S., China, Britain, and the U.S.S.R. to enforce Japanese demilitarization jointly for twenty-five years. At the conclusion of the Allied occupation, a quadripartite Commission of Control would take over the inspection and investigation duties to insure the demilitarization.

For a year after the State Department circulated this draft no official comment from the other three powers was publicized. General MacArthur himself ignored it in his discussions of Japan's future.

The other nations seemed to have no very clear idea of what they wanted done with Japan; they only knew what they did not want done. If any constructive and positive program for Japan's future was to be drawn up, the United States had to do it.

CHAPTER XI

U. S. COLONY OR U N WARD?

At Potsdam the United States had not intended to solve the problem of the Pacific by creating in Japan a "bulwark of democracy" but by stripping the country of its possessions and its war-making potential. After May 1946, when U. S. policy toward the Soviet Union seemed to harden everywhere, SCAP became less concerned with theoretical democracy and paid more attention to practical expediencies. This was evident not only in the plucking out of many New Dealers who were planning or administering SCAP directives, but also in SCAP's milder attitude to Japanese big business and its tougher policy toward labor. In making Japan "America's stronghold in the Pacific," law and order had to be encouraged and social chaos discouraged.

"What has happened in Japan," wrote Far Eastern expert Darrell Berrigan in the March issue of '47, "is that one militarism has been replaced by another, more paternal, militarism. The people of Japan are used to militarism and they accept the new type with as little protest as they did the old." But SCAP with its Pollyanna policy closed its eyes to this basic assumption. Its spokesmen went to ridiculous lengths praising the Japanese. Before the occupation was a year old George Atcheson, Jr. allowed himself to be quoted as saying: "The Japanese have learned the falsity of totalitarian and expansionist ideas, and that with newfound freedoms they will learn to give critical examination to false political ideologies."

The U. S. State Department did not seem worried by all the historical evidence which indicated that the concept of democracy cannot be imposed by an alien army. They never stopped to ask themselves this question: "Can the really democratic elements in a defeated enemy nation be strengthened by an alliance with the armies of the victors?"

Although historic parallels are sometimes only mirages, the

171

present situation in Japan is in certain respects similar to that in Germany under the Weimar Republic. All the faults, failings, and frustrations of postwar reconstruction and reconversion will not be blamed by an unthinking public on the Yoshidas but on the radicals and eventually on the occupation.

In one way MacArthur has attempted to safeguard against this eventuality. To explain his approach to Japan he has quoted Winston Churchill on Germany: "The problem is not to keep Germany down but to keep it up." He reasoned that with increased security and a higher standard of living the Japanese would attribute their better life to the new order. Conversely he realized that increasing unemployment and despair might be blamed on the difficulties and seeming contradictions of democratic processes. Such a state of affairs, MacArthur believed, could lead to Communism. But it is also similar to the postwar background from which Hitler arose in Germany.

It is axiomatic that MacArthur could not encourage liberal democracy in Japan without permitting the rebirth and growth of more leftist opinions including the Communist and pro-Communist movement. He did just that for many months. The release of political prisoners, the return of exiled leaders like Sanzo Nosaka all were meant to prove to the Japanese that a victory for the United States was indeed a victory for democracy.

But the sudden mushrooming of the left gave MacArthur a bad scare. In the first place he thought of anybody who was not violently anti-Communist as a potential member of the Russian fifth column. He looked at the political scene as a military man surveys a battlefield: on whom can I count? In the second place, the mounting hunger marches, demonstrations, strikes, and riots cast doubts on his own frequent assertions that all was well in Japan and that he, MacArthur, was doing an exemplary job. It might give the folks back home the idea that not everybody loved the occupation, Hirohito, and MacArthur.

SCAP had to make a fundamental choice: quick success or continued instability, backing the conservatives or risking a growing left trend, being "tough" or being "soft," shelling out or cashing in. When the trend in United States domestic and foreign policies veered sharply right, MacArthur stopped giving lip service to the progressive directive given him at the beginning of the occupation.

In declaring for the status quo in Japan, dressed up with democratic furbelows, MacArthur thought that this final achievement had assured his place among the greats of contemporary history. The price that the world and the Japanese may have to pay for his greatness will not be known in this generation.

During the first nine months after the war the old guard, the *Zaibatsu*, the Emperor-worshippers and the militarists prayed and worked for a short occupation. The progressives, including the Communists, hoped for a lengthy occupation as the best safeguard against a return of reaction and oligarchy. After May 1946, when MacArthur began more and more to support the conservative Yoshida Government, the situation altered radically. The old guard looked upon SCAP as the savior of the old way and wanted the occupation continued to protect their interests against the rise of trade unions. The progressives, on the other hand, began to believe that while SCAP was in existence they might have to battle them as well as the conservatives and reactionaries in order to win broad social and economic advances. They failed to see that without SCAP's guarantee of civil liberties, Shidehara and Yoshida would have been far more ruthless in their persecution of the opposition.

With the adoption of the new Constitution, the second national elections and the decision on rebuilding the Japanese economy, MacArthur's Japan had come to a turning point. In one direction it could become what *Pravda* called "a U. S. colony or semi-colony." Or it could evolve under Allied civilian control, perhaps as a ward of the U N, into a reasonably democratic society.

2

The elections in April 1947 indicated that the "spiritual change" which MacArthur kept seeing in Japan was actually fairly superficial.

In the month before these elections two important developments had occurred in the Japanese political picture. The Progressives under former Premier Shidehara dissolved and then re-formed into the Democratic Party. This maneuver not only enabled the conservatives to capitalize on the most popular political byword in postwar Japan but also enabled them to incorporate in their ranks Diet members and representatives of various factions previously listed as Independent. Even a handful of dissident Liberals, led by Hitoshi Ashida, quit Yoshida's party to join the Democrats.

The second development, voted by the House of Representatives after many stormy committee meetings, marked a significant victory for the conservatives. Shrewdly put together by Yoshida the new election law outdid even American gerrymandering; it approximately quadrupled Japan's fifty-three election districts. The law also provided for a "single" rather than a "plural" ballot. Under this revised system a voter could cast a ballot for only one candidate in his district even though there were five candidates to be elected. The "plural" ballot had permitted voting for two candidates if the total number of candidates to be elected was ten or less, for three candidates if the number was more than ten. In their losing debate on this critical issue the left-of-center parties, and most of the rank and file Diet members who represented anything new in Japanese political life, pointed out that with only one name to select, Japanese voters would certainly pick the best-known name. But top leaders of the conservative parties pushed the measure through.

Nobody was more pleased with the results of the 1947 elections than General MacArthur. "This is democracy!" he exulted in a statement praising the Japanese for rejecting the extreme right and extreme left. He was, of course, particularly happy that the Communists had been repudiated. This was a hollow victory, since Communism was not and had not been a major issue in Japan. The demonstrated measure of independent thinking was the real issue, and on that score there was room for big doubts.

Final returns in the elections for the Diet's House of Representatives gave the Social Democrats 144 seats and they emerged for the first time as the largest single party. But the Tweedledum Tweedledee conservatives still had a majority with their combined total of 261: Yoshida's Liberal Party had 129 seats, the new Democratic Party 132. The People's Co-operatives elected 31 representatives, the Communists 4, the minor parties and independents 26. Incidentally, among the independents was eighty-nine-year-old Yukio Ozaki who has been elected in every national election in Japan's history.

In the newly created House of Councilors, replacing the Peers, the conservatives and their sympathizers (running as "independents") captured 70 per cent of the seats in an election characterized by heavy disinterest.

The system of plural balloting in the 1946 elections had encouraged voters to pick the well-known names as first choices and then to select a woman candidate because that seemed part of SCAP's new democracy. The new single-ballot system cut down the number of women elected. Seventy-nine women campaigned for office in 1947 but only 15 (including 12 incumbents) were victorious as compared to 39 the previous year.

From the long-term point of view the most significant of Japan's four election days during April 1947 was the first. On April 5 the Japanese in all the cities, towns, and villages throughout the country were supposed to go to the polls to elect their provincial governors, mayors, and headmen for the first time. On this grass-roots level, rather than on the more heavily publicized level of the Diet elections, the Japanese were more likely to behave with less concern for SCAP's wishes. In their own areas the Japanese felt they knew what the local condidates stood for because they knew their faces and their families and their positions in society. As a result, most of the candidates ran without party labels.

In roughly a third of the towns and villages there was no contest. No newcomer to the political scene had the temerity or the following to challenge the accepted administration. Elsewhere, for the most part, the old faces held sway. Of the forty-six incumbent governors, most of them appointed by the Government, thirty-three were re-elected. The political purge changed some of the names but affected few of the ideas. In Osaka, for example, the militarists and the totalitarian-minded who had been purged formed a political clique which nominated, financed, campaigned for, and elected many of its own candidates.

In the little town of Onuki, fifty miles north of Tokyo, Joji Shibata was elected mayor. Joji is a sixty-five-year-old millionaire with questionable connections who, three months prior to the election, bought himself a Buddhist funeral. After an appropriate ceremony attended by thousands of mourners and presided over by Buddhist priests, Shibata jumped out of the coffin. With his name changed from Jo to Joji, Shibata said he was ready for a new start. He declared his decision to run for town headman in the April 5 election, and no one dared oppose him.

The inevitable victory of the reactionaries on April 5 was to a certain extent underwritten by the SCAP-approved regulations on campaigning. House-to-house canvassing was forbidden. Gubernatorial candidates were allowed twenty days to electioneer, while mayoralty candidates were limited to seven days. These restrictions all counted in favor of the old-line bureaucrats or the candidates whom they supported.

If the man who inspired the notorious plan for aggression, the Tanaka Memorial, had been still alive, his close relatives would have been subject to the political purge. But Baron Giichi Tanaka was dead and therefore his son, Tatsuo Tanaka, was permitted to run for governor of an important prefecture. During his own career Tatsuo had worked for the Cabinet Planning Board in the early years of the war and later served as an official in the Munitions Ministry where he was close to Yoshida. Despite a consistent pro-war record Tanaka's son was not purged. In fact, the magic familiarity of the father's name helped to elect the son governor of Yamaguchi Prefecture.

One other example illustrates why the Tokyo newspaper *Yomiuri Hochi* called the April 5 elections "the victory of the old regime." The biggest plum in the elections was control of the Tokyo area, comparable in importance to the mayoralty of New York City. The successful candidate was a man who had stood and fought for the same things which had been reason enough to purge thousands of other bureaucrats. Seiichiro Yasui began his career as a police chief. His ability to make the masses toe the line was so pronounced that in 1931 he was appointed an aide to the governor-general of Korea. His talent as a colonial administrator was quickly recognized and he became Director of the Monopoly Bureau and later a provincial governor in Korea. Then he moved to Formosa and Manchukuo in important posts where he could oversee the task of exploiting colonial resources and peoples for Japan's war effort.

The Yoshida Government, charged with the responsibility for carrying out SCAP's purge directives, maintained a hands-off policy on Tanaka and Yasui and dozens of other "independent" candidates who had tacitly pledged their support to the Prime Minister. The Government was not, however, above using the purge order as a political weapon against their chief opponents in the bid for the conservative vote. Wataru Narahashi, one of the founders of the Democratic Party, and thirteen other Democrats were declared ineligible the day before the election. MacArthur insisted on remaining "neutral" in the face of these shenanigans, but actually his refusal to interfere gave tacit support to Yoshida.

Of forty-five gubernatorial posts, the Social Democrats won only four. The Communists did not win any. Most of the victors were "independents" who were not in favor of a reform program and who had the backing of the Liberal and Democratic parties. In the elections to prefectural councils (state legislatures) the conservatives were voted into more than a thousand seats compared to a couple of hundred for the Social Democrats, less than a hundred for the Co-operatives, and none for the Communists.

The Japanese in the big cities were fairly uninterested in the results. Like apt American-imitators, more of them lined up in front of the *eigakan* (movie theaters) than before the *keili-ban* (bulletin boards). In Tokyo, where Yasui was elected, only about 53 per cent of the eligible voters went to the polls. In Osaka even fewer bothered to vote. Elsewhere a would-be voter suddenly realized he couldn't remember the name of the candidate he was supposed to vote for. "Do what I did," suggested another voter, "just write in the character for rice."

A new Diet was organized in May. In the House of Councilors, Tsuneo Matsudaira was named first President by the overwhelmingly conservative membership. A former Ambassador to London, Matsudaira belongs to one of the old and respected families who are always close to the Emperor. The lower house, with a plurality of Social Democrats, elected the labor leader, Komakichi Matsuoka, as speaker.

After a good deal of behind-the-scenes maneuvering by outgoing Premier Yoshida of the Liberals and the aged ex-Premier Shidehara of the Democrats (formerly Progressives), Social Democrat Tetsu Katayama became Premier. Yoshida attempted to enforce, as a precondition to joining a coalition Cabinet, a split in the Social Democratic Party. He insisted that the Socialists expel their "undesirable" left-wing members. Since this would have wrecked the Socialists' plurality in the Lower House, if for no other reason, they refused.

Due to Yoshida's immense influence among the conservatives, Katayama found it difficult to induce the Democrats to back his cabinet. One faction in the party led by Shidehara was closely allied with the Yoshida Liberals and refused to participate. Katayama offered the post of Foreign Minister to ambitious Hitoshi Ashida, the leader of the other faction. Ashida was editor of the Japan *Times* from 1933 to 1940 and is a close follower of the purged

Liberal chief, Hatoyama. He is slender, sartorially splendid, and shrewd.

At this juncture, when it appeared that no cabinet could be formed and perhaps another Premier might have to be designated, MacArthur intervened with one of his beautifully timed sermons. His statement said that Katayama's election meant a "middle-of-the-road" course. This was the official tip-off to the other parties and to the Socialists, themselves, that the left-wing Socialists would not be tolerated. SCAP also seized the occasion to call public attention to Katayama's Christian faith, an indication, according to MacArthur, "that East and West can find common agreement in the spirituality of the human mind and erect a barrier against the infiltration of ideologies which seek by suppression the way of power and advancement."

SCAP's benediction helped weak-chinned, unobtrusive Katayama. At a Democratic Party caucus Ashida urged that they enter a coalition cabinet without the Liberals. When this proposition won, Shidehara resigned as titular chief of the party. Katayama then formed a cabinet, composed of right-wing Socialists, Democrats and Co-operatives. It was generally considered a weak government, since the Socialists had found it necessary to give up four of the most important ministries to the other two parties: Foreign, Home, Welfare and Finance.

In his first statement as Premier, Katayama sounded like an echo of MacArthur. He expressed the pious hope that democratic government in Japan might be "permeated by a spirit of Christian love and humanism" and "guided by a Christian spirit of morality."

Tokyo newspapers, under stricter SCAP censorship following the general strike threat in February, wrote tongue-in-cheek editorials about the election results. Many of them were happy about the plurality of the socialists in the Lower House but worried about the continued majority of the conservative coalition and the sweep scored by them in the House of Councilors, and in the prefectural and local campaigns.

There was real alarm in China over the elections. The reliable *Ta Kung Pao* found "The Japanese problem is again becoming more and more serious." In an editorial on the conservative victory, the newspaper said: "What we are worried about is the fact that General MacArthur is fully satisfied with the Japanese elections. Due to this, the reactionaries in Japan will remain to the very last. A frightful vision is clearly before our eyes."

The Shanghai *Wen Hui Pao,* further to the left politically, accused MacArthur of influencing the elections in favor of the conservatives. "If within six months or a year a reasonable solution cannot be found for United States–Soviet relations, then in six months or a year we shall see Japan being rearmed so that she may become the United States' defensive and offensive advance post in the Far East against Soviet Russia. The Japanese capitalists are now waiting patiently for the arrival of such a day. On this point we Chinese must be on the alert."

3

Japan is a long way from the kind of democracy which even MacArthur envisions. The roots of evil are still deep in the volcanic soil. It would be naive to expect that two years would be enough time to cut them out and see a fresh, healthy plant growing.

We have done much spadework for the forms of democratic growth; at times we have merely been jumping up and down, clapping hands, and hurrahing before we could honestly say whether a weed or a flower was coming up. The Boy Scout optimism of our leaders about the changes which two years have wrought on an ancient people with deeply imbedded beliefs is not only ridiculous, it is dangerous. All we can safely say is that many Japanese like us, many Japanese follow us, many Japanese seem to understand our ways and to believe in them. There is certainly less bitterness toward Americans and American policy than in liberated Korea or in China.

Thus far, the Allies under MacArthur have done a good job in Japan, but a greater job remains to be done. A good job has been done compared to what professional cynics and MacArthur-haters anticipated. It is a good job compared to what other occupying forces have done in other countries and in other times.

But it is not good enough. Only part of the fault can be attributed to the limitations of MacArthur's wisdom. The wide gap between theory and practice, the failure to understand the significance of the undertaking in Japan, the lack of trained personnel in sufficient numbers—these faults are our own as well as MacArthur's.

In the final analysis, the basic defect of our plan for Japan has been our post-World War I approach. It is an approach which somehow ignored the fact of atomic energy and of a shrinking world. We have treated Japan as a colony and we have accepted Japan's problems as our own, forgetting that the whole world must be considered in any settlement of the Japanese puzzle.

The problem of what to do with Japan's potential industrial and trade position illustrates how we have been guilty of jerry-building peace in Japan. It is reactionary in the dictionary sense of the word to think that Japan's advanced technology can be ignored in providing for the future. Japan must become a producer again. But the production must harmonize with the requirements of the entire Far Eastern area. It must be planned by interested nations in concert and planned in such a way that the old fears of Japanese domination or the new fears of American domination do not arise.

At this stage—if we were not scaring ourselves with the Communist bogey—the best hope for a solution would be within the United Nations. Only under the ægis of a U N civilian commission can the greater job be done. Only that way will the Japanese realize that they must prepare themselves for citizenship in the world and not just for participation in one power bloc as against another.

General MacArthur's remarks at the Tokyo Press Club on March 17, 1947, about the desirability of U N civilian control for Japan came at a moment in world history when American policy-initiators in Washington were preparing to write off the U N as too weak. Yet it seems obvious, and MacArthur's speech only re-emphasizes it, that without international accord on the problem of Japan's peacetime role there are danger signals flying ahead.

Already Japan's neighbors in the Far East are asking uneasy questions about that nation's re-emergence as the economic colossus of Asia. Already (according to a recent public opinion poll) more than 80 per cent of the Chinese believe that Japan will again invade China. The only way to assuage such fears, to build confidence in peace, is to turn the Japanese nation over to the U N until it is ready to become a full-fledged member.

PART TWO

HODGE'S KOREA

Democracy endures on the principle of compromise, not on the compromise of principle.

Lieut. Gen. John R. Hodge
(*September 8, 1946*)

History is repeating itself. Forty years ago, Czarist Russia and Japan struggled for supremacy in Korea. Today America and Soviet Russia are rubbing their shoulders in Korea. It is the eternal story of power politics all over again.

Lyuh Woon Heung
(*in the Christian Science Monitor, March 13, 1947*)

CHAPTER XII

FIGHTS FOR FREEDOM

FOR A THOUSAND years conquerors and would-be conquerors of China have begun their drive for Asiatic dominance by first winning Korea (Chosen). This narrow, mountainous peninsula on Asia's northeast coast occupies eighty-five thousand square miles, an area larger than Austria, Hungary, and Belgium combined. Its 28 million Mongoloid inhabitants are racially neither Japanese nor Chinese—but not very dissimilar. Primarily an agricultural people, they have a national history which dates back to the twelfth century B.C.

Until the end of World War II, relatively few Americans knew very much about Korea and even fewer were concerned about what happened to the country or its people. That was Japan's business. Today the whole world has become everybody's business and Korea, in particular, has become the special affair of the United States and the Soviet Union. And yet internationally minded Americans have been less interested in Korea than in Bermuda.

This is strange and shocking. Today the needle of history which quavers between the magnetic forces centered in Washington and Moscow points directly at Korea. In "The Hermit Kingdom," as nowhere else in the world, American and Russian ideologies and methods have co-existed side by side. Korea is the only country that has been under joint American-Russian domination. Korea, therefore, more than Japan, China, Germany, or Austria, is the demonstration ground for the world's greatest forces. There history's future can be forecast by their rivalry or co-operation, by their success or failure.

The plan which led to this juxtaposition of forces began at the Yalta Conference in February 1945. In military staff meetings, after it had been decided that the Soviet Union would enter the war in the Far East three months after V-E Day, northern Korea was designated a Soviet area of military operations and the southern half as an American sector. Five months later at Potsdam the Joint Chiefs of Staff agreed that the 38th parallel would divide the two sectors as a military expedient. This arbitrary line, drawn without regard to political, geographic, or economic factors, continued to divide Korea long after the military reason for the "line" had been erased.

On the political and diplomatic level, Korea was always near the end of a crowded agenda. Through an exchange of notes, the Soviet Union and the United States appeared in substantial concord on Korea: that after its liberation Korea would have a short occupation of six months to a year followed by a civilian trusteeship (American, British, Chinese and Russian) of approximately five years' duration.

This non-partisan approach to the Korean problem did not work out. With the world-wide growth of friction between the U.S. and the U.S.S.R., the side-by-side military occupations remained and became Military Government—neither of them with the consent of the Korean people. Thus began a kind of competition in the two zones; two concepts of democracy were planted, tended, and watered by two armies.

If the American people have been uninterested in this competition, the Koreans are not. Nor are the millions in undeveloped colonial Asia who wait impatiently watching to see which way of life produces independent, democratic government based on the actualities of social growth and economic security.

Before I left Tokyo for Korea, one of the editors of *Asahi* said to me: "We will be interested to see what you write about Korea. In Japan we are living in the same century as America. In Korea they are a century behind. The Russians have great experience in taking giant strides forward in short times. We are wondering what you will do."

2

The white-clad Koreans in their strange black headgear lined the roads and joyously shouted *"Mansei! Mansei!* (Live One Thousand Years!)" when the Americans marched into their country on September 7 and 8, 1945. There were quickly scrawled signs proclaiming "USA ARMY WELCOME HURRAH" and "AMERICANS-KOREANS FRIENDS IN CHRIST."

From the commanding general down to the lowliest private, the Americans were touched. Unfortunately many of them, after long months of battle, felt they were being hailed as conquerors. The Koreans were acclaiming them as liberators. Disillusionment came quickly for both.

The Americans of the battle-burned 24th Corps knew almost nothing of the zone they were taking over. What information they did act upon was dangerous; it erroneously lumped the Koreans together with the Japanese who were still everywhere in evidence. The conquering liberators or liberating conquerors did not even understand the history or the character of the Korean people. The occupation troops funneled into the scattered towns and cities. Few realized the basic fact of Korean economy: most of the people were submarginal farmers, living in small, crudely constructed thatch-roofed mud or wood huts without chairs or other Western-style furnishings. . . .

Of Korea's 3 million farm families, only one out of every four had a horse or an ox; a draft animal competed with a human for the small amount of available foodstuff. The Americans could not comprehend why they rarely ate meat except at festivals. Their food staples were cereal grains, chiefly millet, rice, and vegetables. In a farmhouse an optimum meal consisted of cayenne pepper soup, dried fish cut into thin strips, radishes soaked in salt water, cabbage, rice or millet, and a cup of rice water. The well-to-do landowner, who frequently was able to find enough for three meals a day instead of the usual two, might also serve such delicacies as pine seeds, lily bulbs, boiled pork with rice wine, dried seaweed, or shrimps. But for nearly two-thirds of Korea's population, a normal meal, eaten in contemplative silence, consisted of a bowl of cereal, a few radishes, and rice water.

This was a picture post-card country that the 7th Division had marched into, less lush than Okinawa but varied and breathtaking. They approached the capital from its seaport, Chemulpo, along the ancient Peking Pass. This was the road on which the envoys from China came in the days of China's suzerainty to collect tribute from Korea. The King used to welcome them outside the West Gate.

The people were high-strung, hot-tempered, proud, and sensitive. "They gotta helluva lot of crust for gooks," the G.I.'s said when the Korean men refused to hurry off their streets in front of onrushing jeeps. When the Korean women resisted their "Here's-a-Hersheybar" advances, the G.I.'s wished they were in Tokyo or Manila, and the less hot-headed quickly learned to differentiate between the willing Japanese and the unwilling Korean girls.

After the first days, many American officials never saw any more of Korea than the area right around Seoul, the capital. Founded in 1392, this walled city of more than one million population is a strange admixture of Western and Oriental styles of architecture, of bicycles and rickshas, of people named Kim (gold) and Li (plum), of wide avenues and narrow alleys, of open sewers and closed gambling dens, of pagoda-topped palaces (all facing south), and windowless hovels. The city's climate is not unlike that of Washington, D. C., but its natural setting is far more fortunate. Seoul is the center of a fertile cup, sided by gaunt granite mountains fringed with greenery only around the bottoms. One of the mountain peaks, *Book Ak San,* towers to the north of the modern-looking granite, be-domed Government General Building. Koreans believe this peak embodies the spirit of an ancient prince and that it is constantly inching closer to the city. Another nearby eminence is called Guest Mountain; it is supposedly a symbol of good fortune for all visitors to Korea, especially when they leave to return to their own countries. This legend was an unspoken joke when the Japanese were in control of Korea, and Seoul was called Keijo; today the people of Seoul have not forgotten its significance.

I was only slightly better prepared for the first sight and sound and smell of Korea than the average G.I. Perhaps I was two books and two conversations ahead.

Korea does not look like Japan: the conspicuous irregularity of the volcanic landscape is missing. Seoul is not like Tokyo: the occasional Western sign or building is an intrusion as it is in Peiping. Most of the foreign homes, red brick houses built by the Japanese, are grouped in the western hills toward the river. The Koreans themselves do not set much store by four walls.

One of the first Koreans I ever talked with, Mr. Hu Heung, who represented an association of Koreans in Tokyo, became scornful when I inquired if Korean houses were in the Japanese style: "To British and Americans, a house is a home," he said. "You have your books and your radios and your pictures and your rugs. Yes, even your working man and farmer has these things. What has a Korean to put in a house? A cup, a bowl, a howling child? I come from peasant stock and so do most of my countrymen. In my village a house is a place to go when it rains too hard or it is too cold."

When I asked about houses in Seoul he continued, "Even in the city you will find my people do most of their living under the sky. Will you be in Seoul this summer? Too bad. You would see that the people cook in the streets and sleep at night on mats in front of their houses."

Seoul was as Hu had described it: from the bustling, wide Chong-on ("Street of the Big Bell") in the center to the narrow twisting passages in the so-called native section. Hu had not mentioned the smell. Great cities have characteristic odors. Seoul's is compounded of the delicate scent of old men smoking long pipes, of redolent ox-dung, and of the penetrating sour vinegar reek of *kimchi*, the Korean pickle.

As Hu said, Korean women were far handsomer than most of the Japanese. Their carriage is beautiful and so is their hair, oiled to shiny black smoothness. The typical Korean costume is certainly more attractive than the dull, workaday Japanese *mompei* or the more formal kimonos with tightly wound *obi* sashes which, although often dazzling, seemed somewhat to deform the female figure. Korean women, at least the better-dressed ones in Seoul, wear brightly colored silk print blouses with a white border around the neck and a ribbon looped over the right breast and falling in two strands below the waist. The full-length skirts are exceptionally high-waisted and usually pleated. Even more vivid outfits are worn by the *keisangs* (the Korean equivalent of *geishas*) as they thump their hourglass-shaped *chang kus* (drums) and fill the air with their emotional ballads.

Traditionally the men wear long robes of white—the color of mourning. Not five minutes from the Government Building their wives can be seen daily with buckets full of clothes washing them in streams. If they are really dirty the robes must be boiled in lye. Then they are beaten with sticks on flat stones, allowed to dry in the sun, and taken home to be beaten again. Doing the laundry has been one of Korea's chief home industries for generations.

In the villages and farms around Seoul less attention is paid to dress, although tradition is not slighted. But men, women, and children work too hard and too long in the fields to worry about daily washing. They have almost no implements and the man of the family is the chief beast of burden. I have seen them trudging slowly along the dusty roads with a wooden structure on their backs called a *jigi*. It resembles a chair with a single pair of legs which the man holds. On top of the *jigi* anything and everything is piled.

With a confused rush, staff officers began to learn statistically about Korea from English-speaking Japanese and anxious-to-please Koreans. The Southern zone's population was 19 million, compared to the North's nine million; the South had the bulk of food supplies, the North most of the mineral and ore deposits. To aid their war effort, the Japanese had developed Korea as a base for coal, chemicals, foods, textiles, and coke. "Between 1929 and 1942," the Japanese reports read, "the value of Korean production increased 500 per cent." Almost none of this helped raise the living standards of the Korean masses; it was fed into Tojo's war machine.

The Americans were much slower to learn and believe that the Koreans were *not* what the Japs claimed they were—a kind of inferior servant class. Many a G.I., given no orientation, has served his tour of duty in Korea without realizing the rich heritage and great potential of its people. Despite periodic incursions from both Japan and China, the Koreans still cling to their own language, their own dress and customs. They are proud of their history which predates that of more renowned European nations. Once Korea was more powerful than Japan and a cultural center to rival even China. Their ancestors invented movable type; they developed a unique system of writing which combined both the alphabet and the syllable; they were among the first to utilize the compass, the cannon, and the ironclad fighting ship.

The American officer who associated privately with the Christian converts thought it peculiar that anyone should still root his religious beliefs in primitive animism and natural folklore, or Buddhism, Confucianism, and Taoism when an enlightened substitute like Christianity was available. By the time the facts about Korea and Koreans were available, an unshakable set of prejudices had been built, based not upon the historical development of the Korean people but upon American conservatism, ignorance, intolerance, and our mistrust of Russia.

3

Until the latter part of the last century Korea, a kingdom under nominal Chinese domination, resisted all other foreign influences.

Since then it has been a whipping boy for both Eastern and Western imperialism. The Japanese began it by breaking into this exclusive Chinese sphere in 1876, using an "incident" to exact a trade treaty with extraterritorial rights from the Korean rulers. It paid dividends and by 1894 Japan had captured 90 per cent of Korea's trade.

Six years later the United States, after several failures, also managed to secure a treaty with Korea. Inspired by the success of Commodore Perry in establishing relations with Japan, another U. S. naval diplomat sailed to Korea. Commander R. W. Shufeldt negotiated a treaty of mutual assistance and trade with Korea on behalf of the United States. This pact, which Koreans have often quoted and Americans more frequently ignored, pledged that "If other powers deal unjustly or oppressively with either government, the other will exert their good offices, on being informed of the case, to bring about an amicable arrangement, thus showing their friendly feelings."

About the same time, Tsarist Russia began to press for closer contacts with Korea. Since the Russian Empire bordered on Korea (in 1860 the Russians had secured Siberian territory as far south as the Amur River and had established Vladivostok), this was not to the liking of the Chinese and of the Japanese who were rapidly coming to consider Korea their rightful prize. In 1884 the Russians sent officers to train the small Korean army. A year later the Tsar's agents attempted to secure a Korean warm-water port for the use of the Russian navy, but they were blocked by combined British-Chinese-Japanese pressure.

In 1893 both China and Japan sent troops into Korea to help quell a rebellion. The Japanese refused to leave, demanding reforms in the Korean government which the Chinese resisted. The next year the Japanese manufactured another incident, attacked the Korean Royal Palace in Seoul, murdered the anti-Japanese Queen, and made the King a prisoner. They installed a pro-Japanese government which asked Japan to assist them in driving out the Chinese. In the interest of Korea's independence Japan declared war on China on August 1, 1894. By the spring of 1895 the Chinese were defeated and the Japanese began plans to strengthen Korea as a bulwark against Russia which was still demanding a Korean warm-water port and a Korean terminus for the Trans-Siberian Railroad.

The next year the captured Korean King and Crown Prince escaped from the Japanese and took refuge in the Russian legation when the Americans were unwilling to help. The King appointed a new government which, for the next two years, was heavily under Russian influence, and the Russians received the best lumber and mining concessions. At this time one of the first clashes between American and Russian interests in Korea was recorded. The Russian envoy, Alexis De Speyer, noting the growing influence of Christian missionaries from the United States, dictated that no Korean officials friendly to the Americans could retain a government post. The Russians further consolidated their position on June 3, 1896, by signing a treaty with China calling for mutual aid against Japanese aggression; the same treaty gave Russia the right to construct its railroad through Chinese Manchuria to Vladivostok.

The Japanese at this juncture offered to divide Korea with Russia along the 38th parallel. The Russians refused and on June 8 signed a treaty with Japan recognizing Korean independence. Both sides secretly were convinced they could acquire the whole country.

Japan and Russia jockeyed for position in Korea for the next few years with the Western nations backing first one and then the other in an attempt to prevent either from becoming a dominating power in the Pacific. The turning point came in 1902 when Britain, then the world's greatest power, made an alliance with Japan, which, in effect, recognized that nation's junior partnership in the exploitation of the Far East. Less than two years later, without advance warning, the Japanese attacked the Russian fleet at Port Arthur. In the event of hostilities between its two potent neighbors, Korea had proclaimed its neutrality. But the Japanese quickly overran the country and on February 23, 1904, the Korean monarch was forced to sign a treaty of alliance with the Japanese which allowed them to make Korea a base of operations against Russia. In return, the Japanese "definitely guaranteed the independence and territorial integrity of the Korean Empire."

Officially neutral, the United States nevertheless hoped for a Russian defeat. "Japan is playing our game," President Theodore Roosevelt wrote to his son. But Japan's easy victories changed the balance of power; Roosevelt interceded for peace, anxious that Russia remain as a counterweight to Japan in the Far East. In 1905, therefore, Roosevelt helped settle the Russo-Japanese war by bringing the warring parties together at Portsmouth, N. H. The

Koreans recalled their treaty of 1882 with the United States and asked for our assistance in maintaining their independence. Roosevelt had sent his Secretary of War, William Howard Taft, to the Orient to confer with Japanese Foreign Minister Count Katsura. Taft and Katsura made a secret covenant under which the United States recognized Japan's right to Korea in return for Japanese disavowal of any aggressive designs on the Philippines, recently acquired from Spain by the United States.

Taft expressed the opinion that ". . . The establishment by Japanese troops of a suzerainty over Korea to the extent of requiring that Korea enter into no foreign treaties without the consent of Japan was the logical result of the present war and would directly contribute to permanent peace in the East."

The ease with which Taft and then Roosevelt acquiesced in this conquest only whetted the appetite of Japan's ruling class for further aggrandizement. From 1905 to 1910 the Japanese governed Korea under a "trusteeship," with the Korean ruler still enthroned in Seoul. But in 1910 the strategic peninsula was gobbled up into Imperial Japan. China and Russia were too weak to risk a fight, and the Korean King renounced his throne for a Japanese pension. The United States, bound by treaty since 1882 to help Korea, did nothing. President Roosevelt scornfully referred to the Korean people as unwilling to strike one blow in their own defense.

Koreans never completely accepted foreign hegemony. In 1906 they began active demonstrations against Japanese rule. As the rioting mounted, thousands of Koreans were killed or imprisoned. Several hundred thousand migrated to neighboring Siberia and Manchuria. Outspoken leaders in the struggle for Korean independence made their way to southern China and even to the United States.

Between 1907 and 1910, the year when Japan completely annexed the peninsula, attempts were made to break up the Korean army. Many units refused to surrender authority to the Japanese commander. Led by Tokyo-trained General Li Tung-hui, about 5,000 Korean troops withdrew across the Yalu River into Manchuria. There they found food, shelter, and support among the villages of Korean farmers who had fled from Japanese control. From this Manchurian base the exiled army began partisan attacks across the border. Japanese sources reported 780 encounters with these "Korean brigands" in the year between September 1908 and August 1909.

When the Japanese retaliated with punitive raids, more and more partisans and farmers resettled in Siberia where they later came under the influence of the young Soviet Republic. Following the example of General Li some even became Communists. On one occasion the Japanese actually invaded Manchuria and wiped out 4,000 Korean inhabitants.

When the deposed Korean Emperor Yi (also pronounced *I* in Korean, *Li* in Chinese, and *Ri* in Japanese) died early in 1919, patriotic Koreans turned the day for mourning him into an occasion for an independence demonstration in Seoul. Korean Christian leaders, many educated in the West, had become enthusiastic over Woodrow Wilson's Fourteen Points and especially his championing of self-determination and the rights of smaller nations. They believed that "the great American President" would break the shackles which Roosevelt and Taft had allowed Japan to clamp on them. On May 1, 1919, almost half a million paraded through Seoul's wide, tree-lined streets in support of the independence manifesto issued by thirty-three Korean leaders, including eleven Christian ministers. This American-style declaration concluded with the optimistic statement that the age of force and arms was ended and the age of right and justice begun.

The demonstrators throughout Korea had been advised:

> Whatever you do
> Do not insult the Japanese;
> Do not throw stones;
> Do not hit with your fist;
> For these are the acts of barbarians.

These instructions had no effect on the Japanese police. Angered and frightened, they called in reserves and systematically launched a campaign of terror against known demonstrators. Koreans have estimated that 7,000 were massacred, thousands more injured, flogged, and thrown into jails. Some rebels were forced completely underground while others had to leave the country secretly.

In the fall of that same year leaders of the Seoul independence movement joined exiled patriots from elsewhere and proclaimed themselves a Provisional Korean Government in Shanghai. They chose Syngman Rhee as President General. The members of this government in exile concurred on only one thing—ridding Korea of Japanese occupation and achieving freedom. They differed on almost every other issue including the means of achieving their one common goal. Representatives of the Manchurian and Siberian exiles advocated active opposition to the Japanese, while some of the Western-educated and Christian-influenced leaders, such as President Rhee, kept hoping for eventual intervention by the League of Nations or the United States. With its limited means, the group was able to carry out two functions. They operated as a lobby for Korean independence in other capitals and they smuggled propaganda and organizers back into Korea under the sharp eyes of the Japanese overlords. They succeeded in gaining official recognition only from Dr. Sun Yat-sen in China (1921).

Within Korea the insurgents continued to work underground, abiding by the advice in their 1919 Declaration of Independence which urged Koreans to be "smart as a snake and humble as a dove." In 1921 a Proletarian Union was illegally formed in Seoul. A General Union of Korean Workers and Farmers was organized in 1924 and continued to meet secretly despite a Japanese ban. In the Annual Report for 1922-23 the Japanese attributed Korean non-co-operation to the "non-comprehension of the true idea governing the Japanese rule." Paradoxically, the same report stated "the new Japanese subjects, moved by the exceeding graciousness of the Japanese Emperor, came to rely confidently on the Japanese authorities."

Forbidden to go elsewhere, Korean students who went to Japan for higher education were quickly absorbed into the radical student movement which flourished briefly after the First World War. Unsettled conditions in Tokyo following the 1923 earthquake resulted in a government-inspired pogrom against the Korean minority who were used as scapegoats. Hundreds of students fled to China to join forces with the revolutionary Kuomintang. They hoped that the militant Chinese nationalist movement under Dr. Sun Yat-sen would eventually aid them in the liberation of Korea.

When Chiang Kai-shek (Dr. Sun's successor as head of the Kuomintang) split with the Communists in 1927, the schism among Korean exiles in Shanghai was considerably widened. Disagreement among the militants revived the influence of the pacifists led by Syngman Rhee. To some extent this conflict was reflected in the Korean underground at home. The Japanese secret police seized upon this confusion and in 1928 cracked down on the ringleaders, the Communists. The Korean underground was almost completely uprooted by wholesale arrests of members and sympathizers, many of whom actually revealed their identity by wearing beards as a mark of their independence.

The Korean independence movement suffered another blow in 1931. The Mukden "incident" quickly lead to Japan's expansion into Manchuria and placed Korean exiles in that area under Tokyo's control, although some of them moved north to Siberia. When China began to fight back six years later, the scattered Korean exiles once again revived their hopes and renewed their struggle against the Japanese. Some joined Chiang's Nationalist forces and still more served the Chinese Communists as guerrillas. One of the latter, Wu Ting, became chief of staff to an Eighth Route Army commander. Even the much spied upon and terrorized insurgents in Korea took heart and plagued Japanese supply lines by marauding attacks from hill hideouts in the North.

No means had been overlooked to transform the Koreans into docile colonial subjects of the Son of Heaven. The Japanese proclaimed insolently: "Koreans should be taught to follow, not to know." The use of the Korean language was forbidden; Korean family names were changed to Japanese; all religions were placed under strict state control and the Shinto doctrine was actively propagated; with one exception, Korean language newspapers and magazines were suppressed; independent labor unions were crushed; public assembly and freedom of speech were banned. For a Korean to entertain ten dinner guests, a special written permit was required. Korean political parties were dissolved; heavy industry, transport, communications, and banking were kept in Japanese hands; Korea's foreign trade was integrated completely into the Japanese home economy.

As Japan's area of aggression expanded, the Japanese were faced with an ever-growing need for Korean loyalty and Korean labor. Not all Koreans were anti-Japanese. Many of them found it extremely safe and profitable to collaborate. They were rewarded not only with land and money but with high-sounding positions in the administration. While the Japanese were making concessions to upper-class Koreans, they impressed several hundred thousand workers for forced labor in Japan, China and Manchuria. They paid Koreans less than half of what Japanese received for equivalent work. They filled their jails with dissidents. In 1935 the Japanese made 206,214 arrests and in 1937 they reported they were holding 6,000 "political prisoners" in Seoul alone.

4

In 1940, to counteract growing admiration and support among Korean factions for the effective Communist resistance to the Japanese, Kuomintang strategists took the Provisional Government out of the diplomatic closet in Chungking. Kim Koo, the aged terrorist, was President and Dr. Rhee the Washington envoy. Rhee actively solicited support for his "pro-American" government as a dike against the flood of Communism in Northern Asia. In Chungking a "Korean Independence Army" was established but it never fought any battles.

The Communists, meanwhile, organized the Korean People's Emancipation League under Wu Ting. Its headquarters in Yenan, the Communist capital, served as a center for militant Koreans in North China and Manchuria, and as a haven for leaders escaping from Seoul. During 1944 and 1945 the League, which had been running a military and political training school near Yenan for its 2,000 active cadres, sent members to infiltrate Japanese lines. These agents helped increase to a fairly high percentage the desertions of Koreans drafted into the Japanese army and labor corps. The Korean peasant conscripts never had proved thoroughly reliable. As early as 1935, 7,000 of them mutinied near Canton, killing their Japanese officers.

In Korea, working with remnants of local resistance groups, the agents from Yenan spurred industrial sabotage as well as uprisings against compulsory military training and conscription. Their leaflets urged the peasants to hide all surplus food supplies, to listen to Yenan's anti-Japanese broadcasts, to resist Emperor worship. The issue of labor conscription (300,000 were sent to Japan from 1941 to 1945) roused the countryside as nothing had since 1919. Men dragged from their families and homes often resorted to suicide to avoid deportation. At a favorite suicide spot, one of Seoul's main bridges, the Japanese posted a sign: "PLEASE WAIT FIVE MINUTES."

Japanese authorities were ruthless in suppressing opposition. But at times it was more than they could handle. As early as September 1940 over 200,000 Christians started a non-co-operation movement patterned after the Hindu example. Despite the danger, an estimated half-million students, farmers and workers were taking some part in illegal anti-Japanese activities inside Korea by the war's end. As an indication of how much this revived Korean nationalism troubled the Japanese, Hirohito granted the Koreans the right of representation in the Japanese Imperial Diet in April 1945—thirty-five years after Korea had become a part of the Empire and less than half a year prior to V-J Day.

This same month the Korean Emancipation League issued a call urging all Koreans in all countries to form a united front based on opposition to Japan and on the principles of democracy. This unity, the manifesto declared, would lead to a democratic Korean republic. Inspired by the Cairo Declaration of 1943 the big powers which pledged Korean independence "in due course," the various organizations in exile committed themselves to unity. This unity lasted only as long as the Japanese occupation.

CHAPTER XIII

AMG: THE LIBERATORS' CONQUEST

IN THE three weeks which elapsed between the announcement of the Japanese surrender and the landing of American forces at Inchon (Seoul's port) the Korean people reacted violently and characteristically to their long-delayed freedom. Nervously the Japanese sent messages to the Americans suggesting that they hasten their landing date. Koreans were going on an unrestrained holiday. They quit their jobs. Fearing reprisals, Japanese paid Korean laborers a year's "tear money"—the Korean equivalent of severance pay. Authorities released stores of rice wine, beer, and food.

The Koreans, for the first time within the memory of most, dared talk back to the puppet police without fear of arrest or assault. They celebrated the release from jail of thousands of political prisoners. They tore down the Shinto shrines where they once had been obliged to show obeisance. They organized law and order patrols and self-government councils under the supervision of resistance leaders, many of whom were Communists.

After so many decades of enforced restraint, Korean political self-expression swept the country like a torrential flood. On August 15, the uneasy Japanese authorities recognized, after the fact, Korea's right to form self-government councils. They tried, but failed, to find a conservative Korean to act as representative of the Korean people. By August 31, there were "People's Committees" in one hundred and forty-five cities and villages. On September 6 these Committees sent six hundred delegates to a national convention in Seoul called by Lyuh Woon Heung, a famous resistance leader. The delegates elected a constitutional draft committee, a group to preside over the central government, and proclaimed a People's Republic. This new "government" claimed the support of a majority of the Korean people with backing from trade unions, peasant organizations, youth and women's federations, Lyuh's People's Party, and the small Korean Communist Party under Pak Heung Nung. The conservatives remained skeptical, the collaborators remained in hiding.

The platform of the People's Republic quickly won it additional popular approval. It was pledged to: (1) confiscate all Japanese-owned land and distribute it free to farmer-tillers; (2) expropriate holdings of Korean collaborators and Japanese and to place public utilities, mines, large industries and plants under State ownership; (3) guarantee civil liberties; (4) establish equality of sexes; (5) lower the voting age to eighteen years; (6) abolish child labor and put into effect minimum wage laws, minimum living standards, rationing and an eight-hour working day; (7) conduct a vigorous campaign for universal literacy and against black-marketeers, usurers and militarists; and (8) place the state militia and police on a volunteer basis.

If the Koreans had specific ideas on what to do with Korea's future, the American liberators whom they awaited had none. At the time of the Japanese surrender neither the United States Army, Navy nor State Department had anybody especially trained to assume command or any occupation functions in Korea. The late General Joseph Stilwell, who knew more about the Far East than any American commander with the possible exception of General Douglas MacArthur, had been penciled in as commander of U. S. forces in Korea. At the last moment someone fairly high up in Washington decided that Stilwell's appointment ought to be cleared with Generalissimo Chiang Kai-shek because Chiang had objected to "Vinegar Joe" in China. No official statement has been made on Chiang's reply, but Stilwell was not sent to Seoul.

In his place went Lieutenant General John Reed Hodge, Commander of the 24th Corps and a hero of the Okinawa campaign. Hodge is stocky and pugnacious, with a gimlet eye and a lantern jaw. When he smokes his pipe he resembles Popeye the Sailor Man. Born in Golconda, Ill. fifty-two years ago, Hodge originally studied architectural engineering. At the age of twenty-four he was commissioned a second lieutenant; in 1918 he was sent to France where he eventually commanded a company in the Meuse-Argonne drive. Since then he has been a professional soldier. Between wars he was trained in military science and tactics, chemical warfare, air corps tactics, and General Staff operations at six different army schools. In the Pacific during the last war he commanded troops in the battles for Guadalcanal, Leyte, and Okinawa. He was wounded near Bougainville.

Hodge landed in Korea with a "draft directive" which failed to include concrete proposals concerning immediate political and economic matters. The one thing on which he had definite orders was the disarming of the Japanese. On September 9, 1945, the day he received the formal surrender of 120,000 Japanese troops in Seoul, Hodge began stepping on Korean's sensibilities. Announcing that Korea's desire for immediate independence could not be granted, Hodge stated that "to prevent chaos" he would temporarily retain Japanese in office including the notorious Governor General Noboyuki Abe.

According to George H. McCune, who at this time in 1945 was chief of the Korean desk in the State Department's Office of Far Eastern Affairs, the draft directive which General Hodge had received prior to his departure from Okinawa "explicitly stated that he was to remove the Japanese administrators, though retaining for the time the general structure of the government. An elementary political sense should have dictated the immediate removal of at least a token number of top-ranking Japanese officials, but apparently Hodge's advisers were too shortsighted to realize this."

The Koreans never forgave Hodge for this initial mistake. They were further enraged when Japanese police fired into a friendly Korean demonstration gathered at Inchon to welcome the Americans. U. S. officers upheld this Japanese action, afraid that Korean parades might interfere with the smooth flow of troop debarkations.

Hodge received little in the way of sound advice from Washington or from his own untrained aides. His political adviser on the spot was a State Department specialist on Japan who had had no previous experience with Korean problems. As Military Governor Hodge installed Major General Archibald V. Arnold, a beefy West Pointer who had been an outstanding football player. At the outset, Arnold's entire staff of officers for Military Government purposes consisted of one hundred and nine men. The vast majority of them had received no instruction for their assignments except a few hurried lectures on geography and past politics before leaving Okinawa or Manila. There was not a Korean language specialist in the entire contingent and they arrived without any adequate translators. Later Secretary of War Patterson "reinforced" Hodge's staff of advisers by sending him a former Brooklyn newspaper publisher and a Russian-speaking former second-secretary at the U. S. Embassy in Moscow under William C. Bullitt. When General Arnold was named to head the U. S. delegation in the talks with the Russians, Major General Archer L. Lerch, a specialist in military law, became Military Governor until his death in September, 1947.

Through no fault of his own, Hodge continued to make embarrassing blunders. On September 11 he told reporters that the political situation among Koreans was "chaotic with no central theme except desire for immediate independence. . . . As a matter of fact the Japanese are my most reliable sources of information. . . ." Hodge also declared that Korea would have independence "in due course." The Koreans, who had lived with this phrase since the Cairo Conference in 1943, thought it now meant "in a few weeks." Hodge hastened to comply with a MacArthur directive which ordered him to replace all Japanese in governmental positions as rapidly as possible "consistent with the safety of operations." MacArthur had been so instructed by the Joint Chiefs of Staff in Washington.

After waiting forty years for independence the Koreans were understandably impatient and irrational. What stuck in their minds was the word "chaotic" and the fact that it took Hodge at least two more months before the last Japanese had been removed from a position of importance. Both Hodge and MacArthur had failed to realize quickly enough that Korea was *not* a conquered country.

For a year and a half the Koreans lived in fear of Hodge while Hodge lived in the green-roofed mansion which had been built for the Japanese Governor General. This was another mistake in psychology by the Americans. In Tokyo, MacArthur could make a sound case for his haughty manner and his regal style of living. Actually, Hodge picked the Governor General's home for its plumbing and other utilities; but the Koreans decided Hodge was just a new overlord residing in the old overlord's high-walled mansion. Even in the spring of 1947 when Hodge embarked on a successful tour of southern Korea to "meet the people," he rode in the pearl-inlaid private car previously reserved for Japanese royalty. Fortunately the man's basic simplicity and his guilelessness, plus the rumored pledges of greater American aid in the form of imported foodstuffs and money for economic rehabilitation, made the countryside respond more warmly to Hodge than they ever had to a

Japanese governor. But in the intervening months there was little real understanding on either the American or the Korean side.

2

It is true that the complex problems demanding solution in Korea might have been almost insurmountable even if the Americans had been prepared for them and had approached them intelligently. In the very first days Hodge's headquarters were barraged by questions and petitioners. Koreans wanted to know: "Why is our country split in two?" and "Where is our provisional government?" Hodge had no answer for the former, reported the latter to his superiors.

A quick decision had to be reached on the question of what to do about the People's Republic. Hodge had no authority to recognize any government. When one of Lyuh's eager and injudicious supporters protested that the Russians in their zone had immediately recognized the local committees of the People's Republic, Hodge instinctively began to oppose them. His junior officers, who had made a superficial survey among English-speaking Koreans in Seoul, reported back that these self-government committees were "little more than armed mobs."

At almost every juncture Hodge demonstrated a brand of diplomacy which during the war might have passed as praiseworthy bluntness; now, however, it led to some uneasy situations. For example, there was Hodge's famous remark that as far as he could see the Koreans "are the same breed of cats as the Japanese." The commanding general's appraisal of Koreans never appeared in the public press but in Oriental countries word-of-mouth transmission has a way of spreading further and more rapidly than any other means of communication. Hodge later denied the remark and said he meant that to Koreans, all Japanese or Korean police "are the same breed of cats." But the harm had been done.

In an awkward effort to give Korea a semblance of self-administration, Hodge appointed an eleven-man Advisory Council headed by a wealthy landlord. This man had also been active as an adviser to the Japanese and was almost universally hated and distrusted throughout Korea. It is almost inconceivable that Hodge could have named him without knowing his background. Reacting against co-operation with the People's Republic, Hodge had placed AMG in at least a temporary alliance with extremely conservative Korean politicians who had the backing of only a small minority. "These mistakes," reported Harold Sugg, a newspaperman who served in AMG under Hodge, "almost destroyed the confidence of the Korean people in Americans and are still hampering all of our efforts."

The Koreans responded to Hodge's seeming lack of understanding with impulsive antagonism. There were threats, boycotts, and strikes. Independent Koreans had long ago adopted the attitude that good citizenship under foreign domination meant fooling the government, hiding foodstuffs, avoiding taxes, and generally making things as difficult as possible. It seemed to them that Hodge had come not to further their freedom but to obstruct it. The direct method of reducing this anarchistic tendency would have been to thrust as much responsibility as possible upon respected Korean officials. Hodge argued that this was not immediately possible. The last three generations of Koreans had not been highly educated; only the sons of pro-Japanese families had been allowed to receive training for administrative positions. Korea lacked a large white-collar class. AMG did not have, by its own standards, one hundred, much less ten thousand, Koreans necessary to fill the gaps left by the departing Japanese bureaucracy who had run everything from railroads to banks.

This lack of trained personnel among the Koreans placed an additional heavy strain on AMG which it was not equipped to handle. In Japan, where the enemy bureaucracy was utilized, the situation was completely different. It served to make it more difficult for MacArthur, who commanded but never visited the American sector in Korea, to understand the enormity of Hodge's problems. After a while SCAP was consulted less frequently, and Hodge could communicate directly with Washington.

To replace the Japanese officials, Hodge and his aides looked around for "cats" who resembled Americans more than they resembled Japanese. Quite naturally they selected the well-dressed and the soft-spoken who had some knowledge of Western manners and methods. Lieutenant Commander George Z. Williams, U. S. N., son of a former missionary in Korea, was assigned the task of obtaining Korean officials. He drew them chiefly from among Korean Christians, most of whom belonged to the Korean Democratic Party. This small ultra-conservative group composed of middle-class landlords and educated Koreans who had collaborated with the Japanese also supplied the key personnel for Hodge's Advisory Council. As an example, Yu Uk Kyum, who made recruiting speeches for the Japanese during the war urging young Koreans "to die for the fatherland," became head of the Department of Education for AMG. Yu's proselytizing for the Japanese was known to many Koreans and his record was presumably available to Hodge's political advisers.

3

Koreans made up for lost time talking and living politics. A disillusioned American officer in Seoul said, "Every time two Koreans sit down to eat they form a new political party." In October, a month after the landings, all political parties were ordered to register with AMG. The national preoccupation with politics was such that by November 2, two hundred and five parties had presented claims for recognition. Among them were the Forlorn Hope Society, the Supporters' Union for All Korean Political Actors, the Getting Ready Committee for the Return of the Provisional Korean Republic Government, and the Boy Scouts. The Boy Scouts, incidentally, proved so dangerous in their efforts to thwart law and order that they had to be disbanded.

Until the war's end Koreans had been united by a common cause. When the need for unity against the Japanese disappeared, Korean politics became "chaotic." The people knew in general what they wanted but they did not have the political maturity to decide which new party offered the best road for reaching the goal. Since few of the parties had any record of performance and their labels were almost meaningless, the Koreans were attracted by the personalities and achievements of various leaders rather than party policies.

Gradually out of the confused political spectrum two dominant bands emerged. On the right was the Korean Provisional Government based in China since 1919, and on the left the People's Republic. The rightists generally agreed with the People's Republic platform, published shortly after V-J Day, on the need for agrarian reform and government direction of large industry and utilities. But the conservatives were not willing to redistribute the lands of Korean absentee landlords (as well as Japanese holdings) and they believed that eventually Korean big business should resume ownership and operation of large enterprises.

The right also had the disadvantage which afflicted every government in exile except the Czech: by default they had surrendered to the left the active leadership of the people in the war of resistance.

During the first year of the occupation in the southern zone the outstanding Korean political figures were: Syngman Rhee and Kim Koo on the right; Kimm Kiusic on the right center; Lyuh Woon Heung on the left center; and Pak Heung Nung on the left. Their careers form an interesting pattern. The labels "right" and "left" are used only for relative identification to each other and are by no means absolute.

The most widely known and respected Korean political figure, at least in the United States, has been Rhee Syngman (in the Western order of surname last, Syngman Rhee). He is also the oldest (seventy-three) and probably the most conservative.

Born of a well-to-do family in Seoul, Rhee first attended a Confucian school and later came under the influence of American Methodist missionaries. In 1897, at the age of twenty-three, after a brief career as a journalist, Rhee was thrown into prison by the Korean Emperor for advocating a constitutional government for Korea. During the subsequent seven years of internment, Rhee wrote a book called *The Spirit of Independence* which won him standing as a scholar and philosopher. In 1904, with the help of his missionary friends, he was able to leave Korea. He went to the United States where he took his B.A. degree at George Washington University, his master's degree at Harvard, and his Ph.D. at Princeton. At the latter university he became an ardent disciple of Princeton's president, Woodrow Wilson.

In 1910 Rhee returned to Korea to help organize the Korean Christian Student Movement. His activities soon ran afoul of the Japanese thought-control police and he was threatened with arrest. Because of the intercession of influential Korean families and American friends, Rhee was released on the condition that he leave the country. Back in the United States he began his long crusade to win moral support for his country's cause.

After the mass demonstration of 1919 in Seoul which was at least partly inspired by Rhee's interpretation of the Wilsonian principles of self-determination for small nations, several thousand other political exiles convened in Shanghai. In the French concession, protected from the Japanese and Chinese police who frequently worked together, they planned to form a government in exile. According to legend, Rhee, with a fancy price on his head, was smuggled into Shanghai in a coffin. The exiles elected Rhee as first president of their Provisional Government.

Rhee preached an admixture of Christian and Wilsonian tenets to his colleagues in Shanghai, all of whom did not agree with Rhee's quiet dependence on moral and diplomatic pressures by the great democracies to obtain full justice for Korea. In fact, Rhee's cabinet was headed by the militant General Li Tung-hui who had led the Manchurian-based Korean guerrillas against the Japanese and who believed in more direct methods than did Rhee.

For the first five years of its existence the Provisional Government was torn by internal disputes. When Rhee and his "American group" supporters proved adamant, Li resigned from the coalition and returned to the north to continue his work with the "Siberian Manchurian group." He died in Moscow in 1928.

Turning over most of his duties to Kim Koo, Rhee returned again to the United States as plenipotentiary for the Shanghai group. He set up a Korean Commission in Washington drawing on the support of Korean residents in America, and operated it as a lobby for U. S. recognition of his government. In 1932, after Japan had invaded Manchuria, Rhee went to Geneva to raise the Korean question before the League of Nations. He was no more successful there than he had been twenty-five years before at Portsmouth, N. H. when Theodore Roosevelt had not shown much interest in Korea's plea for independence. In 1934 he took a different course and went to Moscow seeking financial aid. Turned down, he became more anti-Soviet than ever. At the San Francisco Conference Rhee bid for publicity with an unfounded claim that Korea had been ceded to Russia at Yalta.

On October 16, 1945, Rhee returned to Korea after thirty-five years, ostensibly the guest of General Hodge. "I have no connection whatever with any group or government. I come as a private citizen of Korea," Rhee announced. His return had been eagerly anticipated by Americans and Koreans for much the same reason: they hoped that this almost legendary septuagenarian could end the squabbling among other Korean leaders and political groups and form a coalition.

Hodge personally introduced him to a mass meeting of 50,000 Koreans. In his speech, Rhee blasted Russia and the Communists. By his side at this and subsequent rallies was his Viennese wife, who did not speak any Korean. This heightened the feeling that Rhee had grown away from his native country during his long exile and the leftists wisecracked: "Rhee may be the father of our country but she will never become the mother."

Rhee was not to prove the answer for the Koreans; according to one observer, he turned out to be "a sentimental old man with uninhibited animosity toward the Soviet Union and the leftists." He had failed in exile to get united support and there was no reason to suppose he could do it in hectic Seoul.

Kim Koo, also over seventy, is a hard-bitten, self-educated nationalist and terrorist. In 1899 when he was twenty-three Kim strangled with his bare hands Captain Tsuchida, the Japanese who murdered the Korean Queen. Kim left a note on the dead body identifying himself as the avenger, giving his reasons and his address. Impressed by this last bit of information, the Japanese picked him up, tried him and ordered him put to death. Later, when Kim's sentence was commuted to life imprisonment, he contrived to escape. In 1910 he reappeared to oppose the colonization of Korea by the Japanese and was arrested again. This time they kept him in chains for seven years.

After that Kim went into exile, helped form the 1919 Provisional Government in Shanghai and continued to act as its head when Rhee went to America. Although he believed in acts of individual terrorism, he supported the Rhee non-revolutionary group rather than Li's. His most successful exploit in his own particular field was the bombing in Shanghai's Hongkew Park in 1932. As a result of this the Japanese Commander in Chief, General Shiragawa, lost his life, Admiral Nomura, later Japan's Ambassador to Washington at the time of Pearl Harbor, lost an eye, and Mamoru Shigemitsu, who signed the surrender for Japan aboard the *Missouri*, lost a leg. This made Kim a great Korean hero, a position which he reinforced by marrying the daughter of An Chung Kuen, assassin of Prince Ito at Harbin in 1909.

After Japan invaded China in 1937 Kim lost touch with the underground in Korea and was supported more and more by Chiang's government. He helped organize a corps of Korean agents for Tai Li, the late chief of the Kuomintang secret police. Kim's faithfulness was rewarded in 1940 when the Kuomintang resuscitated the Korean Provisional Government and made Kim its leader.

On November 23, 1946, Kim left China to return to Seoul. In an interview he professed an earnest desire to bring all shades of political opinion together. He said he believed in agrarian and economic reform although he was uncertain how it should be accomplished. On his arrival in Korea, Kim stated further that he did not like the idea of two zones and he did not know whether Koreans wanted to go Communist or extreme right. He, too, came as a "private citizen" to co-operate with AMG in establishing "order." Asked what was the first step in this direction, Kim replied it was necessary to reduce the number of parties. After conferences with General Hodge, Kim met with the other Korean leaders in an unsuccessful attempt to reach a settlement.

Kimm Kiusic, a graduate of Randolph Macon College, is a frail professor who claims he "hates politics." A doctor of philosophy, he was an official of the Provisional Government formed in Shanghai. During his years of exile he taught at a college in Tientsin. In the Provisional Government he was generally considered a middle-of-the-road thinker who helped bridge the gap between Rhee and some of the more radical elements. He was at first by-passed by AMG in their quest for a unity leader, but after Rhee and Kim had failed to win unity, Hodge leaned more and more upon the younger Kimm in his efforts to achieve a coalition without the pro-Soviet left. This attempt to isolate the left continued despite the fact that the early months did little to diminish the standing of Lyuh and the now illegal People's Republic. The *New York Times* correspondent, R. J. H. Johnston, an ardent admirer of Hodge, reported on January 5, 1946, that conservatives supporting the Provisional Government had "fallen far behind liberal as well as radical factions in Korean political groups" and that the People's Republic "continues to gain strength in rural areas."

The leader of the People's Republic was, until his death, the most interesting and baffling character on the Korean political scene. When he was assassinated, Lyuh Woon Hueng was a sixty-two-year-old journalist, robust, handsome, and extremely popular despite his egotism and eccentricity. In his youth he had been a famous athlete. Like the other Korean heroes, he was involved in the 1919 independence movement and later fled to Shanghai. But unlike the others he returned to Korea and began the struggle for eventual freedom, sharing the life of the people who would have to achieve it. During the past twenty years he had several jail sentences for illegal activities. When funds and materials were available, he published a Korean language newspaper in Seoul despite the rigid censorship. This was finally and completely shut down by the Japs.

When his People's Republic was declared illegal by AMG, Lyuh devoted his activities to his left-of-center People's Party. On Rhee's return to Korea, Lyuh offered him the leadership of the party in the interests of Korean unity. Rhee refused, intimating that Lyuh was a "Red." Lyuh was continually criticized by the center and right for his willingness to co-operate with the Communists in a popular-front program. After Rhee and Kim Koo became active in Seoul politics, it became apparent that Lyuh had a much larger personal following than either of them. AMG political strategy then focused on the problem of finding arguments which could persuade Lyuh to drop the Communists and co-operate with the other parties against them. Early in 1946 a unity council was appointed including moderates and progressives as well as the conservatives. Lyuh at first agreed to serve on it but later changed his mind when the Communists denounced the council as "unrepresentative and undemocratic."

The council met on February 14 with Rhee as chairman and Kim Koo and Kimm Kiusic as vice-chairmen. When Lyuh backed out, feeling that Rhee and Kim had too much personal control, a segment of his People's Party (including his own brother) split away from him and backed the new council. After this Lyuh went through various shifts in his political position. In midsummer 1946 he wanted to retire from political life but by September he was as active as ever, announcing, "I am going to start again as head of the People's Party to set a new course. I demand that the Communists should get out of the party." A month later Lyuh was kidnapped and when he reappeared he said "numerous people" had tried to persuade him not to co-operate too much with American efforts to form a South Korean legislature. AMG surmised this was the work of the local Communist Party. After several unsuccessful attempts on his life, Lyuh was assassinated on July 19, 1947, by an unidentified gunman.

The Communist leader in South Korea, Pak Heung Nung, is

under fifty. He is a small, nervous man who wears horn-rimmed glasses over his bright eyes, and speaks little English. He participated in the 1919 independence movement before he became a Marxist. After the flight of the older leaders to Shanghai, Pak remained in Korea, studied Communist literature and became head of the illegal Young Communist League. He was jailed by the Japanese from 1922 to 1924 and 1926 to 1928. He was very ill when he emerged from his second term of imprisonment and was smuggled out of the country through Siberia. He spent a year or more in Moscow recuperating and being trained as an agent of the Comintern. Returning to Korea, he resumed his underground activities. The Japanese caught him again in 1933 and put him behind bars until 1939. In that year he was elected General Secretary of the Korean Party.

After Japan's defeat, many of Pak's supporters were released from jail. With them he helped Lyuh organize the self-government committees which led to the formation of the People's Republic. At that time the membership of the Communist Party was less than 5,000. When the Americans came, Pak favored the coalition government, but not one which would exclude the Communists or be overloaded "with respectable, swell-headed conservatives." He told reporters he would co-operate with all parties and that Korea should have a short occupation with simultaneous withdrawal by both the Russians and Americans. He also favored the abolition of the 38th Parallel.

Because of terrorist threats on his life, Pak has kept in hiding much of the time. But when Kim Koo returned, Pak, as well as Lyuh, conferred with him and agreed to back him. Pak said, "I agree we should all work with Mr. Kim," and added that the Provisional Government plus the People's Republic could merge to become the interim Korean government. This idea appealed to most of the important leaders except Dr. Rhee, who did not like the idea of collaboration with the Communists, and balked at the coalition. In a showdown between Kim and Rhee, Rhee held the high card—the backing of Hodge.

Gradually the split between the Provisional Government grouping and the People's Republic grouping (although they changed their official names and titles many times) widened. In August 1946 Pak announced plans to merge the left into a South Korea Labor Party (including the Communists and the People's Party) which would then merge with the North Korea Labor Party to become the All-Korea Labor Party. Before this program got very far, Lyuh was won over to the support of Kimm Kiusic's plan for an interim legislature for South Korea, half appointed and half elected.

With the Communists isolated from the left-of-center group, AMG began to crack down on them as undesirable elements. In September 1946 several Communist leaders were arrested; three pro-Communist newspapers were banned on the grounds that they were endangering the security of the occupation forces; and Pak was forced to flee to the northern zone for temporary protection.

CHAPTER XIV

TWO SIDES OF THE PARALLEL

A GLANCE at the map reveals why the Soviet Union regards its zone in Korea as vitally important. Northeast Korea is contiguous with Soviet Siberia; the Korean peninsula dominates both Dairen and Port Arthur, where Russia has special interests; and the strategic port of Vladivostok is less than a two-hour drive along a good road from the Korean border, and a few minutes by air. These are the obvious reasons why the Russians are not apt to quit Korea until they can be certain, in the words of Colonel General Terenti Shtikov (chief Soviet spokesman at the joint talks with the United States in Seoul) that Korea will emerge as "a true democratic, independent country, friendly to the Soviet Union, so that in the future it will not become a base for an attack on the Soviet Union."

These are almost the exact words which I had heard Premier Stalin and other Soviet leaders use in 1944 to describe Russia's interest and intent in Poland. It serves to underscore the opinion of a Red Air Force major whom I met in Siberia last summer. He was just returning from six months in Korea. "It is the Poland of the East," he told me, "and the Koreans are just as proud and difficult as the Poles."

This account of what has happened in northern Korea is based chiefly on two sources: Soviet accounts, checked where possible against the reports of the few Americans who have been allowed to enter the Soviet zone; and from the statements of Koreans who have left the area.

The Soviets moved into northern Korea on August 2, 1945, with an army estimated at 200,000 men. They were not the Red Army's finest troops, not the most disciplined. In their ranks were many ex-prisoners who had been banished to the Siberian frontier regions. The units which rushed into Korea carried along with them only

211

limited supplies. They took over existing Japanese storehouses, but much of the food in them had to be dished out to the thousands of surrendered Japanese troops who fell into the Red Army's hands. Almost immediately the Russians began to "live off the land," a process which did not endear them to Koreans, regardless of political hue.

Their occupation of Korea found the Soviets almost as unprepared and untrained for the job as the Americans with one extremely important difference. The Americans, in time, imported a few aged and conservative Korean exiles and looked to them for assistance and leadership. The Russians imported from nearby Siberia as many as thirty thousand of the reported eight hundred thousand Korean emigrés who had become Soviet citizens. They were loyal and thoroughly familiar with Soviet ideology and methodology. This enabled the Russians to set up a Korean-speaking bureaucracy between themselves and the local population. It also enabled them very quickly to turn out of office and imprison not only the hated Japanese officialdom but also Koreans accused as pro-Japanese collaborationists. Local Red Army officials did not have to wait for definitive directives from Moscow. Nor were they lacking in faithful translators or aides who had a knowledge of the Korean nation.

The Soviets never set up a formal Russian "Military Government." Under Marshal Vasilievsky's orders, undoubtedly approved in advance by the Politburo in Moscow, the Red Army occupation officials eagerly co-operated with the locally elected left-wing workers and peasants committees of the People's Republic. To the Soviets, a prison record under the Japanese was a recommendation and a badge of honor. While we put our faith in those who had an interest in the status quo, the Russians backed those who had fought for change.

For five months the Russians supported a leader in Pyongyang (Heijo), their capital, chosen early in August by the Korean patriots. Cho Man Sik, a practicing Christian and a non-practicing lawyer, was often called "Korea's Gandhi" because of his repeated sponsorship of passive resistance to the Japanese overlords and his campaign for home industry and handcrafts. He always wore the traditional Korean costume of baggy white pantaloons, blouse, and stiff horsehair hat. As the purge of pro-Japanese or anti-Russian Koreans spread, Cho resisted Red Army directives.

In January 1946 Cho was replaced by Kim Il Sung. This almost legendary Korean leader was credited with having led guerrilla warfare against the Japanese in Manchuria for almost ten years despite the fact he is now in his mid-thirties. When he returned to Pyongyang from the Chinese Communist capital, Yenan, Kim was met by Korean welcoming committees who hailed him as the new "chief." Korean conservatives in the American zone, worried by the almost magical appeal of the name "Kim Il Sung" among the peasantry, publicly denounced him as an impostor. The real Kim Il Sung, they claimed, was dead.

Dead or alive, the Russian-speaking Kim became Secretary-General of the Communist Party in the northern zone and, in practice, the head of the interim government in that sector. His headquarters were in the former Presbyterian Hospital while the Soviet commanders moved into the Mission Ladies' Home.

2

During the early months, confiscations, cattle-stealing, and watch-snatching purportedly went on almost unchecked in the Russian zone until the arrival of special police troops released from duty in Manchuria. While these taking ways of the Russians were unpopular, the occupiers did win support for their immediate retaliation against Japanese and Korean war criminals; for reducing rents so that tenant farmers could retain 70 per cent of their crops; for permitting Japanese holdings to be operated by committees of Korean foremen and workers, often retaining irreplaceable Japanese technicians under them. The black market in rice was ruthlessly stamped out. A Korean militia was formed under the leadership of Soviet Koreans. Food rationing was instituted and strictly followed. Japanese prisoners of war were put to work building roads and other public works. Japanese paper currency was abolished.

Large landowners, those suspected of collaboration, and others who for one reason or another preferred American to Russian domination, fled across the border to the southern zone. (In all, General Hodge reported, almost eight hundred thousand entered the U. S. sector from the north.) Meanwhile the North Korea People's Interim Committees confiscated their farms and belongings and parceled them out to their former tenants. No family which did not actually cultivate its own land was permitted to receive an allotment. Priority in the distribution of these free twelve-and-a-half acre plots was accorded those who had resisted the Japanese. The local Committees undoubtedly saw to it that those receiving land grants kept in good political standing. On March 3, 1947, Kim Il Sung was able to announce that 2,404,406 acres of land had been distributed free to 724,522 farm laborers, landless peasants and tillers of small plots.

After the return of Kim Il Sung, the occupation authorities issued a directive requiring all Korean males between sixteen and sixty to carry a special passport. Without this passport an individual's life was not worth much; he could not even draw rations. To obtain the necessary papers, the Koreans were obliged to declare their unconditional support for the Moscow Declaration on Trusteeship.

The political and economic pattern in northern Korea developed in a manner similar to that in Yugoslavia, Bulgaria and in other Soviet-influenced countries. A "government bloc" was formed, embracing all political parties which favored nationalization, land distribution and independence under the Moscow provisions. On June 24, 1946, the North Korea People's Interim Committee—a super-cabinet including many labor leaders—issued a series of ordinances providing for compulsory education, social insurance, an eight-hour day, and a child-labor law. It established the right of every citizen to work and declared that "equal wages shall be paid to workers for equal work and skill regardless of age and sex."

In their attitude toward organized religion, the Russians were more liberal than some of the Korean extremists. The Soviets neither condemned nor condoned religion. They immediately granted permission for the reconstruction of the Roman Catholic Cathedral in Pyongyang which had been demolished by the Japanese to build anti-aircraft emplacements. On the other hand, they gave no help in the procurement of materials.

An American missionary who had been stationed in Pyongyang prior to the war was permitted to return in the spring of 1947. He found that forty Protestant churches in the Soviet zone were openly flourishing and that Korean divinity students were being permitted religious training at a seminary.

Elections were held in northern Korea on November 3, 1946. Of 4,516,120 eligible registered voters (half the total population),

4,011,813 went to the polls. The pro-government bloc of parties and non-partisans received almost 97 per cent of all votes. The largest number of those elected to office were from the white-collar class, with peasants forming the next biggest group. Of 3,459 successful candidates (including 453 women) for offices ranging from village committees to provincial councils, only 510 were classified as workers. A Russian newspaper analysis of the election lists 1,102 of the 3,459 successful candidates as "labor party" (Communist) members, 351 as "democrats," 253 as representing the Society of Young Friends and 1,753 as non-partisans.

If coercion or disorders occurred at the polls, no reports leaked out. Only Tass and pro-Government Korean reporters were allowed to cover the campaign and the elections.

Economically, a modified nationalization of utilities was carried out. Despite controls, inflation occurred—although intelligence reports indicate it was not nearly so bad as in the south. Food continued short well into 1947 when the Russians sharply curtailed the size of their occupation forces.

3

Except for the conservative flight south and, to a much lesser degree, the occasional radical retreat to the north, little has crossed the 38th Parallel except the wildest kinds of rumors. Koreans in the north heard about supposed atrocities committed by American troops and about American "coddling" of the Japanese, and the southern Koreans heard charges of Russian persecutions against all who opposed them.

Perhaps the most important rumor which has winged its way from Pyongyang to Seoul is that the Soviets have been conscripting, equipping and training a Korean army of 500,000 men. General Hodge's intelligence officers have made every attempt to substantiate this. They are fairly certain that there *is* a Korean army in the north and that at least a portion of it has been drafted.

When General Hodge returned to Washington in March 1947 for consultation, he finally put Korea on the front pages of U. S. newspapers by charging that the Russians were preparing this 500,000-man army and leaving the reader to figure out what it was prepared for. Hodge indicated this was a "report" and not a fact, but most newspaper accounts failed to differentiate. Hodge failed to say, however, that his own intelligence officers had not rated as "very reliable" any of the sources for the stories about an estimated 500,000 Koreans in a conscript army. The stories may or may not be true.

I have inserted this cautionary word because, particularly in the Far East, rumors based on partial truth often become entirely accepted through lack of better information. Major Frezhenko, a Red Army officer who had been stationed in North Korea, told me in Siberia he had heard that American troops were fighting in Manchuria on the side of the Chinese Nationalists against the Communists. His information was, of course, based on the fact that American forces and ships had helped transport Nationalists into Manchuria to fight the Communists. In North Korea they also believed, according to a dispatch I read in *Pravda* datelined from Pyongyang, that the Americans were training a large Korean army in the south, mostly of former Japanese puppet troops. Actually we were organizing a Korean constabulary and many of the officers had served under the Japanese; but it was hardly an army.

Some of the weirdest tales about the Russian zone atrocities have, when checked into, proven untrue. They were originally gathered by reporters and intelligence agents from the frightened Koreans who fled to the south hoping for American leniency. As Ambassador Pauley stated after his Korean stay, "I was present when many returning Koreans were cross-examined and they all broke down and admitted they were reporting things they had heard, and not the things they had seen."

In rare instances Americans have had an opportunity to verify charges against the Russians. Early in the occupation the Red Army occupied the town of Songdo, fifty miles north of Seoul. They remained there for ten days before it was discovered that Songdo was actually five miles below the 38th Parallel; the Russians evacuated and the Americans moved in. Americans who talked to the Korean officials in the town learned that the Russians had helped themselves to over eight million yen in one of the Japanese-controlled banks, and had also usurped 60,000 pounds of ginseng root from a warehouse. News of this latter "liberation" spread so far and wide that a Chinese pharmacist in Shanghai told me all about it eight months later in explaining the high price and scarcity of ginseng, which his customers sought as a male hormone supplement.

4

Following six months of harrowing American-Soviet negotiations, an agreement was ratified for the exchange of mail across the border once a week. The Russians also agreed to supply the American zone with a certain amount of electric current and once traded northern chlorine for southern cotton yarn.

With infrequent exceptions, the Russians have barred their zone to foreign inspection. After months of waiting, Ambassador Pauley, as the President's representative on reparations, was permitted to tour the north for six days. To his surprise Pauley found "There was little evidence of [factory] stripping. In fact, there was considerable evidence of efforts by the Russians to revive industry." This was contrary to "eyewitness reports" which General Hodge had been cabling to Washington for months.

Pauley and his group of observers reported that the Soviets had embarked on a program to propagandize Communism among the people and to obtain control of all existing government and economic functions. Russian-inspired banners and slogans decorated the streets. But, as Mr. Pauley wrote in his diary, "There have been so many incidents between the Soviet forces and the Koreans after dark that General Chistiakov [the Soviet commander in northern Korea, not to be confused with General Shtikov, the chief Soviet negotiator] was forced to issue an order that after dark a Russian must be accompanied by two others, making three in the group. Still, two or three are killed every night by Koreans who have no weapons other than a rock."

It appears obvious even from the slim evidence available, that many democratic Koreans will fight the Russian occupation in the north as obdurately as others will fight the American domination in the south. Many in the north listen to the American broadcasting station in Seoul, JODK, even though it is forbidden; they resent the fact that the only foreign news in their newspapers comes from the wires of Tass, the official Soviet agency; they are angry that Red Army troops were billeted in their churches and temples. Others hate the idea of nationalization and lack of free speech. This is not rumor. It is the explanation for the stream of refugees to the U. S. zone at the rate of almost two thousand a day.

Rightly or wrongly, the Soviets believe most of the Koreans in the north prefer them to the Japanese and that the Koreans are impressed by the quick, effective economic reorganization which the Russians have encouraged local leaders to undertake. No doubt they have also been impressed by the Soviet charge that the Americans went easier on the collaborators and that there was an avoidable famine in the southern zone which reached its peak in June 1946.

Another factor which the Russians say has helped to establish a favorable impression for Soviet policies is the re-acquisition of southern Sakhalin Island (Karafuto). Under the Japanese there were no schools for the large Korean minority. Today, following the Soviet policy of complete cultural recognition for minorities, more than half of southern Sakhalin's fifty schools are conducted in the Korean language. News of this has reached Korea in the pro-Soviet press and through an exchange of "cultural missions" between Pyongyang and the island off the coast of Russia's Maritime Province.

Many northern Koreans, not only the Communists, undoubtedly recognize that since Russia is their neighbor Korea's policy must be based on friendship with the Soviet Union as well as with the United States. As they read their Tass dispatches about continual U.S.–U.S.S.R. frictions, they may become convinced that the anti-Soviet Koreans "being groomed for power" below the 38th Parallel will never be acceptable to the Russians as a Korean government.

5

Without any positive plan, AMG in Korea hoped that a rapid shove in the direction of free enterprise might start the country's stalled economic machine. In the latter part of September 1945 all price controls on rice were lifted. "We didn't have the forces to police such a system, anyhow," an AMG official explained to me in February 1946. The immediate effect of this abolition of controls was to legalize the black market; it was expected that the lure of black market prices would stimulate the flow of foods and goods. The results of this negative policy are best judged from what happened to rice, the chief food staple in southern Korea.

Under the Japanese 40 million bushels of Korean rice had to be exported to Japan annually. The American-occupied zone, which contains approximately 70 per cent of Korea's cultivated lands, harvested nearly 90 million bushels of rice in the fall of 1945, the

biggest crop in many years. Formerly 50 per cent of this crop would
have been exported to the Japanese mainland and a further amount
shipped to northern Korea. After Korea's liberation the entire rice
supply was retained in the American-controlled sector. Koreans
legitimately anticipated that for the first time within memory they
would have an ample food supply, especially as the 1945 crop was
60 per cent over that of 1944. This anticipation was predicated on
a system of controlled prices and rationed distribution, a policy
which had been vigorously supported and enforced by the People's
Committees after the Japanese surrender.

AMG, however, embarked upon its free-trade program, had
ordered the People's Committees dissolved. When controls were
abolished speculators bought up all the rice they could find; well-
to-do families, able to afford the rising prices, gorged themselves.
Greedy farmers, delighted by the skyrocketing prices, hoarded their
rice supplies awaiting even greater profit. Within three months
the rice supply evaporated from the open market; the black market
became so high that only promoters intending to convert rice into
more profitable products such as wine and whisky were able to
afford it. Prices of all staple commodities on the market were
perilously bloated, the average increase being more than 300 per
cent. The Korean worker, and even the tenant farmer who had
sold his rice early in the spiral, approached starvation in the
spring, touched it in June 1946, when the rice ration was only
20 per cent of the minimum needed for subsistence.

Overworked AMG officials were flooded with complaints and
petitions from the Koreans demanding that price ceilings and rationing be resumed and that the authorities take drastic action to stop
the rice hoarding. In many cases, it has been charged, AMG was
reluctant to move against the principal hoarders because they were
"respectable" Korean businessmen upon whom AMG was relying
for support and advice. General Hodge finally ordered a survey of
rice futures; the outlook was so discouraging that the original
program was abandoned to some extent in March 1946 and directives were issued for the resumption of rationing and the establishment of rice collections under AMG supervision. Since this was
reminiscent of Japanese control, it was not popular with the peasants. The food larder shrank and shrank and in May the Koreans
were receiving only half as much rice as the Japanese. That month
the cost-of-living index reached 14,000 with 1937 as the base period.

Bertram D. Sarafan, an attorney who served with Military Government in Seoul during that period, reported on his return to the United States: "As a result of its handling of the rice problem the Koreans arrived at a complete loss of faith in the Military Government." Koreans, regardless of political affiliation, labeled the American administration "ineffectual and bungling"; increasing numbers of them joined the Communist-led demonstrations against AMG policies.

After the occupation honeymoon was over, Koreans began to ask embarrassing questions concerning AMG's plans for agrarian reform. Everyone, even the Americans, recognized that little had been done under the Japanese to improve the economic status of the peasantry who were 80 per cent of the country's total population.

At the war's end, the historic evils of landlordism, exorbitant rents, usurious interest rates, increasing farm tenancy—with its corollary of concentrated land ownership—and primitive methods of cultivation were still deeply rooted in Korean agriculture. At that time it was estimated that two-thirds of the 11 million acres of cultivated land was owned by 3 per cent of the population. More than half of Korea's farmers were tenants, forced to hand over to absentee landlords from 40 per cent to 80 per cent of their annual harvest. In addition, taxes on rented land were high and the tenant, not the landlord, was forced to pay them.

The official Japanese Year Book (1941-42) which attempts to present Nippon's colonial policies in the most favorable light, reports almost casually about Korea: "Eighty per cent of the farming community may be regarded as having debts, bearing interest at 3 per cent or 4 per cent per month. Expenditure is always greater than income. . . . The farm household generally suffers from a shortage of foodstuffs." The Year Book explains this sad state of affairs with the claim that Korean farmers worked only 100 days per year, while the industrious Japanese farmers labor 200 to 250 days.

The politically expedient policy followed during the first year of occupation by the Americans was to give verbal support to an agrarian reform program which would satisfy the aspiration of the Korean peasant for land of his own. No responsible Korean political party attacked this objective although they began to divide sharply on the best method of redistribution. The more conservative parties believed, in general, that the peasants themselves or the government should foot the bill for the redistributed land. The radical parties, inspired by what had transpired in the Russian-occupied zone, campaigned for free distribution.

Seemingly neither the few experts in AMG nor any of the Korean political leaders had the time, talent, or temerity to investigate the thesis that the smallholders system might not function economically in Korea no matter who paid the initial cost. Korea has a population density of 285 per square mile (U. S.—44 per square mile). Its rate of population growth is 1.1 per cent yearly, greater than that of any European nation except Russia. Even with the improvement of techniques it appears questionable that there is sufficient arable land to support a peasant population working on a private farm basis. Before the war Korea's per capita value of agricultural production was two-thirds less than Japan's—below the minimum required for subsistence. The size of the average Korean farm was less than four acres; the average in the United States is forty-eight times as large.

As in Japan, one approach to higher agricultural productivity may be through mechanization applied to larger farm co-operatives and even collectives. In America where the size of farms is so many times greater, farmers can still enjoy the luxury of disdaining such incursions on individualism and private enterprise. But in Korea the scientific and economical application of farm machinery and modern methods will almost certainly require some kind of controlled planning and communal enterprise on large, contiguous sections of land rather than on the existing cut-up small segments.

To achieve such an end, which goes against the immediate desires of the majority of the Korean people, AMG would have had to embark on a bold, farseeing educational campaign. Not even the Russians, who during the early years of their Revolution found that breaking up the land did not pay, have broached the subject in their zone. As in Poland and the former Baltic States, they have pursued the expedient policy of granting the peasants' desire for land and this policy has won them a certain amount of favor in northern Korea. The Americans, more laggard, failed to cash in completely on the immense popularity of land redistribution. Early in the occupation U. S. authorities seized Japanese-owned property; but a year later they had not yet turned it over to Korean farmers. Theoretically the former Japanese land has been held in escrow. Actually it was AMG's prolonged indecision which gave critical Koreans the opportunity to charge, without concrete refutation, that the confiscated properties might wind up in the possession of wealthy landlords and collaborationists most sympathetic to AMG.

The Communists made good use of AMG's vacillation on the land question in southern Korea. They promised free land to the peasants and claimed that redistribution had been carried out not only in northern Korea but in enemy Japan. As the result of this appeal, an AMG officer reported last winter that in his province, Kyongsang Namdo, the Communists had gained the support of more than twenty thousand indebted share-croppers within a few months.

AMG did little to give Korea confidence by its handling and disposition of Japanese industrial assets. Again policy vacillated. On September 15 it was declared that Japanese property would not be confiscated, but a month later this decision was reversed.

The old Oriental Development Company, largest Japanese holding company in Korea, had owned 64 per cent of Korea's dry lands, 80 per cent of its rice lands, and 350,000 acres of forests; it had controlled the shipbuilding yards, the textile industry, the iron mines, the shoe factory, and the alcohol refinery. AMG renamed this 700 million-dollar octopus "The New Korea Company" and held its assets against future Japanese reparations and Japanese (or Korean) payment of American occupation costs in the southern zone.

To many Koreans this has seemed like American approval for the re-establishment of industrial monopoly in their country. They waited many months in the vain hope that the octopus would be put to work for the good of the Korean people. They were not interested in the wisdom or the legality of the American position. When the New Korea Company slowly began to move its tentacles, Koreans were amazed to find the monopoly's operations still exploited by many of the same people who had been associated with the Oriental Development Company or who had served the Japanese in other capacities. AMG, perhaps guiltlessly, had preordained this reincarnation by requiring ten to twenty years' previous experience in the handling of plant operations from all its Korean executives.

With the stiffening of policy against the Soviet Union and against leftist regimes everywhere which became increasingly evident in May 1946, it was decided to give the Koreans, under Hodge, a 25-million-dollar credit. The left seized on this and claimed it was an attempt to subsidize "special interests." Hodge replied to these attacks that the loan would bring surplus equipment to Korea which the nation needed. He said this charge illustrated the way "well-organized propaganda factories" falsified aims. He reiterated that AMG intended to block any effort of vested interests to operate against the best interests of the Korean people.

Editorial writers in the United States have repeatedly stressed the vital importance of making a first-rate U. S. administrative record in southern Korea. But General Hodge and his assistants, even if they had been supermen, could not have accomplished this end with the quantity and quality of personnel at their command.

For too long a time the American personnel charged with the responsibilities for the New Korea Company consisted of one major and one captain in Seoul, with a field staff of one enlisted man in each province. Regardless of the ultimate wisdom and legitimacy of American policy for disposing of Japanese industrial holdings, the Koreans have not been impressed by our efficiency or our manpower. The Koreans, as well as General Hodge, have had to pay for MacArthur's "I-can-do-it-with-one-hand-behind-my-back" policy.

A lugubrious American colonel with whom I played poker dice in the gloomy bar of the bleak Chosen Hotel in Seoul early in 1946, loosened up sufficiently to remark that MacArthur's economies might make his administrative record look good in the history books and in the publicity releases back in the States. "But I will wager," said the Colonel, "that we are losing twenty dollars or more in occupation costs for every dollar we are saving by skimping on personnel."

Later, when more personnel became available, it was not always judiciously apportioned. The Korean "Department of Commerce" in the spring of 1947 had two hundred sixty-five Americans assigned to it, while the vital "Education Department" had only thirty.

After about the eighth or ninth round of poker dice (the eventual loser footing the bill for that many rounds of drinks), I turned to the red-faced, craggy-nosed Lieutenant Colonel on my other side and asked whether they played this game often.

"Every damn day," he roared, "every damn day. Not another damn thing to do in this place."

"Anybody study Korean?"

"Hell, no. Even the Japs didn't learn the language and they're Orientals. Besides we have enough to do."

"Aren't you training your own translators?"

"What for?" the Lieutenant Colonel bellowed, "it's easier for Koreans to speak our lingo."

I was not surprised some months later when I met a professor from a Seoul college who spoke in scathing tones about our lack of intellect and intellectual curiosity. "You know how to do all kinds of things," he said, "but you do not often know why or where it all leads. Your tempo is too rapid for you to stop and think. But still you waste time because you have an economy built on waste."

When I probed for a fuller explanation, he evidently felt that it was necessary to talk down. His simplification made his meaning clear. "I have a cottage in the hills outside of Seoul. I invited two colonels who are interested in school reform problems to visit me. They got up in the morning and stood for whole minutes debating whether to wear the olive green tie or the khaki tie. Then from the Post Exchange they brought copies of two different magazines covering the news of the week for the same week."

"That's our intellectual curiosity," I pointed out, tongue-in-cheek.

"The wrong variety," said the professor, smiling. "You are lazy, mentally. Do you know I argued with your colonels about education in Korea and when I asked for the source of their erroneous information, they invariably cited their interpreters. That is why the Korean people call your military government 'the interpreters' government.' And the bad thing about that is you will want us to have an interpreters' government, too, when we elect one so that our officials can talk with you."

6

During the first year and even longer, the difficulties of AMG were augmented by the rapid turnover of Army men in Korea. The War Department was slow to begin the recruitment of competent civilian personnel. Even when a belated drive for help was initiated, the importance of the Korean assignment was not sufficiently clarified. Salaries and living conditions did not make the assignment any more attractive. For some regular Army officers Hodge's Korea held a perverse kind of temptation: they believed that in Korea they might be on the spot to get "first crack at the Russians."

Failure to provide proper orientation for the troops has been a factor in permitting U. S. Army morale in Korea to drop dangerously low. Returning from a Far Eastern inspection trip in September 1946, Congressman John E. Sheridan, acting chairman of the House Military Affairs Committee, reported that he found morale of American troops in Korea the "lowest" of any he had seen. He recommended that Hodge be relieved of his post. These charges were not shared by the majority of the Committee and Secretary of War Patterson expressed full confidence in Hodge.

The lot of G.I.'s and officers in Seoul has not been made any easier by the rekindling of Korea's deep-burning anti-foreignism. This antagonism has been fanned by the usual disregard for native customs and sensibilities exhibited by occupying forces. Under the Japanese many Koreans had felt no racial or color barrier. Less adaptive and less eclectic than the Japanese, Koreans did not eagerly embrace American jazz dress, manners, movies, slang, or men. They guarded their women zealously and jealously; fraternization was definitely not encouraged.

"Boy, this sure got my back up," a lieutenant from Seoul told me. "The women just cold shoulder us."

I asked whether he realized that in Korea women were regarded differently, that even married women were not accustomed to being informal with their husband's male friends.

The lieutenant hadn't heard. "I thought they'd get rid of all that feudal nonsense when we bounced the Japs," he said.

Even the Korean Christians did not stretch the admonition "Love thy neighbor" to include lonely G.I.'s. Korea became known as "the end of the line"—a kind of Siberia for American troops. "I'd rather be in prison than in Korea," one G.I. said when he returned to Boston from a year in Korea.

CHAPTER XV

TWO SIDES OF THE ARGUMENT

AT THE Moscow Conference in December 1945 Byrnes, Bevin, and Molotov drew up an agreement on Korea (see Appendix H). Recognizing the desirability of eliminating the arbitrary division at the 38th Parallel, they provided for a Joint U.S.–U.S.S.R. Commission to (1) assist in the formation of a provisional Korean government, and (2) to work with the provisional government and democratic organizations for "the development of democratic self-government and the establishment of the national independence of Korea." It was then stated that the proposals of the Joint Commission be submitted to the U.S., U.S.S.R., United Kingdom, and China "for the working out of an agreement concerning a four-power trusteeship of Korea for a period up to five years."

The first news of this, which reached Korea on December 23, was an incomplete dispatch which only referred to a decision on a "four-power trusteeship." According to General Arnold's aide, "In Seoul, only the dropping of an atomic bomb could have created more excitement. Japan, in 1905, had taken over the land under what was called a 'trusteeship.' Here was the awful word again; Korea had been betrayed!"

Historians may someday be able to fix the blame for this mix-up. Certainly it was not Hodge's fault that the communique was permitted to leak out before he had been fully briefed on its entire contents. The excitable Koreans wasted no time in expressing their reaction. It was violent.

For fear of mass rioting and reprisals, General Hodge, on December 27, ordered all U.S. troops to remain indoors. Koreans, who had closed their shops and declared another informal holiday, demonstrated individually and collectively in the streets. Half-expecting a Soviet invasion to add to his woes, Hodge nervously cabled Washington: "KOREAN REACTION . . . IMMEDIATE AND HYSTERICAL."

When the official text finally arrived on December 28, Hodge undertook to explain the Allied formula to representatives of the local press. He made it plain that the communique provided for a U.S.–Soviet Commission which would lay the groundwork for a new Korean provisional government; that Korean political parties and leaders would be drawn into the discussions and would have a voice in determining their own government. But the bone in the throat was still *sin tak*—"trusteeship." Unable to get around it, Hodge kept repeating that "it" would be limited to five years. But the Korean reporters, like their readers, only knew that "it" meant "trusteeship" and that they were now presumably trading one master (Japan) for two (U.S. and U.S.S.R.).

In the northern zone, the "trusteeship" had been translated into Korean as "guardianship," meaning "help" to an independent nation.

Hodge had no better luck in his efforts to win over Korean politicians. Kimm Kiusic either could not or did not want to understand any rationalization. "Korea had been betrayed again," Kimm kept saying. He realized that this was the feeling of the people. One Korean leader, Song Jin Woo, accepted the Moscow Decision and was assassinated that same day.

Nor could Hodge mollify old Kim Koo who declared on December 31 that he and his rampaging followers were so fed up they had determined to seize the government. They actually did try to take over the judiciary and the police force. That same afternoon they called a mass demonstration and thirty thousand marched menacingly past Hodge's headquarters for an hour and a half, carrying tiny Korean flags and giant banners. Evidently Kim Koo believed that this show of power would induce the Americans to leave or at least to abandon the nonsense about a Soviet-American Commission and trusteeship.

By a strange twist of logic, Kim Koo proclaimed that the left had been responsible for the trusteeship. At the same time Rhee was blaming the U.S. State Department for its "appease Russia at all costs" policy. However, after considerable American pressure, Rhee was prevailed upon to change his mind in public and take a stand against Kim Koo, which he did. During this hectic period Hodge kept signaling Tokyo and Washington requesting amplification, clarification, or explanation. Finally, a cable arrived from Secretary Byrnes. Two doughty Korean members of Military Government were dispatched to locate Kim Koo and appease him. This was not an easy assignment. All the Korean political leaders had surrounded themselves with small private armies of trigger-happy bodyguards and secured themselves in well-protected hideouts. These two unsung Korean heroes found Kim Koo and showed him the face-saving cable from Byrnes which stated, in effect, that Joint Soviet-American Commission may find it possible to dispense with a trusteeship.

Although privately disappointed by the terms of the Moscow Decision, leaders of the People's Republic refrained from public participation in the anti-trusteeship hysteria. AMG has always maintained that they were ready to agitate against the Moscow Decision until they were given the Communist "party-line." For whatever reason, they held a demonstration on January 7, 1946, attended by twice as many as Kim Koo's, and pledged their support for the Moscow Decision. Two days later, after assurances, threats and persuasion from Hodge, all parties signed a joint statement mildly favorable to the Moscow communique.

2

Behind the massive granite pillars of Seoul's pretentious Duk Soo Palace on January 16, 1946, the Joint Soviet-American Commission convened "for the consideration of urgent problems establishing permanent coordination in administrative-economic matters." The American delegation was headed by Major General Arnold, assisted by Lieutenant Colonel Charles W. Thayer. The Soviets sent as their negotiator bull-necked Colonel General Terenti Shtikov, with Simeon K. Tsarapkin, one of their top-drawer diplomats, as his adviser.

After pleasantries had been exchanged through interpreters things got off to a poor start. The Korean and American press were not given free access to any of the principals or their spokesmen. Instead of waiting for the bare communiques, reporters indulged in speculative stories based on unreliable rumors. One story which received a good deal of attention in the American press described how the Russians had behaved like boors, ordering General Hodge's car out of the garage to make room for their own, and generally acting unfriendly and obstreperous. While the Russians were evidently none too friendly, the story of their bad conduct in the local hotel was completely embroidered.

The Americans were too uneasy about the Russian position in

Korea to make their visitors feel at home. This amusing incident which highlights how badly the social program was planned, was described to this reporter by Alfred Eisenstaedt, the photographer, who was present at the Seoul meeting: "I arrived at nine o'clock at General Hodge's house. The Russians and Americans were having cocktails but I am told by Hodge's aide that I can take any picture I want but not one with cocktail glasses or vodka. They didn't want any of that. It was in fact one of the most sober, quietest parties I have ever been at. To me it was like—how shall I say it?—a funeral dinner. I didn't hear any laugh. There was absolutely nothing of life. I personally would call it very dull.

"I was able to take some over-all pictures and got also one where they toast President Truman. But the most exciting thing or incident was when they showed a movie. One operator said to me, 'It is "Sunbonnet Sue" and Gloria de Haven is in it.' I went to General Hodge and told him. He said, 'Eisie, I hope they show a new movie with lots of music and light stuff.'

"Around ten o'clock the movie started and all the Russian generals were placed between American generals and interpreters to explain it. They showed first an Army-Navy football game where we could see Truman, Nimitz, Halsey. I noticed especially when Halsey was shown everybody was making comments.

"Then came the flop. I mean the insult to the American movie industry. Instead of to impress the Russians with say 'Rhapsody in Blue,' they showed a picture called 'Sunbonnet Sue'—a Monogram picture released in 1934. Damn thing. I got excited. I was really mad about that. 'Sunbonnet Sue!' It shows New York in the 1890s. The Bowery, the Bowery, tatatatatat. Big bush-moustached policemen and individuals as in Chaplin's 'Kids' and 'Gold Rush' time. You don't see people like that any more. For five minutes the interpreter tries to explain that badly illuminated, badly scratched, badly outdated, badly photographed movie. The interpreters naturally gave up. Different generals started to smoke and look very often backwards. This was to my mind the worst picture I have ever seen in my whole life. Nobody understands the sense of the whole picture because it was so mixed up and interwoven with nonsense. To top all that they showed a Fleisher cartoon, 'Traphappy Porgy' which is more recently released but could be put in the same category as that other flop.

"After everything was over I mentioned to the men in charge of the household of General Hodge that this showing, especially of 'Sunbonnet Sue,' was an insult to the American movie industry as the Russians might think this is the latest creation of Hollywood. But this Lieutenant Smith didn't understand me. He said, 'I was only interested that the movie lasted exactly eighty minutes. I asked the film librarian, "Give me a movie that lasts one hour and twenty minutes and has some music in it." ' They had about fifty modern reels on file. It's amazing that a twenty-five-year-old lieutenant can spoil a whole lot. Because a lieutenant picks that thing.

"When it was over the operator put on a record, 'Rum and Coca-Cola,' and the Russians went into the other room and disappeared."

The preliminary meeting of the Commission achieved very little and wound up on February 5 with an agreement to reconvene after each side had considered various proposals. Hodge issued a report on the results in which he said its achievements had fallen short of the goals which the U.S. delegates had set. The Russians wanted to limit the conference to discussion of a small number of the most urgent problems. The Americans proposed talking about the removal of capital goods from Korea (i.e., by the Soviets) but the Russians did not think that was an immediate or urgent problem. Then the Americans suggested changing the boundary line at the 38th Parallel to conform with the political divisions of existing Korean provinces. The Russians took this under consideration.

The Americans hoped to discuss the possibility of unifying the Korean broadcasting system and permitting the free circulation of all newspapers throughout both zones. The Russians claimed these questions were not within the scope of the conference and they likewise put off discussion of a unified currency and of reopening telephone and telegraph communications between the zones. The conference did agree on the resumption of some ship, train, and postal service, and voted to permit Koreans to move from either zone to their former residences in the other sector provided they filed appropriate applications within sixty days. Students were allowed to cross the border to attend schools.

Among the Russian proposals the main one was for an exchange of raw materials. They requested rice in exchange for coal or anything else the Americans needed. Arnold truthfully told them that there was no rice to spare, since the southern zone had become crowded with refugees.

The Russians returned to Pyongyang but were expected back in

Seoul by early March. They did not reappear on schedule. General
Shtikov's delay in returning was traceable to the low tide of American-Soviet relations elsewhere in the world. The Iranian issue was
being argued before the United Nations, and the Russians were in
no mood for talking co-operation. On March 20, 1946, when Shtikov
did arrive in Seoul, his opening speech nearly closed the whole session as far as General Arnold was concerned. "We do not intend to
deal with any Korean parties or individuals who have opposed the
decisions of the three Foreign Ministers in Moscow," Shtikov declared categorically.

After weeks of debating procedure, agenda, and the issuance of
press communiques, the Commission began to discuss Shtikov's
opening statement and the whole question of eligibility. When the
Americans insisted that nearly all Koreans in the southern zone had
originally opposed the Moscow Decision, the Russians compro-
mised: they would be willing to concede eligibility to all Korean
organizations which *now* agreed to trusteeship (even if they had opposed it at first) and which would agree to co-operate with the
forthcoming conclusions of the Joint Commission. One such conclusion, the Russians warned, might well be continued trusteeship.

The Americans and Russians then drew up a three-paragraph
declaration which they agreed had to be signed by any Korean
democratic party or social organization before the Joint Commission
would consult with them. The text read:

We ——————————— declare that we will uphold the aims of the
Moscow Decision on Korea as stated in Paragraph 1 of this decision,
namely:
The re-establishment of Korea as an independent state, the creation
of conditions for developing the country on democratic principles, and
the earliest possible liquidation of the disastrous results of the protracted
Japanese domination in Korea.
Further, we will abide by the decisions of the Joint Commission in its
fulfillment of Paragraph 2 of the Moscow Decision in the formation of
a Provisional Korean Democratic Government; Further, we will co-operate with the Joint Commission in the working out by it with the participation of the Provisional Korean Democratic Government, of proposals concerning measures foreseen by Paragraph 3 of the Moscow
Decision.

This statement, called Communique Number Five, was issued on
April 17. Between that time and adjournment on May 8 the Americans and Russians could not agree on anything. The Americans

submitted a list of eligible democratic Korean organizations from their zone and the Russians one from theirs. According to the Russians, the U.S. proposal called for consultation with seventeen "reactionary" groups and only three "progressive" parties. The official government newspaper, *Izvestia,* declared, "The U.S. delegation did not even add to its list such mass public organizations as the All-Korean Confederation of Labor numbering about 600,000 trade union members, the All-Korean Women's Union numbering about 800,000 members, the All-Korean Union of Democratic Youth numbering 656,000 members or the All-Korean Peasant Union representing over 3,000,000 Korean peasants. While depriving mass workers' and peasants' organizations of representation, the U.S. delegation considered it quite proper to include in its list six religious societies and certain minute ultra-reactionary organizations."

The Americans denied these allegations and pointed out that the list from the northern zone did not include any conservative groups. The Russians saw nothing strange in this. "They are not democratic," Shtikov said.

Communique Number Five was not immediately acceptable to any but left-wing organizations in the American sector. In private conversation and in public speeches Hodge tried to win over the dissenters. At first this proved slow and unrewarding work. Finally after consultation with General Arnold, Hodge arrived at an explanation of Communique Number Five which was palatable to the followers of Rhee, Kimm, and Kim Koo. Hodge told them: "Signing the declaration for consultation with the Joint Commission does not indicate that the political party or social organization favors trusteeship, or that the organization commits itself to support of trusteeship. Those who will not sign the declaration, however, will not be consulted by the Joint Commission."

This infuriated the Soviet delegation who claimed that Hodge's interpretation "quite distorted the substance of the Moscow Decision and in point of fact went back on the decision of the Commission on April 17." Hodge's statement, *Izvestia* later charged, "cannot be regarded otherwise than as direct advice to the reactionaries to violate the conditions of consultation with the Commission."

On May 1 the holdouts against Communique Number Five signed the two-paragraph declaration. The Russians heard that Kimm Kiusic regarded this only as a commitment to co-operate with the Commission until a government had been formed; after that he and others in the right-wing bloc reserved the privilege to go into opposition. Such an "insincere" tongue-in-cheek attitude, Shtikov maintained, ruled out the "reactionaries."

Then the Americans became as stubborn as the Soviets, taking a firm stand on the principle of free speech. When this inevitable American-Russian discussion bogged down in a semantic impasse, General Arnold suddenly suggested that the Commission abolish the division at the 38th Parallel. Shtikov roared, *"Nyet!"*, claiming there was no authority in the Moscow Decision for discussing the 38th Parallel before settling the question of the provisional government.

Arnold asked him: "Is this your last word? Otherwise, there appears nothing else to discuss." Shtikov requested a twenty-four-hour delay. At ten o'clock on the morning of May 8 Shtikov spent three hours with General Hodge during which time they argued through interpreters about the meaning of words and phrases in previously agreed upon communiques. At eight that night Shtikov returned and informed Hodge that, after having communicated with higher headquarters, he had received instructions to return to northern Korea with his delegation.

3

In a lengthy review of the Commission's work leading to the breakdown of negotiations, General Hodge categorically blamed the Russians for the interruption. Nevertheless he wrote immediately to Soviet Commander Chistiakov declaring his willingness to resume the talks if the Russians would agree to "free expression" for Korean parties. There was no direct reply. But *Pravda*, on June 3, devoted three full columns to "The Question of Establishing a Provisional Government in Korea." It excoriated Hodge and the Americans for the Commission's failure, charging that "To introduce into the Korean government reactionary leaders who speak openly against the Soviet Union and stand in the way of the democratic development of Korea, and thus to subordinate Korea to U.S. influence—these are the real purposes of the American representatives in Korea, masquerading under talk of 'the defense of democracy.'"

Eventually Chistiakov did answer one of Hodge's letters. On October 26 he offered to resume negotiations, but on Soviet terms.

Hodge replied on November 1, reiterating the American position but agreeing that the Commission could exclude from consultation "individuals, parties, or organizations who foment or instigate mass opposition to the work of the Joint Commission or fulfillment of the Moscow Decision." Chistiakov replied to this on November 26 with three counter-proposals. First, that the Commission consult with those democratic organizations which fully upheld the Moscow Decision. Second, that organizations consulted could not nominate for consultation any representatives who had actively voiced opposition to the Moscow Decision. Third, that consulted organizations could not voice opposition nor incite others to voice opposition to the Moscow Decision and the work of the Commission.

Hodge replied on December 24, modifying these conditions slightly. In regard to Chistiakov's first point, Hodge asked that the signing of the two-paragraph declaration in Communique Number Five be sufficient to make the signatory organization eligible despite any previous record of opposition. This was the American position of May 1, 1946. Taking up the second, Hodge stated for the record that an organization had the free right to pick its best man for the consultation; however, if it were believed that the representative was antagonistic to the implementation of the Moscow Decision or to either of the Allied Powers, "the Joint Commission may, after mutual agreement, require the Declarant Party to name a substitute spokesman." This was an American concession to the Soviet viewpoint.

On the third point, Hodge suggested a revision of the wording, but the Soviet view was accepted.

This last exchange represented considerable compromise on both sides, but no initiative was taken to reopen the talks. During his visit to Washington in February 1947 Hodge said that such action must be taken on a higher level. Although the topic was not on the agenda of the Foreign Ministers meeting in Moscow, Secretary of State Marshall moved to break the deadlock on Korea. In a letter to Foreign Minister Molotov on April 8, he asked the Soviet Government to name a time and place for renewing negotiations. Marshall stated that the Joint Commission should be charged with expediting "its work under the terms of the Moscow Agreement on the basis of respect for the democratic right of freedom of opinion."

Molotov replied on April 19, suggesting that the commission reconvene on May 20. He charged that the Americans and not the

Russians had attempted to bar certain groups from the discussion and that the United States was therefore to blame for the breakdown of the talks.

The exchange of notes continued. In the meantime in Washington a three-year program of unilateral aid to Korea was being drafted under the Truman policy of quarantining Communism. This move may have caused the Russians to become more conciliatory. On May 2, Marshall wrote to Molotov again, trying to nail down the definition of terms under which the Commission would operate. Five days later Molotov agreed that the terms set forth in Hodge's last letter (December 24) to General Chistiakov would be acceptable. Marshall confirmed this procedure on May 13 and the Commission meetings got under way in Seoul a week later.

CHAPTER XVI

THE WAVERING POLICY

In 1946 the American strategists decided that the Koreans were again ready for an election. Early in the occupation, elections had been held in three provinces and coalition candidates backed by the People's Republic had won overwhelming victories. That had discouraged AMG on elections, but the popular clamor now demanded democratic representation.

This time half the members of a new "interim legislative assembly" were to be appointed by Hodge, and the other half were to be elected by popular vote. The safety-valve idea had been proposed to Hodge by a coalition of conservatives and the non-Communist left. AMG carefully retained the right to order new elections for the ninety-man legislature at any time, the right to abolish it and the right to veto any action it might take.

The promised secret balloting for the forty-five elective seats in the new legislature went off badly as a demonstration of American-style democracy. The voting was preceded by a wave of arrests made possible by AMG edicts which Koreans thought were strongly reminiscent of Japanese "peace preservation laws." Any group of more than three people engaged in political activity, under AMG Ordinance 55, was required to register with AMG by March 31, 1946, and to submit a complete file of members' names and signatures plus a thorough financial record. This ordinance met with a storm of protest, both from left and right, and was later rescinded. Newspapers denounced it as undemocratic. The leftist *Min Po* called it "The most cruel ordinance in Korean history." The conservative *Dai Dong Press* said it was "contrary to common sense" and complained that AMG policy was "becoming harsher and harsher, little by little."

Ordinance 72 listed more than eighty miscellaneous offenses against AMG which were so construed as to give the occupying power almost carte blanche in making arrests. Prior to the elections, leftists including intellectuals and labor leaders were picked up by AMG's Korean police on charges of "publishing, importing, or circulating printed, typed, or written matter which is detrimental or disrespectful to the occupying forces" or for "attendance at any public gathering, parade or demonstration for which no permit has been granted."

AMG's original explanation for such action was based on the fact that the Communist Party and its sympathizers opposed the election plan and called upon the people to oppose it. In this connection the unfortunate parallel between defeated Japan and liberated Korea is difficult to push aside: Japanese Communists were permitted much more freedom of expression than the Koreans.

The harsh policy in Korea boomeranged against AMG. In the six-week period before the elections, the southern portion of the U.S. zone was swept by strikes, riots, and even by open rebellion. Accounts of exactly what transpired were conflicting at the time, but a non-partisan report later gave weight to this interpretation: AMG tried to characterize the entire chain of unfortunate events as a Communist-inspired plot to discredit the elections.

Actually the first link in the chain was economic, and not political. And political concession would not fill rice bowls. During the summer of 1946 conditions in the American zone had, if anything, grown worse. On August 29 AMG estimated that food costs were one hundred times higher than in prewar days. Two days later, in an effort to appease the unrest among the Koreans, Hodge directed Military Governor Lerch to turn over the running of Korean government departments to Koreans. That solved very little. On the same day, August 31, the conservative *Chosun Ilbo*, with the largest circulation in Korea, printed an open letter to Hodge in its editorial column. Pointedly but politely it summed up what most Koreans were thinking about the U.S. occupation:

To General Hodge:
We thank you and your officers and men. The Korean people will always remember that your country, making great sacrifice in this war, swept away the Japanese from our land. We also thank you and your subordinates for the effort made to govern Korea with all its inconveniences.
Let us look at the present situation in Korea, General Hodge.
The Korean people are now suffering more than they ever did under

the Japanese rule. We do not believe that this suffering is due only to the political confusion and lack of patriotism among the Korean people. . . .

We can glibly say that this present economic confusion is due to the postwar inflation but how to relieve the sufferings of the people is a difficult problem. . . . The prosperity of every country depends upon the policy of the Government.

We believe that the Military Government in Korea has not been successful in its efforts, and that this failure is due to your country's lack of understanding concerning Korea, the interpreters' administration, the permission of free economy without any preparation and to your wavering policy.

These accusations against the Military Government in Korea are not slanderous but true. We hope that your country will heed the public opinion of the Korean people more than it did in the past and that your country will reflect this quickly and positively in the policies carried out in Korea. . . .

It can be imagined that if the conservatives felt this strongly about AMG, the leftists, including the trade unionists, expressed themselves even more strongly. Early in September the Korean Federation of Trade Unions, claiming to represent two million workers, asked AMG for higher wages and specified rice allotments to meet the still-rising inflation. AMG did not deign to reply to the petition.

On September 23, the railroad workers walked out at Pusan, a port in the far south and Korea's second largest city. The Federation appealed again to AMG, without avail. A general strike order was issued. The railroad men were joined by the chemical and textile workers in the Taegu district, only fifty miles away. Before long, over three hundred thousand workers were on strike.

Then the firecrackers began popping, most of them in Taegu, the southern zone's third most populous city (*circa* 150,000). Korean police smashed up a picket line while union spokesmen protested that democracy guaranteed them the right to strike and picket. When a crowd of citizens gathered in a protest meeting at the Taegu railroad station, the nervous police fired into them. Three were killed, many wounded. In the fighting that ensued, thirty-eight policemen were killed by the enraged mob.

AMG declared martial law on October 4. U.S. troops were used to "restore order," which included arresting any strikers who "exhibited signs of violence." This action by the Americans made the Koreans so angry that they sided with the strikers whether they were pro-labor or not. An estimated hundred thousand students in high

schools and colleges walked out to show their sympathy and to
protest U.S. tactics.

Then followed what Koreans call "a reign of terror" in which mass
arrests were made and quite a few who resisted were killed. Ultimately 16 of the 1,342 arrested were condemned to death for their
roles in the insurrection, and 557 more were sentenced for various
crimes against the occupation by a Military Government court.

The leftist parties stated categorically: "During the tyrannical
rule of Japanese imperialism for thirty-six years the Korean people
rose in revolt on numerous occasions against the Japanese oppression and exploitation, but none of them can be compared with the
present affair."

Less heatedly, the conservatives agreed. Seoul newspapers, lawyers' associations and even some of the anti-Communist politicians
urged clemency and pointed out that AMG was at least responsible
for the conditions which had caused the "People's Uprising." Nearly
all of them compared "American democratic methods" to "Japanese
tyranny."

Hodge appointed a balanced Korean-American Commission to
investigate what had happened in Taegu and to determine, if possible, the causes.

2

Less than a month after this unpleasantness the elections were
held; they resulted in almost total victory for the extreme right. The
returns were embarrassing to AMG and to Hodge personally, since
he had predicated the logic of his severest orders and policies on
the potent influence of the "Communists."

Mark Gayn reported to the Chicago *Sun* that "The election has
resulted in an overwhelming victory for a coalition of landlords,
city moneyed interests and officeholders which regards Syngman
Rhee, seventy-three-year-old politician, as spiritual leader." The
conservative Korean Democratic Party and Rhee's ultra-conservative National League for Acceleration of Korean Independence won
forty seats. To establish some kind of balance Hodge and Lerch,
in selecting people for the forty-five appointive seats, named supporters of Kimm Kiusic and Lyuh Woon Heung. This infuriated
Rhee who told anyone who would listen to him that the people
would no longer follow him if he "collaborated with Communists."
By "Communist" Rhee meant anyone not prepared to follow Rhee's

program. One of the most vociferous protests on the election came from Kimm Kiusic. A Korean Board of Elections had reported the elections were "undemocratic and non-representative." He claimed in a letter to Hodge that the elections had been fraudulent and pointed out the victory in Seoul of two notorious collaborationists. He demanded a new election since the elections just held "were not democratically carried out, owing mainly to the manipulations of certain groups and parties acting for selfish interests."

Still more serious were the little-publicized reports of American correspondents that universal suffrage was not carried out. Instead, the old Confucian system remained in force: heads of family only were given the vote; and in some cases, the heads of the ancient ten-family groups. In many villages the headman simply filled in the candidates' names for the voters (usually his own) and in others messengers were dispatched to collect "chops" or name seals which were then affixed to the ballots by officials.

AMG's attitude was to give the bungled election and the labor unrest as little publicity as possible. It became increasingly difficult for accredited U.S. correspondents to move out of Seoul. One Intelligence officer frankly told an American reporter that AMG didn't like newspapermen snooping around. "The Army will tell the American people what they ought to know," he said.

The tendency was to dismiss complaints of vote irregularities as "sour grapes" on the part of defeated candidates and parties. Nevertheless the opening of the assembly was postponed until mid-December. There was more bad news for Hodge at this period. According to an A.P. dispatch from Seoul, two investigating groups (Americans appointed by MacArthur) uncovered "a considerable number of cases of fraud or attempted fraud by Korean officials."

When the intense popular pressure for an investigation of the elections in various districts kept up, Hodge named a committee to look into it. As the result of their findings, he disallowed the elections of six candidates, all considered ultra-conservative and collaborationist. In the re-elections, five rightists and one leftist were picked.

The Assembly finally opened on December 12. General MacArthur, never one to overlook any historic event, said that South Korea had made its "greatest step forward in the democratic processes of self-rule."

The left propaganda claimed, without basis, that the Americans were, in effect, going ahead with a separate government for South Korea in defiance of the Moscow Agreement. The right, led by Rhee, claimed that the Americans were *not* going ahead with a plan for a government and that they should. Hodge did his best to clarify the controversy and to emphasize the fact that the interim legislature "is not a government within itself, nor is it the governing body of southern Korea. It is exactly what the name implies, an interim legislative assembly with legislative powers to make laws for enforcement by the executive branch of the government." Such functions were to continue until a unified provisional government was established, Hodge repeated, and were subject to AMG approval.

At the convocation of the Assembly, thirty-one of the elected rightists walked out in protest over the seating of a few "Communists" and because their members had not received any appointive positions. They came back nine days later, having saved face.

The best work of the legislature was the drawing up and passing of a child-labor bill which became law on June 1, 1947. The ruling made the employment of children under the age of fourteen illegal. In Korea, where approximately a third of the cotton mill workers are below that age, this was a drastic move. The Assembly also wanted to pass a bill making collaboration with the Japanese a crime as far back as the year 1910. AMG was willing to consider this, but it put its supervisory foot down hard when the Koreans insisted on a "family guilt" system; this would have made a son punishable for the political errors of his deceased father.

During the second year of the occupation the temper of the Korean people simmered down somewhat. But Korean politics were still full of explosive paradoxes. The right-wing leaders and parties were applauded for demanding outright and speedy independence; the left-wing groups were followed for their economic and taxation programs and particularly for their agitation in favor of land redistribution. Hodge and Lerch, finally, were staying in the middle of the road and trying to balance off the extreme right against the extreme left. They had learned something from the elections and they should have learned even more from the report of the Joint Korean-American Commission investigating the October riots. Hodge thought the group's findings were sincere and that they were "patriotic and industrious." The Commission informed Hodge that there were five basic reasons for the uprising: (1) enmity toward the police; (2) the continued presence of Japanese collaborators in

Military Government posts; (3) the effect of too many interpreters in the government; (4) the corruption of some Korean officials; and (5) agitators against the best interests of Korea.

The General promised to use the recommendations. But in his official statements in Seoul and in Washington, Hodge stressed only the point about agitators—a problem not his fault, but one caused by that increasingly popular whipping boy, "The Russian Bear."

Hodge began to see that a real economic improvement was necessary. For if the independence issue were removed, the leftists could gain strength rapidly, due to the economic plight of the people. Hodge was indignant that for so many months more had been done to raise the living standard in Japan than in Korea. The General's requests for more food shipments, as well as supplies, to quicken the recovery of Korean industry received little attention until the formulation of the Truman Doctrine. Then it was decided on highest levels to aid Korea's economy with 528 million dollars.

CHAPTER XVII

CAN KOREANS GOVERN KOREA?

THIS account of the trials and tribulations of Hodge's Korea would not be complete without re-emphasizing the tremendous problems which had to be faced and listing some of the positive accomplishments.

In addition to disarming and deporting the Japanese, the southern zone had to handle the eight hundred thousand refugees from the north and nearly a million more who returned from Manchuria and Japan.

Even if Hodge had been a perfect diplomat, he would have been hated by Korean hotheads who were prepared to resist any foreign occupation, American, Russian, or Swiss. AMG policy did force into opposition a large group of Koreans who could have been useful. This same shortsighted procedure had distinguished U.S. policy in China. By throwing U.S. support only to the right in a country which demanded and needed radical reform, AMG alienated a healthy segment of the left which could have been wooed and perhaps even won by a living exposition of American democracy. Excluded from office-holding, spurned by Kim, Rhee, and even Kimm, many militant Koreans were pushed further left and closer to the Communists. As AMG's Harold Sugg reported: ". . . The left soon became what the American command had assumed it was. Military Government made it easy for the Communists to capture the left-wing organizations and to spread to thousands of bitter, disillusioned Koreans the allegedly good news from the Russian zone."

Hodge undeniably learned on the job, but America's reputation paid for his upgrading. His second year was far better than his first. Nevertheless he kept resisting any changes for the better in personnel or conditions if such changes were advocated by the Communists. He believed it would show that he gave in to their demands. In practice his stubbornness helped the Communists win support on several popular issues.

Completely aside from politics, the Korean temperament frequently clashed with the American. "The Koreans are like the Irish," Americans kept pointing out to me. "They've gotta chip on their shoulders about being Korean. They think they can handle any job that comes along even if they don't know the first thing about it. They are the most independent, cocky, sassiest people in the world. . . ." This attitude is much like that of the Russian major who compared the Koreans to the Poles.

The occupying forces did not seem to realize that the traits which they had ascribed to the Koreans were understandable ones in a people who had lived under foreign rulers for so long before the arrival of new "masters."

The split at the 38th Parallel was more than a political headache; it was an economic problem of the first order for Hodge. Physically the line, which does not even conform to the borders of existing Korean provinces, is an unmarked row of rocky ridges stubbled with short pines. Behind it both Russian and American patrols are scattered. The failure for so long to find a formula for removing the Parallel as a barrier to trade has been costly to both sides. As an example, there are mines in the north which have little value unless the ore can be shipped to the smelter which is south of the Parallel. Also in the north are large reservoirs which in past years had been opened periodically to help flood the rice lands of the south. The north, in exchange for food, used to supply fertilizer to the south. Such instances could be multiplied many times.

The Soviet zone suffered from the division even more than the Americans. Colonel M. Preston Goodfellow, one of General Arnold's political advisers, continually advised following a tough policy in negotiations with the Russians because he believed that the United States had the better half of Korea. The northern section, he pointed out, was a food-deficit area and the Russians could not afford mass starvation. He also reasoned that the Russians could be made to look bad by their intransigency and that world opinion might force them out of Korea as it had done already in Iran.

2

Korea has a considerable industrial potential, once real unification is achieved. Korea's rivers, properly harnessed, could generate five million kilowatts of power per year. That is about twice the current total output of the TVA. The country has iron reserves of a billion tons; coal (chiefly anthracite) of two billion tons; it has a wealth of unmined light metals—lead, gold, zinc, graphite, mica, magnesium.

Indecision as to whether a political and economic settlement with the Russians could be achieved prevented the Americans from properly organizing their zone for reconstruction and trade for almost a year. Once the first series of Joint Commission talks broke down, concrete efforts were made to revive business and improve the living standards in the south. Beside the 25-million-dollar loan, a plan for barter with Japan was approved by SCAP. Up to January 1, 1947, Korea received sixty million dollars in foreign aid, three-fourths of it from the United States. Medicines were imported for Korean hospitals; a public health program and mass inoculations were begun; surplus Army rations were distributed for relief purposes; a campaign was initiated to teach Korean farmers how to increase crop yields; Japanese Army horses were sold to Korean farmers; and demonstrations were given on how horsepower could save manpower in farm work. The New Korea Company was permitted to lease former Japanese airfields to farmers. Other unused tracts were used to start a great reforestation program.

Slow but steady progress was achieved in helping the Koreans equip themselves for the twentieth century. Well-meant but limited assistance was rendered in modernizing and expanding their police, fire, judicial and school systems, their museums and libraries, their factories and transportation. More than seventeen thousand Japanese schoolteachers were dismissed and thousands of Korean teachers put through a re-education course. Today, despite a textbook shortage, a larger number of children attend school in South Korea than ever did before in the whole country. To help in mass education radio was employed for the first time; talks were broadcast on domestic science and the meaning of democracy; lessons were given in oral English as well as Korean history and language. Athletics were encouraged as a method of developing "fair play," and a Korean soccer team was sent to Tokyo to enter international competition. With privately raised funds a Korean delegation was sent to the United States for the annual Boston Marathon and Yun Bok Su, one of the Koreans, won.

To help the transport problem, one hundred locomotives were imported, some from Japan. On May 20, 1946, the Korean Liberator, a ten-car, streamlined train built by Koreans, made its first official trip. Also in May the merger of three privately owned railroads into one national railroad system was ordered by AMG.

In addition to locomotives, Korea obtained salt, seeds, and tungsten (for electric light bulbs) from Japan and sent back in return graphite, talc and pyrophyllite (used in making slate pencils).

These and many other material gains have been praiseworthy attainments for AMG and the Koreans, despite the limitations of trained personnel. Such successes may not be enough to match the real failures in the over-all application of political and economic democracy induced by ignorance, lack of experience, fear of a people's free will, and, of course, the bogey of Russia.

3

As the record in Korea shows, American democracy cannot be taught by "getting around" American principles. Fine speeches mean nothing when the people find out how the voting took place; when they learn that U.S. troops were used to break a strike; when labor leaders are arrested, newspapers suppressed for being "shrill," and wages held down while prices soar. They want to know why, for example, Seoul's West Gate prison is jammed with political offenders and there are "more political prisoners now than ever." They cannot understand how AMG tolerated police chiefs known to be corrupt and cruel.

The disagreements, the demonstrations, the strikes, the boycotts, the name-calling that have been evoked in southern Korea cannot be dismissed, as General Hodge would have it, by attributing them solely to "professional trouble-makers" and "vicious agitators" who infiltrated into the U.S. zone. The Korean people are still confused by our high words and our low performance.

Six months after the American "liberation" Koreans in Seoul told me that "there is one discernible difference to us between American M.P.'s and Japanese M.P.'s—you Americans are taller."

It is doubtful that AMG really believes the trouble is all Soviet-inspired. But the Red scare has made a convenient if hoary scapegoat for the things which have gone wrong. So wrong that in May 1946 a poll conducted for American Intelligence by Koreans revealed:

53 per cent of Koreans questioned said they had an "unfavorable" impression of the Americans.

At the height of the food crisis in 1946, another poll indicated that:

49 per cent of Seoul's citizens would have preferred the hated Japanese to the Americans.

AMG must know that this cannot be entirely passed off as the fault of the southern zone Communists or the Russians. Time after time the secret polls have shown that a majority of the Koreans were anti-American. This does not mean they are pro-Soviet. An impartial poll in the Russian zone might produce similar anti-Russian results.

But that is no excuse for the American occupation. In fact, once the Japanese were disarmed and repatriated there was no moral reason for any military occupation of Korea by any powers. A United Nations commission could certainly have done no worse in advising the Koreans than we and the Russians have done in bossing them.

A decent, long-lasting solution of the Soviet-American deadlock in Korea is not easily outlined. Even with the U.S. and the U.S.S.R., their armies and Military Government officials simultaneously withdrawn from Korea, the struggle for ideological domination would go on. The tug of war between Korea's left and right is certain to involve the United States and Russia long after the military occupation is over. As in China, both sides would be wooed with loans, broadcasts, news services, religious and cultural missions.

The United States is not likely to leave entirely until two major conditions are fulfilled: (1) the establishment of a sound, competent, trustworthy Korean government for all of Korea, a government which can be counted upon to maintain stability and keep Korea friendly to the Western powers; (2) a complete withdrawal by the U.S.S.R. and a renunciation by Russia of any further interest in Korean matters.

The Russians will certainly not be willing to leave as long as they believe, as *Pravda* has noted, that independence under present conditions (*i.e.*, anti-Soviet leaders in South Korea) "would inevitably lead to a new enslavement of the country by foreign capital and the seizure of power by a small group of adventurers, backed by inveterate enemies of democracy—large-scale Korean landowners and capitalists."

After the enunciation of the Truman Doctrine, the State Department requested 528 million dollars for Korea. This money can be well invested or it can be wasted—all under the excuse of aiding Korea. If the U.S. remains in Korea, and it seems likely to do so at this writing, the job should be and must be carried out more intelligently, more constructively. The first step would be to cut down the elaborate administrative structure which finds the War, Navy, State Departments and the Far Eastern Commission in Washington all having a say on policy, and sending it to Tokyo where there is an even more complex structure before word reaches Seoul.

The next step would be to find top-flight civilian personnel and pay them enough to make the task of helping the Koreans attractive. Military men of General Marshall's caliber may be dependable in almost any situation. But there is a discernible gap between the top rung which Marshall and Eisenhower represent and the kind of personality and background which General Hodge brings to his functions. He is an honest fighting man with little flare for government. His thinking is tuned to military wave-lengths. He is constantly looking over his shoulder and trying to anticipate a Red invasion. His favorite question to startle visitors is: "Do you know how many planes we could get into the air if the Russians attacked tomorrow?" Many of his political and economic advisers were born a century too late; they are busily applying nineteenth century colonial administration to a twentieth-century situation.

Many Koreans disliked the Military Governor, General Lerch, more than they disliked Hodge. And at times Hodge, himself, didn't seem to be very fond of his top-ranking assistant.

The major fault lies not only with the implementation of the Hodges or of the Lerches but also with the policies (or lack of them) of the State and War Departments—and with the American people. Responsible government agencies failed to provide the needed leadership and we, as a people, have accepted representation that is not worthy of us. The State Department, for example, sent no basic program on Korea for nine months after Hodge arrived. On more than one occasion Secretary of War Patterson asked that the State Department assume responsibility for and control over Korea; he was turned down flatly until General Marshall became Secretary of State.

Perhaps our grandchildren will be consoled by historical accounts of this phase of the Korean misadventure. The process of synthesis will leave this kind of historical residue: "In the southern zone the Americans established a multi-party system with freedom of press and of speech, while in the north the Russians installed a one-party system with a controlled press and severe restrictions on free speech." The account might not add, however, that in neither zone were the Koreans satisfied or free.

There seems little sense in the idea that more charity, faith, and friendliness should be extended to our former Japanese enemies than to our Korean allies. American educators should go to Korea. Korean students from all segments of society should be brought to U.S. schools. Korean industrial managers and skilled workers should be trained here if sufficient teachers cannot be sent there.

The military-minded in both zones of Korea believe it will be many years before the Koreans are able to govern themselves even when the Americans and Russians negotiate their difference about the establishment of a unified provisional government. This view, however, is not shared by all the Americans who have observed the Koreans at firsthand. Dr. Horace Underwood, a prominent American educator and an adviser to AMG who has lived many years in Korea, told Edgar Snow that the Koreans "are as capable of governing themselves on their own level as we are. They had centuries of independence and sovereignty before the Japanese conquest—a history almost as long as China's and much older than Japan's. Naturally they'll have difficulties. But there is no reason to suppose they won't run an honest or efficient government."

Mr. McCune, from his vantage point in Washington at the Korean desk of the State Department where he had access to unpublished reports, agreed with Dr. Underwood. "Much has been written on the capacity of the Korean people to govern themselves, a subject which has been greatly over-emphasized in all discussions concerning the future of Korea," Mr. McCune wrote after leaving the State Department. "The experience of American Military Government and the Soviet regime has proved the Koreans can govern themselves without a lengthy 'training period,' despite inevitable inefficiency in the transitional period."

I have questioned many Koreans about this matter. They agree almost entirely with Underwood and McCune. They point to their long tradition of village self-government which even the Japanese could not wipe out; their net of co-operatives which claimed more than two million members in 1944; their Western-trained university graduates.

This writer believes that the answer is probably somewhere be-

tween the pessimism of a Hodge and the optimism of an Underwood. With friendly help from both Allied powers and the U N,
Korea can develop personnel which will be able to assume full administrative responsibility within a short span. They will make
many mistakes, but they will have the virtue of being Korean mistakes. Their errors can be no more stupid than ours. In the mean·
time there is no reason why, if the Korean people vote for it, American and Russian engineers and experts cannot assist Korea in
building up its industry. Not so long ago Americans extended such
aid to the Russians themselves, and we are still supplying technical
personnel and equipment to China.

Politically there is not much hope for a lasting coalition among
Korean politicians or parties until there is a basic world-wide agreement between Russia and the United States and, as a corollary to
that, between the Nationalists and the Communists in China. Until
such a greater problem is solved, the lesser one cannot even be
honestly or seriously discussed. The alternative, as General Hodge
told me, is for the United States to "sit Russia out." Since presumably the Russians will be doing the same thing, nothing but a
stalemate can result, and, despairing of real freedom, the Korean
people will quietly prepare to take things into their own hands
once again.

PART THREE

MARSHALL'S CHINA

To make China strong and independent, it is necessary that all citizens, from the highest to the lowest, must be united in one purpose; that we rouse ourselves for thorough reform, eliminate frivolity by insisting upon honesty, and discourage indolence by upholding active endeavor. Our thinking must be realistic, our living disciplined; our duties must be performed with a sense of responsibility, and our actions must be orderly; and we must seek the truth through practical work, and progressively strive for improvement.

Chiang Kai-shek
(in *China's Destiny*)

I do not believe any nation can find justification to suspect our motives in China. We are asking no special preference with respect to economic or similar matters. We are placing no price on our friendship. We have a vital interest in a stable government in China—and I use the word vital in the accurate sense.

George C. Marshall
(March 16, 1946)

CHAPTER XVIII

OPPORTUNITIES AND OPPRESSIONS

MOST Westerners see China and her problems through her cities, and usually her port cities where there is more trade in foreign goods and, perhaps, in ideas. The Asiatic, however, sees China through her thousands of villages. It is in these rural areas where 90 per cent of the Chinese people live, where three-fourths of them strive to eke out a livelihood from the tired earth.

During the war years and in the months following the peace with Japan, more Americans had contact with China and the Chinese than in all of the previous history of the United States. The troops who were stationed in China did not react very favorably to most of the Chinese they met or dealt with. The barriers of language, custom, and living standard were enormous. The unrehearsed G.I. opinion of the Chinese would probably be a compilation of abusive adjectives such as dirty, stupid, lying, thieving, and inefficient.

This picture of the Chinese is valid to about the same degree as the frank opinion I have heard Chinese express about us: impatient, intolerant, uncultured, immoral, disloyal, arrogant, and cruel.

Such generalizations do not hold true for diplomats, politicians, and high-ranking army and navy officials on either side. Among them the disparity in living standards is less likely to be noted. At a social gathering, the wives of a Chinese official and of an American consul general may both wear a $150 dress from Hattie Carnegie's, although the styling be as different as East and West. An American colonel and a Chinese general may hold a conference, both shod in G.I. boots, both smoking Camels, and then both depart in Chevrolet staff cars.

But the gap between the American G.I. and Chinese coolie, whether he be in the Chinese army or pulling a ricksha, is insurmountable. The difference between an American UNRRA official and a hungry Chinese peasant is just as great, although the UNRRA official may have a deeper comprehension of the peasants' problems.

The coolie and the peasant in China, the minor bureaucrat and the shopkeeper, have the same basic problem: keeping alive. In times of peace, this primarily means getting enough food; housing, clothing, and medical attention are matters of secondary concern. In time of war, especially civil war, this not only means getting enough food but escaping the more violent and sudden forms of death. In times of civil war food is more scarce and more expensive. Tillers of the soil are conscripted, and less land can be cultivated. Hoarding, inflation, speculation, the ravages of battle, and higher grain taxes make the job of getting enough to eat a full-time occupation, and not always a successful one, in country and city, in Szechwan or Shanghai.

2

Shanghai is as different from Seoul or Tokyo as the rest of China is from Shanghai. It is a slag heap of modernity linked by a bridge of gold bars to a morass of medievalism. It has a Chicago skyline and the stench of a pigsty. It has a harbor full of goods-heavy freighters and sleek warships, a creek full of lice-ridden *sampans* and barges, all heavy with humanity.

Shanghai is a Gropper cartoon of the fat man with the thick gold chain and the too-thin worker with hollow cheeks. It is as impressive as a train wreck, as depressing as flypaper swarming with stuck flies.

You can see Shanghai and never know about the hundreds of dead-from-starvation children carted off the streets and burned every week. You can see the International Settlement, the busy, modern Bund teeming with rickshas, pedicabs, jeeps, bicycles, limousines, peddlers, and foreigners; the shops full of postwar fountain pens and prewar Swiss watches. You can smell the good smell of leather brief cases and wallets, the scent of incense in the curio stores. You can walk by the myriad temples of the money-changers; the handsome Eurasian girls and the glad-eyed, sad-faced White Russians; the high-priced restaurants and the high fashion salons of the modistes; the drugstore windows full of ginseng roots and other "elixirs of life." You can get the indelible impression that the current civil war and the Japanese occupation were nothing more than salable myths for export; only after your eyes grow accustomed to the neon brilliance do you recognize the incredible compression, on opposite sides of a gutter, of plenty and poverty, of surplus and starvation, and wonder about the indifference of those with plenty, Chinese or foreign, to everything but the frantic quest for more.

Among the postwar money-mad cities of the world, Shanghai was definitely schizophrenic. Money was everything and, at the same time, nothing. A man did not feel rich if he had several million dollars in the bank—he would rather have several thousand *piculs* of rice in his *godown*. (One *picul* is about 133⅓ pounds.) Nobody was investing in money, at least not in Chinese money. If a Shanghailander felt exceptionally well he said, "I feel like a million dollars—U. S." If he just looked good but didn't feel so hot, he said, "I feel like a million dollars—CNC" (Chinese National Currency).

This fine disdain for paper currency did not prevent those who had some from trying to make more. In fact the only thing that could keep pace with Shanghai's frenetic inflation was Shanghai's frantic speculation.

"You cannot stop speculation in Shanghai any more than you can stop war," a White Russian merchant philosophized to me. "If you dropped an atomic bomb on the center of Shanghai today, survivors in the suburbs would be buying and selling radioactive calcium powder tomorrow."

The Russian picked at his three gold teeth and launched into the familiar illustration of Shanghai speculation. A case of sardines was repeatedly bought and sold at steadily soaring prices—always by means of a paper transaction. Finally one buyer asked to inspect the case of sardines. A prolonged search turned it up at the bottom of a *godown* (warehouse) some miles from Shanghai. The latest buyer pried open the box, smacked his lips, then peeled back the cover of a can. The tin was empty. Enraged, the buyer stormed into the office of the reputable merchant who had sold him the case, charging fraud. The reputable merchant became equally enraged. "You idiot," he cried, "everyone knows those sardines are not for eating but only for buying and selling!"

Experienced Shanghailanders scoffed at such stories and said that the postwar speculation was no worse than it had always been. It just seemed much dizzier than usual because, like everything else in Shanghai except the pavements, it is tied to the most astronomical inflation spiral since the twenties, when German marks became as worthless as campaign leaflets after election day.

At the end of the war, the Chinese dollar was set at five hundred to one U. S. dollar. In 1946 it was revalued at two thousand to one. By 1947 it was bought and sold at the ratio of twenty thousand to one—with no end in sight. The Government called in all bills under five hundred dollars, issued crisp new ones at ten thousand dollars.

Using Shanghai's last prewar year (1936) as a base, it is calculated that food costs had risen 1,896 times, housing 543 times, and clothing 3,461 times by the end of February 1946. Despite governmental gestures to achieve stabilization the kite strings of inflation were still unslacked. The general cost-of-living index which had climbed to 1,464 times over the 1936 average by February's end, increased 40 per cent more during the first ten days of March 1946. (By June 1947 the cost-of-living index hit the unbelievable high of 20,000 times the prewar average.)

In the ten-year period (between 1936 and 1946) wages inched up a measly 500 per cent, which made it obvious that Shanghai workers had to starve a little, operate a "squeeze," or do a little speculating to induce both ends within meeting distance. Americans, who in past years have frequently reaped benefits from foreign exchange, were no exceptions to the new lack of rules. That good old stand-by, the American buck, was buying only 20 per cent as much as it did before the war in Shanghai. Instead of wage increases, Government bureaus and private companies "loaned" money to employees. Interest rates shot up to 15 to 20 to 25 per cent. Labor unrest led to the Government prohibiting strikes and holding union leaders legally responsible if a strike did occur.

The only price control which worked in Shanghai was the ceiling on rents, and even that had a twister. The municipal government thoughtfully stipulated that landlords could increase rents only 60 times over prewar fees. But a little thing like a regulation in Shanghai does not prevent eager landlords from rubbing their thumbs and forefingers together in the familiar Shanghai gesture. I heard about a family which was lucky enough (or gave enough of a bribe) to obtain a fair five-room apartment boasting what the Chinese call *wei sheng she pei* or "hygienic establishments"—flush toilets. The rent was nominal but the family had to pay the landlord $4,500 (American) *ting fei* or "key money." That is the only way to squeeze into living quarters in Shanghai today. The key money practice has become a universal and reluctantly accepted custom. I asked a Chinese landlord how he'd define *ting fei*. Blandly he replied, "A deposit which is not returnable."

Speculation in places to sleep was not confined to regular landlords. The "have-nots" willingly propositioned any "haves" in an attempt to buy a lease. A friend of mine who lived in a compact two-room suite on accessible Nanking Road was offered $8,000 in gold bars as *ting fei* if he'd move out. My friend was willing—but for $10,000 gold. He got it.

Some innocent UNRRA representatives, seeking to avoid the key money racket, sought to buy a house. They soon discovered that few owners were willing to sell, as there is a 40 per cent tax on property transfers. A lady who owned a modest six-room home which might be worth $10,000 in the U. S. at boom prices, turned down an offer of $100,000. Major General Lu Chiu-chih, publisher of Shanghai's reform *Daily News*, boasted that a house which he appropriated from a Japanese at the war's end for $7,000 (CNC) was resold for $100,000,000 (CNC)—a neat profit of over 10,000 per cent. "Which," said the General, "is even better than *ting fei*."

The Shanghai municipal government has a simple and logical explanation for proclaiming an interest in rent ceilings and disclaiming any interest in the *ting fei* squeeze. "We allow rents to rise only sixty times while the price of rice has risen three thousand times," said a city official, "because municipal employees like myself can only afford to pay that much rent increase. If we set rent ceilings higher, we would have to raise salaries of our employees."

Anyone lucky enough to have an apartment protected by the 6000 per cent increase ceiling still had to shell out for other living expenses. An American couple living moderately well, figured out that their living expenses—mostly food—cost them $800 a month. Any U. S. housewife who wonders how a couple living "moderately" could spend $800 a month might ponder these sample Shanghai prices: one scrawny chicken for four—three dollars; a pound of American coffee—three and a half dollars; one pair of nylons (which cost thirty dollars a dozen in the States)—$35; cigarettes—six dollars per carton. These are not black market prices. The cigarettes, for example, cost the importer two dollars a carton to land in Shanghai from the States, with duty and shipping charges. The wholesaler sold them to the retailer at three dollars, who then doubled the price and resold them to the consumer.

The importers, wholesalers, dealers, distributors, and retailers who cleaned up on Shanghai's postwar boom were those who have been persevering, shrewd, or lucky enough to acquire scarcity goods for a quick turnover. In addition to cigarettes, the biggest profits—ranging from 500 to 5,000 per cent—were made in cosmetics, drugs, and stockings. Exporters had a more trying time than importers. Immediately after the Japanese surrender, those businessmen who came into Shanghai and bought up stockpiles and then managed to ship them out, did very well. Furriers especially made a killing. During the war Chinese weasels, sables, and kolinskys from Harbin and Mukden, lamb and kidskins from Tientsin, and Japanese mink from Hokkaido accumulated in Shanghai with little prospects for sales in Japan's conquered southern empire. In November and December 1945 these furs were available at low prices and fur exporters in Shanghai made a tremendous profit.

Old-time exporters and importers were not bullish on immediate prospects for "legitimate business." "Money is being coined in the black market," they told me somewhat dolefully. Old China hands also complained that their business futures were not up to expectations. One said it was "because too much is coming into China through UNRRA." The local Dodge dealer did not feel very sanguine about his next year's sales curve because the China market was already cluttered with UNRRA Dodge trucks sold by CNRRA (UNRRA's Chinese affiliate) for just under the black market price. A third lament from American firms concerned taxes. Since March 1, 1946, the Chinese have seriously tried to enforce tax payments. "And we get it in the neck," one U. S. corporation executive explained to me, "because we keep the kind of books where we don't hide our profits. Chinese companies just keep cash accounts and it is hard to tell how much profit they have made. That gives them a decided advantage over us—at least until they learn how to keep proper books."

As a result of these headaches many U. S. firms did not cash in on the Shanghai boom even though they contributed to it. A big cotton firm such as Clayton Anderson sells raw cotton at its usual 5 or 10 per cent profit. Chinese mill owners (most of them in or connected with the Government) after they have spun cotton into yarn, sell their produce at a 500 per cent profit.

American dealers who trusted that the Shanghai bubble would not last forever, were passing up the quick kill in favor of the slow, steady bloodletting. An automobile importer, expecting his first shipment of Packards shortly, carefully screened his customers to make certain they would not resell their cars for profit. Since he expected to do business in Shanghai for a long time, he charged them reasonable prices. Less responsible dealers easily sold Packards, or any other cars for that matter, in Shanghai for ten to fifteen thousand dollars and more.

Until Army officials cracked down on them, U. S. troops stationed in China were making free with enterprise in a big business way. One G.I. almost succeeded in tying up all future cosmetic delivery contracts to give himself a virtual monopoly in China. An officer who purchased foodstuffs for the army made over a million dollars' worth of private contracts on the side in anticipation of establishing his own export-import business after discharge from the army.

Before civilians were permitted to fly in any planes between Shanghai and North China, an army private who knew furs and flew regularly from Shanghai to Tientsin on army duties, bought up furs for a Shanghai dealer and cut himself into every transaction for a healthy commission. Other G.I.'s, without wings, remained in Shanghai and invested their monies and talents in bars and nightclubs. One such entrepreneur even worked behind the bar until yanked out for disgracing his uniform. In most instances these ventures ran into trouble when soldier-businessmen tended to supply their enterprises with army fruit juices, peanuts, cigarettes, and beer.

The favorite army game in China, until the official ban made it slightly more dangerous than profitable, was money exchange. With China's currency fluctuating like a malarial fever chart, G.I.'s who knew the curve of expectancy cashed in while ostensibly ferrying Chinese troops from the interior and Shanghai northwards. They bought Chinese dollars in Kunming at two hundred to one U. S. dollar, sold them in Peiping at five hundred to one, bought gold bars in Peiping for four hundred and fifty dollars and then sold them in Shanghai at seven hundred dollars. With their profits they returned to Kunming and triangulated their deal all over again.

With stricter army supervision, profit-minded privates have been taking their discharges in China and joining organizations like UNRRA so they can run their own "squeezes" on the side with impunity and immunity. Several former Flying Tiger and CNAC (China National Aviation Corp.) pilots have bought up surplus army transport planes and begun flying goods into Shanghai for quick cash turnovers. Such deals are generally quite legal, but early in 1946 a surplus C-46 flown from China was intercepted in Japan with seven tons of opium for transshipment to America.

Chinese operators, probably because they are so busy working angles themselves, do not seem to mind the Americans working simple black market rackets. "In Shanghai there is a black market, a *black* black market and a *black, black* black market," a foreign stockbroker informed me. It is illegal to trade in gold bars, U. S. and Chinese dollars, but it is done quite openly on every street in downtown Shanghai. That's just ordinary common black market.

In mid-February 1946 the Generalissimo ordered Shanghai's stock markets shut down. Police ripped out 1,130 telephones in the Stock Exchange Building on Chung Yang Road. During the ban stocks were bought and sold over and under the counter—not in the closed Stock Exchange Building but almost everywhere else. Daily newspapers still quoted bid and asked prices while stocks rose from 500 to 1000 per cent.

If you knew somebody who knew somebody you could walk into a large room on the fifth floor of a prominent Shanghai bank building and watch millions of dollars in securities change hands before you could say "Chiang Kai-shek." This sort of thing is considered a *black* black market because not everybody and his brother Wang can deal in it.

The *black, black* black market is something nobody wanted to talk about even if they recognized that it existed. It seems, just for example, that UNRRA sold flour to CNRRA which sold it to the public (or what passed as the public) for CNC $9,000 per *picul*. Somehow the flour found its way up the coast by junks to Tientsin where it was sold at CNC $20,000. The Government did not interfere with this process because otherwise, they argued, Tientsin would not get any flour since the Government had no shipping and the railroads were not running and the American planes had no gas and no maintenance crews. The Government was sorry about the extraordinary *black, black* black market price of the flour when it found its way to Tientsin, but they realized the Chinese businessman must make a profit and the man who owned the junk must make a profit.

Few Chinese were very happy over the Shanghai inflation except those who had had so much money for so long that they stopped counting their happiness in dollars, U. S. or CNC. The little man who cannot afford key money and the little woman who never sees the flour UNRRA sent her were not happy. The inflation has ruined China's export trade, impeded postwar production, tended to advance the interest of bureaucratic capitalists and Government monopoly. It has turned small businessmen, the white-collar class, and the organized workers violently against the continuation of the civil war. And even the successful speculator writhed in a thin skin of frustration. Mr. Wang, the overstrained, stubby, shiny-faced secretary to Shanghai's harassed Food Commissioner summed it all up this way: "It's nonsense, you know." Mr. Wang approached the subject of speculators making money, "Suppose I buy goods for one million dollars and sell them for two million. Then suppose I buy something else at two million and sell it at four. You say I make three millions on my one. Then suppose I want to buy the first thing again. It now costs five million. So I lose one million. How can do?"

3

But Shanghai of the 4.5 million is not China of the 450 million. It is an inflamed sore on the skin of China's body politics, a body which is bleeding to death internally. The sore will not clear up until China itself is healed.

A country of 450 million people with a land area thirty times bigger than that of Japan and Korea combined, China is a nation great in its past and great in its potential. Today, except for the few who sit on the backs of the many, China is poor—poor in resources and poor in spirit. China has been denuded by war, eviscerated by hatreds, bound by ignorance as no other country of modern times.

When my Chinese friends search for a simile to describe their country, they often say—"like a wounded giant."

Newspaper editorial writers speculate about China's illness, compare symptoms, prescribe cures, and the patient cries for quiet and rest. There has been no real peace in the vastness of China for as long as most of my friends can recall. Since 1911, revolution and counter-revolution, riot and revolt, invasion and resistance have been the rule rather than the exception.

Toward the latter part of the eight years' war against the Japanese, the Chinese people were apparently united in a common cause for the first time in two decades of internecine struggle. Then the surrender of Japan in 1945 removed the powerful unifying factor of resistance to a common enemy.

Desperately weary of the long war, the Chinese people wanted, needed, and demanded peace. There were indications that the Government, victorious under its Generalissimo and President, Chiang Kai-shek, would at last live up to its great expectations. In that brief flush of world-wide optimism it seemed that China's immediate internal problem—what to do with an armed minority party, the Communists—would be settled over a conference table.

The United States and Russia both gave assurances that they favored a strong, unified and democratic China. On August 26, 1945, the U.S.S.R. and the Government of China concluded an "alliance of good neighborliness." The United States urged Chiang to put his house in order by making a deal with the Communists. On September 3 Chiang definitely stated that he would institute liberal domestic reforms: the legalizing of all political parties, convoking the National Assembly to set up a constitutional government, removing all wartime restrictions on freedom of speech and freedom of the individual, democratizing of the land system, controlling of monopolies.

In an historic meeting with Mao Tse-tung, Chairman of the Communist Party, Chiang and the rival leader agreed to deliberate their differences at a Political Consultative Conference. With Japan defeated, China was invited to the peace table as one of the Big Five. American supplies, loans, and personnel were ready to help reconstruction. Americans were sincerely interested in aiding China and its people far more than they were Japan or Korea or India.

Despite these signs of tranquillity and good intentions, China was seething with internal unrest. It was the unrest of destiny unfulfilled, of revolution frustrated. Its seeds were in the ancient soil of China, in the longing of men to be secure, to feed their families, to work their own fields, to live and learn, to live and let live.

For Westerners it is difficult to understand the interminable struggle in China. We tend to interpret it only in terms of two parties fighting for power. Our knowledge is bounded by yesterday's wire service dispatch and last week's newsmagazine. From them we will probably never learn that in China today the greatest and most effective (and most expensive for the United States) organizing force for Communism is the Kuomintang Party and in particular its hard core of reactionaries who believe in monolithic government and monopoly economy. Most of these men are in the "CC" clique, led by Chiang's friends and collaborators, the brothers Chen.

The Kuomintang is also the Government, the National armies, the secret police. Its ruthlessness, greed and corruption drive people to seek an alternative. "The only realistic alternative when you are being chased by a bad man with a gun is another man with a gun who may or may not be bad," explained my young friend, Liao Wei-chen. Liao is a philosophy student who works for the Kuomintang, watching helplessly as it loses more and more ground, but still pinning his hope in "good men," the beleaguered liberals left in the party. Liao, incidentally, is not his real name.

But there is honest despair even among Kuomintang liberals. The authoritative newspaper, *Ta Kung Pao*, which represents the thinking of the moderate Political Science Group in the party, wrote frankly on February 7, 1947:

In looking over the compilation of our past editorials, the pain one suffers is as if one were by the bedside of a sick man suffering from a hundred diseases. For example, among the things that happened after V-J Day, besides the two big diseases of civil war and the face-losing resumption of sovereignty process, there have been all sorts of strange diseases every single day. Loans for foodstuffs and for industrial development in China have become a shortcut for treacherous merchants to make a fortune; fire-fighting, a necessary thing in modern countries, has become a means for looting and extortion in China. In the streets of Canton men often sell their wives and daughters; in the city of Taiyuan (Shansi) decapitated heads are often hung up as a warning to the masses; hundreds die in airplane crashes, a thousand die when a steamer sinks; last year, in Shanghai alone, 3,500 died under the wheels of automobiles, and the sound of drought and graft is louder than a tolling bell. . . . Conscription, in a modern country, is not strange; the strange thing about conscription in China is that recruits are bought with money, bound up with ropes, and driven to the place of slaughter to kill our own people. . . . As for the living standard of the people, beautiful sounding posters are up on all the walls all over China, yet the Principle of the People's Livelihood (one of Dr. Sun Yat-sen's three People's Principles) written thirty years ago, is confined in a high tower; tenant farmers are panting their last under the double squeeze of the Rice Administration and the landlords, foreign goods are flooding the market, loans at high interest are as fierce as a tiger, and all China is speeding toward bankruptcy. The disaster is as general and cruel as the plague.

It is perhaps just as well for the Kuomintang that the Chinese people do not understand all the delicate ramifications of Western democracy. Recognizing China's backwardness, Dr. Sun had called for a period of "political tutelage" under the then revolutionary leadership of the Kuomintang to achieve nationalism, democracy, and livelihood. Of the three People's Principles, the one that still interests the Chinese most is livelihood. When they have a sufficiently full rice bowl they can think then of democracy and then Nationalism. But under two decades of Chiang's leadership, the Kuomintang has not measurably helped the Chinese people to improve on their livelihood.

What makes China's common people hate government and turn toward anything that holds out a flickering hope? In Hunan, according to Chao Heng-ti of the Hunan Political Consultative Council, an all-party group, the Central Government directed its officials to purchase "surplus" rice for the army at a low price. The rice was seized from the peasants by force and paid for at a low price, although there was no surplus in Hunan during February 1946. In fact, there was famine and American correspondents actually saw Chinese making their daily meal on a soup of grass and earth. Such conditions also existed in Hupeh according to Chen Pao-nan, an official of CNRRA.

In South China cities the situation is such that Government clerks insert advertisements like this in newspapers: "BOY CHILDREN FOR SALE: A friend who has been for many years a civil servant in an administrative office is now unemployed and unable to earn a living. He is willing to sell his five- and nine-year-old sons, both in primary school. Prices may be discussed personally. Please apply at Number 45 Hsueh Men Chien."

In the village of Kuolutang in southern Honan the Government ordered that each *pao* (about one hundred households) should give sixteen able-bodied men to the Army. Many of the families used nitric acid to blind their men to escape conscription, even though some died from over-poisoning.

A letter to the editor of the "CC" clique's newspaper, *Hsin Wen Pao* complains about the Government's methods in the draft:

Since it has started, the men have fled to Shanghai. Then the Government switched to drafting men at night. Plainclothesmen and members of the Self-Defense Corps with guns knock on doors in the middle of the night and take any young men they see. Those who resist are thoroughly beaten. The men of my village do not dare to go back home at night now and they sleep in the fields. At 2 A.M. on the 30th six members of the Self-Defense Corps took away an only son. The father knelt and plead with them because his son was an imbecile, but in vain. They bound up the boy and took him away without showing any official order.

These are a few isolated instances in the record of day to day existence in China which indicate why the common man mistrusts government. It is not helping him.

4

The conflict in China is not primarily caused by a struggle between the "Ins" and the "Outs," although it is that, too. It is not primarily a struggle between capitalism and communism, between freedom and regimentation, between pro-Americans and pro-Russians. It is not a conflict of practical politics on a theoretical level but of theory on the most practical level: which group offers the coolie and peasant a better chance for survival. And survival in China today, as it has been for thousands of years, is based on land—who owns it, who tills it, who taxes it, who eats from it. The party which can best solve the land problems, not from the standpoint of the leaders of the party but from the standpoint of fuller rice bowls for the millions, will eventually win in China.

Because the Communists held out some hope of improving the people's livelihood, the National Government was for years unable to crush them by superiority of arms. Then the Japanese, with even greater superiority of weapons, could not eliminate them.

Almost every Chinese with whom I talked about the Communists agreed they were a "menace" or a "promise" which continued to exist and grow under oppression because they appeared to give the peasants more than the Nationalists or Japanese appeared to offer.

Support for anti-Kuomintang opposition has come from millions of non-Communists in China, people who have not read Marx, people who, in fact, cannot even read. Without the sympathy of these people, chiefly peasants who make up more than three-fourths of China's population, the Communists would have been wiped out many years ago. American Army intelligence reports, for example, indicate that Communist-led forces have a higher ratio of volunteers to draftees than any other major army.

Support has also come from hundreds of disillusioned intellectuals, writers, teachers, students, artists who are what we would call "individualists" and who have decided, often reluctantly, that their chances for full development were better running against the Government than being run by it.

There is a saying in China that "where starvation visits, the weak eat grass and the strong challenge the law." This is based, like so many Chinese sayings, on experience. In May 1946 UNRRA, as a result of its limited investigations, announced that there were thirty-three million destitute people in China. Chinese economists with whom I talked always estimated in terms of fifty or sixty million who were in desperate need of assistance.

Manifold are the reasons given for China's widespread famine, and most of them have a certain measure of validity. Professor Ma Yin-ch'u, a jolly, fat man who taught economics to the Generalissimo, enumerated some of them for me one night: the population-land ratio; the eight years of the anti-Japanese war; the long years of civil war preceding the war of resistance; corruption in the Government; continuation of feudal influence; the conservative land system; technological backwardness in cultivation; the collection of taxes in kind; the breakdown in transportation; uncontrolled inflation.

Until the Japanese war, the Kuomintang did make slow progress in solving China's immense problems. But invasion and civil war turned the clock back again. Reform ideas which once made the people rally to the Kuomintang are still on the ledgers of village, country town, province, and National Government. But they are not being applied.

After the end of the Japanese war, Chiang's Government promulgated a program of help to those in the recovered areas: no tenants could be evicted from lands they were farming; no collection of back rents by absentee landlords; no collection of taxes for one year. The program was implemented, too. Landowners did not have to pay their land tax, the only one to which they are subjected in most provinces. But the peasant—he had to pay surcharges "as numerous as the hairs on a cow's back." He had to pay his household tax, his food tax, his tax on slaughtered animals, his taxes for the army. In addition rice levies were collected, by force when necessary, for repairing hospitals, for the upkeep of schools, for celebrating Chiang's sixtieth birthday, for renovating jails. And in some provinces taxes have been collected five and six years in advance to support Chiang's armies.

Chinese peasants may be ignorant of political freedoms in our sense, but they understand taxes, conscription, greed and graft. They know or have heard that in the Communist "liberated" areas rents were reduced, the properties of collaborationist landlords redistributed and all taxes reduced into a single tax based on income. They believe that no Communist leaders have fattened on expropriation or graft. That, to the hungry and untutored peasant, holds the magic that political democracy does for us.

Recognition of the tremendous significance of this factor in China today is fundamental to any understanding of the civil war and of the two contesting parties. The factor is not a hidden one. American representatives know about it, but too often prefer not to give enough weight to its importance.

In this connection it is interesting to refer to a confidential postwar report made for the U. S. State Department by its Interim Research and Intelligence Service. The unpublished document was discovered by Hugh De Lacy, former Congressman from Washington.

Analyzing the chief difference between Kuomintang and Communist agrarian policies, the report underscores one reason why the Communists have received so much popular following and help from the peasants. It states:

The Kuomintang also endorses this principle of "land-to-the-toilers" but differs with the Communists as to its interpretation. . . . The Kuomintang, which is dominated by big landholders . . . advocates making more land available to the people as tenants rather than as owners. . . .

The decisive dividing line between the Kuomintang and the Communists may be drawn between a Kuomintang policy of safeguarding the emoluments of land ownership and the Communist policy of demanding enough land to guard the economic security of the peasant.

The Communists have clearly identified the Chinese Communist Party as the party of the peasants. Its present program—reduction of rent and interest, progressive taxation, assistance to production, promotion of co-operatives, and institution of popularly elected governments—is designed to meet needs felt by the peasants and to bring about their participation in the solution of their problems.

Congressman De Lacy, in a speech to the House of Representatives, went on to summarize the programs of the two parties for China's future industrial development:

Chiang and his official family dream of a state-controlled heavy industry, run of course, by the present corrupt officialdom, with a light consumers' goods industry part owned by government and part by private Chinese capital, to utilize cheap labor and export into world markets to build up credits.

. The Communists, according to this unpublished State Department report, "argue that the Kuomintang policy of controlling completely the course of economic development will limit foreign participation and adversely affect China's industrial growth." They consequently inveigh against "bureaucratic capitalism," which they contend discourages private enterprise and the initiative needed in China's further growth.

Thus, in the new postwar era, victorious China is worse off than defeated Japan; victorious China grows weaker while defeated Japan recovers. While the Japanese are grateful for American assistance, the Chinese people grow to feel more and more that their ally, United States, is partly responsible for their worsening conditions. The Japanese have new hope, the Chinese have the old despair.

The Government of the United States has not acted deliberately to protract China's misery. It has tried now for years to bridge the difference between the Kuomintang and the Communists, but every time the breach is closed by pressure it widens even further when the pressure is relaxed.

In the first winter after V-J Day the United States made an unparalleled effort to bring about peace in China. The effort failed. Only by carefully reviewing what happened and trying to figure out why it happened, can the American people hope to understand China's problem and the shortcomings of our own policy.

CHAPTER XIX

"THE GOD OF PEACE"

AFTER General Patrick Hurley resigned as U. S. Ambassador to China on November 27, 1945, the President appointed General George C. Marshall as special envoy to China. James F. Byrnes, then Secretary of State, declared on December 4 that the United States "favors the creation of a strong, united, and democratic China and feels that collaboration among China, United States, Britain, and Russia is essential to Far Eastern peace."

When the former Army Chief of Staff departed for Chungking by air on December 15, President Truman attempted to strengthen his hand and to clarify the U. S. position. In a firm statement of policy (see Appendix I), the White House announced that economic assistance would be granted to China only when "a broadly representative government" was established, one that would give "all major political elements in the country . . . a fair and effective representation."

In the final communique on the results of their conference in Moscow a few weeks later, the Foreign Ministers of the Soviet Union and Great Britain again declared themselves in full agreement with Secretary Byrnes on the necessity for a unified and democratic China under the National Government. Restating their policy of non-intervention in China's internal affairs, the communique emphasized the desirability of withdrawing all foreign troops from China as soon as they had completed their assignment in aiding the Chinese to disarm and evacuate Japanese forces.

Marshall wasted no time on preliminaries. His C-54 landed at Shanghai's Kiangwan Airport where he hurriedly inspected the honor guard of the 65th Regiment of the American-equipped New Sixth Army. He drove to Cathay House for a business conference, side-stepping the military music and flourishes in his honor. As his five-starred car weaved through the packed streets, flags were waved and school children were paraded.

Since the Generalissimo was temporarily in Nanking, Marshall stopped to see him there. Then in Chungking he began his assignment immediately. He was at home to representatives of all political factions. They came bearing gift scrolls and problems for *Ma Hsieh-erh* (the transliteration of "Marshall" into Chinese which means "Resting Horse"). In his turn the General asked perceptive questions, listened attentively to the answers, made few comments. In a week he felt well enough briefed to try and reach a military solution to the civil war.

The Government and the Communists eagerly accepted Marshall as mediator on January 1. The Kuomintang appointed as its negotiator stocky, conscientious General Chang Chun, a former classmate of the Generalissimo's. Chang, fifty-eight, who looks like an American Indian, was once Minister of Foreign Affairs, Mayor of Shanghai, and later Governor of Szechwan Province, his birthplace. Spokesman for the Communists was their unofficial "foreign minister," dark-eyed, handsome, lean General Chou En-lai. Born in Chekiang in 1899, Chou was a French return student who became an active member of the Kuomintang until it drove out the Communists in 1927. He had been Chief of the Political Department of the Whampoa Military Academy under Chiang Kai-shek.

The discussions were held at Marshall's Chungking residence, Yu Gardens, in a stone bungalow which had been called "Failure House" because it had been the scene of earlier unsuccessful peace efforts. Marshall listened to the demands of both sides. Then he boldly suggested compromises. All went well for a few days, surprisingly well. Then as the three men sat around the open charcoal fire in Marshall's living room on January 9, a bad snag broke the smoothness. General Chang insisted that the Government must take over the Communist-occupied border provinces of Jehol and Chahar before a truce could be declared. Chou balked at that and refused to hear of any compromise.

On the evening of the 9th Marshall went over Chang's head, spoke directly to the Gimo (a popular contraction of Generalissimo). "The Government," he said in effect, "is certainly strong enough to make this concession to peace in return for having the railroads into Manchuria and other lines of communication opened up."

After a two-hour talk, the Gimo concurred and the truce was drafted the next morning.

Not long afterwards when a Kuomintang army invaded Jehol, it is reported that Chang Chun was furious because he felt he had lost face with Marshall. He reproached the Gimo, saying that it was contrary to what he had agreed upon in the negotiations. "You do the negotiating and I will do the fighting," Chiang Kai-shek replied.

In the famous "Agreement on the Cessation of Hostilities between the Government and the Communist Party" the three Generals stipulated three conditions for peace: (1) an immediate end to all fighting; (2) cessation of all troop movements except for certain specified areas (including the movement of Nationalist troops to take over sovereignty in Manchuria); (3) clearing of all lines of communication. Marshall, who from the outset had worked toward a practical means of enforcing these pledges, suggested that the agreement be implemented immediately. He proposed the establishment of an organization to be called Executive Headquarters, composed of American, Communist, and Nationalist members, which would carry out the three steps. At first the Generalissimo balked, feeling that this procedure raised the Communists to equal status with the Government. The difficulty was ironed out by allowing the Generalissimo to order the activation of the organization and to appoint the commissioners of all three sides.

In Peiping, Marshall had already begun assembling as a nucleus, a small, capable staff of American officers and civilians which would help Executive Headquarters get away to a fast start. A man of direct action, he was suspicious of too much talk. It could lead to dissension as well as agreement. U. S. planes were placed at the disposal of the Communists to enable them to fly some of their representatives from Yenan and other parts of North China. It was quickly arranged with the Rockefeller Foundation to borrow the huge hospital of the Peiping Union Medical College for the duration of the emergency.

Never before in history had two opposing factions in a civil war signed a truce, formed an organization to enforce that truce, and then invited a foreign nation to join it as an equal member. In fact, the Americans were more than equal members. The chairman was to be the American commissioner (Walter S. Robertson, Chargé d'Affaires of the U. S. Embassy) and under him an American director (Brigadier General Harry Byroade) was to run the staff work. In addition the United States contributed all the office and field equipment and most of the administrative know-how. Throughout the whole organization the Americans were to be the dynamic, yet magnetic force which linked two antagonistic bodies together and kept them moving in one main direction.

Within two weeks Executive Headquarters was a going concern. General Cheng Chieh-ming of the National Military Council represented the Generalissimo and General Yeh Chien-ying, Chief of Staff of the Communists' 18th Group Army, spoke for Yenan. American planes scattered a half-million leaflets across the North China countryside proclaiming the truce. The three commissioners met for the first time on January 13, the day the cease-fire became effective. They wrangled a bit about the location of the chief "danger point." On the 17th, however, the first truce team was dispatched to Ch'ih-feng to deliver the Gimo's cease-fire order, to mediate local fighting and to maintain communications with the Headquarters. A week later seven more teams, all consisting of Americans, Nationalists, and Communists with a U. S. Army colonel as the chairman, were scattered through North China. They traveled by plane and jeep and truck, employing the tools of war to bring peace.

Initially the teams radioed back encouraging reports, and the Americans in their cables to the Pentagon optimistically labeled the three-ringed undertaking as "Operation Dove." An insignia was drawn up and worn as a patch by all three sides: it consisted of three interlocking circles similar to the Ballantine beer trademark of "purity, body, and flavor."

2

Marshall did not personally announce this unprecedented success. The good news of the truce was first proclaimed at the opening session of the Political Consultative Conference (PCC) by the Generalissimo himself. The PCC, which was an all-party conference (agreed upon in the fall of 1945 by President Chiang and Chairman Mao Tse-tung of the Communists) to work out a program for unity, heard other almost unbelievable good news from its wartime leader.

The handsome, bullet-headed Chiang concluded his inaugural

speech with these remarks which, if carried out, meant a new day for China:

I wish to take this opportunity to further inform you gentlemen what the Government has decided to carry out:

Freedom of the People: The people enjoy the freedom of person, creed, speech, publication, assemblage and association. The existing laws and regulations will be either repealed or revised on the basis of this principle.

Authorities other than the judiciary and police shall not cause any person to be arrested, or punished.

The Legal Status of Political Parties: All the political parties shall be equal before the law, and may operate openly within the law.

Popular Election: Local self-government will be actively promoted in all places in China and popular election will be held from bottom up in accordance with the law.

Release of Political Prisoners: Political prisoners, except traitors and those found to have committed definite acts injurious to the Republic, will be released.

The applause which greeted these pledges was as thunderous as that which had responded to the news of the truce. Thus, the PCC on January 10, 1946, began its deliberations in an air of great achievement and expectancy. Personal animosities were temporarily subordinated to national benefit. Debate was unusually dignified and restrained.

On the second day Sun Yat-sen's son, round-faced, roly-poly Dr. Sun Fo, told the PCC the government's plan for broadening its base. It was the kind of measure which ordinarily the Communists might have violently attacked as "half-way." This time they listened politely and offered polite suggestions for amendments which were, in most cases, defeated by a majority vote.

In this atmosphere of hope and unity the PCC reached a series of important and far-reaching decisions. The Conference was composed of eight Kuomintang delegates, nine from the middle-of-the-road liberal grouping (including Socialists) called the Democratic League, seven from the Communists, five from the pro-Government Youth Party, and nine representing non-party elements. Within three short weeks these men drew up a blueprint which, if followed, might have become the sturdy framework for democratic rule in China.

Among the constructive suggestions which the PCC worked out were agrarian, educational and industrial reforms and revisions of the 1936 Kuomintang Draft Constitution. The delegates voted that the new Constitution should be presented to a multi-party National Assembly which was to be convoked by all parties in May 1946. It was further decided that a three-fourths vote of the National Assembly would be required to ratify the Constitution. Therefore the apportioning of the number of assembly delegates to each party was extremely important. Unless the minority parties could muster one-quarter of the total votes, the Kuomintang could ride roughshod over the constitutional convention. The PCC agreed that the Kuomintang should have 220 members, the Communists 190, the Democratic League 120, and the Youth Party, 100. In addition there were 950 delegates "elected" to the 1936 National Assembly of which all but 50 were Kuomintang. Finally there were to be 70 "non-partisans" about equally divided in sympathies between the Government and the opposition. This apportionment gave the pro-Kuomintang bloc approximately 1,250 certain votes to about 400 or more from the opposition groups. Another block of 400 seats were to be contested for in an election.

Significant changes which the PCC wanted written into the draft Constitution included the following: (1) that a bill of rights grant unrestricted civil liberties; (2) that the Legislative Yuan (Congress) would have sole power to introduce new laws, that it would be directly elected by the people and that the Executive Yuan (Cabinet) would be directly responsible to it; (3) that a majority "no confidence" vote by the Legislative Yuan would force the Executive Yuan either to resign or to request the President to order a national election; (4) that the President and Vice-President be elected by direct popular vote; (5) that the provinces be permitted to write their own constitutions, elect their own governing officials and in general be granted privileges and rights similar to those of the forty-eight states in the United States; (6) that the military be placed under the civilian control of an all-party National Defense Committee; (7) that the mechanics for holding democratic elections be established.

The government had made concessions on a number of issues, while the opposition parties had accepted a formula for the projected coalition government which greatly favored the Kuomintang. The Communists had been willing to cede central power to the government in exchange for assurances that they would have a greater say in local provincial administrations within the national framework.

While General Marshall had no direct connection with the summoning of the PCC, it is obvious that the unanimity and harmony achieved would not have been possible if the dissident groups had not had complete faith in his mission and in his personal integrity. For the first time in twenty years the Chinese peasant and worker, scholar and bureaucrat saw "a bright break in the dark clouds." The Associated Press reported that January 18, 1946, was the first day in eighteen years without any fighting in China.

Addressing the final session of the PCC, President Chiang congratulated the delegates on their great work and in his thin, piping voice, prophesied: "From now on the leaders of the various parties of society will all participate in the government and shoulder jointly the great responsibility of shaping the future of the country. From now on the heavy task . . . rests not on the Kuomintang alone and much less on me as an individual. . . . From now on, whether in the government or out of it, I will faithfully and resolutely observe, as a citizen should, all the decisions of this conference, sincerely work for peace and solidarity, and urge the nation to take the road of unification and democracy."

The PCC had agreed in principle that there could be no political unity in China so long as there remained personal or private armies; the Communists indicated their willingness to place their forces under a non-political Minister of Defense.

Actual details of combining the three hundred divisions in the Kuomintang and Communist armies was left to a subcommittee headed by Chou En-lai and the Government General Chang Chih-chung. Marshall sat with them as adviser. On February 25 in a Chungking office they signed a document calling for the fusion and reorganization of the Government and Communist armies. It not only ended all private armies but forbade area commanders from meddling in civilian affairs. Within eighteen months there was to be only one army in China consisting of sixty divisions, of which the former Communist armies would comprise ten divisions. It was further agreed that the reorganization and retraining of the new unified army would be aided by U. S. officers. The knotty problem of how the Kuomintang would exercise control over top-level Communists was solved by a Marshall compromise: that the Generalissimo retain the power to appoint and relieve all officers but if he dismissed a Communist commander he was pledged to replace him with a man nominated by the ranking Communist member of the Government.

Marshall called this pact "the great hope of China" and pleaded "that its pages will not be soiled by small groups of irreconcilables who for selfish purpose would defeat the Chinese . . . desire for . . . peace and prosperity."

With Communist Chou and Nationalist Chang Chih-chung, Marshall flew around North China, covering 3,500 miles and visiting ten cities and towns in less than a week early in March. Everywhere he was greeted with wild enthusiasm by Communists and Kuomintang alike, hailed by banner-bearers as "The God of Peace," "Terror of the Evildoers," and "First Lord of all Warlords." News of the truce teams' successes in Hopei, Shantung, and Shansi had preceded the triumphal tour. Marshall was tremendously moved by the unfeigned joy and gratitude he read on the faces of the thousands who lined the streets to see him. Later it was charged that fighting ceased as he arrived and resumed as he departed. But the effect of the junket was tonic to the people's hopes.

In Yenan Marshall met and conferred with Mao Tse-tung for the first time. At Hankow he made a speech, saying that "Military agreements will be carried out" and that he found the situation "most encouraging." He concluded: "Last month and the next two are the most critical months in the history of China."

He may have been right. History might also add a footnote that the course of events in one of those two months might have been different if George Marshall had remained in China. Instead he departed for Washington on March 11 after getting the two sides to agree that the cease-fire order and truce agreement be extended to Manchuria. He left as his substitute an earnest soldier but no diplomat, Lieutenant General Alvin C. Gillem, Jr.

3

In Washington Marshall drove straight to the White House to confer with President Truman. What the two men said is not known, but the next morning Special Envoy Marshall optimistically reported to a press conference what he thought had been accomplished. Characteristically he did not mention his own role except to point out that the Executive Headquarters, which he had created, was the "most important instrument we have in China":

The Chinese people are engaged in an effort which should command the grateful co-operation of the entire world. It is an effort almost without precedent. Their leaders are making daily progress toward the settlement . . . deep-seated and bitter conflicts which have lasted for twenty years. . . . They are succeeding in . . . ending hostilities . . . and are now engaged in the business of demobilizing vast military forces and integrating the remainder into a national army. They have agreed to basic principles for the achievement in China of political and economic advances which were centuries coming to Western democracies. . . .

If we are to have peace—if the world wants peace, there are compelling reasons why China's present effort must succeed. This depends in a large measure on actions of other nations. If China is ignored, or if there is scheming to thwart her present aspirations, her effort will fail. . . .

The next few months are of tremendous importance to the Chinese people and . . . to the future peace of the world. . . .

Up to this point Marshall had been phenomenally successful because the Government and the Communists both trusted him. It was not necessary for him to remind Chou that if the Communists would not co-operate, there would be those in the United States demanding that America give more aid to the Kuomintang; nor to tell Chang that if the Government were intransigeant about reform and peace, American investors would consider China a poor risk and Congress might withhold loans. Both sides knew that the Special Envoy held almost absolute control over all aid-to-China programs, both civilian and military. They felt, at least until he went home, that he would not use his power unfairly.

Marshall brought to his job certain attributes which Generals MacArthur and Hodge lacked. One such asset was summed up by Henry Stimson, former Secretary of State and War, who observed that "General Marshall's ability has no ceiling, it expands with the job." In China, the General lived up to this estimate. He was a man who had the important faculty of being able to see the woods and the trees at the same time. Time and again he was able to find validity in diametrically opposed viewpoints and to make the opponents acknowledge, at least to him, this validity.

Throughout the year of his mission, Marshall's tactics were admirable. When the Chinese were remote and polite, Marshall was straightforward and definite. When the Chinese were opinionated and obstinate, Marshall was polite and unhurried. His capacity for patience was almost as great as his capacity for learning.

In all, during his mission, he held over three hundred formal recorded conversations with the Government and the Communists, sometimes singly, sometimes together. Frequently when things were at an impasse, he wisely called a halt for a few days to give the negotiators time to think things over and to check with their party colleagues. At other times he cut through generalizations and pressed for a minimum agreement *on paper*.

His personality stood the insidious test of the cold, damp Szechwan winter in Chungking, and later the moist, enervating heat of summer in Nanking. He kept his temper and his good will during the irritating backing and stalling, during the deceit and name-calling on both sides, during unending hours of droning translations. Repeatedly the other negotiators tested him, entrusting to him items of information which they asked that he not reveal to the other party. They found him above reproach at keeping secrets but were somehow incredulous when he expected the same silence from them on certain touch-and-go negotiations.

Marshall's physical stamina wore out his small staff. His capacity for work seemed to increase with the urgency of the objective situation without relation to his own bodily well-being, the climate or hours of sleep. On some days he would conduct negotiations two or three times, and if a "break" occurred late in the evening he would be willing to meet again for as long as there appeared to be a rewarding discussion.

Shortly after his arrival in China leading members of the Democratic League called on Marshall to present their analysis of the situation. During the discussion one of them asked Marshall for his understanding of democracy. The General's reply was similar to the definition which he gave Soviet Foreign Minister Molotov in Moscow more than a year later. Modestly he apologized for talking in conceptual terms to a group of intellectuals. "I might say," the General began, "that there seem to be a great many definitions of democracy in the world today. . . . The Russians have one, the British have another, we have our own." He paused and frowned. "I can only tell you what many Americans consider to be the definition of democracy. We think of it as a system which gives us an inherent right to have a voice in our own affairs, the right to speak freely, the right to assemble peaceably, and to go about our own affairs without interference unless we interfere with the rights of others."

The liberals who listened to him agreed that China had never had such democracy, and that a government which could introduce and safeguard such a happy state of affairs would surely be loved and respected by the Chinese people.

On another occasion Marshall impressed General Chou by his application of American history to the current Chinese scene. One day when Chou was discouraged by the bickering in the PCC, Marshall handed him the translation of a paragraph which he had found while rereading Benjamin Franklin's autobiography. Later the quotation might have made an eloquent epitaph on the demise of Marshall's mission itself. Referring to our own Constitutional Assembly, Franklin had observed: "When you assemble a number of men to have the advantage of their joint wisdom, you inevitably assemble with those men all their prejudices, their passions, their errors of opinion, and their selfish views. From such an assembly can perfection be expected? It therefore astonishes men to find this system approaching so near to perfection as it does. . . ."

4

The great weakness in the picture of peace which Marshall had patched together was that the military truce was only effective so long as there was strong hope of a political settlement and so long as Marshall was around to maintain the delicate balance. Even before Marshall flew home to report, minor cracks appeared in the picture: there were elements in both camps which were not satisfied with peaceful compromise. Right-wing Kuomintang gangs raided meetings in Chungking where earnest discussions were being held on PCC issues. A happy, boisterous Chungking demonstration celebrating the successful conclusion of the PCC was turned into a riot. Several liberals were attacked and beaten. Following the old adage that the best defense is a vigorous offense, the Kuomintang-controlled press accused the liberals of fomenting and leading the riot.

The Kuomintang press and party agitators were also quick to seize and use the issue of Soviet Russia's factory-stripping in Manchuria. Genuine popular indignation against what was regarded as an unfriendly act was fanned with fervor. Anti-Soviet demonstrations were organized in several cities. The Communists, while they did not approve the stripping either publicly or privately, kept silent. Chou En-lai, when I asked him what he thought of the Russian action, said: "You know I cannot answer that question. No matter what I would say it would be used against us by our enemies." I inquired whether he considered what the Russians had acquired could be called "war booty," and Chou replied: "I have heard that during T. V. Soong's talks with Stalin that Stalin told Soong what the Red Army was prepared to remove from Manchuria as war booty, and Soong made no strong objections."

At about the same time a Kuomintang representative, traveling from Mukden to Fushun to take over the great Manchurian coal mines, was pulled off the train and murdered, although he had a safe-conduct pass from the Russians. This Manchurian tragedy had a second act later when the Nationalists seized Fushun from the Communists and proceeded to intimidate the Soviet engineers and their families left behind by the Red Army.

The first major political setback came in March just after Marshall's departure. The Kuomintang Central Executive Committee (CEC) met to approve the PCC decisions. They did—with certain amendments which negated the chief gains of the PCC. By this show of strength the reactionaries proved that they still controlled the Kuomintang Party. Chiang, despite his pledges at the PCC, did nothing effective to fight their ultra-reactionary stand. In fact, John Hersey in a dispatch from Peiping to the New Yorker, stated flatly that they were "acting on an explicit O.K. from the Generalissimo." Under the "CC" leadership of Chen Li-fu and his brother, Chen Kuo-fu, the Kuomintang Executive Committee demanded that in "the new democratic government" the president have almost dictatorial power; it repudiated the principle adopted from the British system of a cabinet responsible to the elected legislature; it pared down non-Kuomintang representation in the proposed coalition government; it resolved that provincial constitutions were unnecessary. Most of this retreat was accomplished under the sanctimonious guise of adhering to Dr. Sun Yat-sen's wishes.

The Communists saw this as the familiar handwriting on the wall of Chinese history. "Another sell-out," said Chou En-lai. Thus when the PCC itself met again later in March the multi-party delegations promptly split over Communist and Democratic League charges that the Kuomintang, by the actions of its Central Executive Committee, had "sabotaged" the January agreements.

On the military front, Communist armies were rapidly filtering through Manchuria. They had disarmed many Japanese divisions and now they managed to move into strategic spots ahead of the

Nationalists as the Russians evacuated them. Whether or not this was a plan arranged by the Chinese Communists and the Soviet Army is still a matter for conjecture; the fact is that the Russians put no major obstacles in their path. The wholesale sabotage of the war potential in the area, however, left little doubt that the Soviet high command anticipated that the Central Government, and not the Communists, would eventually control Manchuria.

CHAPTER XX

"OPERATION DOVE" IN MANCHURIA

ALTHOUGH General Marshall had persuaded the Chinese factions to extend the cease-fire order to Manchuria before he flew back to Washington on March 11, both sides deliberately delayed on taking any action. Not until March 27 did the Committee of Three, representing the top-ranking officials of the Americans, Nationalists and Communists in Executive Headquarters, sign the order permitting the tripartite truce teams to enter Manchuria where the civil war had become most intense. Two days later all available U.S. planes were mobilized in Peiping and a giant air lift began. Within a few hours the DC-3's and DC-4's had transported the men and officers of four field teams to Mukden, including their clothing, food, trucks, jeeps, fuel, radio transmitters, and other inpedimenta.

In Nationalist-held Mukden an operational base was established. But the machinery of peace stalled again while the officials argued over the scope of Executive Headquarters' authority in Manchuria. The Nationalist command for southern Manchuria, General Hsiung Shih-hui, at first refused to grant permission for teams to operate in his area. Brigadier General Harry Byroade, the youthful American executive director of "Operation Dove," failed to budge General Hsiung. Then, through channels, Byroade threatened to cable Marshall in Washington that the Government was sabotaging the truce. This brought results. The Generalissimo sent instructions to General Hsiung and General Hsiung informed Byroade that he had "changed his mind."

Still nothing happened, although rumors and reports poured into Mukden daily about large-scale fighting within a radius of fifty miles. The Communists, who were holding most of Manchuria's key cities with the exception of Mukden, appeared anxious to preserve the Manchurian status quo especially as new Government armies were being rapidly transported to the northeast by the U.S.

Army and Navy. By the same token, the Nationalists were not eager to put the truce into effect until they had a chance to regain certain strategic areas and their badly defaced military prestige.

Byroade, who worked tirelessly despite his poor health, threatened, cajoled, begged. Finally by getting the representatives of both sides in the same room and "knocking their heads together" for thirteen hours, Byroade achieved a compromise on the original compromise. The morning of April 8, almost two weeks after reaching Mukden, the first team actually set out from Mukden for a troubled zone. Its instructions were vague enough to suit both sides. The team was to collect military information which would ultimately be valuable to General Marshall and his Chinese colleagues in arriving at a settlement of the Manchurian issue. In addition to the fact-finding, the Americans hoped the team could attempt to arbitrate local hostilities on the side and on the *q.t.* to negotiate an unofficial "black market peace."

I was fortunate enough to be one of three American correspondents permitted to accompany that first field team (Number 29). What follows is an account of its adventures, its efforts, and its frustrations. The experience of Team 29 perhaps illustrates better than anything else the mundane and many problems of peace-making which must be met and solved by men on the actual operations level. By comparison, the jobs of policy-makers often seem simple.

2

The ninety *li* (one *li* is approximately one-third of a mile) from Mukden to the great coal mining center of Fushun were uneventful. About 11 A.M. an L-5 circled prettily above our small convoy and dropped information about the condition of roads ahead: "Bad but passable." At another point we switched off the ignition while our radio jeep tried and failed to establish contact with the main transmitter in Mukden. The Manchu peasants didn't flock around our vehicles with curious eyes. They would have gone their own way by foot or oxcart or donkey, but a motley patrol of Nationalist troops materialized from the nearest house and threw a protective cordon around us. With a great show of efficiency they jabbed bayonets at every straggler, searching for hidden arms. When I asked why it was done, a Nationalist colonel said, "Maybe *chien fei* [bandits]. Must be careful these times."

Since I had made the journey to Fushun previously, I rode in the first jeep with the three team commanders during the last leg of the trip. The American and nominal spokesman, Lieutenant Colonel Robert Drake, a red-faced, beak-nosed telephone engineer from Uniontown, Pa., General Marshall's birthplace, drove the jeep. He was a forty-one-year-old veteran of the Burma campaign. Huddled in the back were his Nationalist and Communist opposite numbers. The Nationalist was short, silent, handsome Major General Kuo Chi, a forty-year-old landlord's son from Szechwan. The Communist, tall, homely Major General Hsu Kwan-ta, had been on the Long March, the Communists' epic trek northward. In the middle of the one good bridge leading into Fushun the jeep became ensnared with a bunch of oxcarts loaded with coal. While trying to extricate ourselves a little Japanese jeep flying a Chinese flag weaved through the traffic, honking angrily. It stopped nose to nose with our Willys. General Liu Y. Foo, Nationalist commander of the Fushun garrison hopped out. Drake introduced himself and his colleagues, then directly explained his business. "I want to get the disposition of opposing forces in this neck of the woods," he said. Then he waited patiently for his words to be translated.

General Liu, who started nodding agreement even before the translation was completed, replied, "I only take care of this area . . . Fushun."

"Where do I get the information I want?" Drake asked. The Chinese General when he talked looked directly at Kwang, Drake's translator, Drake always kept his eyes fixed on the man he was questioning.

Liu told Drake he'd have to go to the headquarters of Lieutenant General Chao Kung-wu, Commander of the 52nd Army, about one hundred *li* away.

"What's the condition of the road?"

"The road is destroyed."

Drake played with the peak of his garrison cap. "All I want to know is whether it's possible to get through or not."

Liu replied, "For about ten *li* the road is all right. After that it disintegrates. But about twenty *li* away you will find some Communist troops."

"O.K. about the Communists. We intend to visit them too. Can I go to Chao's headquarters?" Drake pulled back the sleeve of his parka and looked at his wristwatch.

"If you want to see the General, I will have to send a telegram first to ask . . ."

"Tell General Liu we have a passport which will permit us to go anywhere," Drake cut in on the translator. Liu shook his head. "I will send the telegram to ask for instructions," he said smiling.

Drake smiled too but his voice had snap in it as he addressed his translator: "Kwang, tell the General we are here to give instructions, not to ask for them." He paused and repeated, "Can we go on right away?"

"The road . . ." began Liu.

"We'll push on as far as the road will permit us to go," said Drake.

Liu was puzzled. "But the Communists . . . the fighting . . . ?"

Drake was direct: "Our instructions are to push on and get to the fighting."

Liu looked at Nationalist General Kuo. Kuo cleared his throat and said to Drake, "The Communists are only twenty *li* away. Maybe it would be better to investigate there first."

Communist General Hsu lit a Camel.

Drake didn't seem to hear Kuo's suggestion. He pointed his forefinger at Liu. "If the General will be kind enough to furnish us with a guide we'd better get a move on. If we can't get through we will come back here to Fushun tonight."

Liu glanced at Kuo again, but Kuo's eyes were on the ground. Hsu was grinning. He looked like a Philadelphia dentist. Liu took off his cap and mopped his round bald head, although it was a cool day. "I am only responsible for this area," he repeated. "I am not even sure where General Chao's headquarters are, so I will have to send a telegram."

Some of the oxcart drivers began to shout their impatience. All traffic on the bridge had been halted.

Drake insisted he'd get what local military information Liu could give him and then go on as far as possible toward Chao's field headquarters. He climbed back into his jeep and followed the little Jap car back to Nationalist Divisional headquarters high on a hill overlooking Fushun. The headquarters were in a very fashionable Japanese house, surrounded by pillboxes, electrified barbed wire, and guards. We filed in, nobody bothering to remove his boots in the sitting room. Tea was served by soldiers. Then Liu introduced his chief of staff, Colonel Ching, who unrolled a handmade map and began to explain in a musical voice, "Yesterday here," he pointed to the well-worn map, "at four o'clock Communists came—one hundred of them and destroyed the water tower and the power plant."

"How far is that from Fushun?" Drake wanted to know.

"Twenty *li* south. At the same time yesterday one thousand *palus* (8th Route Army soldiers) appeared at Chien Kuo Cha, twenty-five *li* south."

Drake took out his notebook. "How many battalions in your division?"

Ching answered without hesitation, "About ten, including artillery."

"How much artillery?"

"One artillery battalion."

"How many men in a battalion?"

"About six hundred."

"Good. What information do you have on any other Nationalist forces in this area?"

Liu coughed. "None," said Ching quickly, "but we have some on Communist troops on the other side of Fushun."

"That's fine," Drake said, "let's have it all."

"At Huan Chi Ying yesterday at 11 A. M. about two thousand *palus* including cavalry show up. That's about eighteen *li* north."

"What regiment?"

Ching said they had no information on that. "At 1 P.M. yesterday," he continued, "about six thousand Communist troops showed up here." He bent over the map. "That's about twenty-five *li* southwest. At Sha Chang Tang at 9 A.M., two thousand Communists destroyed the railroads and at the same time asked food from the people there and one village head was shot by these *palus*."

"How far?"

"About thirty *li* northeast. This is about all the activities of Communist troops yesterday," Ching concluded with a slight bow. "Maybe there is some more in some other area."

"Where are Communist main headquarters?" Drake asked.

"Penki." (This was spelled *Penhsihu* on my map.)

Drake thought a moment. "Can I get a copy of this map? Mine is not large enough to show the detail."

General Liu, in a flowery little speech, said it was his only copy, otherwise he would be only too glad to make Colonel Drake a present of it. "That's fine," said Drake, "then you won't mind if I have my lieutenant make a tracing of it."

Without awaiting a reply, Drake hurried on: "How many Communists would you say there are in this area? Troops, I mean." Drake rummaged in his briefcase for the tracing paper and found it.

"About sixty thousand," said Liu. He put on his hat. "But sometimes there are only a very few thousand."

Drake asked about the possibility of arranging quarters for the teams. There were twelve Nationalists, six Americans, and eight Communists. Liu readily agreed to furnish billets. "But the senior members of the team," Drake said, indicating Kuo and Hsu, "we want to get to Chao's headquarters right away."

"It is impossible," Liu said politely.

"Why?"

Liu took off his hat again. "In the first place, it is rather dangerous. We cannot inform the Communists. They may shoot. In the second place, I do not know the actual place of General Chao's headquarters. That is all the difficulties," Liu said.

Drake put on his hat. It seemed to make him taller and the big brass eagle insignia in front made him look very official. "I appreciate all the difficulties. But tell the General we came on this mission with the understanding we might get killed trying to do a job. I'd like to go on. My jeep has an American flag. That will give us a certain amount of protection. I also have passports for each man."

Liu sighed, not comprehending Drake's impatience. "I still have to send a radio message," he protested. "I do not know where Chao's headquarters are."

"Fine," Drake agreed, "send the message. If we don't find Chao today we will know where to find him tomorrow."

Liu put on his hat this time with an air of finality. "Go if you want to," he drained his dish of tea and stood up, "I will not accept responsibility for your lives or your safety."

Drake took Liu's hand and shook it, beaming as if Liu had just given him a thousand *taels* of silver. "General, we don't ask you to take that responsibility. There's danger and we are prepared to meet it." They shook hands. "If you will just give me a guide to the edge of town and have him point out the road . . . ?"

"Yes," said Liu, "but surely you will stop for tiffin. We are already preparing a small banquet."

"That's fine," said Drake. "The other members of the team can eat, but General Kuo and General Hsu and I must start as soon as the guide comes." He looked at his watch. It was a little past noon.

3

The guide came in half an hour and rode with us to the last Nationalist outpost southwest of Fushun. Drake roared ahead in his jeep with Kwang, his interpreter, and Generals Kuo and Hsu. We followed at a dusty distance in a truck. About one hour and ten miles later we stopped at a village which consisted of about thirty squat mud huts. A semicircle of villagers stood off a few paces watching Drake's jeep. Drake climbed out, approached the oldest man in the group, introduced himself and then began firing questions. How many soldiers were here? Government or *palus*? When did they leave? Which way did they go? Where is that? How far?

The oldest man replied that Government forces had left his village yesterday morning and had gone west towards Mukden.

"Which way is Penki?" Drake asked next.

"One hundred and twenty *li*," said the oldest man. "Follow this road."

"How far are the Communists?"

"You'll see some just south of here. About ten *li*."

"Was there fighting in this village?"

The oldest man shook his head. "The fight was in another place, four days ago."

"How many Government troops?"

"About ten thousand."

"Who won the battle?"

For the first time the oldest man hesitated. He whispered with several of his neighbors, then said, "Neither side wins the battle." Drake asked more questions about this, but the old man refused to elaborate.

Our two vehicles moved on again along the narrow, rutted dirt road, winding through an almost treeless valley. We didn't move far. In the next village Communist patrols stopped us. After Communist General Hsu had explained the mission of the truce team, the Communists convoyed us to Ying Shao Pao. Their regimental headquarters was a farmhouse undecorated by flag or insignia. Chickens, geese, hogs, and horses were jammed together in the front yard, guarded by one lone sentry. Bread was being baked in a blackened brick stove just outside the house. We sat on the *k'ang* (a straw-matted, brick, heated platform about three feet high and five feet wide, where the whole family sleeps) and sipped tea in the big dirt-floored room. On the wall was a color reproduction showing Chinese quintuplets.

Drake addressed his questions to Colonel Nan Ping, Deputy Commander, and Lieutenant Colonel Han Fou-tung, Deputy Chief of Staff of the 8th Route Army's Third Brigade. This time by unwritten protocol, little Shen Yin-chih, the Communist General's interpreter, did the translating. Kwang, a Cantonese, had been in the Nationalist army and was on loan to Executive Headquarters for this assignment.

Drake quickly found out the names of commanding officers, the disposition of Communist and Nationalist troops in the immediate area. It checked with the information he already had from General Liu.

"Where can I get such a map?" said Drake, pointing to the one the Deputy Chief of Staff was using.

"In Penki. That is the headquarters of the United Democratic Army of which we are a part."

"Who is the top man in Penki?" Drake asked.

"In Liaoning Province it is Chang Hsueh-shih," replied the Deputy Brigade Commander respectfully.

"That's the Young Marshal's brother," I told Drake.

"How do you spell it?" Drake asked. He wrote it down. "How many brigades are there in this United Democratic Army, and are there fifteen thousand men in each?"

"Nine brigades and the number varies."

"Have there been any battles near here?"

"At Shih Wan Kwan, the place you just passed," said the Colonel.

"Were many killed?"

"The number of casualties was great."

"On both sides?"

"On both sides," said Nan Ping.

Drake pressed for more specific details, failed. Suddenly Deputy Commander Nan said, "We do not want fighting, we want peace."

"That's why the Americans are here," Drake said cheerfully. "All we expect to get out of it is to see the fighting stop and make a friend of China."

"Thank you," said the Colonel.

"Where's your home," Drake asked.

"In Honan, near the Yellow River."

"How long have you been here?"

"I grew up here," said the Colonel, "I was only born in Honan." The Colonel said he was thirty-two and not married "because there's been no chance to marry." He had been in the army constantly for twelve years.

"Where can I get complete information on all your troops in this province?"

"Penki."

"That's fine. We will go there day after tomorrow. Can you inform your people that we will be there?"

The Colonel agreed to do it. The sun was sinking and Drake decided if we were to make Fushun before dark we'd better get started.

"The road is pretty bad," he said to Kuo and Hsu. "We'll get to Chao's tomorrow with an early start." They agreed.

The bamboo circuit had been working. In the gathering dusk, the shadowy streets of the villages were strung with bright-eyed people, people who had lived for fourteen years under Japanese oppression. Mothers held up their small children who had never known the real meaning of the word "peace" and whispered into their ears the sounds that might bring real peace to Tungpei. "Mei kuo. . . ." Older boys and girls rushed from the millet fields like children flocking to see a parade. They did not wave or shout. Once in a while when our truck slowed down for an exceptionally bad hole in the road a villager would smile shyly and say, "Mei kuo—ding hao. . . ." Americans—very good."

It was almost dark as we drove the last miles between the Communist lines and the Nationalist outposts at Fushun. A few shots rang out from the breast-shaped hillocks. Drake speeded up. We made it into the city limits.

Next morning General Kuo sent his aide from the house where he was quartered to the house where Drake was staying to report that he was sick. Drake, the only one of the three who didn't give a damn about "face" as long as he accomplished his job, went around to see Kuo. The Nationalist General said he would be unable to make the trip to General Chao's headquarters. Drake expressed regret, but said he counted on Kuo's Colonel representing him on the trip and he hoped the General would be well enough the next day to go to Penki. Kuo said he did not know how anybody could go to Penki because there was so much firing.

"The Communists said they'd stop it for us," Drake reminded him.

Kuo said he was not even certain whether he was supposed to go that far through Communist lines. Maybe they should first check with Mukden.

Drake went to see General Liu. Had General Liu gotten a message through to General Chao's headquarters? General Liu said he had bad news. The radio transmitter was not working. But he had good news, too. The Mayor was giving a party with dancing girls for Colonel Drake and the peace mission that night at five.

Drake held on to his temper and intimated that he wasn't going to any parties until he had made an effort to get to Nationalist headquarters.

"I understand," said Liu, who obviously did not. "I can tell you where headquarters was three days ago."

"That's fine," said Drake, "and perhaps someone there can tell me where it is now."

It was almost eleven before Drake set out. When he came back about five, he was tired, dusty, and discouraged. He had been mired five times but he'd gotten to within five miles of Chao's headquarters when a Communist patrol stopped him and ordered him flatly not to proceed further because there was too much fighting.

The Mayor's party was a gala affair with Chinese food, Japanese hostesses, Russian beer, and a bastard kind of brandy made in China by Japanese according to an American formula. If the formula called for a minimum of flavor and a maximum of alcoholic content, then the brandy was an unqualified success. So was the party. Even General Kuo, now recovered, had some fun.

A local Nationalist General who spoke English introduced me to Mr. Koan Ta-cheng, who wore a dark Western-style suit and a heavy gold watch chain across his ample stomach.

"He is Mayor of Penki," said the General whose name was Lio, which was confusing to an untrained New York ear, since the Mayor of Fushun was a General Lo and the garrison commander was Liu.

I took Mr. Koan's card, shook his hand, and said conversationally, "I am going to Penki tomorrow."

"Yes," said General Lio, "and the Mayor will go there in three or maybe four days." The Mayor beamed.

"But the Communists are holding Penki," I said.

"Yes," said Lio, "but in three or four days? I will tell you something. There is now a big battle near Penki . . ." he winked and repeated, "Mr. Koan will be going there in three or maybe four days."

For every speech there was a *kan pei* (dry glass) drunk. There were fourteen or fifteen courses and almost as many speeches as courses. Drake, who had never had any particular trouble standing up to the liquid onslaughts of the coal miners back in Uniontown, Pa., and who could outdrink his men in Burma, kept up with his hosts handsomely. His face got beet red and he used more slang in his speech but few people were sober enough to notice or care.

4

The next morning when heads were bursting, Drake was up at six and eager to start for Penki. Nationalist General Kuo had made up his mind not to go. He and General Hsu were closeted with Drake for several hours. Kuo maintained that the team's authority, as he understood it, was strictly confined to the Fushun area. Penki was one hundred and sixty *li* away and he did not consider it within the team's jurisdiction. Drake overruled him. Kuo stood firm. He said he recognized that the American official was the chairman of the triumvirate, but on something as basic as this he believed it wiser to get a clarification from his superior in Mukden. Hsu sided with Drake. Drake, trying to avoid an open break, agreed to radio Mukden for instructions. By the time contact was made, and an answer came back, it was too late to set off for Penki that day. The answer was, in effect, "The American officer has the right to make such decisions unless there are directives to the contrary." Kuo accepted this edict with good grace.

At six on the morning of the eleventh we set off for Penki. As usual Drake and the two Generals rode ahead in the jeep. We followed in a weapons carrier which we were driving ourselves. Behind us in a six-by-six truck were additional members of the Chinese teams. Not many *li* from Fushun it became obvious that the journey was going to be very slow and arduous, if not impossible. Somebody, presumably the Communists, had dug three or four foot deep slit trenches varying in width from a foot to a yard across the road every hundred feet or so. In most cases it was impossible to drive off the roadbed without bogging down in the thaw-soaked fields.

We managed to get over the first few trenches. When the road was unexpectedly good for a brief stretch, Drake's jeep went from second to high for the first time in an hour. Then we saw the jeep suddenly halt. I slowed down. Drake's jeep was surrounded by five wild-looking characters dressed in an odd assortment of civilian clothes. When we rolled up closer I could see they were carrying big pistols in their right and homemade grenades in their left hands. The pistols were cocked. Drake had his hands up. So did Kuo. So did Hsu, the Communist General. They had all been ordered out of the jeep. Drake shouted at us: "Stop and get out!"

We got out. Then Drake yelled, although we weren't more than twenty feet away, "Don't take out your cameras. Don't move. They'll shoot."

"Who are they?" I asked.

"Reds, I guess," said Drake. "They are uncertain whether to take us prisoner or kill us."

The wild-eyed youths waved for us to join the others, standing in a soggy field. The gunmen paced around us, nervously, continually jabbing their cocked pistols at us. Shots sounded in the hills. We saw a company of bayonet-carrying troops dotting the ridge of the nearest blue-green hill. As we watched, they fanned out and deployed around us in a big circle.

Hsu, the Communist General was trying to talk like a Dutch uncle to one of the youthful plainclothesmen. But they kept walking away from him. "He won't recognize the Communist General's credentials," explained Kwang, the translator, with a weak grin. He kept grinning. "There's an old Chinese proverb," he said. "You can't shoot a man with a smiling face."

Presently we could hear the six-by-six groaning along the road. The *palus* dispatched some men with rifles to stop it.

"Colonel Li is on that truck. Maybe they will recognize him," said Drake hopefully. Li was a pock-marked *palu* whom Hsu had shrewdly added to his team that first day during our visit to the Communist brigade headquarters.

Li probably saved our lives. The Communists kept us prisoners for a long hour while Li went with one of them to locate their company commander. When Li returned he was smiling and the company commander was smiling and pistols and bayonets were lowered, slightly.

"They were not expecting you today," Li reported cheerfully. "It's all right now, we can go ahead."

"Whew!" said Drake. "I don't mind telling you boys that I was plenty scared. I didn't get through the worst of the Burma campaign to come out here and lose my life settling someone else's war."

Everyone tried to talk at once, describing how he had felt. Only Kuo was silent. He called for his aide and translator, Colonel Tzai, and talked quietly to him. Then Tzai reported to Drake. "The General says let us go back to Fushun at once."

Drake was thunderstruck. "Why?" he asked. "Why turn back?"

Kuo's answer was indirect. "We have made a decision to go to Penki. The Communists sent a radiogram to their people that we were coming. This outrageous hold-up makes no sense."

"It would be bad news for the world that we allowed ourselves to be stopped by one patrol," said Drake.

"I was insulted," said Kuo, "they used cursing words." He inclined his head towards the *palu* patrol.

"I don't know what they said," said Drake, "but there is always bitterness in civil war. Look at our own civil war. . . ."

"I am the Government representative," said Kuo proudly.

"I have my orders," said Drake. "We must go on."

"We must go to Penki," said General Hsu, who looked very unhappy.

"I cannot agree," Kuo said.

Drake began speaking slowly. "I feel it is to the Government's best interest and to that of our mission if the General would accompany us further. But that is up to the General."

"I cannot agree," Kuo repeated.

"All right," Drake said patiently, "I will give you the truck and you can go back. The Communists will give you safe conduct."

"The other two should not go ahead if one turns back," Kuo said.

"Did the General not see the directive from Mukden yesterday that the American representative shall make the decision?" Drake asked.

Kuo glowered, did not speak. Drake went on. "It is my decision that the Communist and American forces should go on ahead."

Unexpectedly Kuo asked, "And what is the attitude of the Communist member?"

Hsu said, through his own translator, "This is a fighting place. So it is natural they guard the roads. All three of us must go for the fulfillment of our mission."

Drake was sweetness itself. "If General Kuo doesn't care to go that's up to him." He knew that Kuo was weighing face. "I will accompany the General back to the Nationalist lines myself, and then return."

The Nationalist Colonel, Tzai, suddenly said, "If our team is willing to go, who will take the responsibility if this happens again?"

Drake looked at Hsu. "The side that does the harm will be responsible. We are guaranteed safe conduct. It is not my responsibility."

Kuo, who had been some paces away, walked up to Drake. "In the past two or three days the Government troops have respected *all* members of the team. But the Communists used cursing words against me and have shown no respect. Maybe later the Government troops will say cursing words to other members."

Drake climbed into the front seat of the jeep. "That's too bad," he called, "but that should not hold us up. Yes or no?" Kuo hesitated. Drake went back to working on relative face. "I can tell you I felt as scared as anybody else when that guy was shoving his gun in my teeth."

That seemed to do it. Kuo could not have anyone think he wanted to turn back because he was more scared than Drake. "I agree to go ahead," he said, "but if the same thing happens again we *all* go back to Fushun."

"That's fine," said Drake, stepping on the starter, "but I refuse to go back unless someone stops me physically." Kuo didn't budge. Hsu climbed into the jeep behind Drake. I started the weapons carrier. Drake raced his motor. Slowly Kuo walked to the jeep and fitted himself into the seat next to Hsu.

There were more trenches in the road. But now that we had made our peace with the Communists, local villagers with shovels trotted along behind our convoy. When we stopped, they caught up with us and filled in the gaps. A horseman was dispatched to the villages ahead and the peasants were mobilized to repair the roads in advance. The sixteenth trench was a small canal. We sent the truck back to pick up still more villagers. Everyone on the team went to work throwing rocks into the gully and gathering logs to bridge the bad spot. Only Kuo remained seated, as solemn and majestic as anyone can look in the back of a jeep.

Each time we had to stop the pock-marked Communist, Lieutenant Colonel Li Chang-kwan would say apologetically in English, "Sorry," and the Nationalist Colonel Tzai would always say, "Very interesting."

When we came again to the village where the Communists had their regimental headquarters, we waited forty minutes while they sent word ahead to their patrols. The wall of the biggest farmhouse facing the road was whitewashed with this slogan in Chinese: LET THE KUOMINTANG GOVERNMENT HELP SOLVE THE PROBLEM OF THE NORTHEAST PROVINCES BY POLITICAL MEANS INSTEAD OF BY FORCE.

It had taken four hours to achieve the thirty *li* from Fushun to Ying Shao Pao. We made the remaining one hundred and thirty *li* to Penki in seven hours, bumping over winding mountain roads, forging bridgeless rivers. The jeep made the best time. Our six-by-six bogged down in the mire at one point and we tried in vain to pull it out as our wheels spun without friction. Eventually a company of 8th Route Army soldiers put their collective shoulders to the back of the weapons carrier and shoved it onto drier land. The big truck was less fortunate. It settled in a river bed, had to be hitched up to horses, and finally reached Penki at three o'clock the next morning under its own power.

5

Penki was a surprise. After traveling eleven hours through wild, undeveloped steppes we came over a mountain rise at dusk and there below was a kind of industrial Shangri-La, its water towers, smokestacks, and power pylons jutting into the sky. We had expected Penki would be a fairly big town but not a thriving city of one hundred and fifty thousand with coal, copper and iron deposits, steel works, coking plants, and machine-tool factories.

The local officials had prepared a monster demonstration with twenty thousand citizens rallied to greet the truce team. But like Drake, we entered the city on the wrong road and had to satisfy our hosts by listening to accounts of the prepared welcome.

Drake met with the local leaders in the reception room of the former Japanese military hospital. The place was draped with homemade flags of the Big Five. On the wall were rather poor portraits of Attlee, Truman, Stalin, Chiang, as well as Communist leaders Mao Tse-tung and Chu Teh.

In Penki Drake wanted most to consult and question Chang Hsueh-shih. He is the youngest brother of Chang Hsueh-liang, the Young Marshal who kidnapped the Generalissimo at Sian in 1936 in an effort to bring compromise and peace to China. The attempt had failed and the Young Marshal was still held in custody. On August 10, 1945, Communist Chairman Mao Tse-tung had asked thirty-year-old Chang Hsueh-shih to assume command of all non-Communist, anti-Japanese, anti-Kuomintang forces in Tungpei. Since Chang's father, Chang Tso-lin, had been one of the last great Manchurian warlords and his elder brother had led a great army, Chang's name carried great prestige in the Northeast provinces. On his return to Manchuria he rallied to him remnants of his brother's troops, helped the Communists capture a large sector of territory around Mukden.

But Chang wasn't in Penki when we arrived. Boyish, buck-toothed Lieutenant General Shaw Hwa, Communist political commissar, explained that Chang was off on an "inspection tour." Drake said to me, "I'll tell them what I want tonight. If they decide to play ball that will give them a chance to produce the Big Boy tomorrow without loss of face."

Drake may have been correct. Chang returned the next morning and came to see us almost immediately. He had a simple, informal manner, plus the poise of a royal heir. His oxford-gray uniform had no trace of brass or insignia, although he had the rank of lieutenant general. Carefully choosing his words, Chang gave us a sketch of life in Liaoning, the province which he was governing for the Communists. A few points seemed to make a profound impression on all the Chinese as well as on ourselves. According to Chang, there had been seventy-two different kinds of taxes in Manchuria; now there was only one—a sliding scale assessment against income. Free schools were open (the Communists had rewritten the history books). Among the ninety-seven members of the provincial Political Council, thirteen were described as "large landlords." This, Chang believed, was good enough evidence that rule by one class or party had not been tolerated. When Chiang finished outlining his program, we asked if he were a member of the Chinese Communist Party. (General Shaw had said that he was.) Chang replied, "I am a New Democrat." This referred to Mao Tse-tung's doctrine for China called "New Democracy."

I inquired whether Chang thought the Central Government should be allowed to establish sovereignty over Manchuria.

He replied, "The people of the Tungpei have the right to receive the sovereignty of Tungpei. The establishment of this provincial government here is tantamount to taking over sovereignty by China. After all, this is a *Chinese* government."

"If the civil war ceased, would you agree to a new election with all political parties represented?"

"Yes," said Chang, "when and if the National Assembly in Nanking agrees upon a democratic constitution."

"I suppose you've heard that the Central Government has appointed its own Governor for Liaoning Province?"

"Quite ridiculous," Chang said easily. "Nobody elected him. The highest principle of democracy is election by the people by secret ballot. Whoever heard of a secret ballot in a Kuomintang province?"

The General was asked how he felt about the transporting of Central Government troops to Manchuria by the United States. He smirked slightly. "If it helps bring peace to Tungpei, I am sympathetic to it," he said.

That afternoon while wandering around Penki's streets we saw six hundred Nationalist prisoners being marched to internment from the front. We requested and received permission to question them. Without any coaching from our hosts, we picked out First Lieutenant Tong Ping, twenty-seven, a native of Hunan Province who was a company commander in the American-equipped New Sixth Army. He had been taken prisoner on the evening of April 10 during a Nationalist attempt to break through to Penki before the truce team arrived. A veteran of five years of fighting in Kwantung, Kiangsi, Indo-China, and Burma, Tong said that he had been told he had to come to Tungpei only to disarm the Japanese. "If I were allowed to leave I would go home and resume farming," he said.

Chang Kwei-chu, twenty-four, a warrant officer, said he had been a member of the Kuomintang Youth Corps in Kweichow. Two years ago he had volunteered for the Burma Expeditionary Force. He, too, had been told he was being sent to Tungpei only to disarm Japanese. In his opinion, morale was very bad among Nationalist troops because the men did not know why they had to fight against fellow Chinese. When we had finished our questions the student volunteer asked if he could interrogate us.

"Do United States military men and politicians both desire peace in China?"

We said that they did. "Then," challenged Chang Kwei-chu, "why does the United States help to transport Chinese troops to fight Chinese troops in Tungpei?"

A political officer listening to the conversation beamed happily. "I'll bet in three months you'll have him as a political commissar if he continues like this," I said. The Communist officer did not disagree.

While we were sipping tea after supper, more than half a hundred men and women crowded into the reception room of the hospital. They said they represented Penki's intellectuals, workers, unions, farmers, teachers, students, and women and had come to petition the truce team for peace.

Chao Tze-shu, a bearded fat man wearing a coolie's indigo-blue Chinese gown and a European soft, gray felt fedora, spoke for the local Peoples' Political Council. Reciting the wonders of peace and the people's hatred of civil war, he demanded that "The National Government stop any attack on this region and that Generalissimo Chiang carry out the decisions of the [Chungking] Political Consultative Conference." Next Si Sha-yueng, a giant, unwashed coal miner, spoke. Graphically he depicted the horrible life under the Japanese and told how the people of Penki had fought against them. In an eloquent conclusion he pleaded: "We do not understand, sirs, why if we give peace to the Japanese, cannot we give peace to the Chinese people."

The team members listened: Drake, the red-faced, Pennsylvania Signal Corpsman who had fought in Burma and led two successful truce teams in North China; Kuo, the solemn but cherubic-looking forty-year-old rich farmer from Szechwan Province, who had been fighting the Japanese since 1930 and had been twice wounded; and Hsu, reared in a well-to-do Changsha family, who had left Whampoa Military Academy to fight in the Chinese Revolution alongside Sun Yat-sen and Chiang Kai-shek. Drake was the lone proletarian; he understood coal miners. They talked his language. His frank blue eyes roved around the room. There was a pregnant woman, a lame man, a mother with her small children, a farmer still smelling of hogs. Most of them were dressed in dark, bulky cotton quilting, bound at the wrists and the ankles.

Drake was attentive as Kwang translated the words of Wang Pao-ling, another miner, who said: "More than thirty thousand workers have been organized in Penki since August 13. Most of the factories here are in operation now. . . . The life of the worker is improved and we are living the happy life and enjoying freedom and happiness. . . . But now in recent days we have heard the song of battle in Penki and we are very sorrowful, as we have felt war for fourteen years. We know that the troops who attack Tungpei are also Chinese and this makes us more sorrowful. . . . We heard the team of truce arrived in Mukden some days ago . . . but why is the war still going on . . . ?"

At this point one of the hosts tried to wind up the meeting, explaining to the people that a concert had been arranged in honor of the team. He was interrupted by cries of "No! No!" The hosts looked at Drake for a decision. Drake said, "We came here on a peace mission. I have to leave tomorrow, but if these people have a problem I will sit here all night and listen to it."

"Don't go tomorrow," cried one old woman with a dirty bandage wound around her head.

"We must," said Drake. "I must visit the Kuomintang headquarters."

The old woman sobbed, "If you go, we are afraid there will be war here."

Drake reassured her, "Have faith . . ." he said.

Another woman, with several front teeth missing, said, "I had to dig trenches for the Japanese. I prayed for peace. Perhaps I can live one more year so I can enjoy the free life under the Chinese Republic. . . . There would be laughter among the defeated Japanese at this civil war."

Wang Pao-yuen, a farmer, said, "If Chinese fight Chinese they will destroy industry and natural resources. Before the surrender we had to give a large part of our harvest to the landlord. We could not eat any good food, only the flour of water chestnuts. Now we can even eat the flour of red corn. We are afraid of the civil war. If the Kuomintang troops come here we may eat water chestnut flour again. We support the *palus* because they brought us happiness and well-being."

Another farmer, Chieng Kiang-feng, who represented the Farmers' Self Guards, added: "We suffered fourteen years from the Japs like living in a fire. Now the *palus* have delivered us from the fire. . . . civil war may only give us more fire. If the Kuomintang troops come here we will help the *palus*. Not much. Only to carry ammunition, food, and water. The main thing we beg of our American friends is peace."

Around the room the standing people spoke. Some with bitterness. Some calmly with logic. Some bordering on hysteria. For hours the team listened patiently. Once Chang Hsueh-shih himself made another attempt to end the session, but the people said they had come a long way and had waited a long time to speak.

Chao Tze-shu, the fat, bearded man, spoke again. "We have some questions for the team members which we would like to have them answer." The questions tumbled out, dozens of them, some shouted, some whispered. Why did not Chiang carry out his four promises to the PPC? Why was not the Young Marshal released from prison? Why were the puppet traitors who escaped to Mukden not punished by the Kuomintang? Why are American arms used to attack us? Why does the Government have concentration camps for progressives? Why does the Kuomintang come back now when fourteen years ago they gave Tungpei to the Japanese without firing one shot?

An old man with a face of infinite wrinkles, spoke in a thin, raspy voice. "I remember before the republic. The Emperor knew how to love the people. Chiang is a great leader, the leader of all China, but he does not know how to love his people. Why does he not use peace instead of a sword to solve the problem of Tungpei?"

The delegates applauded in quick, short bursts. Drake got up. He spoke with dignity. "The fact that you have come here shows that you wholeheartedly believe in peace," he said. He told the people truthfully that the problem of peace was complex but that it would be solved. "A people divided against itself cannot stand," he paraphrased. "You have mentioned many wrongs and rights tonight. The mission of the team is peace. It is not within the province of this team to right the wrongs. That must wait the establishment of a truly democratic state in China. If people have patience a while longer with Executive Headquarters and this team, I believe peace will come."

General Kuo spoke next. Softly he defended the Generalissimo's leadership. The delegates shouted out against him. Kuo went on doggedly, "All parties want peace, President Chiang Kai-shek wants peace. The Kuomintang is here in Tungpei now because it was planned that the Russian Red Army would evacuate and the Chinese Government would come to take over sovereignty. But someone destroyed this plan. . . ."

A man's voice from the back of the room cut in, "It is obvious to the people that this plan was destroyed due to the liberation of the people themselves."

Kuo sat down and closed his eyes. I felt rather sorry for him at that moment. There was no applause. Hsu arose to speak. He praised Executive Headquarters, General Marshall, Colonel Drake. "Let the people have unity and support the field teams. Let them have patience and we will yet have peace in Tungpei."

Chao Tze-shu thanked the team on behalf of the delegates. "We hope you will do your best," he said. "We will support you. We offer our highest respect to the field team."

Applause again. Then the delegates filed out. Drake stood by the door and tried to shake hands with all of them. Some of the miners were ashamed because their hands were still black. They hid their hands and bowed in humility.

I asked Chang Hsueh-shih, "What do you really think, General? Can there be peace in Tungpei?"

He thought for a moment, clasping and unclasping his long, strong fingers. "If the field teams made peace in North China, then they can do the same thing in the Northeast provinces. Under one condition," he warned, "that with American help everyone must have faith in democracy and sincerity in their wish for peace."

It was after ten-thirty, and there was still a concert. In the Penki Municipal Theatre, almost two thousand young, uniformed *palus* were gathered. They cheered us long and heartily as we walked down the aisle to our seats in the front row. In the array of Allied flags, I noted that the big American emblem at the right of the stage had twelve stripes—thick red ones and thin white ones. There were slogans tacked on to the bright, canary yellow cyclorama. In front of us were tables covered with offerings of watermelon seeds, apples and cigarettes (called "Waldorf") manufactured in the Communist area.

The program, delayed more than three hours, opened with speeches. Communist General Shaw, acting as master of ceremonies, introduced Drake. He pledged "peace, unity, and prosperity in

China." The *palus* chanted: "Long live Colonel Drake!" Colonel Tzai, speaking in place of General Kuo, who had gone to bed, promised, "Peace will come, and a stable peace." General Hsu concluded the oratory and the troops sang their inspiring marching song.

Two girls and two boys were on the stage when the curtain went up, and they sang a propaganda cantata written for the occasion, called, "Establishment of a Coalition Government." The girls singsonged, "Under what government will the people have a happy land?" and the boys came back with, "Under a democratic coalition government." In between other musical selections, including "The Merry Widow Waltz," "The Democracy March," and "Old Folks at Home," there was a farmer's traditional jig which concluded with a vocal tribute to President Truman, General Marshall, President Chiang, and Chairman Mao.

Thus the entertainment stretched on until long after midnight, winding up with a fascinating *Yang Ko* presentation in folk dance form called "Mid-Autumn Festival." This commemorated the fifteenth day of the eighth moon when the Japanese started their seizure of the Tungpei fourteen years ago.

6

The next day we returned to Fushun, but only after Kuo had staged another scene. He sent word to Drake that he would not travel on a new route which the Communists promised would be smoother and shorter. Kuo did not put it into words, but possibly he foresaw an ambush by "bandits." Drake did not force an immediate decision. When Kuo appeared, Drake said: "Let's toss a coin." Before the General replied, the other correspondents and myself announced that we were willing to try the smoother route despite any potential perils. Kuo agreed to the tossing of the coin and he won. We entered Fushun long before the jeep and met nothing along the way more threatening than a few wounded *palu* stragglers and an occasional farmer dragging coal on a small sledge.

In Fushun on the following day we invited General Kuo to lunch and asked him to comment on the team's visit to Communist territory. "Self-government in Penki?" he scoffed. "Take those representatives we met last night. From their dialect and attitude I am sure some of them are from Szechwan and Hupeh provinces. They are not representatives of the Tungpei people. I have never dealt with the Communists before, but I have heard they are very tricky. Last night it was proved to me. All the speeches and questions were prepared."

"Were all those people Communists?" we asked.

"No," said Kuo deliberately. "Among them were non-Communists last night. How do you prove it? When the Government representative makes a speech giving the Government viewpoint some Communists try to stop me because I am trying to explain our mission. They try to stop me because they do not want the non-Communists to hear me. I think the Government in Penki is not a truly representative government. Take Chang Hsueh-shih, the Governor, for example. You gentlemen all know that the General's father and brother were both very powerful in Manchuria before. The Communists are trying to use him to gain power. And he is using the Communists to regain his family's ascendancy. Fourteen years ago it was his brother, Chang Hsueh-liang who gave Manchuria away without firing a shot. . . ."

The General complained that what the Russians had not stripped in Tungpei the Communists were now destroying.

"But factories are working in Penki," I said.

"Maybe that's all they wanted to show us."

"What do you think of the tax reforms and the opening of free schools?"

Kuo struggled to be fair. "In this they really do something good. You cannot say all the Communists are bad."

"Isn't the Communist program winning converts?"

Kuo admitted that it was. Then he was asked why the Central Government had not publicized and implemented a program of its own to give the people an alternative.

"Perhaps it is not so simple," Kuo said. "I talked to army officers of the former puppet government who are with us now and also to some plain people in Changchun. They knew all about the Generalissimo's speeches and about Sun Yat-sen's Three Principles. But the Communists force the local people to agree with them."

"Why doesn't the Government use its planes to drop leaflets in territory it has not entered?"

Kuo said that maybe the Government had not thought about that. "Besides," he said, "if we drive the Communist troops away, the people will follow the Central Government."

I returned to Mukden and three days later the Committee of Three arrived. Colonel Drake and the senior members of Team 29 were called back from the field to report on their findings. Then the Committee of Three flew back to Chungking to report to General Marshall.

The atmosphere in Mukden had changed. There were signs and slogans plastered around the city which hadn't been there a week before. Angry words proclaiming THE NATIONAL ARMY SHOULD LIBERATE THE PEOPLE IN THE BANDIT AREAS. . . . THERE ARE NO COMMUNISTS IN TUNGPEI ONLY BANDITS. . . . WE DONT WANT MEDIATION, WE ONLY WANT EXTERMINATION. They were written in English, a special plea to the Americans.

The Americans were not hopeful. Even with their best efforts they were learning that trust and faith could not be molded and baked in a day like bricks. The angry words of Kuomintang Mukden had their echo in the angry words at Communist Penki. Peace was, as Drake had said, a complex problem which needed patience.

Despite the hopelessness and complexity, there were many Americans as represented by Drake and Byroade and Marshall who understood that without peace in Asia there could be no peace in the world. They knew, too, that millions of Chinese, plain people without party or cause, had faith that the Americans would bring an end to suffering and civil war. One reason for the eventual failure of "Operation Dove" was that we could not maintain that great faith. In Penki that old woman with the bandaged head had sobbed, "If you go we are afraid there will be war here." Drake had reassured her, told her to have "faith."

Less than a month later the Nationalists attacked Penki, relying heavily on American arms and equipment. After a fight, the city fell. With it fell American prestige. Whether or not the Government armies had access to the military information which Team 29 gathered in Penki, I do not know. But it would be difficult to convince the people of Penki otherwise, whether they are Communists or not.

I for one, as an American, would not want to face the people of Penki again.

CHAPTER XXI

CHIANG, CHOU AND CHEN

DURING the spring of 1946 Manchuria was undeniably the scene of much severe fighting. The four truce teams with whom I had entered the northeast provinces were nearly always in the vicinity of the battles but they were never able to halt them for longer than a banquet.

The Manchurian muddle was evidence that Executive Headquarters was losing, perhaps irretrievably, the things which had held it together: honesty, mutual trust, and a closed mouth. On the last count, it had been agreed from the outset that Executive Headquarters officials would not give out individual policy statements or interviews and that they would refrain from public charges and counter-charges. When the radio stations and newspapers at both extremes began blabbering claims and rumors, it was symptomatic of the fact that honesty and mutual trust in Executive Headquarters were disappearing.

After advocating a half-billion-dollar American loan to China and testifying in the Senate's Pearl Harbor investigation, Marshall flew back from Washington. A headline in a Shanghai paper proclaimed: GENERAL MARSHALL MAY ARRIVE IN CHINA TODAY—IT IS LIKE LOOKING FOR RAIN CLOUDS DURING A DROUGHT. Another Shanghai daily was more philosophical about the peacemaker's return. In an editorial entitled "We have no face to see General Marshall," the independent *Wen Hui Pao* wrote:

In the month General Marshall has been away, our political and military affairs have gotten into a mess. . . . The people have been anxiously looking forward to General Marshall's early return. Now he is just about to return to China, and everybody welcomes him from the bottom of their hearts . . . but, General Marshall is not a god that can do everything and he cannot stay permanently in China to make peace between the Kuomintang and Chinese Communists and "lead" China's politics. And then, to speak of America's basic policy toward China, there is still a difference between the direction which the State Department in Washington has taken, and the direction which the Chinese people should and are willing to take. . . . General Marshall is very warm-hearted in returning to China once more to make peace! But at a press conference on February 8th, American Secretary of State Byrnes said very frankly that both in the past and at present America has always held that China's door should be opened. From this we know that if we ourselves do not unite and brace up, our future and our position in the world will be much to be feared for. The Open Door policy is one which the powers adopted fifty years ago to share their booty in colony-like China. And today, it is actually uttered by our democratic friend America! Before Byrnes said that, Chairman John Abbink of the National Foreign Trade Council in a speech set China and India side by side as the two big markets in the world that are waiting to be opened, and that in China the plans for industrialization should be led by America and participated in by England. This and a United Press dispatch from Washington: "Marshall and other U.S. officials in China have found that it was not possible for them to act merely as advisers and umpires, but that they must actually take the lead if any progress is to be made" sounds as if they come from the same idea. What kind of position and what kind of a country are we now in the eyes of our friends? If things go on like this, in the near future, we will not be "one of the four powers" but we will be "restored" back to our position of semi-colony. . . . Of course we welcome General Marshall's return for emergency's sake. But depending excessively on outside (foreign) strength is not very wise.

This editorial appealed to me because the day before it appeared I had dispatched a gloomy cable to *Time* on the prospects of peace, concluding:

I doubt if Marshall will come up with anything more than a temporary solution. If he does even that, he deserves a half-moon halo to go with his five stars. If China is to remain in one piece, the lasting leadership for achieving this peace must come from the Chinese people themselves and not from a foreigner, however wise or well-meaning or well-loved, whether he be American, Russian, Japanese or Tahitian.

That cable was dated April 18, 1946, the day Marshall landed in China.

For a while after Marshall returned all parties attempted, officially, to pick up where they had left off. But it was not the same, neither in Marshall's living room nor in the field. In Kaiyuan, Manchuria, the Nationalist First Army Commander gave a truce team a big welcome and then put the Communist members in "protective custody." There were skirmishes in the area and the

Communists sent the bodies of slain Nationalists back in coffins "as an expression of a sincere desire for peace and unity."

A few weeks later three Communists and two Americans from Executive Headquarters arrived in Mukden from Peiping by plane. While they were waiting at the Mukden airport for an American C-47 to take them to Changchun, two B-25 bombers warmed up. They were American planes, now painted with the blue and white star of the Chinese National Air Force. As the truce team members looked on, the two planes with their bomb racks loaded and their machine guns ready for action, roared into the air to attack Communist positions north of Mukden. Then the Nationalist commander of the airport emerged happily from the operations shack and politely invited the Communists and the Americans to join him for tea.

In instance after instance the Communists attacked or claimed they were attacked by former puppet troops fighting under the Government banner. The Communists used the presence of puppet garrisons as a justification for marching into towns. When the matter was brought up at Executive Headquarters the three Commissioners debated for days on a press release concerning the matter. They could not settle on a definition of "puppets," and the agreement was never forthcoming.

This necessity for complete accord by all three parties (like the Big Three veto in the United Nations) was a constant brake on Executive Headquarters' progress. Another basic weakness was that the truces, where effected, were not followed up by an over-all plan for the withdrawal of warring parties. The rival camps were just frozen to the spot, usually with the Nationalists occupying the towns and the Communists surrounding them, still within striking distance of the lines of communication.

In retrospect it seems remarkable that the American colonels who headed the teams managed to be as impartial as they were. Their traditional sympathies, as army men, were heavily on the side of legality and order. These virtues they naturally associated with the Government. In purely military matters, however, they remained fairly neutral. When the military flowed over into the political realm, they were more outspoken in favor of the recognized central power and the status quo.

Generally a good deal of tolerance for both sides was demonstrated by the Americans when the Chinese bogged down badly in their administrative paper work at Executive Headquarters. But at times their lack of Western-style competence in routing and returning memos, compiling summaries, and issuing directives moved the Americans almost to the point of violence.

By mid-April there were twenty-two truce teams in the field. Since the peace formula was not working in Manchuria, both sides attempted to put it to the test again in North China. Which group made the initial move cannot be determined. The Kuomintang simply announced that the Communists were starting "an all-out offensive" and so they countered with new drives in Jehol, north Kiangsu, and Shantung. On the other hand, General Chou En-lai stated that the Kuomintang's aggressive actions in Manchuria had indeed forced "a general civil war."

2

What happened to "Operation Dove" in North China is perhaps best exemplified by a summary of the extended negotiations in the Central Plains Liberated Area, in the Hupeh hills north of Hankow. Here portions of the Communist New Fourth Army under General Li Hsien-nien, a former Hupeh carpenter, had established an effective anti-Japanese base. The number of men under Li grew from two score in 1938 to more than twenty thousand by the end of the Japanese war. By the spring of 1946, linked with other irregulars from the south, Li commanded ninety thousand men.

Li, a lean, humorous man with strong, gnarled hands, is a nonconformist with an immense popular following. One of the stories I have heard told and retold about him concerns the morning the Japanese unexpectedly surrounded the village where he had his headquarters and a political training school. Li called a meeting and proposed a plan to sift through the encirclement that night.

"Lighten the load," he ordered, "throw away everything not essential, do not even take your books. Never mind Marx, Lenin, Stalin, Mao—bury them and we will get them back another day."

Several of the political students objected. "We must take our Marxism with us on the march, who knows when we will return—books are scarce and valuable. . . ."

"Comrades," said General Li, "let us examine the objective situation. What does Marxism mean to us at this moment of history? It means that when we are running across the fields we must run a little faster than the Japanese."

After the formal conclusion of the anti-Japanese war, the New Fourth was evidently still under attack from Chinese Nationalist troops aided by the Japanese. Despite the "Cease-Fire" Agreement of January 10 the skirmishes continued. Executive Headquarters dispatched a team to arrange, if possible, a supplementary truce between the area commanders. They agreed to cease fighting, demolish their blockhouses, and pledged that each side would remain "frozen" in the sectors they already controlled. The truce team then left the field and set up headquarters in the city of Hankow.

General Li, advancing the slogan "Peace is Precious," demobilized part of his forces for spring planting, destroyed his fortifications, and sent gifts to the nearest Nationalist commander. The truce team later discovered that the Nationalists did not destroy their blockhouses, but actually built new ones, conscripting peasant labor under the *pao chia* system. Local Nationalist raids and Communist retaliations occurred sporadically. The truce team finally went back into the Central Plains Liberated Area and traveled from community to community settling disputes like a frontier marshal in America during the latter part of the nineteenth century. Wherever they went, the rivals became temporarily peaceful. When the team commander journeyed to Executive Headquarters to list his successes he was greeted by reports that the Kuomintang had launched another, larger offensive against the New Fourth Army.

The Communists at Executive Headquarters asked that the New Fourth, which by now was operating within a shrinking amœba-like pocket (approximately one hundred miles by two hundred miles) surrounded by Kuomintang forces be allowed to march peaceably to a recognized Communist region. This request was voted down by the Nationalist Commissioner. Although American officials were inclined to see the merits in the Communist suggestion, it was useless for them to take a public stand since unanimous consent was needed for any action.

The problem went to higher levels. The Government military men, led by General Ho Ying-ching (then the Generalissimo's Chief of Staff) argued that the New Fourth could be wiped out with relative ease. Why let them escape possibly to fight the Government again?

The first week in May General Chou went to General Marshall and said he had evidence that "the Kuomintang is about to launch an all-out annihilation campaign against the New Fourth area." He had already complained to Marshall that the Nationalists were cutting off all UNRRA supplies from the region. Marshall asked the Generalissimo's headquarters if Chou's information was true and received only a vague reply. Chou, whom Marshall trusted, insisted that an attack was coming and that it would spread the war through all of Nationalist China. Marshall summoned Byroade from Peiping and sent him with Chou to investigate the facts on the spot and to mediate.

The "first-string" team flew to Hankow where it was joined by the Deputy Chief of the Government's Hankow headquarters. The three then embarked on a rough overland trip by jeep. At a rain-swollen river the jeeps had to be carried across on poles. Chou rolled up his pants and waded across. So did Byroade. The natty Kuomintang representative decided that a General should display more dignity and allowed himself to be ferried on the backs of his aides.

When they reached the Communist base the Penki pattern was repeated. All three men made speeches to the populace. Byroade explained the workings of "Operation Dove." "The Americans are not in Executive Headquarters to judge who is right or wrong," he told them through his interpreter. "Our mission is to form a framework of personnel and equipment in which the Chinese themselves can work to reach agreements." The Nationalist pledged: "I have full authority to guarantee that there will not be an attack on this area." Chou said, simply, "What is there left for me to do but to call upon you to recall this promise, so that in the future you may all be assured that the Deputy Chief of the Generalissimo's Hankow headquarters had personally guaranteed you against attack."

The first-string triumvirate was then replaced by an ordinary team, Number 32, which supervised an arrangement permitting General Li to evacuate over a thousand of his seriously wounded men.

The big drive was delayed until late June. The Government closed a pincers using from three hundred thousand to half a million men against the sixty thousand left in the New Fourth. When the battle was engaged the New Fourth seemed to disintegrate. Perhaps a third were killed outright or captured and then executed. The rest dispersed into the countryside in small groups. The Government felt it had scored a great victory.

Weeks later General Li's forces began regrouping in South Shansi, far to the northeast of the Hupeh fighting. Whatever number of men he had left, that was the number which no longer revered George C. Marshall as "The God of Peace."

3

The Chiang Government maintained, and many American observers agreed, that the Communists first disrupted the military truce in March by grabbing Changchun and holding the rail lines from Mukden to the north. This prevented the Nationalists from getting to Szepingkai, Changchun, Harbin, and Manchuli as the Soviet Red Army withdrew.

In defense of their actions the Communists have reiterated two principal arguments. First, that the Americans had not been neutral when they transported Nationalist troops and equipment in Manchuria. They recalled that the military agreement signed by the three groups on February 25 stipulated that the Nationalists should have only five armies in Manchuria and that they had moved in seven or more. Replying to this, the Americans correctly pointed out that the agreement had permitted the Government to move troops into Manchuria and that the limitation of armies had nothing to do with the size of the forces needed by the Government "to take over sovereignty" and that the five-army limit was to be reached only at the end of eighteen months.

The second Communist line of debate was that the Nationalists did not need to "take over Chinese sovereignty" in areas where the Communists had moved in, because they, too, were Chinese. Furthermore they argued that the Nationalists, wherever they assumed control in Manchuria, abolished the local self-governments instigated by the Communists. This they felt violated the spirit of the democracy encouraged by the PCC, the promise of some provincial autonomy, and the February 25 ban on army commanders meddling in civilian affairs. They asked a pledge of free, all-party elections in Manchuria. But a Kuomintang spokesman said "Unity and sovereignty of the Chinese Government must first be restored."

The Communists, who had little faith in the Kuomintang after the Central Executive Committee backslid on the PCC decisions, found new reasons for reinforcing their belief that the only guaranteed protection was their fighting force. The Kuomintang had tried to add two hundred and fifty more seats to their National Assembly delegation by boosting the allotment of the People's Political Council which they appointed. When this caused a great hue and cry the Kuomintang changed tactics and concentrated on efforts to control the May 5 Assembly by capturing the four hundred delegates still to be selected. About half of these were to be nominated by Kuomintang organizations such as Chambers of Commerce, the General Labor Union and the General Farmer's Union. The rest were to be elected by "popular vote."

The only Chinese election which I witnessed was the one perpetrated on Shanghai. It was rigged from start to finish in such a heavy-handed manner that even the English language newspapers published in the city had no trouble exposing it. In most precincts only tax-paying heads of families were granted the franchise to vote. The list of candidates from which they could choose had been carefully pruned by the Kuomintang Bureau of Social Welfare. No representatives of opposition parties were nominated. In proportion to the total population of Shanghai, the number of voters was infinitesimal. It occasioned no surprise that the "elected" candidates were Kuomintang stalwarts or their relatives, civil service employees, and a few "non-partisans" of predetermined sympathies.

In several Kuomintang areas the Democratic League attempted to organize pre-election rallies which were broken up by Kuomintang strong-arm gangs. On such unfortunate occasions, the Chinese police never appeared until it was time to arrest a few of the beaten-up liberals for disturbing the peace.

4

Although he perhaps did not realize it then, Marshall returned too late. When he landed in Chungking the third week in April, nearly all his good work had been undone. There was still high regard for him as an individual, but not the same respect for American neutrality. Supplies kept rolling into Government warehouses, the U. S. Navy kept moving Nationalist troops. Perhaps General Gillem, Marshall's substitute, had said too many sharp, even if true, things about the "Reds" which had grapevined back to Chou.

Marshall discovered that Chiang was in a different mood. The Gimo now felt that coalition must come as a gift from a Kuomintang at the peak of its power and prestige. The Communist victories in Manchuria had "shattered the face of the Government." The Gimo meant to repair the damage and punish the Communists before resuming any talk of peace.

The Communists' attitude had hardened, too. Marshall did his best with Chou. The Communist merely said that he was responsible to the Central Committee in Yenan which had told him, "Marshall may be a man of peace and good will as you say, but American ships are transporting Kuomintang soldiers to fight us and the democratic peoples of Tungpei. American experts of every kind are coming to help the Kuomintang. American aid, sent to the Chinese people, is being sold by Kuomintang profiteers to enrich their war chests."

The first two weeks he was in Chungking, Marshall impressed his co-workers by his "caution." He moved very slowly, as if he too had suddenly realized that he was responsible to a larger political body back home which might not entirely back him up. He was also handicapped by the physical fact that a great deal of Chinese and American energy at this juncture was strained by the immense effort of moving the capital of China from its wartime base at Chungking down the Yangtze to its former home at Nanking.

The Government formalized its return to Nanking with an impressive ceremony the first Sunday in May. Under a rich blue sky wisped with white clouds, several thousand dignitaries drove out through Nanking's East Gate in a strange procession of town cars, sedans, jeeps, and trucks. They moved along the smooth macadam highway shaded by *wutung* trees, through the bright evergreen woodland to the tomb of Sun Yat-sen at Purple Mountain.

Politely declining sedan chairs, the Generalissimo and Madame Chiang slowly mounted the two hundred and eighty-three flag-decked steps to the marble tomb. At the top they paused momentarily, out of breath. Then they bowed three times. From within the tomb's outer room the Generalissimo intoned Dr. Sun's will. As the Gimo descended the immense crowd greeted him, shouting good wishes.

Later, at the parking lot alongside the gray granite building constructed in 1936-37 for the National Assembly, the Gimo made a moving speech to the twenty thousand people assembled. That same afternoon the Chiangs held a tea for the diplomatic corps, including General Marshall. As usual, the Americans crowded around Madame Chiang while the Chinese seemed inclined to ignore her.

After the Government was installed, I went to Nanking to interview various officials. It was easy to see why General Marshall had found the city "depressing." There was not much optimism among the populace or the bureaucrats. The one positive factor in the move was that the Central Government was now closer to the source of many of the nation's troubles, and therefore presumably better able to cope with them. The capital itself was, in microcosm, a mirror of urban China. It lacked the artificial financial nervousness of Westernized Shanghai, the placid beauty of historic Peiping, the cohesive urgency of wartime Chungking. Like all of China, Nanking still bore the tragic scars of its "rape" by the Japanese invaders in 1937. Behind its massive stone wall, the sprawling city had the rough and unfinished appearance of a frontier town despite the fact it was founded over six hundred years ago. There were no streetcars on its wide, dusty avenues and meandering herds of goats and pigs mingled with the traffic contentedly, seemingly no more out of place than American jeeps.

Nanking was taking its problems very seriously. Nobody was having very much fun—the diplomats, the government workers, nor the local population. The foreign colony of embassy personnel were busily trying to write sense-making reports on China's vacillating peace and trade prospects. The government workers, many of whom had taken the long trek from Chungking without their wives and children, were casting anxious eyes at the rising price of rice and wondering if their salaries would be raised. The local people, physically and mentally undernourished and lacking adequate medical care, were understandably apathetic. For almost eight years under the Japanese and the puppets they had had any lingering political initiative beaten out of them. Not even the sudden arrival of the Chinese Government in their midst, and of a civil war around them, roused more than casual interest at first.

Almost everybody in Nanking complained about the housing shortage. The embassy set which once longed for the day when they could leave exile in Chungking, already reminisced about "the good old days" in the interior. The Russians, for example, had one huge old mansion atop a commanding hill in Chungking where all the Soviet citizens could live together in collective harmony. They hoped that the capital would be transferred to Peiping where they are among the larger landowners, boasting forty acres of fine walled-in property in the legation section of town. However, the capital was returned to Nanking partly for sentimental and partly for practical reasons (cautious Chiang thought Peiping too close to Communist territory and the Soviet Union) and the Russians were forced to make do with several smaller houses, none of them impressive.

General Marshall, as the highest ranking American in Nanking, was given the home of the former German ambassador. This commodious seventeen-room dwelling was more than ample as living quarters and offices for the General, Mrs. Marshall, and the small staff of officers who worked with the special envoy. With the German house the Marshalls inherited table silver and linens boldly monogrammed "DR" (*Deutsches Reich*). In a city of shortages like Nanking the Marshalls were more pleased than embarrassed by this happenstance. They even had a fine lawn where the Marshalls liked to play croquet in the cool of the twilight.

Of all the strangers to Nanking, the Communist delegates probably had the most serious housing headache. The Government publicly announced that it had set aside two houses for them at a cost, to the Government, of 114 million Chinese dollars. Actually all this provided were two rather small middle-class stucco houses, each suitable for a family of six and not for the eighty persons in Communist negotiator General Chou En-lai's entourage. The Reds set up dormitory-style living and dispatched some comrades to Shanghai. The Party members utilized one of the two houses as a headquarters and with a small radio managed to monitor daily the news broadcasts from Yenan and to issue communiques in Chinese and English based on these reports. General Chou made himself more readily available to the press than either his American or Nationalist opposites in the delicate peace negotiations. Almost daily Chou climbed into his beautiful black Buick, probably sent to him by a rich admirer as a hedge against revolution, and drove across town to confer with General Marshall.

5

The finest domicile in all Nanking, the seventy-room mansion built for the Chinese puppet ruler, Wang Ching-wei, was set aside for the Generalissimo. But the Generalissimo, puritan that he is, spurned such obvious luxury. Besides, it would not be fitting for him to live in an edifice built for a lesser man, and a Kuomintang traitor at that. Instead, he chose to return to the plain red-brick house which was built for him in 1927 in the compound of the Central Military Academy. The Generalissimo and Madame Chiang were living in this modest house when the Japanese attacked Nanking. Although he does most of his work at home, the Generalissimo still goes to Government Headquarters every Monday at 9 A.M. to lead a memorial service. Dr. Sun's will is read punctiliously and then, as customary, the Generalissimo and members of his Government bow three times. After a brief report on outstanding governmental problems, the Generalissimo holds conferences with his various ministers and advisers.

The question of who would eventually acquire the puppet's palace was second only to war rumors in Nanking's daily gossip. The palatial offices on the estate had been turned over to Americans as an officers' club (and later became the U. S. Embassy.) The mansion itself, with adjacent swimming pool and tennis courts, was still empty. The foreign correspondents, who lived rather humbly in Chungking, were among the bolder petitioners for at least a portion of the rooms as a press hostel. Meanwhile they were residing and working in the city's second-best hotel.

This hotel, which for an inexplicable reason is called "Central" in Chinese and "Nanking" in English, was transformed into a high-class brothel for Japanese officers during the occupation. Times and customers changed. The bored American officers who inhabited the third floor discovered that one could still procure a girl for the night by pressing the button over any bed and asking the roomboy to bring one as you would ask for a glass of water. The Japanese, if they were so disposed, paid about $200, while the postwar fee rose over $15,000. Nobody paid much attention to the sign in each room, posted when the hotel was built several decades ago, which says that "The hotel begs to draw the guest's special attention that opium smoking, gambling, prostituting, and other bad conducts are strictly forbidden."

The fact that these restless Americans ever inhabited the third floor of the Nanking Hotel was one of the by-products of the civil war. Almost one hundred officers were sent out from the States to train Nationalist and Communist armies in modern warfare. This operation was known as MAGIC (Military Advisory Group in China). Some of them were in Shanghai preparing to go to Communist-held Kalgan when fighting erupted again on a large scale. They raised so much hell in Shanghai it was deemed wiser to move them to the more rustic setting of Nanking, away from fancy prices and fancier White Russians. But Nanking did not prove very enervating; there was not much to do for exercise or entertainment except to climb the two hundred and eighty-three steps up to Dr. Sun's impressive mausoleum on Purple Mountain or to picnic among the tombs of the departed Mings. Army authorities, sensing their growing restiveness, sent one-third ahead to await developments in Peiping and introduced compulsory Chinese language courses for the remainder.

Tea-drinking, politics, public abluting in bathhouses, and negotiating were just about Nanking's only industries. As a result, Nanking, like Washington, manufactured nothing original—except rumors. Last summer twelve new political parties announced themselves and there were rumors that at least two dozen more would shortly declare themselves. The sole new enterprise that one heard about in Nanking was indirectly the result of American aid. Most of the used clothing contributed by kind-hearted Americans was a nuisance to CNRRA. Little could be done with a half-dozen huge cases of shoes, all of them for the left foot. Evening gowns and swallow-tailed suits were not practical and did not look particularly snappy on China's poverty-stricken refugees. As a solution to an embarrassing situation, UNRRA advanced a sum of money to open a factory in Nanking to remake second-hand wraps from Jay Thorpe into garments for school children.

The largest employer in Nanking is the Government and it pays the poorest wages. An average middle-class government clerk last summer made the equivalent of thirty-five U.S. dollars per month (the price of one pair of Nylon stockings) and a man of Cabinet rank was paid less than one hundred U.S. dollars per month. Nevertheless, by one means or another, many officials seemed to have unlimited sums of money to spend on almost anything. With famine in Hunan and Honan, this was frowned upon by powers that be. The Generalissimo tried to set an example by his abstemious living. But since few who had the money seemed to follow the Gimo's example, the Executive Yuan adopted stringent restrictions. There was little straight thinking about the basic causes of inflation and starvation. Instead the capital was filled with Alice-in-Wonderland arguments over blue laws. Government employees were officially forbidden to dance, officially instructed to observe frugality in giving presents and holding ceremonies. If any government personnel entered ballrooms where there were taxi dancers "or into any improper place," or if they "invited prostitutes, taxi girls, singsong girls to amuse them" they were to be summarily fired. In the future, it was decreed, government officials should tender teas instead of banquets, serve tea instead of wine, and let their guests bring their own cigarettes. The Executive Yuan urged all municipal governments to follow this new edict, which is in accord with the New Life Movement favored by the Generalissimo.

Before Nanking's mayor could act, the *Central Daily News* (official government organ) belabored his administration and charged Nanking was becoming as corrupt as Shanghai. This is about the same as the *Christian Science Monitor* editorially declaring that Boston's Back Bay was becoming like New York's Greenwich Village. The *Central Daily News* beat its editorial drums loudest about the ballrooms which it said were "standing like a forest" in Nanking. "We will plunge into a life or death struggle with the city government which advocates luxury until it surrenders unconditionally," the paper declared. All this horrified and astonished Nanking's mild-mannered Mayor Ma who has been careful to be known for his abstemiousness. He said he had felt very self-conscious at the ceremony marking the return to the capital on May 5 because he had only a shabby old Chungshan uniform to wear while Premier T. V. Soong looked so elegant and grand in his double-breasted blue suit.

Mayor Ma quickly closed all ballrooms and then probably regretted it. Another influential Nanking newspaper began berating him for forcing girls into prostitution by robbing them of "an honest livelihood." To his bare office at City Hall one morning after the edict marched five hundred ballroom employees including musicians, and seven hundred taxi dancers. They demanded that Mayor Ma feed the girls and allow the jazzmen to play public concerts at city expense. Since the Mayor was watching his municipal budget even more closely than municipal morals, he refused. The result was that sin went undercover. There were places which Americans called "dance-quietlies" in Nanking where, if you knew the right people and had enough money, you could smuggle a snuggle on an unvarnished dance floor. Many taxi dancers not fortunate enough to be thus employed became singsong girls in tea-houses while others, to quote a Kuomintang newspaper which disapproves of this blue law, "have been compelled to walk along another more tragic road." All this furor raged in the Party press while civil war raged in the countryside. It was supposed to give the bureaucracy a fine moral uplift; actually it was the shallowest kind of hypocrisy. It was as if, during the depression, the United States Government had urged people on bread lines to stand up straight.

Another superficial thrift measure, motivated politically rather than morally, backfired in Nanking while I was there. The National Assembly, scheduled to meet on May 5, had been postponed indefinitely. When the government blandly announced that after May 15 it would no longer meet the expenses of delegates who remained in Nanking, there was the devil to pay. At a tea party—the guests smoked their own cigarettes—given by the government's representative, venerable Shao Li-tze, the delegates shouted down his attempt to explain the economy move. One delegate became so agitated and so eloquent that his false teeth fell out. Delegates yelled at the white-haired Shao that the Assembly should never have been postponed in the first place and that they would not leave Nanking unless driven away by guns. "The Communists are bandits," charged one delegate who blamed not only the postponement but also the elimination of expense accounts on them. The rumpus soon became general and the four hundred Kuomintang Assemblymen, most of them elected more than ten years before, pounded tables, broke up chairs, threw tea cups.

Shao restored order long enough to say, "It's like asking people to dinner and when the guests come and the host's food is not ready, a postponement is necessary." The delegates hooted. Shao, a trained diplomat, took off his glasses and tried another simile, saying, "It is as if a large company had called a meeting of stockholders and because so many did not come the meeting had to be put off."

These explanations only infuriated the delegates. "Your examples are no good!" they yelled. "*Ta! Ta!* (beat him, beat him)," they screamed.

At this critical juncture someone had the presence of mind to announce in a booming voice: "This tea party is adjourned. Let's talk it over with President Chiang tomorrow."

Next day at another tea, this one less rambunctious, the General-issimo mollified the delegates. He explained why it had been neces-sary to cut off their expenses, why the Assembly had been post-poned. A delegate who had been angry the preceding day, and was still angry, accused the government of placing too much importance on political parties and not enough on the plain people whom he claimed to represent. The Generalissimo calmly replied that not only the political parties but the Government wanted the Assem-bly postponed.

Half-soothed, half-disgruntled the delegates filed out. Those who had come from far-off Tibet and Mongolia and Sinkiang could not go home, but those who lived in nearby cities went back to them. Some got fat Party jobs to tide them over until they could go back on a government expense account. Still others, with money of their own, spent it on singsong girls and tried to bribe their way onto a train for Shanghai.

Meanwhile the plain people of Nanking were wishing there were more doctors and more medicines and more to eat. They had come to understand in a vague sort of way that the fighter planes and transports taking off from Nanking's airfields, the troop trains chug-ging through Nanking's station, the beautiful, big, black Buick of General Chou's gliding to General Marshall's and the beautiful, bigger, black Cadillac of General Marshall's gliding to the Gener-alissimo's, all had something to do with eventually bringing them more food and medical care.

They hoped it would be soon but none of them I talked with were overly optimistic.

6

The afternoon that *Life's* George Silk and I were invited to call on the Chiangs the big news in Nanking was the Government's drive on Changchun, the capital of Manchuria. There was some question as to whether or not the Communists would put up a major defensive battle for the Manchurian capital or whether they would withdraw in the interests of unity. Chou seemed willing to discuss a peaceful withdrawal if Marshall could guarantee that the Nationalist armies did not then attempt to penetrate further into Communist-held territory.

Dr. Li Wei-kuo, an affable Vice-Minister of Information who had a jeep, arranged the meeting for us. George had an assignment to make a series of informal shots on "The Chiangs at Home." The reception room was perfectly balanced, completely ordered. On the wall were two charming scrolls. On them were inscribed couplets written by the Generalissimo, himself. Dr. Li translated the first as: "The meaning of life is to create the continuously growing life of the universe." The second read: "The purpose of living is to increase the happiness of the whole of humanity."

We had not been in the reception room for more than five minutes when Madame Chiang swished in, carrying a rich scarlet wrap and a smart handbag. She wore a carefully fitted print dress, Chinese style, and toeless shoes with spike heels. Her lips were freshly painted and diamond clips sparkled on her delicate ears. She seemed older and more brittle than at our previous meeting in New York during the war. She greeted us perfunctorily, inquired about mutual acquaintances in America, and announced that her car was waiting and she had only a few minutes to spare. The Generalissimo, she explained, was busy at the moment but he would be along presently and then he would have us to tea but she was not sure that she would be back in time because she had so many things to do which she was sure we would understand and where did Mr. Silk want the picture taken?

George, a little confused by the high tension sentences which Madame generated at us, suggested a setting. Madame said all right but she did not really think that was the best place but she presumed Mr. Silk knew his business and would he please hurry up because she had so much to do.

It seemed to take George an incredible amount of time to open his cases, remove his equipment, arrange his extension cords and lights, set up his tripod and load his camera. In the long meanwhile, the following conversation took place, as nearly as I can recall it.

MADAME CHIANG: "Dr. Li, you are looking well. I think you are getting fat. You must be eating too many sweets."

DR. LI: "Thank you, Madame. I am about the same weight as always, and at present prices I cannot afford to eat many sweets."

MADAME CHIANG: "I trust your wife is looking as healthy as you are."

DR. LI: "Thank you for asking, Madame Chiang. My wife is fine. (Pause, then turning to me.) You know during the war Madame Chiang used to send us vitamin pills. . . ."

MADAME CHIANG (interrupting): "I am terribly sorry but I only have enough vitamins now for myself and my immediate family."

DR. LI: "Oh yes, I understand that, Madame. I only wished to point out your extreme kindness."

MADAME CHIANG: "Is this going to take much longer? I am really in a terrible hurry."

DR. LI: "During the war in Chungking Madame was also good enough to send my wife milk and . . ."

MADAME CHIANG: "I do not have my cows any longer, therefore I cannot give milk away."

DR. LI (bowing and apologetic): "Please do not misunderstand, Madame Chiang, I only wanted to explain that . . ."

SILK: "Will Madame take that seat, please?"

MADAME CHIANG: I photograph better against a plain background."

DR. LI (trying to say something *really* nice): "You know during these very hard times for China, Madame Chiang sets a wonderful example. No matter how important the dignitaries she only serves four courses for dinner."

At this point, recalling the banquets at private homes which I had attended in Shanghai, Chungking, Peiping and Mukden—where the number of courses often exceeded twenty, I remarked: "That's a fine example, Dr. Li, but judging from my own experience, very few wealthy people seem to be following it."

MADAME CHIANG: "That just *proves* we are a democracy."

SILK: "Will Madame look this way?"

I asked Madame Chiang what she meant.

MADAME CHIANG: "In China we set the example but we do not *force* others to follow it. That is democracy."

Then I'm afraid I made a little speech about my own non-Confucian concept of democracy having to do with the greatest good for the greatest number. I said: "In America where we have, through good fortune, more food than is available in China, it has been necessary to institute rationing. I don't believe that's been tried in China, with all the famine."

Madame Chiang positively beamed: "Exactly. That just shows we are a higher form of democracy. We do not dictate what people shall or shall not eat."

Silk took a few pictures and then the Generalissimo came in. He was smaller and slighter and pleasanter than I had expected. He wore a summer uniform, its blouse—a little too big for him— streaked with many-colored campaign ribbons. Whenever he was addressed, or I caught his glance, his lips smiled. His eyes were as bright and hard and cold and unchanging as agates.

George seated him in a chair near the Madame.

"Ask the Gimo to fold his hands," George said.

"Darling, fold your hands," said Madame Chiang, in English.

"Hao," said the Gimo, grinning, but not moving and obviously not comprehending.

"Fold your hands," Madame repeated in English. Neither Dr. Li nor the Generalissimo's aide, who had entered, said a word. They explained later that it was the custom that only Madame Chiang should translate for the Generalissimo when she was present. Finally Madame Chiang rose, leaned over her husband and folded his hands.

"Hao," the Gimo grinned. He jiggered his foot nervously up and down, up and down.

This kind of embarrassing performance continued for ten more minutes while George kept frustrating the Madame's always imminent departure by saying, "One more please, Madame. I want to be sure we have you looking your best."

She left without saying goodbye to Dr. Li, to Silk, or to me. Very casually, as she snatched up her wrap, she called back to the Generalissimo, "I must go now, darling. I may not be back in time for tea."

The Generalissimo looked as if he understood the sense of the words, if not their meaning. He beamed affectionately at her disappearing back and said, "Hao."

When she was gone and the aide began translating my questions, the Generalissimo appeared thoroughly at ease and most communicative. We talked briefly about the civil war. I was struck by the Gimo's carefully paternalistic tone; he literally spoke of the civil war protagonists as though they were children—his children—one just and forthright and loyal, the other mean and underhanded and disloyal. Then abruptly he inquired about American public opinion in respect to Russia.

"I think they are in favor of Russia, most of them," he said with a straight face.

I shook my head. "I would not say so. Certainly not."

"*Hao*," said the Gimo. He smacked the palms of his hands against his knees.

Silk said, "Let's take the Gimo inside. I want some shots of him sitting at his desk. Please?"

We all went into the Gimo's study, a long, handsome, comfortably furnished room with thick, blue carpets and modern chairs and sofas covered in beige.

The Gimo's large, carved wood desk was down at the far corner and behind it was a painting by Ping Hung. The artist, now dead, dedicated his drawing of a tree trunk to the Generalissimo with this inscription: "Chuang-tzu [Chinese philosopher] says 'eight thousand years for spring, eight thousand years for autumn. This is the symbol of longevity and humanitarianism. Here is the quintessence of the virtues of nature. It is nothing incidental.' "

Over the fireplace was a portrait of Dr. Sun Yat-son, the only photograph in the room. On an end table were large white dahlias in a handsome Ming vase.

Another military aide rushed in with a "dispatch from the front." It was a bulky manuscript written in Chinese on parchment. The Gimo studied it while George focused. The flash bulbs went off, but the Gimo, unblinking, concentrated on the report.

"Tell him to flip some pages over, it'll look better," George ordered. Nobody said anything. Impulsively George leaned across the desk and flipped the pages. "Like this," he said. The Gimo looked up in surprise. It was impossible to tell if he was angry.

"That's fine," George said.

The Gimo smiled.

"Put your head down," George ordered.

The Gimo resumed reading.

"No one dares treat him like this except the Madame," an aide whispered to me.

Then a bulb exploded with an unexpected frightening pop. The aides crouched; one looked as if he were reaching for a pocket pistol.

"God, I'm sorry," Silk said.

The Gimo had not moved a muscle.

"Please tell the Gimo I'm sorry," George said.

The aides and I helped hold flash extensions. George worked fast.

"Sit up," he said to the Gimo. Then he caught himself. "I mean, please ask the Generalissimo to sit up straighter in his chair."

An aide whispered and the Gimo straightened up. Dr. Li said softly in English, "He has a bad back still. Be quick. It is from the time of the kidnapping in Sian—you know about that? The Young Marshal . . .?"

The Gimo called to an aide, who came over to me. "Will you excuse the Generalissimo for a few minutes. He must examine this document closely."

We went into the dining room. George photographed a painting on the wall which depicted the harbor of Hong Kong—with no British warships anchored in the bay. A servant brought in ice cream and cakes.

"Austerity," I said to George.

"Democracy," he said, eating some ice cream, "and bloody good, too."

Presently we went back to the study. The Gimo was sipping tea with General Adrian Carton DeWiart, Britain's special military envoy, and the Canadian Ambassador, General Victor W. Odlum. DeWiart, who wears two Victoria Crosses and has lost an eye, a leg, and an arm in his country's service, had just returned from Japan and the Generalissimo asked him questions about MacArthur. De-Wiart was enthusiastic in his praise. "A remarkable chap," he said, concluding with a typical understatement. George made some group pictures.

The Gimo, who told me he read a summary of American newspapers every day and a translation of certain *Time* stories weekly, asked about the accuracy of the atomic bomb spy story in Canada. General Odlum said, rather sadly, that it was all too true. "I cannot understand," he said, shaking his head, "how Canadian citizens could think more of the Soviet Union than of their own country."

When this was translated, the Generalissimo laughed and slapped his knee, almost upsetting his teacup. "That is easy to understand for me," he said. "Look at the Communists in China."

Odlum and DeWiart nodded.

At this point T. V. Soong barged into the room, and the study suddenly seemed to shrink. George set up another picture and we tried to persuade the Gimo to go outdoors. He said he was too busy and came to shake our hands.

"The Generalissimo thanks you very much for coming," said an aide.

"Thank *him*," we said.

"No, he appreciates *your* coming very much."

The Gimo smiled and bowed. We shook hands again. His aide said: "The Generalissimo asks you to excuse him for not showing you to the door."

We said we understood and left.

7

That evening I had supper with Chou En-lai at a Hunanese restaurant. There was plenty to eat there, too. Among the questions I asked Chou was one about the Young Marshal, Chang Hseuh-liang. I wanted to know why he was not released.

Chou said, "At the PCC this question was asked. The Government explained that the Young Marshal could not be released like any other political prisoner because his relationship to the Gimo was like that of son to father. And so the punishment is that of a parent to a disobedient, disloyal son."

Chou was tired; he did not want to talk about the war. He wanted to hear about America—what was the farmer's life like, what was studied in our public schools and public colleges, how did a young man enter politics. Although he had been told I had spent part of the war years in the Soviet Union, Chou never asked me a question about Russia. This is not probably of any significance, unless one would like to call it politics.

During this and other talks with Chou and the Communists I found them supremely confident of the ultimate success of their program, no matter how badly off their chances appeared at any one moment. Simplified, their reasoning developed something like this. If there is peace and all parties have the right to appeal to the voters, the only way the Kuomintang can defeat the Communist reform ideas is by espousing them and carrying them out on a national scale better than the Communists were doing in their areas of local autonomy. (In this connection the Communists nearly always stressed the revolutionary background of the Kuomintang, noting that many of the so-called Communist reforms were long ago pledged to the Chinese people by the Kuomintang itself.) In a period of peace, the capitalist-democratic coalition government

would speed China's industrialization. With this industrialization
would come a larger working class and greater mass education, two
factors which the Chinese Communists believed would help them
win support.

In the event of war, the Communists point out that it would be
a long, drawn-out affair. In the past the Nationalists and the Japanese drove the Communists from the towns but could never entirely defeat them. By waging a yearly anti-Communist campaign,
the Government would have to depress the standard of living to
support military expenditures, continue conscription by force and
the suppression of freedoms. This, the Communists believe, would
lead to economic chaos, widespread non-co-operation, peasant revolts, and eventually to the collapse of Chiang's Government. In
the "warlord period" which presumably might follow, only the Communists would have staunch followers throughout China, only the
Communists would have a unified program and a unified army to
stabilize the peace. "We would, in that case," Chou En-lai said,
"welcome and actively co-operate with all other groups, not for
the immediate establishment of socialism, but for the preservation
of peace, a decent living standard for the people, mass education,
and industrialization. We might even want to borrow money from
you."

The one thing which Chou feared, he said, was a world conflagration with the United States and the Soviet Union as the chief
flame-throwers. Paradoxically, this was the very thing which Chen
Li-fu, one of the "CC" brothers, told me he counted upon to solve
the civil war. "Our problem with the Communists," the patrician-
looking Chen confided over lunch at his Nanking home, "is the
same as yours with Russia. When you are ready and able to wipe
out Russia, then we will be ready and able to wipe out the Communists." Chen was the suavest Chinese official I ever met, with
wavy white hair, a benign face, a disarming way of looking you
straight in the eye.

Until recent years, Chen's name and reputation were little known
in the United States, just as, I suppose, James A. Farley was not a
familiar figure in foreign countries despite his importance in the
Democratic Party during the thirties. In China there is a saying,
"The country belongs to the Chiang's, but the Party belongs to the
Chen's."

Chen Li-fu was born forty-eight years ago in Chekiang Province.

His uncle helped to finance Chiang during the early days of the Gimo's fight for power in the Kuomintang and Chen has helped Chiang retain that power ever since. By the moral code to which Chiang adheres, he is indebted forever to the Chens and no amount of pressure from a General Marshall or a General Chou could induce the Gimo to dispense with the nephew of his benefactor.

When the Communists were driven from the Kuomintang, Chen masterminded the purge. Since then he has represented "reaction" both in the Kuomintang and in the Government to the Communists. This fact has been used in Chen's favor by his defenders who like to picture him merely a gallant and frequently misunderstood crusader against Communist infiltration.

They are inclined to forget that as Minister of Education (1938-44) this same mild-mannered, patrician-looking man terrorized China's schools and universities with his "Red hunts." Invariably felling more liberals than Communists, his "thought police" even reached out to report on what Chinese exchange students were doing and saying while in foreign countries. Since then he has represented "reaction" both in the Kuomintang and in the Government to Chinese progressives who believe in civil liberties.

As I talked with Chen, I tended to forget these things, too. He told me about his year at the University of Pittsburgh School of Mines, about the success of recent Kuomintang recruiting drives, about the danger of superficial comparisons between China and Western nations. We did not discuss how Chen ran the Party apparatus through his control over local magistrates, although I broached the topic more than once. But he was more than willing to continue the discussion about the war against the Communists.

I asked Chen if the Government would stop its armies at Changchun if they managed to recapture it. "Why should we?" he demanded. "If we can keep taking over sovereignty, we should. No matter what we say for diplomatic reasons, we understand that the Communists are completely insincere in these negotiations. Today they give their word, tomorrow they break it, the next day they raise a new question."

When asked if the Kuomintang always kept its word, Chen said: "We are often forced to employ the weapons of our adversaries, not for our own personal good, but for the interests of the people."

Later, in answer to my repeated question about continuing the civil war if Changchun were returned, Chen explained: "It is frankly a question of tactics. If we go on fighting, we may not get the loan from your country immediately. Of course, you need us against Russia, so we will get it eventually. But we may need a period of peace to get it now. The Communists may keep fighting just so we do not get that money. But as for ultimately—let me tell you a very funny story. The world will get pinker and pinker and one morning it will wake up and see red."

That day one of General Marshall's colonels went to the Generalissimo's headquarters to determine the latest military situation. He was told that the Nationalist armies were held up just north of Szepingkai and that Changchun was not about to fall.

The following morning the Generalissimo borrowed General Marshall's plane for a trip to Mukden. Without informing Marshall, he flew to Changchun which his forces had just occupied. The Communists had withdrawn without a major battle. The news reports of the Government's Central News Agency characterized the conquest of Changchun as an epic military victory for the Nationalist armies. Actually it was a victory, concocted half of Communist submission to Marshall's persuasiveness, and half of American tanks driven by Nationalist soldiers.

8

Before the meeting with the Generalissimo I had dispatched a long "iffy" cable to *Time*, evaluating the significance of a Cabinet reshuffle which introduced a few independents into the straight Kuomintang deal. The evaluation was based on off-the-record talks with members of the Democratic League, the Kuomintang, the Communists, and one or two of the people in our Embassy. This was written on May 18, while the battle of Szepingkai was still raging, while there was still some public debate as to whether or not the Gimo would exert his influence for peace or war.

May has always been an uneasy, critical month in the history of China's revolution. This May which was trumpeted in with Red victories in Manchuria and the Gimo's less than triumphal return to Nanking, has been no exception. Before the month is over, most observers believe, the die will be cast for the molding of China's destiny. The Gimo is the man who, by his decision or continued indecision, can bend the form that the mold will assume.

Thus far in May his indecision has increased rather than decreased the importance of his position. When Marshall returned to China, it was the American who was thought to have the greatest power to shape the future. But Marshall, despite the obvious positive deeds he has achieved, is near the end of his rope of gold. He can plead, propose, ponder, pontificate just so much. Even the vaunted veto over the loan avails him little. There are Communists who believe the foreign loan is meaningless and even dangerous unless there is at least a coalition government to direct its dispersal. There are Nationalists who believe that the loan is not enough—that no loan could be enough—to make it worthwhile postponing what they consider to be the ultimate conflict for power with the Communists.

The Communists, as usual, are more unified in their demands—whatever they are. I don't know, but it certainly includes readjustment of the ratio of troops in Manchuria, possibly even a majority of provincial governorships in Manchuria and/or multi-party elections. By now Marshall has received from Chou Yenan's minimum demands. These he has presented to the Gimo.

The indecision which tugs at the Gimo's hands is tied to the split in his own party. The die-hards, the realists, or the idealists—depending on how you evaluate their viewpoint, base their arguments on the inevitability of a knock-down, drag-out fight with Yenan. From this they argue that postponement is slow suicide: Yenan will grow stronger; they have industrial bases for the first time; in Manchuria they are already manufacturing munitions; American aid to Nanking will diminish; UNRRA aid will be over in a year; Russia is weary of war and less likely to aid the Communists now than later.

The tug of war on the right is matched by the tug of peace on the Gimo's left. Many in the Kuomintang, loving the Communists no more, argue that open civil war in China will lead to a world war involving America and Russia on opposite sides, that China will become the battlefield, that even a military victory will leave little of China—Nationalist or Communist. They urge the Gimo to press for a coalition government in which the Kuomintang can still play a leading and dominant role. Then with American financial and also technical aid, the Gimo can rebuild the country. In raising the standard of living, he can combat the Communists' spread, revive the people's lagging faith in Kuomintang leadership. (At this point tug-o-war shouts: "But you can't trust the Communists to keep agreements.") At which point tug-o-peace talks about army unification, the new network of Kuomintang-owned radio stations which will preach capitalist democracy, continuing American supervision and large loans.

Meanwhile the Gimo grazes thoughtfully in his valley of indecision. Now he throws a bone to General Marshall and liberal American opinion by approving the removal of General Ho, who had become the symbol of die-hardism and who was personally disliked by Marshall. At the same time Chiang appeases Ho's faction by allowing Ho to help name his own successor. This change to Generals Chen and Pai also pleases the tug-o-war faction because both men are considered more efficient and more clever in military matters than Ho.

But the "Cabinet reshuffle" is not really a decisive decision. It is a trial balloon. The appointment of two "non-Party" people is not a step toward coalition government in the sense that the Democratic League or the Communists understand it. But it might be a broader base for the Kuomintang if it were settling down to an all-out attack on Changchun militarily and on Yenan politically at the danger of rekindling civil war throughout China.

And then again, it might just be the weeding out of the die-hards before the big reshuffle that a coalition would dictate.

At week's end the Gimo was calculating the effect of this balloon. T. V. Soong and the new Information Minister, Peng, were busily scanning editorial reports from America. How far would American public opinion go? Would it stand for war? In the long run, many Americans in Nanking thought that would be the decisive pull. For despite Marshall's careful, cautious (and all sides emphasize these two words in describing Marshall's work since his return) bargaining, his striving to achieve a coalition agreement, there were those around the Gimo—both Americans and Chinese—who whispered that majority opinion in America was rabidly against the Communists, that war with Russia was near anyhow, that more indecision might be the way out of the dilemma. In the meantime a successful attack on Changchun might topple the Reds from their cocky military position, make bargaining easier.

Nanking, the new capital, has a quiet deserted air at week's end. Americans sitting on the ridge overlooking the Gimo's valley were moved to fresh pessimism. "It is no longer a question of whether this government can continue as it is," said one American political observer from Nanking, summing up the present economic chaos. "Now the question is how long can it last—maybe a week, maybe a month." Wiser heads recalled that these same words had been murmured before about Chiang's government during the long war with the Japanese, but somehow it persisted. It will still persist. But the heavy air of indecision may be due for streaks of lightning.

Looking for a sign, the Gimo might well be rereading his favorite volume of Confucius, pausing over the passage which describes how Tze-kung, one of the sage's most faithful pupils, asked Confucius to name the principles of good government. The master said: "Let the people have enough food, enough armament, and have belief in you."

"What shall we omit if we can attain only two ends of the three?"

"Omit the principle of letting them have enough armaments."

"What shall we omit next if we can only do one thing of the two?"

"Let them lose the food but keep their faith in us."

Looking back now, I believe I was guilty of an error which most fair-minded American observers want to make. That was in picturing the Generalissimo as a victim of the die-hards in his own party.

The course he followed was exactly the opposite of Confucius' advice to Tze-kung.

It appears more and more clearly that the only indecision about what to do with the Communists was our own, transferred to Chiang by sleight-of-mind. Chiang's own mind was made up, undecided only on the best approach to his goal. He will negotiate when it serves his purpose. But so long as Chiang holds the ultimate power, there will be no basic compromise with the Communists unless he is forced into such a deal to retain his position.

CHAPTER XXII

"THE GOD" GOES HOME

WHEN I left China in June I was convinced that the Marshall Mission would be a failure for two fundamental reasons, one internal and one external. The military truce had been violated by both sides; which party did it first or deserved the greater share of blame is relatively unimportant. These breaches in the peace could have been healed by Marshall if the political agreements had been kept. There is no question in my mind that the Kuomintang reactionaries doomed the Marshall Mission the week of March 15, 1946, when they refused to abide by the PCC decisions.

Externally, the determining factor was the rapid deterioration of relations between the U.S. and the U.S.S.R. This was reflected in the "tough" policy of American diplomacy against Russia and left-wing groups throughout the world. It was not necessary for President Truman, Secretary Byrnes or War Secretary Robert Patterson to give General Marshall a directive on implementing this "tough policy." He was well-briefed in Washington in April 1946. The ramifications of the tough policy were evident to the Kuomintang leadership long before they became apparent to the American public. Therefore when Marshall returned to China in mid-April, his position as mediator had actually been weakened. Chiang understood that in the shaping of things to come he was a cornerstone of Truman's Arch of World Freedom and Democracy. He could afford, as never before, to stall Marshall, deceive him, give him false or incomplete information, and still be certain that the course of U.S. diplomacy forbade any open censure of his personal attitudes. He was content to let the "CC" be the whipping boys for liberal opinion in the United States.

At home the Kuomintang-controlled press printed new sensations almost daily. The Communists, they screamed, were attacking Nationalist forces in the northeast, they were about to enter Tsinan, the capital of Shantung Province. Few of the reports were ever confirmed by fact. On their part the Communists in their scattered newspapers and over their official radio station in Yenan blasted the Government's "daily duplicity" and also protested Nationalist Army movements which were rarely sustained by investigation.

The cross-fire of propaganda inflamed tempers, created an almost impossible atmosphere at Executive Headquarters and among the truce teams. General Marshall was so irritated by the irresponsible behavior on both sides that on May 23 he issued his first official statement in China. Characteristically, it was written in the third person. The statement said:

General Marshall is daily engaged in discussions with representatives of Chinese political parties and others concerning the restoration of peace in Manchuria. He is deeply concerned over the critical situation in North China and is endeavoring by every means within his power to avoid the spread of the fighting in Manchuria to this region. The present publicity or propaganda campaign conducted by both sides naturally inflames feelings and increases the possibility of some hot-head precipitating a general conflagration. This reckless propaganda of hate and suspicion seriously aggravates the present serious situation and can lead to results that would be disastrous for the people of China.

Operation of truce teams has been made especially difficult by the spreading of propaganda among the officers and soldiers of both sides, and it is on the success of these teams that China must largely depend for the effort at least to localize, if not suppress, conflict. The American members of the team are coping with conditions that involve, not only hardship, but the risking of their lives in a determined and impartial effort to better the situation.

For a brief period the newspapers and radio transmitters were contrite and relatively calm. Then an unfounded rumor dropped in a partisan paper set off the chain reaction of "reckless propaganda" once again.

Marshall continued his efforts through the summer and fall. Month after month the same problems arose, becoming more rather than less difficult to solve. One month the Government would be stronger and unwilling to compromise because it saw an opportunity to become even stronger. The next the Communists would be intransigeant because they feared that advantage would be taken of their attenuated military position.

In June Marshall seemed to make encouraging headway for a while. Chiang, hell-bent for war, suddenly agreed to call a fifteen-day truce on June 7. Lo Lung-chi observed. "The Generalissimo is the kind of a man who will rein in his horse at the edge of the cliff." Then Marshall got the two sides to reach an accord on cessation of hostilities and on the relative strength and disposition of their armies in Manchuria. The Communists had demanded an upward revision of the 1 to 5 ratio of their troops to Kuomintang troops. "At the time we signed the agreement [February 25]," Chou En-lai told Marshall, "we did it with a view that we had made a large concession to secure the peace. This failed, and the situation in Manchuria has undergone much change."

Just when things were apparently going well in June, the negotiations collapsed again. A Communist offensive in Shantung was reported. Chiang demanded that the Communists evacuate from large sections of Hopei, Shantung, Shansi, and the Yangtze Valley into stipulated "pockets." The Communists, under pressure from Marshall and a pledge of a more secure status in Manchuria, agreed. Then Chiang insisted that the Communists pull out of all northern Kiangsu and southern Jehol, including the capital, Chengte. The Communists, to safeguard their holdings in the northeast, insisted on keeping three divisions in these areas. They also wanted Marshall to guarantee that the North China areas which they evacuated would not be occupied by the Nationalists and that existing civil (pro-Communist) administrations could remain until free, democratic elections were held.

Chiang refused to hear of this. "The Central Government must assume full military and civilian control in these areas," he said. He knew what heavy investments the Kuomintang, and the Chen brothers in particular, had in Kiangsu. As a last concession, the Generalissimo extended the truce eight days and proposed that both sides agree on Marshall not only as mediator but as "supreme arbiter."

Chou, who claimed he had sensed a change in Marshall's attitude shortly after the Special Envoy returned from Washington, replied to the Gimo: "We have trusted General Marshall, but to trust him and give him arbitrary power are two different things."

In July the Government widened its "retaliation campaign" into a sweeping summer offensive. Kuomintang armies drove into the areas which Chou had agreed, with conditions, to evacuate. Fighting spread from North Kiangsu to Hupeh and Shansi and north to the Great Wall.

Politically, the Kuomintang began putting the squeeze on liberal elements operating within its areas who did not have Marshall's protection. In Kunming on July 11 Professor Li Kung-po was assassinated and within a week another advocate of coalition government, Professor Wen I-to, was murdered. Eleven other members of the Democratic League, fearing that they, too, might be wiped out, took refuge in the American Consulate at Kunming.

At this point the intellectuals and progressives who were neither Kuomintang nor Communist began to lose their hope that Marshall would or could help China. Fifty-six Chinese educators addressed an appeal directly to the American people, asking them "to prohibit . . . [their] Government from destroying our chances for peace and democracy." Simultaneously Soong Ching-ling, the widow of Dr. Sun Yat-sen and the sister of T. V. Soong and Madame Chiang, broke a long silence to send a message to Americans urging that they ask the United States to withdraw assistance from Chiang.

Madame Sun, educated in America, is powerful in China as a political symbol. Those who believe in the ideals of her late husband (and feel that Chiang has not been true to those ideals) regard Madame Sun as the inheritor of Dr. Sun's mantle just as some Americans already feel that Eleanor Roosevelt carries on her husband's traditions.

"We are threatened," Madame Sun said, "by a civil war into which reactionaries hope to draw America, thus involving the whole world. Civil war cannot bring unity, liberation or livelihood. . . . The first flame of a world conflagration is burning in our land."

Ordering an investigation of the political assassinations, the Generalissimo went to Kuling to avoid the summer heat. Tireless General Marshall and the new U. S. Ambassador to China, John Leighton Stuart (appointed July 9), visited him at that mountain resort in an attempt to keep the negotiations alive. Kuomintang newspapers devoted columns to lauding the delicate shadows of trees reflected in the Kuling streams, the sweet smell of pines outside of the Gimo's house, the new furniture inside it, and the carpet especially woven out of fine straw. When Marshall reached Kuling he found that a bed had been built for him. It was seven feet long and five feet wide. Asked the significance of the extra large bed, one of the Generalissimo's servants replied: "It is hard to be a mediator—he is expected to spend sleepless nights tossing around in his bed."

The envoys' visit was not rewarding. Chiang understood that he was riding high in the United States. President Truman had announced the continuation of Lend-Lease to China on June 14, so that Marshall could no longer use the promise of that aid as a bargaining point. The Gimo was further encouraged by the passage of a bill in Congress authorizing the transfer of an additional two hundred and seventy-one United States naval vessels to the Chinese Government. Despite advice from General Marshall, Chiang widened the breach by unilaterally announcing that the National Assembly would be held in November, although the PCC had agreed that it would be called together by all parties.

2

August was a month sultry with gloom and sickly with deceit. That Marshall continued his efforts is a tribute to his determination, though not his clairvoyance. The July fighting was not intensified, but the political fighting was. During the first week the Government carried out its first air raid on Yenan, bombing and strafing the population of the Shansi cave-city with six P-47's and a B-24 Liberator. This was the signal for a renewed barrage of Communist propaganda about the Government's insincerity and the duplicity of U. S. policy.

About the same time a group of U. S. Marines were ambushed and shot by Communist guerrillas in Anping. While there is no justification for the incident, the Marines had also indulged in unjustified "hunting expeditions" against the Communists. Bored by their prosaic "guard" duties in Peiping and Tientsin, no longer able to channel their energies into the task of rounding up and repatriating the Japanese, little bands of Marines literally went out in jeeps hunting "Reds." These proclivities were naturally not authorized nor were they condoned by U. S. officials. How often they occurred, I cannot say, but like all other such stories from China most of the reports were exaggerated. That such hunting did occur, however, I had heard from a Marine who admitted he went on a shooting party "just for the hell of it."

Toward the end of the first week in August Marshall and Stuart paid another visit to the Gimo, still cooling himself at Kuling. They tried to persuade him that this was the time to announce at least a partial step toward coalition government. The Gimo, thumbing through his daily news reports of American-Soviet squabbles at the Foreign Ministers' meeting in Paris, promised to think about it.

Discouraged, Marshall and Stuart attempted to prod both sides into new concessions by issuing a joint communique about the deadlock on August 10. Their statement said:

General Marshall and Dr. Stuart have been exploring together every possibility of terminating the present growing conflict in China and for the initiation of preliminary steps in the development of a truly democratic form of government.

The desire for a peaceful solution of political problems appears practically unanimous on the part of the people. The economic situation demands prompt solution if disastrous collapse is to be avoided.

Fighting, daily growing more widespread, threatens to engulf the country beyond the control of those responsible.

Government and Communist leaders are anxious to put an end to the fighting, but there are certain issues concerned in the immediate settlements involved regarding which agreement has not been found.

It appears impossible for the two parties to reach a settlement of these issues which would permit a general order to be issued for the complete cessation of hostilities in all of China.

Certain of the unsettled issues relate to the military redisposition of troops. However, these apparently present less difficulty for settlement than the more fundamental issues concerning the character of local or county governments to be maintained in regions which will be evacuated as the result of military redispositions pending the basic decision on such matters by the Constitutional Assembly.

At this point Marshall could have returned home, for all that was to be achieved in the next five months. His reason for staying, at least in part, was that his return would have formalized the failure of American unilateral action at a time when politicians in Congress were talking about mysterious "vacuums" into which a Red flood would pour the minute there was any lessening of American pressure.

Four days after the joint communique, on the first anniversary of Japan's defeat, the Generalissimo released a message to the Chinese people. It was apparently aimed more directly at public opinion in the United States than at the Chinese people, who could judge from their daily lives whether Chiang's statements corresponded to fact: Reviewing the year, Chiang heaped the major blame for the nation's woes on the Communists and their failure to live up to agreements. The Government, he said, was demobilizing its armies and had removed "or amended" wartime restrictions on civil liberties and "will continue to favor a peaceful settlement . . . [and] will always abide by the agreement and formulas to which it is a party."

At the moment he spoke, the armies under his command, numbering perhaps two million men, were stronger and better equipped than at any point in Chiang's long military career. He had at least one hundred divisions which U. S. military observers rated as "good," fifty which were called "very good," and of these fifty, there were thirty-nine with complete U. S. equipment. In addition the Government had a small air force against which the Communists could not muster a single plane.

Two days before the Generalissimo praised the benevolence of his Government, Chu Hseuh-fan, President of the Chinese Association of Labor, had appealed to world opinion against the attacks of the Kuomintang. Chu reported: "In Chungking on August 6 at 6:30 A.M. the Chinese Association of Labor office, our workers' hospital, and two welfare centers built and maintained largely by contributions from American trade union brothers, were surrounded and seized by uniformed and plainclothes police. Twenty of our staff were arrested with no charges preferred against them, and have not been released. . . . In Hankow and Kwangsi we have suffered a similar fate. Our existence is in danger, and free trade unionism is the object of attack everywhere. And who is the inspiration of this attack? Who has turned against us, as against all other liberal movements in China? The very people who have given their solemn promise to initiate China into an era of democracy and reform. This is indeed a sickly democracy, a democracy that is being starved until it is nothing but a skeleton, a bag of bones."

For fear of his life, Chu did not name names. He had originally been appointed with Kuomintang approval and was regarded as "trustworthy." But in order to keep the support of trade-unionists Chu had been forced to lead the fight for higher wages and better working conditions. This cut into the profits of the Kuomintang bureaucrats who were getting control over more and more of Chinese industry. Chu was branded as an enemy. Shortly after issuing his plea, he had to flee China for haven in Hong Kong. The long arm of the Kuomintang reached him there. He was run down on the street by a Kuomintang agent and badly injured.

The Communists, of course, found nothing to their liking in
Chiang's speech. The middle-of-the-road Democratic League found
it ludicrous. Chiang had implied the Communists would be accorded a welcome and given liberties if they had no army and
were just a peaceful party. Dr. Lo Lung-chi, speaking for the
peaceful League parties, reminded U. S. officials that his groups
had no armies and no mass following. And yet they were not allowed to organize in most Kuomintang areas. Two of their liberal
leaders had recently been assassinated in Kunming. As for other
civil rights, Lo pointed out that eighty newspapers of varying
shades of opinion had just been suppressed by the Government.

While Marshall went on mediating, time was favoring the Central
Government. American supplies continued to bolster the Nationalist
armies. MAGIC, the American military mission sent to China to
train both sides, was actually training only one side: the Nationalists.
Chiang had refused permission for the Americans to enter a Communist area.

As the Government military power expanded, Yenan was moved
to its first public criticism of General Marshall. The Communists
claimed that for all the General's neutrality, the U. S. Navy consistently helped the Government. Marshall, they admitted, was the
victim of his Government's policies but he, personally, was thought
to be "not above blame."

Chou En-lai, nevertheless, was not anxious for Marshall to give
up in his efforts. He felt the American alternative was all-out
support for Chiang. He told Ambassador Stuart that if mediation
ceased, the Communists might ask the United Nations to consider
the case. Since the Communists had no legal standing as a nation,
the U N could not have intervened without the Chinese Government making the request—which it was not likely to do.

3

Tired, discouraged and frustrated by the daily duplicity, Marshall
nevertheless remained and tried another "committee." A five-man
board was set up to study and consider procedures for hastening
coalition government: two Communists and two Nationalists, with
Ambassador Stuart as chairman. This effort was doomed to slow
death from its birth. Chiang appointed as Government represent-

atives second-rate people, both anti-liberal and anti-Communist and one an inner member of the "CC" clique.

For two weeks in September these men sipped tea and talked in circles in Nanking. Meanwhile the Communists were spreading their virulent and vituperative, anti-foreign, anti-American campaign, which the Kuomintang newspapers could not easily combat. The people of China were growing tired of "the pretense of mediation" while their brothers were being killed and their children starved. The popular scapegoat became the few thousand U. S. Marines who were still in North China. Atrocity stories, most of them completely fabricated, were whispered from village to village. The Communist press also accused Chiang of being the agent of American imperialism and spoke more and more harshly about General Marshall. Charges were leveled that the American colonels on the truce teams were doing the work of Kuomintang intelligence officers.

Calling them "senseless," General Chou walked out on the Nanking negotiations on September 18. He said they were designed "to camouflage the true civil war situation and black out the truth from the American and Chinese publics." After that, although he was later persuaded by the Democratic League to resume the talks, there was not even the pretense that Marshall could pull anything out of the battered hat. As the Gimo piled up victories in the field, his terms became harder for the Communists to meet.

The Nationalist armies climaxed one drive in October when they marched into Kalgan, although Marshall and Stuart had tried to dissuade the Generalissimo from this move. Then it became apparent to all that the Government was interested only in peace on its own terms. The Gimo, leading from strength, offered a truce proposal which he knew the Communists could not possibly accept without putting their collective heads in a noose.

Marshall, still forced to deal only with Chiang for obvious reasons, began to lean more heavily on Ambassador Stuart's long-term view. That gentle scholar, formerly President of Yenching University in Peiping, reasoned that "gradualism" from within the Kuomintang was the only change that could lead to stability in China now that coalition with the Communists was out of the question. Stuart reasoned: "If the Government is liberalized, the Communists may later be willing to lay down their arms and join."

Liberals in the Kuomintang exerted a concerted effort to bring about Governmental reform. The Generalissimo was especially anxious to broaden the scope of his Government at the time of the National Assembly by bringing in minor party representatives. Flattering overtures were begun toward certain of the more opportunistic chiefs in the Democratic League. The Gimo was already confident that the Youth Party could be counted upon to "come in," especially if one other non-Kuomintang group would also join.

Prior to the Gimo's unilateral "peace offer," a lot of fireworks went off simultaneously on October 10, the anniversary of the outbreak of the 1911 Republican Revolution. The Kuomintang reappointed Chiang as President of China. The Gimo celebrated the holiday by ordering the resumption of nation-wide conscription for men between eighteen and forty-five. He also re-established the fascist-like wartime administrative system which subordinated provincial civilian officials to regional military commanders. The next day his armies announced the capture of Kalgan, the Communist stronghold in Inner Mongolia.

Another firecracker went off in the United States, where the Communists still received a surprisingly good press and the agitation to withdraw the Marines and terminate U. S. aid was becoming more vocal. This had worried the Generalissimo and his advisers who pondered over the daily analysis of American newspaper coverage and opinion on China. Needling messages were dispatched to China's graceful, suave Ambassador in Washington, Dr. Wellington Koo. On October 10, 1946, Dr. Koo handed the Washington reporters a lengthy statement which ably summed up his Government's argument in the civil war.

He sketched the PCC decisions, paid tribute to Marshall's "good offices," and then went on to charge:

"The present struggle in China is not just a struggle between two political parties for power. The Communist movement in my country is not a movement for local self-government. . . . Nor is it a movement for peaceful agrarian reform, for their method of the liquidation of the landlords, including very small landlords, has always been confiscation and expropriation by force. . . . It is the challenge of a minority party with an independent army against the authority of the established Government in the hope of gaining political control of the country. . . ."

On the same date, an American in China published a statement on Chinese politics with a different emphasis. Ambassador Stuart, writing in the *China Press*, a Chinese-owned daily in Shanghai, hoped for "another internal revolution" in China against what he termed "the narrowly partisan" and "ignorantly reactionary forces among her own people." He left no doubt that he hoped for this change under Chiang, "the present, thoroughly worthy successor" of Dr. Sun.

Koo's statement was the first salvo in an attempted campaign to counteract adverse reports by reputable U. S. correspondents and scholars on conditions in China. The Government hoped by passing a democratic Constitution at the National Assembly and reshuffling its Cabinet it could win Marshall's blessing, further loans, and the respect of American public opinion.

Although the Communists and most of the Democratic League had categorically refused to send delegates while the Civil War went on, the Assembly was set to open in Nanking on November 12. In the critical week before, Marshall and Stuart had persuaded Chiang to order his troops to cease fire "except as necessary to defend present positions." This took effect on November 11. On that afternoon, five moderate non-partisans called on the Generalissimo and beseeched him to order a postponement of the Assembly until December 1 in the hope that all parties would join. When General Marshall had previously advised the postponement of the Assembly as long as possible, the Gimo had refused. But when he learned later that there was a chance of swinging over some of the Democratic League's Social Democrats led by Carson Chang, he agreed to postpone the session—not for three weeks but for three days—"in the interests of China."

The Assembly met on the 15th and heard Chiang's new promises of constitutional government. It was a speech which sounded the same eloquent notes that the Gimo had struck at the PCC early in the year. The majority of the delegates, who had been chosen more than a decade earlier for their subservience to the Kuomintang, howled their approval. There were empty seats for the Democratic League parties—except the Social Democrats—and for the recalcitrant Communists. General Chou, living ten minutes' walk from the National Assembly building, scornfully called the gathering a "one-party, nation-splitting Assembly," and said it ended completely any hope for peaceful negotiations. Four days after the Assembly opened, Chou flew back to Yenan. To worried delegates who asked questions about full-scale armed conflict, General

Chen Cheng, Chief of the Nationalist Army Staff, replied that the Reds would be completely defeated in three months.

Appearing before the Assembly as Government head, Chiang spoke extemporaneously for a half-hour. He said he no longer had any political ambitions and "I fear I can no longer do the job as well as formerly. I must give the responsibility back to the people, and the people must learn to protect their rights. . . . Don't pass an inadequate or impractical Constitution, lest China be harmed. Consider the rights and welfare of the people. Only then will Dr. Sun Yat-sen and all our revolutionary dead be consoled in heaven. . . ."

The Kuomintang reactionaries in the steering committee and various subcommittees on the Constitution tried to railroad through two amendments which would have kept the one-party dictatorship as absolute as before. The Youth Party and the Social Democrats threatened to walk out. If this had happened, the Communists would have been proved right and China's "face" in democratic states abroad would have fallen to a new low.

As Kuomintang head, the Generalissimo called a party caucus and read the riot act to the die-hards, telling them that they had to consider external (foreign opinion) as well as internal factors. He had given his word to the Youth Party and the Social Democrats for now, but there would be other National Assembly meetings at which amendments could be offered. In groups of two and three he invited the recalcitrant delegates to lunch and bluntly threatened to read out of the Kuomintang anyone who failed now to follow him as head of the state. Reluctantly, the steering committee dropped the "CC" proposals and the Assembly a few days later passed the draft almost as presented to it.

4

The new Constitution, effective on Christmas Day, 1947, could be a democratic one if properly implemented. Some of the thinking on it goes back to Dr. Sun Yat-sen. Less in the Western tradition than the new Japanese Constitution, its Government apparatus bears only slight resemblance to any other. The original work accomplished by the PCC Draft Committee was modified by suggestions from Dr. Wang Chung-hui, Dr. John C. H. Wu, and Carson Chang, head of the Social Democrats.

The Chinese Government, at least on paper, will have a rather intricate system of checks and balances. The structure starts with the National Assembly itself, a concept of Dr. Sun's, which is not to be confused with a parliament or congress in the Western sense.

The National Assembly is a large body to be elected on a geographic and an occupational basis for a six-year term. In addition to electing the President and the Vice-President, this Assembly has the right to amend the Constitution and, eventually, to initiate referendum.

At first reading the President appears to have fewer prerogatives than the Chief Executive of the United States. Elected for a six-year term, he may be re-elected only once. With the consent of the Legislative Yuan he appoints the head of the Executive Yuan or Prime Minister, declares war or martial law, negotiates peace, concludes treaties, grants pardons and amnesties, and issues emergency orders which must be ratified within a month by the Legislative Yuan. In the event of disputes between Yuans, he can consult with them in an effort to reach a decision. With the consent of the Control Yuan he appoints the members of the Examination (Civil Service) and Judicial Yuans. But several articles make it possible for the President to wield almost unlimited power. As the New York *Herald Tribune* noted editorially, "a president with dictatorial ambitions might make himself an absolute ruler without serious infringement of the Constitution if he could control a few key officials."

The Executive Yuan must comply with all laws passed by the Legislative Yuan or resign. However, it can ask reconsideration of any measure that has been passed; the Legislative Yuan can then make it stick only by repassing the bill by a two-thirds' majority over the veto. The British system requires only a simple majority to force a Cabinet change, and it was this example which the PCC had voted to follow. The Executive Yuan must present reports to the Legislative Yuan, which can also question Cabinet members at any time.

The Chinese "Congress" is called the Legislative Yuan, elected for a three-year term by popular direct vote of provinces, municipalities, frontier regions, overseas Chinese and occupation groups. The budget, which is set by the Executive Yuan, can be slashed by the Legislative Yuan but not increased. This would appear to be one of the weaknesses of the set-up.

The adoption of the new Constitution received a lukewarm reception among the Chinese people, who preferred to wait and see how it affected their livelihood. For although, like most constitutions, it looked good on paper, the wording by itself solved nothing. In any future election campaign the Kuomintang would still have infinitely more money, control most presses, all the effective radio stations except the illegal Communist transmitter, the educational system, the police, the trade unions, and presumably the electoral apparatus itself. While multi-party elections would be held, many thought they would be no more meaningful than free elections in Japan during the prewar and war years.

The chief opposition parties did not support the new Constitution. The liberal Democratic League groups (except Carson Chang's Social Democrats) declared that the document was illegal because the Assembly which framed it had been convened in violation of PCC decisions. The Communists went further. They not only called it "illegal" but criticized the failure to provide for more provincial autonomy (as agreed by the PCC) and the "abridgement of civil liberties." Civil liberties are guaranteed but there is a loophole: they may not be restricted by law *except* "for preventing infringement of the freedom of other persons, averting an imminent crisis, maintaining social order, or promoting the public interests." Non-Communist Chinese intellectuals and trade unionists were equally skeptical about these provisions, having suffered previous Kuomintang "guarantees" of civil liberties. Until this loophole clause had been subjected to trial and interpretation, no one could say how broadly such a phrase as "promoting the public interest" for example, might be stretched, nor was it easy to define "an imminent crisis."

5

From April, the month of the Manchurian fiasco, until early 1947 the Executive Headquarters existed but did not function as "Operation Dove." Peiping was studded with beribboned, middle-aged American colonels and their long-tongued wives, busily shopping for jade earrings, cloisonné vases, and brass curios. Chinese students demonstrated against American "intervention" from time to time.

But the colonels living comfortably at Peiping's best tourist hostelry, the Grand Hotel des Wagon-Lits and working at Peiping Union Medical College (which was locally called "The Temple of a Thousand Slumbering Colonels"), thought it all just a Russian propaganda trick. They knew how naive the Chinese could be, judging from their bargains won along Peiping's Jade and Embroidery Streets.

Without political agreement, the truce teams were as ineffective as company police during a United Mine Workers' strike. The organization continued to exist long after its principal *raison d'etre* had vanished only because it had secondary uses for all three partners. For Marshall and the United States it represented an organism which could be revived if ever a political settlement were, by some miracle, reached. It was also a source for information, a kind of personal Pinkerton service, which enabled Marshall to check the claims and counterclaims of the Nationalists and Communists. For the Communists it was undoubtedly their best and at times their only means of communication with various pockets of resistance. The Nationalists, too, found Executive Headquarters worthwhile as the nerve center of a communications and intelligence network. But in the long run they recognized it was of more value to the Communists than to the Government, which had other means at its command.

The proposal to abandon Executive Headquarters was pressed several times during the summer and fall. Toward the end of November all eight field teams were recalled from Manchuria, and when Marshall gave up and returned to Washington in January 1947, Executive Headquarters was closed. The colonels packed their trinkets and sailed home.

A month after Marshall departed, General Gillem (who had succeeded the disillusioned Walter Robertson as U. S. Commissioner for Executive Headquarters) summoned a final press conference to his large PUMC office in Peiping. "I have called you here to witness the blowing of taps over the most unique mission the American Army has ever had," he said. "We are going down with our colors around us. We are sorry we have not been successful."

During the round of farewell cocktail parties, the Nationalists and Communist senior members, who had learned to work together, toasted each other. When the Communist commissioner left Peiping at dawn on February 21 for Yenan, General Gillem and the Government member appeared at the airport to see him off.

"Peace will prevail!" proclaimed stocky, rosy-cheeked Communist General Yeh Chien-ying. "Long live Chinese-American co-operation!"

Gillem replied, "I hope we meet again."

The *Ta Kung Pao*, with eloquent and elemental brevity, wrote an editorial valedictory for the experiment: "The Committee of Three, the Executive Headquarters, and the truce teams have really suffered in the past year," the newspaper recalled. "They came with the great hope of stopping China's civil war, they go disillusioned. We wish here to thank our American friends and to hate our own stupidity. The weather of dying winter is changing. Smoke, fog, wind, rain, snow, and hail have concentrated in the skies above China. A lot of changes, perhaps, will take place before warm spring comes."

CHAPTER XXIII

CHINA BLEEDS; THE U. S. PAYS

RESPONDING to public pressure for clarification of United States actions in China, President Truman issued another policy statement on December 18, 1946. This reviewed the year since his previous declaration of intention regarding China and resounded a warning about China's civil war. In 3,500 words of postulates and platitudes, the President said that China's war was a threat to world peace and must be ended and that the United States would continue to respect China's sovereignty and continue to help the Chinese achieve peace and economic recovery. "We believe our hopes for China are identical with what the Chinese people themselves most earnestly desire," the President said. The New York *Herald Tribune*, trying to find some reason for a statement which "adds nothing," observed that it was "apparently written in the hope that it would please conservatives and not be too offensive to leftists."

The President or his statement writers were not well briefed. He claimed that U. S. personnel were no longer training Chinese troops, completely overlooking MAGIC which was still busy training Nationalist forces. Whatever "our hopes" for China might be, our actions definitely had not been what "the Chinese people themselves most earnestly desire." Unless, of course, President Truman mistakenly identified the desires of one man, Chiang Kai-shek, with those of the Chinese people.

During the period of the Marshall mediation, the Chinese Government received more Lend-Lease supplies than had been shipped to that country during the Japanese war. In addition, more than 800 million dollars' worth of surplus goods were "made available" to Chiang. What the Nationalists could not use for war was then offered to Latin America in exchange for credits with which the Chinese could purchase arms. The President in his statement claimed that the U. S. was no longer selling military supplies to

China; only copper, which was all that the Government needed to manufacture bullets. While Marshall sought peace, we arranged to transfer two hundred and seventy-one naval vessels to the Chinese Government and encouraged U. S. Navy men to remain in China to train the Nationalist crews.

UNRRA supplies (for which the United States taxpayers met 70 per cent of the cost) went into building up Chiang's war machine. Conservatively, less than 2 per cent of all UNRRA materials ever reached two-fifths of the population—those in Communist areas. The other 98 per cent benefited the Chinese people in Nationalist regions too little. The supplies were bought and sold on the black market like stocks.

Documentation of the National Government's disgraceful handling of UNRRA supplies has already filled a half-dozen book-length reports filed with UNRRA officials. In July 1946 a cable was made public which three hundred UNRRA employees, representing sixteen nations, had sent to Director-General Fiorello LaGuardia accusing the Chinese Government of "persistent misuse" of relief supplies. The charges covered everything from theft and graft to employing relief as a political weapon. "The disregard for agreed policies has resulted in the sale of UNRRA food on the black market while many people died," the employees informed LaGuardia.

It appeared that an honest Chinese UNRRA or CNRRA official was an exception. Senator Allen J. Ellender, Democrat from Louisiana, returned from an investigating junket in China and informed reporters: "Every local official handling UNRRA relief was expected to extract a 10 per cent graft fee just for handling." The gamut of graft ran crookedly from the barge-owners in the harbors up to the statesmen in Nanking. The higher the official, the bigger the cut. The barge-owners settled for a sack of flour; the statesmen had no particular need for a sack of flour, but it did get awfully hot and sticky in Nanking in the summer and. . . .

UNRRA had ordered thirty-six air-conditioning units for the skin disease wards of Chinese hospitals. At the dock they were turned over to CNRRA. Weeks later Chinese public health officials were still asking about them. UNRRA investigators then got busy and found that most of the units had been quietly sold for U. S. dollars. Two units were later discovered in Shanghai's Park Hotel and twenty more were traced to Government officials and agencies. None of the offenders was successfully prosecuted.

Again in the spring of 1947 a group of UNRRA employees in China publicly denounced the National Government for violating its agreements by keeping relief from Communist areas. "Every device has been used by Government agents, from passive blocking to outright military attack," the sixty UNRRA workers related. "Relief truck convoys have been bombed and strafed by air. Hospitals set up by UNRRA have been bombed and strafed. Relief and medical supplies have been held up by military commanders guarding roads into Communist territory."

Chiang himself was not overly concerned by the humanitarian aspects of UNRRA. His Government had signed the protocol agreeing that UNRRA goods could be distributed impartially. But to Chiang, UNRRA aid was a weapon that he wielded to maintain power. When he could use it to his best advantage unofficially, that was done. Yet he was bold enough to come right out in the open and baldly request permission to peddle 200 million dollars' worth of UNRRA supplies on the open (black) market to raise money to check the inflation which was discrediting his regime. The Gimo's suggestion was blocked but he wasn't.

This sort of transaction became the pattern. In the spring of 1947 UNRRA shipped sixty thousand tons of food to Anhwei Province to meet an emergency food shortage; only nine thousand tons "officially" arrived. Shortly afterwards the Kuomintang Governor of Anhwei sent one hundred twenty thousand tons of food to Shanghai to be disposed of on the black market. The money was used to further the Nationalist conscription drive in Anhwei.

2

Despite Mr. Truman's glib assurance, the Chinese people did not "earnestly desire" intervention by U. S. men and money. Dr. Lo Lung-chi, one of the liberals praised by General Marshall, publicly stated: "I cannot understand why the United States has persistently supported the Kuomintang, which has denied the people freedom and liberty. The United States is actually aiding the fascist elements in China. Does the United States want to see Fascism in China?"

Throughout the summer of 1946 General Marshall received

genuine appeals signed by university professors, writers, students, and religious leaders urging him to withhold all aid from Chiang until a "new representative and democratic coalition government is formed." Most of them understood they might be risking a Gestapo-like persecution by signing their names to such a request.

The month before President Truman passed his platter of platitudes to the public, the United States had demonstrated its "respect for China's sovereignty" by engineering a new pact with Chiang. A Treaty of Friendship, Commerce, and Navigation was signed in Nanking on November 4, 1946. One of my Chinese friends wrote me about this "equal footing" treaty that "It gives me as much right to buy Rockefeller Center as it does Mr. Rockefeller to buy Cathay Mansions [a Shanghai hotel], but he has the potent resources to do so and I do not even have the potential. How is that an equal treaty?"

Yeh Kung-chao (also known as George Yeh), who worked in the Chinese Ministry of Information and is now a Vice-Minister of Foreign Affairs, expressed the same idea, slightly differently: "It is just as if you were fifteen years old and I five. We two draw up an equal treaty saying that if I hit you, you can hit me too. Of course this is very fair, but how can I who am five years old win a fight over you who are fifteen?"

The *Ta Kung Pao* called the treaty "a new concession." After analyzing provision after provision and showing how it "opens the door" for the United States but does very little for China, the newspaper concluded more out of sorrow than wrath: "We do not blame the United States, we are only surprised that our Government does not seek to protect our country's industry, economics and the people's living."

Chinese reaction to the Treaty was so bitter that Ambassador Stuart called a press conference in Shanghai to tell newspapermen that the criticisms of the agreement were not true. He said that the United States had not sought nor had it been accorded any special rights in China. The next day the independent Shanghai newspapers politely called him a liar. They pointed out that Articles 2 to 8 on the mutual protection of immigrants did not even give Chinese in the United States the "most favored treatment" of Cubans and Filipinos, and that Articles 21 to 24 gave U. S. ships the special right to use any port in China and to use any short cut. "The Americans say that a diplomat should be an honest man who is sent to foreign countries to lie," remarked *Lien Ho Wan Pao*, a Shanghai paper for businessmen. "This is very true."

3

At the White House news conference on December 18, the date his statement on China was released, the President gave no hint that General Marshall was coming home. In fact he indicated Marshall would stay on.

General Marshall quit China on January 7, 1947, and returned to become Secretary of State. His weary, year-long efforts in China could not be considered wasted if the new director of U. S. foreign policy had learned a few truths about China. In a lengthy, searching report (see Appendix J, p. 417) issued in Nanking before he departed, Marshall indicated that he had acquired a sound appreciation of most of the forces at work against peace and democratic unity in China.

Perhaps because of his new assignment Marshall did not mention names in blaming the irreconcilables among the Communists and Kuomintang forces. Perhaps because Marshall believed it, the statement left the impression that Chiang himself was on the side of the angels. Or perhaps Marshall felt, as the Communists did during the war and the negotiations, that Chiang was still the only symbol under whom all factions could unite.

"I think the most important factors involved in the recent breakdown of negotiations are these," Marshall said. "On the side of the National Government, which is in effect the Kuomintang Party, there is a dominant group of reactionaries who have been opposed, in my opinion, to almost every effort I have made to influence the formation of a genuine coalition Government." Marshall observed that "This has usually been under the cover of political or Party action, but since the Party was the government, this action, though subtle or indirect, has been devastating in its effect."

The General then went on to evaluate the Communists: "On the side of the Chinese Communists Party, there are, I believe, liberals as well as radicals, though this view is vigorously opposed by many who believe that the Chinese Communist Party discipline is too rigidly enforced to admit of such differences of viewpoint. Nevertheless, it has appeared to me that there is a definite liberal group among the Communists, especially of young men who have turned to the Communists in disgust at the corruption evident in the local governments—men who would put the interests of the Chinese people above ruthless measures to establish a Communist ideology in the immediate future. The dyed-in-the-wool Communists do not hesitate at the most drastic measures to gain their end as, for instance, the destruction of communications in order to wreck the economy of China and produce a situation that would facilitate the overthrow or collapse of the Government, without any regard to the immediate suffering of the people involved."

General Marshall's analysis expressed this hope of a possible solution:

The salvation of the situation, as I see it, would be the assumption of leadership by the liberals in the Government and in the minority parties, a splendid group of men, but who as yet lack the political power to exercise a controlling influence. Successful action on their part under the leadership of Chiang Kai-shek would, I believe, lead to unity through good government.

In fact, the National Assembly has adopted a democratic Constitution which in all major respects is in accordance with the principles laid down by the all-party Political Consultative Conference of last January. It is unfortunate that the Communists did not see fit to participate in the Assembly since the Constitution that has been adopted seems to include every major point they wanted.

This last statement, as pointed out in the previous chapter, is not quite accurate, unless Marshall's interpretation of the PCC decisions on the proposed constitution are different from my own. The Constitution in its final form failed to include several of the important guarantees which the Communists wanted and which the PCC had agreed upon.

As to the future, Marshall talked of a "major reorganization" in the Government and said that "practical measures" would be the test. "The first step," he stated, "will be the reorganization of the State Council and the Executive Branch of the Government to carry on administration pending the enforcement of the Constitution. The manner in which this is done and the amount of representation accorded to the liberals and to non-Kuomintang members will be significant."

Enough time has elapsed to judge the success and sincerity of this "first step." The State Council, the fundamental power in China until the new Constitution takes effect, consists of twenty-nine members. Of these, seventeen are Kuomintang Party members who are required to vote as a solid bloc; eight represent the two minority parties (Youth and Social Democrats), and the other four are non-partisans, three of whom are closely allied with the Government. This assures the Kuomintang of twenty votes out of the twenty-nine. Neither of the Chen brothers was elevated to the Council because Marshall had told Chiang that this would decrease China's chances for a loan.

The "minority parties" were also invited into the Cabinet or Executive Yuan, which was reorganized with Chiang's old friend, honest Chang Chun, as Premier. The China Youth Party and the Social Democrats were given three Ministries without Portfolio and two other minor posts. Some of their leading figures, however, refused to accept their assignments in the Chiang Government.

As is so often the case with one of Chiang's reshuffles, the re-action is more apparent in the United States than in China. *Lien Ho Wan Pao* accused Marshall of a change of strategy but not of policy towards China. This newspaper believed Marshall helped "seduce" liberals into Chiang's Government so that when it was reorganized, however slightly, the United States would be able "to point at a deer and say that it was a horse." A Kuomintang-controlled newspaper in Peiping reported rather frankly on the reorganization that "Although the response from American public opinion has been favorable, most of our own countrymen are rather indifferent to it. We have not heard any cheering or inspired talk about the reorganization, which on the contrary has been discussed with suspicion."

The Chinese understand that the new Government is still the sounding board for Chiang and the dominantly reactionary Central Executive Committee of the Kuomintang, which *does* include the Chen brothers and their satellites. It is not Marshall's "major reorganization" by a long shot.

The *Ta Kung Pao* was both penetrating and scathing in its editorial comment on the reorganization. The paper charged that the new Government was "a multi-party Government responsible to one party. . . . The reorganized National Government will continue to be a political tutelage Government and to be responsible to the Kuomintang. . . ." *Ta Kung Pao* underscored this point by quoting Article 10 of the revised Government Organizational Law which stipulates that the President and Vice-President are to be elected by the Central Executive Committee of the Kuomintang and that "The President of the National Government shall be responsible to the Central Executive Committee of the Kuomintang."

The editorial continued, "Therefore, the administration of state affairs from now on, whether good or bad, or whether it proves a success or not, will continue to be the sole responsibility of the Kuomintang which cannot in the least deny the responsibility. For what, then, are the Youth Party and the Social Democratic Party and the few independents joining the Government?"

It is a little difficult for Chinese to believe Chiang can bring democracy to the National Government when he still runs his own outfit as Mussolini ran the Fascist Party in Italy.

As Director-General of the Kuomintang, Chiang selected twenty-two members of the party's Central Executive Committee to "run" for eleven seats on the presidium. Before the one hundred eighty-three members of the C.E.C. cast their ballots most of them made sure which candidates the Gimo wanted elected. He said he didn't care, and then indicated that he had been personally hurt by the manner in which T. V. Soong had resigned from the Premiership. Of the twenty-two candidates, T. V. finished twenty-second.

There was no immediate comment from Marshall on the reorganization. But shortly afterwards thirty-five Marine munitions dumps in North China were turned over to the Nationalists. U. S. military authorities said that the transfer was hastened by a Communist raid on one of the depots on April 5 in which five Marines were killed and sixteen wounded. To neutral Chinese, turning over millions of rounds of shells, grenades, bombs and rockets to the Generalissimo's armies indicated renewed U. S. support in the most realistic sense of the word.

In his report on China, Marshall laid down another rule of thumb for judging the democratization process. He observed: "If the termination of one-party rule is to be a reality, the Kuomintang should cease to receive financial support from the Government." It seems obvious to anyone who knows the behind-the-scenes machinations in China that such a change will occur—but only on paper. In Chungking last year when possibilities of a genuine coalition appeared brighter than they do now, the Kuomintang was already preparing to have the Government transfer many of its assets to the Party. Instruments of propaganda, the Central News Agency and the big radio transmitters, were being refurbished and put on a sound financial basis in readiness for a "paper" switch in ownership without any actual change in control.

Ever since V-J Day the Government has been insuring that the Party would be well provided with funds to pay for its propaganda, to hire agitators and organizers and functionaries, to buy arms, votes and elections if necessary. The Party has been given full charge, and full profits, from several lucrative trading monopolies. The Government has also helped put some of its big financial backers into new businesses and then made cheap Government bank loans and cheap Government transportation available to them.

Most of this was accomplished secretly in preparation for the ending of tutelage. Knowledge of the smaller deals reached the public's attention only because, by accident, someone was not cut in. Nearly all of the known deals involve the Chinese Government's Alien Property Administration which took over former enemy holdings on V-J Day. In the spring of 1947, for example, the Alien Property Administration "allotted" to the Kuomintang three lucrative Tientsin concerns: the East Asia Tobacco Company, the China Match Company and the East Asia Flour Company. The Tientsin edition of *Ta Kung Pao* also revealed that the Kuomintang had possession of forty-three other properties which, on paper, belonged under the jurisdiction of the Alien Property Administration.

Christopher Rand of the New York *Herald Tribune,* cabled the report that one of the leading trading companies in Central and South China, the Chung Ho Industrial Corporation was set up by the Kuomintang and largely financed by the Government's Farmers' Bank, which the Chen brothers dominate.

This deal was exposed by a Kuomintang newspaper owned by men opposed to the "CC" clique. It pointed out that although the Chung Ho Company was capitalized at only four billion Chinese dollars (and most of this money came from the Central Headquarters of the Kuomintang) that Government banks lent them ten billion dollars at low interest rates. The manipulations reminded U. S. State Department officials of *Zaibatsu* tactics in prewar Japan.

The newspaper, *Hsin Min Wan Pao,* also described how the salt monopoly was being converted to fill party coffers. Wang Tien-hsin, chief of the Government's Salt Control Bureau, resigned. With the backing of the Chung Ho Company, he organized the Yungyeh (Everlasting Business) Salt Company. Then the new head of the Salt Control Bureau gave Wang special priority in buying salt, the Chung Ho Company contributed the ships which they rented from the Government-controlled National China Merchants Steam Navigation Company, and in short order Wang's concern had the salt monopoly for five southeastern provinces—Kiangsu, Chekiang, Anhwei, Fukien and Kiangsi.

A contributing factor to T. V. Soong's resignation from the Premiership was the competition among him, his brother-in-law H. H. Kung, and the Chen brothers for control of China's economy. Charges were made that representatives of T. V.'s big Fuchung Company were able to get places faster than agents of the other groups and it was suggested that they frequently traveled on special passports. In this way one of Soong's associates apparently managed to contract for nearly all of the steel exported from America to China. The Fuchung Company also obtained the exclusive agency for Willys jeeps in China; they imported more than ten thousand of them while other companies found it uneconomical to import any due to the lack of shipping space, high taxes and the difficulty of obtaining import licenses. This business activity leads an observer to be rather cynical about Soong's explanation for the slowness of China's reconstruction: "The house is burning down and I am too busy putting out the flames to plan rebuilding."

Growth of Government and Party monopoly has forced small businessmen and private American trade representatives into sympathy with the Kuomintang opposition. The unchecked inflation also made enemies for the Government, except of course for its special friends, who somehow profited by it. In an unprecedented move, eighty independent business, financial and professional leaders met in Shanghai early in 1947 on "God of Wealth Day" and issued an appeal for peace. These conservatives were activated, perhaps, by the fact that during 1946 more than one thousand five hundred firms had failed, including two hundred and twenty-five industrial enterprises desperately needed in reconstruction.

"Ah," said Liao Wei-chen when I sailed from China last summer, "the American people have meant to be kind to wounded China. When you go home please ask this question: 'What good does it do to give only a blood transfusion to a patient who is still bleeding?' Help us, please, also to heal our wounds."

The people of the United States, through various national and international agencies, have already sent close to four billion dollars in blood money to Chiang. This would not be too much if it were underwriting peace and progress. World War II cost us 335 billion dollars to fight. But then we knew what we were fighting against and possibly what we were fighting for.

If the American electorate and Congress realized what happened to the taxpayer's dollar in Chiang's China, not another dollar would go. Even the most rabid anti-Communists would have to see definite proof that Stalin's legions were masquerading as Chinese Communists to keep the funds flowing to Nanking. They would have to ignore, as they are doing now, General Marshall's statement to the press in Honolulu on his way home from China. Marshall said he knew of no evidence that the Chinese Communists were aided by the Soviet Union.

In the economy of China the word "crisis" is an understatement. There has been little else for two decades. Relatively, the last years of the anti-Japanese war almost marked a kind of stability for China. The opportunities for large-scale swindles were restricted in scope and became more dangerous. Even so there were commercial sell-outs and illegal traffic across Japanese lines; raw materials and resources were manipulated for private profit while Chungking factories, according to Donald Nelson, were unable to obtain Government contracts to produce the necessities of war.

No minor reorganization can instill confidence in the Chinese Government or its currency. The week Chiang announced his "coalition" Cabinet and the mock end of one-party rule, commodity prices in Nationalist China reached new highs. The Chinese dollar, fixed at two thousand to one U. S. dollar a year before, and which had been repegged at twelve thousand to one on February 17, 1947, went to twenty thousand to one by the end of April and thirty-three thousand to one in June. Benjamin Welles, in the New York Times, reported that:

It is generally agreed by Chinese and foreign critics that the recent jump in prices, which is creating extraordinary hardships for the poor and the salaried workers, is the result of speculation by wealthy merchants and Government officials who can no longer dabble openly in foreign currency or in imported luxury articles.

Vast sums are now invested in foods, textiles, and other necessaries, and prices are forced up to make huge profits. There is a general belief that the Government knows these speculators but, because corruption is rampant throughout the administrative structure, such men run no risk of arrest.

There is, of course, graft and corruption in every Government, whether it be the capitalist United States or socialist U.S.S.R. The difference in China is that it has become a way of life. It pervades the entire structure of the bureaucracy from top to bottom, making impossible the efforts of honest men to perform a public service. In turn the odor of this political gangrene has turned the stomach of the Chinese public against government.

It is impossible for Chiang's Government to plan; and if a plan is made, the chances of its being carried out are rather small. There is no certainty about any future, which results in the impulse on the part of bureaucrats and businessmen to extract what reward they can as quickly as possible. An anti-Communist lawyer, quoted in *Time*, aptly summed up honest, non-partisan opinion about Chiang's administration this way: "The Government is not a government. It is a dirty, venal lot of officials trying to get what they can while the getting is good. They have lost their confidence."

The Government cannot curb crooks and speculators because they are the Government apparatus. The Government is up to its knees in financial finagling. Under T. V. Soong, the Government absorbed all of the textile industry which the Japanese had run. Three Shanghai Guilds claimed that the Japanese had confiscated a lot of their raw materials and they wanted them back. The Executive Yuan did not deny the validity of the claim but voted against it, and the Guilds sued. The case did not get very far. The private businessmen were not even paid in paper money.

A loan from the Government enabled one private syndicate to corner the Shanghai black market in rice for several months, long enough to make a killing of several million dollars. The fact that this "killing" indirectly led to the death by starvation of thousands of Chinese in the interior was never investigated by the Government.

Some Americans think our four billion dollars has gone to protect free enterprise in China by bolstering Chiang. While I was in Shanghai the Government acquired fifteen thousand trucks from the U. S. It seemed a poor investment even at the low price, since the trucks were designed primarily for the tough Burma and Ledo Roads and were, therefore, tremendously expensive to operate: only four miles to the gallon of gas. The Government was prepared to make the deal profitable by hook or crook. A decree halted the importation of all trucks into China until the fifteen thousand

Government vehicles were disposed of at high prices. This arbitrary action again adversely affected the livelihood of Chinese in the interior as it cut down the potential amount of transport available to ferry foodstuffs and medical supplies from the coastal ports.

The Government has openly become the chief owner of China's power plants and mines as well as silk, cotton, and sugar production. All of this is being done, Chen Li-fu explained to me in Nanking, "in compliance with Dr. Sun's economic theories." However, Dr. Sun, advocating national control in certain fields, believed it would be used to build up the people's standard of living and the national income. His present-day interpreters have identified themselves as the "people" and "the nation." During the 1947 crisis the Government began selling some of its textile holdings, not because it had changed its theory but because it needed money to pay salaries and continue the civil war.

The four billion has not saved free enterprise in Chiang's China, nor has it safeguarded U. S. business interests or bought us new friends. At the end of the war the "old China hands" couldn't wait to get the first boat back to Shanghai. One of the first boatloads of civilians, mostly businessmen, arrived in Shanghai during the spring of 1946. When the next ship sailed for San Francisco more than half of the Americans were ready to go back. "The golden age of exploitation is over," a mercantile man told me. "The Chinese are onto all the angles. If there is an honest dollar to be made, or a dishonest one, the Government is going to make it and no one else. I'm going home."

For all of America's attempts to help, we are today more unpopular among the people in China than we are in Japan or even Korea. Nationwide student demonstrations protested the presence of U. S. troops before they were withdrawn. The Communist press, echoed by some of the more scurrilous Nationalist papers, kept up an insistent and poisonous propaganda campaign, depicting Americans as "drunkards, rapists, murderers, bandits, worse than the Japanese." All of this fed the fire of Chinese nationalism. A "Love Local Goods" mass meeting in Shanghai issued a manifesto urging Chinese to "protect native industry by boycotting American products." The slogans were similar to those used by the Hearst press during the thirties in its "Buy American" campaign.

Those American businessmen who have been sticking it out in China are giving U. S. Consul General Monnet B. Davis a bad time of it. They continually tangle with the Chinese laws, now that extraterritoriality has been abolished, and they expect their consular officials to support them on every issue. A group of them quietly sent an official protest through Davis to the State Department in Washington charging that Chiang's Government sponsored a drive to put them out of business. One Shanghai importer pounded Davis' desk and shouted, "Plainclothes police are regularly stationed in my offices. Our files and desks have been systematically searched. Naturally we're in no position to complain publicly, but you've got to do something."

Old and respected U. S. firms with American representatives in China have been badgered into turning over their agencies to Chinese firms. An American company official explained that "this hurts most Chinese businesses as much as it hurts us. Career politicians with power are forcing their way in and us out." A State Department official backed this up, saying: "That's a pretty good statement of the facts."

During the week that Executive Headquarters broke up, Chinese soldiers closed down Radio Station XMHA. This was an American-operated English-language station in Shanghai which had been transmitting U. S. Armed Forces network programs and news from America. The U. S. Catholic group which owned the station wanted to continue it, but their request for a license renewal was never approved. The silencing of XMHA left the English-language broadcasting field exclusively to XORA, which is owned by Chen Li-fu.

Under new trade regulations (some say as a face-saving revenge for clauses in the over-all Trade Treaty) U.S. concerns are permitted to import strictly limited supplies. Major reconstruction projects, including new communications networks, power plants, textile mills and heavy industry have been delayed for more than eighteen months. Projects only begin to move when a sufficiently highly placed Government official is "cut in." Or, as has often been the case, the whole deal is turned over to a Chinese firm which can guarantee priorities because of high connections.

American technical experts are still welcome in China if they work at fixed salaries for Chinese organizations and keep their fingers out of the graft pie. But even more welcome have been Germans, many of them formerly influential Nazi Party members. The Government set the example on this, too, by hiring Adelbert Schulze as an intelligence agent not long after V-J Day. He had been Chief of the Gestapo in Peiping during the Japanese occupation. Carl Gadow and Walter Kaumann of Defag, a great German dye cartel, were employed as business advisers while T. V. Soong was Premier. This practice was followed by other Chinese importers and exporters. In several cases the Nationalist Government actually intervened with Americans to prevent immediate apprehension of key Nazis in China.

"They are on our side now," an aide of H. H. Kung's remonstrated with an American investigator. "Why waste their talents by arresting them now?"

4

Along with the recurring economic and political crisis, there is a spiritual crisis in Kuomintang China. It is marked by growing demoralization and by a dangerous apathy among the very people who are needed to avert disaster, which makes it increasingly difficult for decent officials to operate honestly. Without drastic change, public-spirited Chinese are reluctant to enter Government service lest they be tarred with the same brush as the corrupt leaders. Fewer and fewer people believe in the possibility of reform. They keep saying "Things have gone too far."

After the July 1946 political assassinations in Kunming, apologists in Nanking said this was all very embarrassing to the Government, which wanted to curry public favor. "Why would we kill these liberal leaders?" they asked. Assurances were given that it would never happen again.

But assurances in China have come to mean as little as one-hundred-dollar bills. In February 1947 a new wave of repression against liberals began. The much-feared, omnipotent Chinese Himmler, Tai Li, was gone. His plane, symbolically, crashed against Purple Mountain where Sun Yat-sen is buried. But a Chiang can create a new Tai Li overnight. Tai Li's successor is Cheng Chieh-ming who carries the pleasant title "Chief of the Second Bureau of the National Defense Ministry." He also carries on Tai's unpleasant work. Ironically, Cheng had previously been the Nationalist's top representative at Executive Headquarters.

In February, while the Americans were pulling out, the local police suddenly rounded up two thousand persons in Peiping without warrant or ostensible reason. They were held without the right of habeas corpus. Days afterward the Peiping police bureau announced that these jailed had included: 17 opium addicts, 1,165 accused of "ambiguousness in answers, inappropriateness in filling out blanks"; 43 guilty of "suspicious behavior"; and 176 held because their "past records were not clear." The "criminals" included university scholars and professors, students, doctors, publishers, and the chief of the Tientsin-Peiping branch of CNRRA.

As a result of this incident there were mass protests throughout China. Liberals pointed out to the minority parties that the newly promulgated Constitution had already been infringed upon and that Chiang's personal pledges of personal freedoms had been violated.

The campaign against any organized opposition increased. In Shanghai there were unpublicized arrests and frequent disappearances of people suspected of liberal or pacifist views. Communist newspapers and magazines were, of course, proscribed by the Government. Throughout the country nine non-Communist newspapers were smashed up in the first three months of 1947. Editors wondered how much they could say.

The Chinese newspapers cited herein are published in Shanghai, where the Government generally resists applying the rigid censorship in force elsewhere in China. But in May 1947 when there were Communist military victories in the North and rice riots in Hangchow, Soochow, Chengtu and Shanghai, when university professors and students protested and went on strike against the civil war and the lack of food, the Government closed down three Shanghai newspapers. A day or so later a fourth paper was suspended for reporting that the suspension of the other three had "the approval of Chiang Kai-shek." The Generalissimo's liberal face had to be preserved in Shanghai even if fascist methods were employed in doing it.

During the February "Reign of Terror" Shanghai newspapers were filled with letters from relatives and friends of people who had disappeared. Ultimately, in typical Chinese fashion, they formed an "Association of the Families of People Who Have Disappeared." A month passed, and the disappeared did not reappear. The Government said it was not responsible. The military commander of the Shanghai garrison, Hsuen Ti-wu, issued warnings that he would hold local police bureaus responsible for any further disappearances. He assured the public that "anybody illegally arrested may refuse to be arrested and make charges against the persons undertaking to make the arrest."

Ta Kung Pao published Hsuen's assurances and then appended a fable called "The Snake and Its Law":

To respect the rabbit's freedom of residence, the snake set a law and proclaimed to the rabbit:
"From now on, if I break into your house without knocking on your door and getting your permission first, you have the right to make charges against me."
But the snake was afraid that the rabbit's conception of law was too weak. Neither was it sure that the rabbit's psychology of having no faith in the snake had been corrected. So the snake decided to experiment first.
Purposely, the snake did not knock at the door, but glided straight in, bit to death a small rabbit, glided out, and sat there waiting for the rabbit to accuse it.
It waited for a long time, but the rabbit did not come to accuse it. The snake got very mad at the rabbit:
"Why don't you obey the law?"
"Sir, towards whom should I obey the law, and whose law should I obey? Ai, Ai," the rabbit whimpered.
"Don't you dare come and make charges against me?"
"Ai, Ai, sir, the one who was the robber just a while ago is you; the judge right now is you. Which robber should I accuse, and to which judge shall I make the charges against?"
"Hiss, hiss!" The snake was so angry, it gobbled the rabbit down. No matter what happened, this time the law demanded that the rabbit should be killed. The procedure of law was accomplished.

About the same time there occurred in Formosa (Taiwan) a massacre carried out by representatives and troops of the National Government which made its acts of individual terrorism appear relatively unimportant. Formosa had been under the Japanese even longer than Korea. After V-J Day the National Government moved in and lost no time squeezing as much gain as possible out of the island. Formosa's biggest industry is sugar, and Chiang's representative took that over. They grabbed ownership of 70 per cent of the land. A moderate in the Kuomintang, General Chen Yi, was appointed Governor. Despite his liberal utterances, the Chinese officials began to exploit and to loot the people "worse than the Japanese." The Taiwanese, who are basically of Chinese stock, became bitter, then angry, and finally exploded. They organized a mass protest demonstration. The Governor appeased them, fearing their mass power. When armed reinforcements arrived from the mainland, however, the unarmed demonstrators, including women and children, were shot down indiscriminately. Conservatively, five thousand were slaughtered.

When the bloody affair was over, *Ta Kung Pao* could write impassively: "Yet the record of the administration in Taiwan is not worse than that of any province in the Motherland. Governor Chen Yi's integrity and diligence makes him one of the best of China's officials inside and outside China. Unfortunately, China's entire bureaucratic construction is inefficient and corrupt."

The sad truth of this admission was underlined when *New York Times* correspondent Welles, after a trip through the northeast provinces, reported in June 1947 that Chiang's Government was in danger of losing all of Manchuria "unless early and sweeping changes in policy up here are made by Nanking." According to observers in Mukden, the danger was not in a sudden growth of Communist strength but "through a continuation of the present dry rot" and "the growing feeling that Nanking regards Manchuria mainly as a colony to be exploited . . ."

5

Such maladministration tends to break down intellectual resistance to the penetration of Communist ideas. The Communists have been branded as ruthless in their methods; they are said to be anti-religious; their theory is authoritarian; they care little for legality. But I have never heard them charged with wholesale graft or corruption.

Thus it becomes difficult for Chinese liberals, for any honest person, to fight Communism because it is "ruthless," "anti-religious," "authoritarian," or "extra-legal," when the Kuomintang is also all those things in a much more real and immediate sense.

The dilemma of Americans is that they, unless they have what *Pravda* would call "ulterior" or "Fascist" motives, are in the same boat as the Chinese people who want decency in government. The United States has supported Chiang's Government primarily because it is anti-Communist, and in the last analysis likely to be our ally in a conflict with the Soviet Union. To a lesser degree we have supported Nanking because it is the legally recognized government; because we thought our economic interests might be better protected under this government. Sincere advocates of all-out support for Chiang may believe he is more susceptible to change and "democratizing" than what would replace him, that only through him can a strong and unified China be established.

Most of these arguments stand critical examination only if it is assumed that the government of the United States is irrevocably committed to fighting Communism and/or potential allies of the Soviet Union wherever they may appear, by supporting governments and leaders of any variety so long as they are anti-Soviet. Even so, this is a tenuous argument. In a military battle with the Soviet Union, China would not even be a reasonably secure supply base. In fact, our Army men in the Pacific have long ago decided that Japan would be a better risk.

The legality of the present government is like that of Santa Claus, more apparent than real. It can be argued, perhaps not by international lawyers, that without our moral and economic support, the Chiang Government could not have retained power this long, legally or otherwise.

Economically, the great age of exploitation in China is over under any form of government. The Chinese people, Kuomintang, Communist or non-partisan, no longer want to be milked by any foreign power. Any government which supported such a program could probably not carry it out except under continuous martial law, which is about what exists in most of China today. As for trade, China has never figured as importantly in our export-import picture as most Americans believe. Under the present regime the living standard is being depressed to support a heavy armament program, a large army, and an inefficient, graft-ridden bureaucracy. This does not create an expanding market for America's consumer goods.

Many base their continued support for Chiang on the hope for "slow change." This reasoning is a little difficult to follow if checked against the program in Chiang's book *China's Destiny*, if checked against the record of Chiang's promises for the past twenty years. He has made at least fifteen annual pledges of constitutional government; time after time he promised the Chinese people full civil liberties. He did not promise these things to "some Chinese people"; he promised them to all—at the PCC in Chungking early in 1946 the Generalissimo made the pledge to *all* parties. Since then liberals have been murdered, newspapers of varying shades of opinion suppressed, mass arrests and persecutions carried on and the right of assembly denied even to non-Communist groups.

The only people in the United States who are fooled by Chiang are those who want to be. State Department officials and many of the more perceptive military men have seen through him. The terrifying thought is that *having seen through him* the U.S. Government still prefers to deal with him—not because it is believed he can or will bring peace and democracy to China but because he can be relied upon to hold China, technically at least, in our bloc of powers.

In other words, our China policy today is based neither on diplomacy nor democracy but rather on military strategy. This may secure us an ally in an immediate war with the Soviet Union, it may help contain Communism for the present. In the long run, however, this policy, if continuously followed and implemented, will array us against the majority of Asia's millions.

To many of us stationed in China, it became apparent in March 1946, when General Marshall made his ill-timed trip to Washington, that our unilateral attempt to help China would lead only to disillusionment and failure. No crystal ball was needed. I recall the furor at Executive Headquarters and in Nanking when Phil Potter, the Baltimore *Sun's* very able correspondent, cabled a story that "the Marshall mission is a failure." We did not want to believe it, but it seemed inevitable. I cabled that no matter who won, we would lose the friendship of China's people.

At that time elements in the Kuomintang were already saying, "If you Americans had given us all the aid which General Hurley promised, we would not have all this trouble with the Communists." The Communists, for sure, liked us less and less. A 1947 New Year's Day broadcast from Yenan, before the Gimo captured the city, announced flatly: "The Chinese people must now carry on a struggle to death with Chiang and American imperialism, their two natural enemies." Six weeks later Chiang Kai-shek blamed us, too. He said that the Communist problem could have been liquidated more quickly if the United States had continued supplying him with enough guns, ammunition, and credits.

The hundreds of millions in cash and credits we had supplied were not enough. The forty divisions we had equipped were not enough. The nine armies we had transported to strategic spots, thwarting the Communists, were not enough. The missionaries, technicians, advisers, and editorial support we had placed at Chiang's disposal were not enough.

Despite all this, and our moral support, Chiang has not diminished the Communist problem in China. He has increased it. For every one Communist his troops have killed, his Government has created two by being oppressive, bureaucratic, corrupt, and incompetent.

If this is the end result, and I believe it is, the action of the U.S. Government in backing Chiang does not match either our sentiments or our policies. It appeals neither to progressives nor conservatives.

6

Since Marshall's return from China, America's world outlook has been stated by the President in a message now called the "Truman Doctrine." It proclaimed with special reference to Greece and Turkey, that we were going to support free peoples everywhere to preserve their democracy and unity.

In China there is neither democracy nor unity. Since Chiang has been in power more than twenty years, it is necessary to stretch several points to fasten the blame for his failure to establish democracy and unity on the Soviet Union. Russia tried to interfere in China in the twenties, and failed. We have tried since then, and failed. If democracy and unity are lacking in China, we presumably bear as much if not more responsibility than any other foreign power—even though our intent may have been worthy.

The question so many Americans keep asking returned correspondents about China is: "What are the Communists getting from Russia?" In theory, much. In practice, nothing. I could find no evidence myself. I met O.S.S. men and G-2 operatives who were devoting all their energies to this problem from V-J Day on. They never collected a good enough case to float a first-class rumor, which in China is the pinnacle of failure.

After a visit to Communist areas, the New York *Herald Tribune's* reliable A. T. Steele (perhaps the best-informed American correspondent in China) reported that "Despite the proximity of North Manchuria to the Soviet frontier, there still is no evidence of direct material aid by the Russians to the Communist forces." Marshall said the same thing on his return from China after having had access to the fullest U.S. and Chinese secret intelligence reports.

It is hard for fair-minded Americans to buttress the case for practical and moral support to Chiang's regime solely with the argument that its chief opposition has the theoretical support of the Soviet Union.

The Communists, I found, were not popular in China as Communists or Marxists. In Manchuria, near Mukden, I asked peasants, "What do you think of the Communists?" They were reluctant to answer. They had undoubtedly heard much anti-Communist propaganda from the Government and from the Japanese. Perhaps they identified my uniform with the Central Government. Whatever the reason, most of them replied that they had no use for Communism, and some were quite violent on the subject. I felt they were sincere. A little later I asked these same farmers, "What do you think of the 8th Route Army?" Their faces brightened and in almost every instance they quickly responded that they approved of the *palus*.

In most areas, the Communists have never had time to preach socialism. The peasants learned only that villages which fed the *palus* could deduct an equal amount of grain from their annual taxes; that Communist garrison troops helped with the sowing and the harvesting; that free schools were instituted where possible.

I never made the trip to Yenan so I cannot compare it with what I saw in Nationalist China or in parts of Manchuria that were ruled by the Communists. The famous cave city had a remarkable effect on Americans who did visit Yenan, however. Regardless of their political hue, they would return rather embarrassed and begin by enumerating all the generally accepted things wrong with Communism and Communists. Then they would launch into a glowing description of what had been accomplished in Yenan, "even if it is a show window."

Adie Suehsdorf, a newspaperman and editor who served with the Office of War Information in China, summed up his reaction to Yenan this way: "Communist China resembles what I imagine the United States must have been in Jefferson's time. It is energetic, fearless, its people sure of themselves but uncertain of the responsibilities of freedom; the goals are set but not yet achieved; above all, headway is being made. In Communist China you can see it happening. In all spheres of human activity, all at once, the people are learning what it means to have a stake in their own future."

Even if Communist China were only as democratic as Hague's Jersey City or Curley's Boston, it is not the present concern of the United States. There is no possibility we will recognize any more merit in the Communists than Marshall has already done. For the near future we seem fated to direct our actions toward Chiang or his heirs.

What these actions will be affects every Chinese and every American. It does not make much sense to continue what has been a failure. President Truman's policy statement on China, made in December 1945, is not a failure. The U.S. has never lived up to it. The President, in the Roosevelt tradition which he is now busily living down, set certain democratic pre-conditions for our help to China. If we never give China another cent we could still help the cause of peace by fashioning our actions to that policy.

As Secretary of State, George C. Marshall is in a better position to hammer out a realistic reshaping of American *actions* in China than anyone else. He does not have to bother about a change in policy. The policy is still as fresh and untested as a bathing beauty's swim suit.

China's conflict cannot be permanently solved by anybody but the Chinese. With the current divergence between U.S. and Soviet views on what constitutes "friendly nations" or "democracy," a joint intervention in China would only complicate an already impossibly complicated situation. The Chinese would resent it twice as much as they did our unilateral intervention.

Theoretically, it appears that the United States could follow several lines of action. We could cut off all aid, cancel all credits. Or we could continue to play along with Chiang, pressing him publicly and continually to improve and broaden his Government. In practice that is probably what we will have to do. Not because it is moral or just or best for the Chinese people, but because our present anti-Communist world policy predicates such action. The only way to change the logic of the part is to change the logic of the whole.

The civil war will go on as long as Chiang wants it to go on. That is reason enough for withholding all but bi-partisan relief from China in the hope that this will speed the necessity for peace. Writing of our dilemma in Greece, Walter Lippmann observed:

> For only if and when the civil war is terminated, can we hope to begin to pass from mere relief to rehabilitation and reconstruction. A government fighting a civil war cannot, even if it had the competence and the will, rebuild anything. As long as it is fighting the war, as long as we merely subsidize it to go on fighting, and refrain from "intervening" to end the fighting, Greece will be a rat hole into which we shall pour not only

money—that is the least of it—but our prestige and our good name, which are infinitely precious and are to be guarded jealously and fiercely.

The same will obtain, and in the past has proven true, of China. The bulk of Chiang's budget (approximately 70 per cent) has gone and will go for military expenses. Down that "rat hole" has flowed our aid. Until the fighting stops we should send only direct relief, administered by a United Nations or even an International Red Cross mission. If the Chiang Government blocks this aid from Communist zones, as it has in the past, it should be barred from participation in such international relief groups and aid should be withheld from its areas too. Then every publicity means should be used to let the Chinese people know why their American friends have let them down.

7

The wisest person I met in the Orient was Madame Soong Chingling, the gentle, soft-spoken widow of Dr. Sun Yat-sen, China's first President. Last July in her appeal to the American people to withdraw their armed forces from China Madame Sun said: "Every person with human feeling must speak out. The present crisis is not a question of who wins, the Kuomintang or the Communists. It is a question of the Chinese people, their unity, and livelihood. It cannot be settled by balancing armies or bargaining for this city and that territory. Not party rights, but human rights, hang in the balance."

Millions of Chinese who are not Kuomintang, not Communist, realize, as Madame Sun does, that only by the mightiest collective effort of all its people will China ever rise from its bed of anguish. They understand that this probably cannot be accomplished peaceably, by legislation, in the American or British tradition. China does not have that tradition. China has a warlord tradition, and the men who hold power, who profit from vast monopolies, who own huge acreage, who control raw materials, are not going to surrender their personal privilege to the common good without a fight. Education will help, but it may be too slow.

After a while I began to believe that every decent non-partisan in China, if forced to make a choice (which they would not want to make) between the Kuomintang way and the Communist way, would probably choose the latter. Although she has never said this to me, I feel that Madame Sun would, too. And it would not mean that she was endorsing a Soviet system for China, or that she was forfeiting civil liberties, or that she was delivering China into "the Russian orbit."

China is faced with the choice of change or death, and to progressives like Madame Sun who understand its history, the Kuomintang under Chiang spells death.

PART FOUR

EPILOGUE

Without a full stomach one cannot speak of high principles . . .

Confucius

The roots of democracy, however, will not draw much nourishment in any nation from a soil of poverty and economic distress. It is part of our strategy of peace, therefore, to assist in the rehabilitation and development of the Far Eastern countries.

President Harry S. Truman

April 6, 1946

CHAPTER XXIV

TOMORROW'S ASIA

THE inherent danger of America's present position in Asia, if not in the whole world, is that we may force people to make a choice (which they do not want to make) between the American way and the Soviet way. It is dangerous to us because our way will be represented to the peoples of Asia by the Chiang's, the Yoshida's and the Syngman Rhee's whom we have at some time supported and befriended. Our propaganda will stress civil rights while our friends in Asia are denying them; it will sing of the bounty of free enterprise when people are starving for lack of an honestly administered rationing system.

For years the British Empire sharpened its claws on the grindstone of history, opposing the nationalist yearnings of colonial peoples. During most of those years, however, it was profitable in terms of trade balances, British living standards, empire security, and costly only in terms of wasted people. If the Japanese accomplished nothing else in Asia, they have made a return to this kind of system much more costly—if not altogether impossible. The success of their "Asia for the Asiatics" slogan, demagogic as it was, fertilized the soil of Asia for growth and change.

In its wake, the storm of Japanese aggression irrigated deep and restless channels of mass nationalism and resistance movements. The flood tide of these movements is now directed against any power which attempts to rebuild the old containing walls. It will run against stability, against property rights, against the old discriminations of color, class and creed, against collaborationists. And a few grenades, a few machine guns, a few sticks of dynamite, make the price of rebuilding in the old ways of imperialism too costly.

We had no old empire to reconquer in the East. In the Philippines we granted political if not economic independence. In southeast Asia our hands were as clean as a British Foreign Office "white paper." Our troops did not help the Europeans to fight their way back so they could rebuild the old containing walls. But this fooled nobody who saw French, Dutch, or even Japanese troops operating to re-establish the status quo ante with tommy guns and supplies, unmistakably "Made in the U.S.A."

In a paper delivered at Princeton's Bicentennial Conference in Far Eastern Culture and Society, John K. Fairbank, Associate Professor of History at Harvard University, made "certain assumptions" about the continued exertion of America's vast power in the Pacific. Professor Fairbank, who speaks from practical experience (he has lived in the Far East for many years and during the war was head of the State Department's Information Service in China), predicted that:

> . . . Our fear of Communism, partly as an expression of our general fear of the future, will continue to inspire us to aggressive anti-Communist policies in Asia and elsewhere, that the American people will be led to think and may honestly believe that the support of anti-Communist governments in Asia will somehow defend the American way of life. This line of American policy will lead to American aid to establish regimes which attempt to suppress popular movements in Indonesia, Indo-China, the Philippines, and China. This will in turn help Communist leadership of those popular movements to become firmly established, since they will be able to champion the people's cause and focus anti-foreign and anti-imperialist sentiment against the United States. Thus, after setting out to fight Communism in Asia, the American people will be obliged in the end to fight the peoples of Asia, in the effort to make them develop liberal political and economic institutions which are outside their tradition and beyond their means.
> This American aggression abroad will be associated with an increasing trend toward anti-Communist authoritarianism within the United States, which its victims will call fascism and which may eventually make it impossible to have discussions like this one today. This American fascism will come, if it comes, because American liberals have joined the American public in a fear of Communism from abroad rather than fascism at home as the chief totalitarian menace, and both the American liberals and the American public are too immature politically to distinguish between the very real dangers of a totalitarian Communism and the great possibilities of developing an American democratic collective economy of our own. In other words, we are too well off materially and too unsophisticated politically to save ourselves by following the example of the British people.

2

One of the most interesting things I learned in Asia was that the pattern of U.S. foreign policy is far more apparent to the supposedly poorly informed Asiatic than it is to the supposedly well-informed American. They know what makes us tick. Perhaps it is because they have seen us before, carrying another flag, speaking another language, shouting different slogans.

Not all Americans look at Asia from the outside. Some are able to look at Asia and at what we are doing from another vantage point. Pearl S. Buck, the author and Nobel Prize winner who, like Professor Fairbank, has lived in the Orient for many years, recently warned a gathering of American statesmen and educators that "The unreal and fantastic processes which are now going on in the name of realism will lead us straight into world destruction."

Mrs. Buck flatly stated that our foreign policy is "based upon military ideas." Because of these military ideas, she claimed, we have taken steps which lead away from peace: the State Department decided against lending money to countries which feel that the U.S. is trying to enslave them; we have withdrawn support from the world food board in order to use food unilaterally as a political weapon; we joined the Russians in opposing a change in the U.N. veto power despite the insistence of smaller nations that it was "hateful privilege"; and finally, in Mrs. Buck's words, "Our policies and action in Japan and Korea are building a cynicism of democracy which centuries can scarcely efface."

The trend which Mrs. Buck sees in our current foreign policy leads to this: we switch our approach to problems from a political to a military orientation. By any objective standard, China remains the most pressing political and economic problem in all of Asia. It cannot be solved by military means unless several million Communists are extinguished, taking care, of course, that several millions more are not spawned in the process. Since military action cannot solve the China problem and even an economic settlement cannot secure China as a base, we have shifted our emphasis in Asia to Japan. The Japanese and Chinese realized what we were doing before we had even formalized the decision.

This decision has not been taken for humanitarian reasons but for reasons of what is called "our own security." It is the decision of statesmanship and diplomacy trained to add up bases and military potential rather than well-being and human beings. It is a program formulated on postulates antithetical to Franklin Roosevelt's "Four Freedoms" or Wendell Willkie's "One World." For today's planners, these are the foolhardy phrases of dreamers. Today we are realists, balancing so many dollars for so much oil.

In a world still quaking with the tremors of power politics, there is nothing wrong with such a program calculated "for our own security." It is the job of our global-minded brass hats to figure out how to circumvent a new Pearl Harbor; and if one occurs, to figure out how we can emerge victorious. But hand in hand with that, in a democracy, should go a civilian-sponsored plan for peace and a world outlook based on the concept that peace is not only possible but probable.

The men who plan and execute our global policy today are not primarily trained to understand the bases for peace. One of the President's close confidants on world affairs—during several changes of Secretary of State—has been Admiral William D. Leahy. George C. Marshall, the current Secretary of State, is for all his real capabilities, trained and experienced as a military man. With him as Under Secretary is Robert Lovett, a man whose previous government post was in the War Department. Major General John H. Hildring has been Assistant Secretary of State for Occupied Countries. Two of our last embassies to China have been headed by generals: Marshall, himself, and Patrick Hurley. Lieutenant General Walter Bedell Smith is our envoy in Moscow. Major General Frank R. McCoy is the U. S. delegate on the Far Eastern Commission. Brigadier General Frank T. Hines is our Ambassador in Panama, Marine General Thomas Holcomb in South Africa and Rear Admiral Alan G. Kirk in Belgium. In Germany Generals Joseph T. McNarney and Lucius Clay have been our top representatives, and, until recently, General Mark Clark in Austria. In Korea, it is General Hodge, and over him, in Tokyo, Douglas MacArthur. And on July 11, 1947, the President appointed a new "special representative" with the rank of Ambassador to "make an appraisal of the over-all situation" in China and Korea: Lieutenant General Albert C. Wedemeyer.

Even more important in considerations of over-all policy is the power of SWNCC—the State-War-Navy Coordinating Committee. In this council the two departments which must be prepared for war have cut heavily into the "civilian authority" of the department which should be prepared for peacemaking.

In the interests of America's integrity and to preserve our high moral position, the State Department under Byrnes and Atcheson was eager to turn the six hundred and fifty former Japanese mandated islands over to a United Nations trusteeship. President Truman had pledged:

"We have assured the world time and again—and I repeat it now —that we do not seek for ourselves one inch of territory in any place in the world. Outside the right to establish necessary bases for our own protection, we look for nothing which belongs to any other power." (*From Army Day Speech, April 6, 1947.*)

But under pressures from the Army and especially the Navy, the State Department changed its mind.

"Even if military agencies and persons soon cease to make and execute foreign policy," a Foreign Policy Association report on this subject concludes, "and military considerations cease to guide civilian policy-makers, the Army and Navy will have left a lasting imprint in the nature of our relations with other powers."

3

"As the curtain falls on Europe, it rises on Asia," a Hindu newspaper in Calcutta observed at the opening of the Asian Relations Conference in New Delhi. "It would show complete lack of historic sense not to realize that the Asian Relations Conference arises as a purified phoenix out of the ashes of Japan," the paper said.

More than two hundred and fifty delegates representing over a billion people in twenty-five different countries met in March 1947 to consider their mutual economic, social, and cultural problems. Included among the delegates were representatives of the Asiatic republics in the Soviet Union. It was not considered abnormal that agricultural experts from Malaya were as interested in the progress of vast irrigation projects near Tashkent as they were in hearing about U. S. assistance to Siam.

The peoples of Asia were not unaware that their minds and cities are the likely ideological and/or military targets for impending conflict between America and Russia. From the opening address by Pandit Jawaharlal Nehru to the closing remarks of Mohandas K. Gandhi, the underlying theme was how the peoples of Asia could avoid being "used as pawns by others" in war or peace.

Declaring that "the day after the terrible war, there is talk of further wars in the atomic age that is upon us," Pandit Nehru warned the delegates: "Asia will have to function effectively in the maintenance of peace. Indeed there can be no peace unless Asia plays her part. . . . Peace can only come when nations are free and also when human beings everywhere have freedom and security and opportunity. We have, therefore, to think in terms of the common man and fashion our political, social and economic structure so that the burdens that have crushed him may be removed and he may have full opportunity for growth."

"For too long," Nehru said, "we of Asia have been petitioners in the western courts and chancelleries. That story must now belong to the past. We propose to stand on our own feet and co-operate with all others who are prepared to co-operate with us. We do not intend to be the playthings of others."

The Asian conference recognized certain truths which are not yet widely held in this country. The first is that unregulated capitalism, at least in Asia, is a failure. There it is associated emotionally with imperialism, exploitation, the white man's burden. It is associated practically with a system which has failed to supply enough clothes, enough food, enough housing, education, or medical care. Obviously this overlooks vast improvements made in certain areas of development.

I recall listening to an Indian employed by the United Nations who calmly pointed out that peace could be more costly in terms of human lives than war.

"In our province of Bengal during 1943 there was a famine," the Indian said. "The total deaths were between one and one and a half million. This is fifty or sixty times the number of casualties of the entire Indian Army and—excluding Germany and Russia—greater than the total casualties of all other countries in World War II."

The Indian then documented his statement that the famine was "man-made"—due to lack of planning, of price controls, of proper distribution facilities. "The famine was preventable," he concluded sadly.

4

In the struggle of ideas, the United States will need to export more than dollars. It is not enough to give loans and credits to Chiang. Millions in loans have increased our domestic taxes but not our foreign prestige. It would be far better to export TVA's than to back corruption and inefficiency. The Reverend Dr. Henry Sloane Coffin, president emeritus of Union Theological Seminary, returned in the spring of 1947 from a seven-months' tour of the

Far East and reported that the prestige of the United States is now so low that it "simply cannot go any lower." "The United States," he said, "must show that our economy must provide the poor man with basic subsistence requirements in order to defeat the notion among many generous and intelligent Indian and Chinese students that Russia has succeeded where we have failed; we must defeat racial prejudice at home, because every racial incident in America is broadcast to race-conscious Asia, and we must defeat the soaring prices that have ruined the Eastern economy."

Dr. Coffin has, in a negative way, pointed out what Stalin once called the Soviet "power of attraction" for Oriental peoples. Economic security is not the whole story of this magnetism, although it is of primary importance. Owen Lattimore, in his brilliant book, *Solution in Asia*, illustrated other facets of this "power of attraction" in the following passage:

If this Uighur learns . . . that among near kinsmen the Soviet Uzbeks, a poor man's children may attend, free, a school at which they are taught in their own language and taught to take pride in their own history and culture; that they may go on to the university and become doctors, engineers, anything in the world; that they may be elected to powerful positions in which they can give orders even to Russians, because Uzbeks and Russians are equal and it depends on a man's position, not his race, whether he gives orders—then he is going to think that the Uzbeks are free and have democracy.

5

"The Pacific," intoned Congressman Ed V. Izac of California on a visit to Tokyo, "is definitely our ocean." Tomorrow's Asia cannot be America's nor can it be Russia's. There is perhaps much in both systems from which Asiatics can borrow. But the choice must be their own and not one forced upon them from Washington or Moscow. Nehru, for example, is a Socialist but he leans heavily on the initiative and resourcefulness of India's young capitalists to develop heavy industry.

This is no plea for isolationism or for smug disinterest in what that choice will be. A world order must come tomorrow. If it is to be a world order established through force of arms it would not be worth fighting for. Today the most hopeful force pointing toward a world of peace is the United Nations.

If it is true, as I have been told, that our present military-minded policy-makers have in reality given up the U. N. as anything more than window dressing, it is not true that the people of this country have abandoned the U. N. idea. As MacArthur said, foreseeing the eventual triumph of democracy in Japan, "You cannot stop the power of an idea." The U. N. idea is one that cannot be stopped. The institution may become a shell before its lofty edifices in New York are completed. It may become an ideological debating forum like the Allied Council in Japan. It may ignore practical politics and economic reform by bogging down in international semantics as the Joint Commissions have done in Korea. As our negotiators did in China, it may talk peace while fighting continues and men are killed. But there is something that has been started in the U. N. that cannot be smothered in words.

Pious phrases will not dress up the inescapable fact that any immediate world recovery must be financed by this country. In two world wars we were the only great nation which relatively prospered. How we spend our money and our talent in helping recovery is just as important as whether we do it or not. We can spend it politically, using "enlightened American self-interest" as our yardstick. This will eventually lead us, as Professor Fairbank indicated, into a fight with the peoples of Asia.

We can spend our money and our talent through the U. N. and possibly insure the peace for our sons and grandsons instead of for our generation alone. We can spend it to plant new crops in old countries, to organize world communications and transportation, to build TVA's and medical centers and universities. We can make nuclear fission an economic open sesame and not just a military passport to oblivion.

We have nothing to fear by spending our money for a higher standard of living throughout the world. We have everything to fear from using it to buy arms for reactionaries.

In China our trump card is neither our military might nor our great Army, Navy or Air Force. It is that we and not Russia are in a position to help China modernize—immediately. We have the know-how, the money, and the exportable equipment. Unless China modernizes it is not a threat to anyone. Thus even a left coalition government in China, including or even dominated by the Communists, would have to get along with the United States. We have nothing to fear in China but the loss of our moral position and we are losing that by backing Chiang.

Looking at the globe not only as Americans but as citizens of the world, we can insist that the profit from our labor and our investments be used to broadcast a "Voice of the United Nations" and not just a "Voice of America" or the "Voice of Moscow."

We will not soothe the Russian's fear of war by telling him of America's might. We may—just may—by telling him of the hope for world co-operation through the U. N.

This requires vision which we now dismiss as "visionary." This requires faith in ourselves which we now call "Jeffersonian idealism." As one who hopes to count himself a world citizen as well as an American, I believe the peoples never had more need of such vision and such idealism.

Archibald MacLeish, former head of UNESCO, who speaks with the voice of Thomas Jefferson, has crystallized the major problem which we Americans must face and answer for ourselves today and tomorrow. Mr. MacLeish wrote in the *Atlantic Monthly* recently:

The character of our time is such that our conception of the role we are to play in it—which is to say our conception of the kind of people we are—has become a factor of critical significance, not only in the shaping of our own future but in the shaping of the future of mankind. If we conduct ourselves in this generation as a young, creative and revolutionary people, capable of thinking of the world in new and creative terms, our future and the world's future will be very different from the future either can look forward to if we think of ourselves as an old established power with our eyes fixed upon the past and our own security. . . .

For the next many years the labor of politics, the labor of statesmanship, the labor of government will be the labor of learning to live with other nations in a world in which no nation, no society has lived before. The problem of our time is not the problem the political commentators talk about. It is not the problem of "making peace." It's the problem of making a world in which peace will be possible. Or rather, it is the problem of learning to live in the new world we have already made, in such a way that peace will be possible.

Perhaps the most hopeful indication that a responsible American official was ready to undertake such a "labor of statesmanship" was Secretary of State Marshall's speech at Harvard on June 5, 1947. Although he referred specifically to the countries of Europe and what was needed from us to insure their recovery, his remarks had meaning for Asia as well. "Our policy is directed not against any country or doctrine," Marshall said, although the Truman

Doctrine had been thus interpreted and implemented, "but against hunger, poverty, desperation and chaos. Its purpose should be the revival of a working economy in the world so as to permit the emergence of political and social conditions in which free institutions can exist."

6

The world is ready to start from scratch today as it never has been since the time of Noah's Ark. Most of the material things for rebuilding it are in this country. We can build an American house and say this is the way it is, this is the way we like it and anyone who lives in a different political or economic or social climate can rot for all we care.

Or we can help build a modern house, a functional house, designed not solely by our own architects but in collaboration with the people who will live with it and in it. This house must have a garden big enough to feed the people who live in it or they will be so busy scratching for weeds to eat that they will never have any time for stepping into the American-style living room to discuss yesterday's vote in the Diet or tomorrow's elections to the National Assembly.

Tomorrow's Asia, we must recognize, is not MacArthur's nor Hodge's nor Marshall's nor ours. Nor is it Asia for the Asiatics or for the Russians. Any such limitation will breed new wars. Only when we have recognized that fact will we be able to begin thinking of the world "in new and creative terms."

APPENDIX A

The Cairo Conference

United States of America: President Roosevelt
China: Generalissimo Chiang Kai-shek
United Kingdom: Prime Minister Churchill

(Statement released December 1, 1943)

The several military missions have agreed upon future military operations against Japan. The Three Great Allies expressed their resolve to bring unrelenting pressure against their brutal enemies by sea, land, and air. This pressure is already rising.

The Three Great Allies are fighting this war to restrain and punish the aggression of Japan. They covet no gain for themselves and have no thought of territorial expansion. It is their purpose that Japan shall be stripped of all the islands in the Pacific which she has seized or occupied since the beginning of the first World War in 1914, and and that all the territories Japan has stolen from the Chinese, such as Manchuria, Formosa, and the Pescadores, shall be restored to the Republic of China. Japan will also be expelled from all other territories which she has taken by violence and greed. The aforesaid three great powers, mindful of the enslavement of the people of Korea, are determined that in due course Korea shall become free and independent.

With these objects in view the three Allies, in harmony with those of the United Nations at war with Japan, will continue to persevere in the serious and prolonged operations necessary to procure the unconditional surrender of Japan.

APPENDIX B

Yalta Agreement Regarding Japan

Between the Leaders of the Three Great Powers—
The United States of America
The Union of Soviet Socialist Republics
and the United Kingdom of Great Britain and
Northern Ireland

(*Signed at Yalta February 11, 1945*)

The leaders of the three Great Powers—the Soviet Union, the United States of America and Great Britain—have agreed that in two or three months after Germany has surrendered and the war in Europe has terminated the Soviet Union shall enter into the war against Japan on the side of the Allies on condition that:

1. The status quo in Outer-Mongolia (The Mongolian People's Republic) shall be preserved;

2. The former rights of Russia violated by the treacherous attack of Japan in 1904 shall be restored, viz:

(*a*) the southern part of Sakhalin as well as all the islands adjacent to it shall be returned to the Soviet Union,

(*b*) the commercial port of Dairen shall be internationalized, the preeminent interests of the Soviet Union in this port being safeguarded and the lease of Port Arthur as a naval base of the USSR restored,

(*c*) the Chinese-Eastern Railroad and the South-Manchurian Railroad which provides an outlet to Dairen shall be jointly operated by the establishment of a joint Soviet-Chinese Company, it being understood that the preeminent interests of the Soviet Union shall be safeguarded and that China shall retain full sovereignty in Manchuria;

3. The Kuril islands shall be handed over to the Soviet Union.

It is understood, that the agreement concerning Outer-Mongolia and the ports and railroads referred to above will require concurrence of Generalissimo Chiang Kai-shek. The President will take measures in order to obtain this concurrence on advice from Marshal Stalin.

The Heads of the three Great Powers have agreed that these claims of the Soviet Union shall be unquestionably fulfilled after Japan has been defeated.

For its part the Soviet Union expresses its readiness to conclude with the National Government of China a pact of friendship and alliance between the USSR and China in order to render assistance to China with its armed forces for the purpose of liberating China from the Japanese yoke.

February 11, 1945

J. STALIN
FRANKLIN D. ROOSEVELT
WINSTON S. CHURCHILL

The Potsdam Proclamation Defining Terms for Japanese Surrender

(*July 26, 1945*)

(1) We—the President of the United States, the President of the National Government of the Republic of China, and the Prime Minister of Great Britain, representing the hundreds of millions of our countrymen, have conferred and agree that Japan shall be given an opportunity to end this war.

(2) The prodigious land, sea and air forces of the United States, the British Empire and of China, many times reinforced by their armies and air fleets from the west, are poised to strike the final blows upon Japan. This military power is sustained and inspired by the determination of all the Allied Nations to prosecute the war against Japan until she ceases to resist.

(3) The result of the futile and senseless German resistance to the might of the aroused free peoples of the world stands forth in awful clarity as an example to the people of Japan. The might that now converges on Japan is immeasurably greater than that which, when applied to the resisting Nazis, necessarily laid waste to the lands, the industry and the method of life of the whole German people. The full application of our military power, backed by our resolve, *will* mean the inevitable and complete destruction of the Japanese armed forces and just as inevitably the utter devastation of the Japanese homeland.

(4) The time has come for Japan to decide whether she will continue to be controlled by those self-willed militaristic advisers whose unintelligent calculations have brought the Empire of Japan to the threshold of annihilation, or whether she will follow the path of reason.

(5) Following are our terms. We will not deviate from them. There are no alternatives. We shall brook no delay.

(6) There must be eliminated for all time the authority and influence of those who have deceived and misled the people of Japan into embarking on world conquest, for we insist that a new order of peace, security and justice will be impossible until irresponsible militarism is driven from the world.

(7) Until such a new order is established *and* until there is convincing proof that Japan's war-making power is destroyed, points in Japanese

territory to be designated by the Allies shall be occupied to secure the achievement of the basic objectives we are here setting forth.

(8) The terms of the Cairo Declaration shall be carried out and Japanese sovereignty shall be limited to the islands of Honshu, Hokkaido, Kyushu, Shikoku and such minor islands as we determine.

(9) The Japanese military forces, after being completely disarmed, shall be permitted to return to their homes with the opportunity to lead peaceful and productive lives.

(10) We do not intend that the Japanese shall be enslaved as a race or destroyed as a nation, but stern justice shall be meted out to all war criminals, including those who have visited cruelties upon our prisoners. The Japanese Government shall remove all obstacles to the revival and strengthening of democratic tendencies among the Japanese people. Freedom of speech, of religion, and of thought, as well as respect for the fundamental human rights shall be established.

(11) Japan shall be permitted to maintain such industries as will sustain her economy and permit the exaction of just reparations in kind, but not those which would enable her to re-arm for war. To this end, access to, as distinguished from control of, raw materials shall be permitted. Eventual Japanese participation in world trade relations shall be permitted.

(12) The occupying forces of the Allies shall be withdrawn from Japan as soon as these objectives have been accomplished and there has been established in accordance with the freely expressed will of the Japanese people a peacefully inclined and responsible government.

(13) We call upon the government of Japan to proclaim now the unconditional surrender of all Japanese armed forces, and to provide proper and adequate assurances of their good faith in such action. The alternative for Japan is prompt and utter destruction.

APPENDIX D

Imperial Rescript Announcing Surrender to the Japanese People

(September 2, 1945—Tokyo Time)

Accepting the terms set forth in Declaration issued by the heads of the Governments of the United States, Great Britain and China on July 26th, 1945 at Potsdam and subsequently adhered to by the Union of Soviet Socialist Republics, We have commanded the Japanese Imperial Government and the Japanese Imperial General Headquarters to sign on Our behalf the Instrument of Surrender presented by the Supreme Commander for the Allied Powers and to issue General Orders to the Military and Naval Forces in accordance with the direction of the Supreme Commander for the Allied Powers. We command all Our people forthwith to cease hostilities, to lay down their arms and faithfully to carry out all the provisions of Instrument of Surrender and the General Orders issued by the Japanese Imperial Government and the Japanese Imperial General Headquarters hereunder.

This second day of the ninth month of the twentieth year of Syōwa.

Seal and Signature of HIROHITO

APPENDIX E

Instrument of Surrender

(September 2, 1945—Tokyo Time)

We, acting by command of and in behalf of the Emperor of Japan, the Japanese Government and the Japanese Imperial General Headquarters, hereby accept the provisions set forth in the declaration issued by the heads of the Governments of the United States, China and Great Britain on 26 July 1945, at Potsdam, and subsequently adhered to by the Union of Soviet Socialist Republics, which four powers are hereafter referred to as the Allied Powers.

We hereby proclaim the Unconditional surrender to the Allied Powers of the Japanese Imperial General Headquarters and of all Japanese armed forces and all armed forces under Japanese control wherever situated.

We hereby command all Japanese forces wherever situated and the Japanese people to cease hostilities forthwith, to preserve and save from damage all ships, aircraft, and military and civil property and to comply with all requirements which may be imposed by the Supreme Commander for the Allied Powers or by agencies of the Japanese Government at his direction.

We hereby command the Japanese Imperial General Headquarters to issue at once orders to the Commanders of all Japanese forces and all forces under Japanese control wherever situated to surrender unconditionally themselves and all forces under their control.

We hereby command all civil, military and naval officials to obey and enforce all proclamations, orders and directives deemed by the Supreme Commander for the Allied Powers to be proper to effectuate this surrender and issued by him or under his authority and we direct all such officials to remain at their posts and to continue to perform their noncombatant duties unless specifically relieved by him or under his authority.

We hereby undertake for the Emperor, the Japanese Government and their successors to carry out the provisions of the Potsdam Declaration in good faith, and to issue whatever orders and take whatever action may be required by the Supreme Commander for the Allied Powers or by any other designated representatives of the Allied Powers for the purpose of giving effect to that Declaration.

We hereby command the Japanese Imperial Government and the Japanese Imperial General Headquarters at once to liberate all allied

393

prisoners of war and civilian internees now under Japanese control and to provide for their protection, care, maintenance and immediate transportation to places as directed.

The authority of the Emperor and the Japanese Government to rule the state shall be subject to the Supreme Commander for the Allied Powers who will take such steps as he deems proper to effectuate these terms of surrender.

Signed at Tokyo Bay, Japan on the second day of September, 1945.

Note—Signatures to the above document, signed on the USS *Missouri*, are of Foreign Minister Mamoru Shigemitsu and Gen. Yoshijiro Umezu of the Imperial General Staff, and for the United Nations the signatures are of Gen. Douglas MacArthur for the Allied Powers, Admiral Chester W. Nimitz for the United States, Gen Hsu Yung-Ch'ang for China, Admiral Sir Bruce A. Fraser for the United Kingdom, Lt. Gen. Kuzma Derevyanko for the Soviet Union, Gen. Sir Thomas Blamey for Australia, Col. L. Moore Cosgrave for Canada, Gen. Jacques Le Clerc for France, Admiral C. E. L. Helfrich for the Netherlands, and Air Vice Marshal Leonard M. Isitt for New Zealand.

APPENDIX F

U. S. Initial Post-Surrender Policy for Japan[1]

(August 29, 1945)

PURPOSE OF THIS DOCUMENT

This document is a statement of general initial policy relating to Japan after surrender. It has been approved by the President and distributed to the Supreme Commander for the Allied Powers and to appropriate U. S. departments and agencies for their guidance. It does not deal with all matters relating to the occupation of Japan requiring policy determinations. Such matters as are not included or are not fully covered herein have been or will be dealt with separately.

PART I—ULTIMATE OBJECTIVES

The ultimate objectives of the United States in regard to Japan, to which policies in the initial period must conform, are:

(a) To insure that Japan will not again become a menace to the United States or to the peace and security of the world.

(b) To bring about the eventual establishment of a peaceful and responsible government which will respect the rights of other states and will support the objectives of the United States as reflected in the ideals and principles of the Charter of the United Nations. The United States desires that this government should conform as closely as may be to principles of democratic self-government but it is not the responsibility of the Allied Powers to impose upon Japan any form of government not supported by the freely expressed will of the people.

These objectives will be achieved by the following principal means:

(a) Japan's sovereignty will be limited to the islands of Honshu, Hokkaido, Kyushu, Shikoku and such minor outlying islands as may be determined, in accordance with the Cairo Declaration and other agreements to which the United States is or may be a party.

(b) Japan will be completely disarmed and demilitarized. The authority of the militarists and the influence of militarism will be totally elim-

[1] Prepared jointly by the Department of State, the War Department, and the Navy Department and approved by the President on Sept. 6, 1945. The document in substance was sent to General MacArthur by radio on Aug. 29 and, after approval by the President, by messenger on Sept. 6.

inated from her political, economic, and social life. Institutions expressive of the spirit of militarism and aggression will be vigorously suppressed.

(c) The Japanese people shall be encouraged to develop a desire for individual liberties and respect for fundamental human rights, particularly the freedoms of religion, assembly, speech, and the press. They shall also be encouraged to form democratic and representative organizations.

(d) The Japanese people shall be afforded opportunity to develop for themselves an economy which will permit the peacetime requirements of the population to be met.

PART II—ALLIED AUTHORITY

1. Military Occupation

There will be a military occupation of the Japanese home islands to carry into effect the surrender terms and further the achievement of the ultimate objectives stated above. The occupation shall have the character of an operation in behalf of the principal Allied Powers acting in the interests of the United Nations at war with Japan. For that reason, participation of the forces of other nations that have taken a leading part in the war against Japan will be welcomed and expected. The occupation forces will be under the command of a Supreme Commander designated by the United States.

Although every effort will be made, by consultation and by constitution of appropriate advisory bodies, to establish policies for the conduct of the occupation and the control of Japan which will satisfy the principal Allied Powers, in the event of any differences of opinion among them, the policies of the United States will govern.

2. Relationship to Japanese Government

The authority of the Emperor and the Japanese Government will be subject to the Supreme Commander, who will possess all powers necessary to effectuate the surrender terms and to carry out the policies established for the conduct of the occupation and the control of Japan.

In view of the present character of Japanese society and the desire of the United States to attain its objectives with a minimum commitment of its forces and resources, the Supreme Commander will exercise his authority through Japanese governmental machinery and agencies, including the Emperor, to the extent that this satisfactorily furthers United States objectives. The Japanese Government will be permitted, under his instructions, to exercise the normal powers of government in matters of domestic administration. This policy, however, will be subject to the right and duty of the Supreme Commander to require changes in governmental machinery or personnel or to act directly if the Emperor or other Japanese authority does not satisfactorily meet the requirements of the Supreme Commander in effectuating the surrender terms. This policy, moreover, does not commit the Supreme Commander to support the

Emperor or any other Japanese governmental authority in opposition to evolutionary changes looking toward the attainment of United States objectives. The policy is to use the existing form of Government in Japan, not to support it. Changes in the form of Government initiated by the Japanese people or government in the direction of modifying its feudal and authoritarian tendencies are to be permitted and favored. In the event that the effectuation of such changes involves the use of force by the Japanese people or government against persons opposed thereto, the Supreme Commander should intervene only where necessary to ensure the security of his forces and the attainment of all other objectives of the occupation.

3. Publicity as to Policies

The Japanese people, and the world at large, shall be kept fully informed of the objectives and policies of the occupation, and of progress made in their fulfillment.

PART III—POLITICAL

1. Disarmament and Demilitarization

Disarmament and demilitarization are the primary tasks of the military occupation and shall be carried out promptly and with determination. Every effort shall be made to bring home to the Japanese people the part played by the military and naval leaders, and those who collaborated with them, in bringing about the existing and future distress of the people.

Japan is not to have an army, navy, air force, secret police organization, or any civil aviation. Japan's ground, air and naval forces shall be disarmed and disbanded and the Japanese Imperial General Headquarters, the General Staff and all secret police organizations shall be dissolved. Military and naval matériel, military and naval vessels and military and naval installations, and military, naval and civilian aircraft shall be surrendered and shall be disposed of as required by the Supreme Commander.

High officials of the Japanese Imperial General Headquarters, and General Staff, other high military and naval officials of the Japanese Government, leaders of ultra-nationalist and militarist organizations and other important exponents of militarism and aggression will be taken into custody and held for future disposition. Persons who have been active exponents of militarism and militant nationalism will be removed and excluded from public office and from any other position of public or substantial private responsibility. Ultra-nationalistic or militaristic social, political, professional and commercial societies and institutions will be dissolved and prohibited.

Militarism and ultra-nationalism, in doctrine and practice, including para-military training, shall be eliminated from the educational system. Former career military and naval officers, both commissioned and noncommissioned, and all other exponents of militarism and ultra-nationalism shall be excluded from supervisory and teaching positions.

2. War Criminals

Persons charged by the Supreme Commander or appropriate United Nations agencies with being war criminals, including those charged with having visited cruelties upon United Nations prisoners or other nationals, shall be arrested, tried and, if convicted, punished. Those wanted by another of the United Nations for offenses against its nationals, shall, if not wanted for trial or as witnesses or otherwise by the Supreme Commander, be turned over to the custody of such other nation.

3. Encouragement of Desire for Individual Liberties and Democratic Processes

Freedom of religious worship shall be proclaimed promptly on occupation. At the same time it should be made plain to the Japanese that ultra-nationalistic and militaristic organizations and movements will not be permitted to hide behind the cloak of religion.

The Japanese people shall be afforded opportunity and encouraged to become familiar with the history, institutions, culture, and the accomplishments of the United States and the other democracies. Association of personnel of the occupation forces with the Japanese population should be controlled, only to the extent necessary, to further the policies and objectives of the occupation.

Democratic political parties, with rights of assembly and public discussion, shall be encouraged, subject to the necessity for maintaining the security of the occupying forces.

Laws, decrees and regulations which establish discriminations on ground of race, nationality, creed or political opinion shall be abrogated; those which conflict with the objectives and policies outlined in this document shall be repealed, suspended or amended as required; and agencies charged specifically with their enforcement shall be abolished or appropriately modified. Persons unjustly confined by Japanese authority on political grounds shall be released. The judicial, legal and police systems shall be reformed as soon as practicable to conform to the policies set forth in Articles 1 and 3 of this Part III and thereafter shall be progressively influenced, to protect individual liberties and civil rights.

PART IV—ECONOMIC

1. Economic Demilitarization

The existing economic basis of Japanese military strength must be destroyed and not be permitted to revive.

Therefore, a program will be enforced containing the following elements, among others; the immediate cessation and future prohibition of production of all goods designed for the equipment, maintenance, or use of any military force or establishment; the imposition of a ban upon any specialized facilities for the production or repair of implements of war, including naval vessels and all forms of aircraft; the institution of a system of inspection and control over selected elements in Japanese economic activity to prevent concealed or disguised military preparation; the elimination in Japan of those selected industries or branches of production whose chief value to Japan is in preparing for war; the prohibition of specialized research and instruction directed to the development of war-making power; and the limitation of the size and character of Japan's heavy industries to its future peaceful requirements, and restriction of Japanese merchant shipping to the extent required to accomplish the objectives of demilitarization.

The eventual disposition of those existing production facilities within Japan which are to be eliminated in accord with this program, as between conversion to other uses, transfer abroad, and scrapping will be determined after inventory. Pending decision, facilities readily convertible for civilian production should not be destroyed, except in emergency situations.

2. Promotion of Democratic Forces

Encouragement shall be given and favor shown to the development of organizations in labor, industry, and agriculture, organized on a democratic basis. Policies shall be favored which permit a wide distribution of income and of the ownership of the means of production and trade.

Those forms of economic activity, organization and leadership shall be favored that are deemed likely to strengthen the peaceful disposition of the Japanese people, and to make it difficult to command or direct economic activity in support of military ends.

To this end it shall be the policy of the Supreme Commander:

(a) To prohibit the retention in or selection for places of importance in the economic field of individuals who do not direct future Japanese economic effort solely towards peaceful ends; and

(b) To favor a program for the dissolution of the large industrial and banking combinations which have exercised control of a great part of Japan's trade and industry.

3. Resumption of Peaceful Economic Activity

The policies of Japan have brought down upon the people great economic destruction and confronted them with the prospect of economic difficulty and suffering. The plight of Japan is the direct outcome of its own behavior, and the Allies will not undertake the burden of repairing the damage. It can be repaired only if the Japanese people renounce all military aims and apply themselves diligently and with single purpose to the ways of peaceful living. It will be necessary for them to undertake physical reconstruction, deeply to reform the nature and direction of their economic activities and institutions, and to find useful employment for their people along lines adapted to and devoted to peace. The Allies have no intention of imposing conditions which would prevent the accomplishment of these tasks in due time.

Japan will be expected to provide goods and services to meet the needs of the occupying forces to the extent that this can be effected without causing starvation, widespread disease and acute physical distress.

The Japanese authorities will be expected, and if necessary directed, to maintain, develop and enforce programs that serve the following purposes:

(a) To avoid acute economic distress.

(b) To assure just and impartial distribution of available supplies.

(c) To meet the requirements for reparations deliveries agreed upon by the Allied Governments.

(d) To facilitate the restoration of Japanese economy so that the reasonable peaceful requirements of the population can be satisfied.

In this connection, the Japanese authorities on their own responsibility shall be permitted to establish and administer controls over economic activities, including essential national public services, finance, banking, and production and distribution of essential commodities, subject to the approval and review of the Supreme Commander in order to assure their conformity with the objectives of the occupation.

4. Reparations and Restitution

Reparations

Reparations for Japanese aggression shall be made:

(a) Through the transfer—as may be determined by the appropriate Allied authorities—of Japanese property located outside of the territories to be retained by Japan.

(b) Through the transfer of such goods or existing capital equipment and facilities as are not necessary for a peaceful Japanese economy or the supplying of the occupying forces. Exports other than those directed to be shipped on reparation account or as restitution may be made only to those recipients who agree to provide necessary imports in exchange or agree to pay for such exports in foreign exchange. No form of reparation shall be exacted which will interfere with or prejudice the program for Japan's demilitarization.

Restitution

Full and prompt restitution will be required of all identifiable looted property.

5. Fiscal, Monetary, and Banking Policies

The Japanese authorities will remain responsible for the management and direction of the domestic fiscal, monetary, and credit policies subject to the approval and review of the Supreme Commander.

6. International Trade and Financial Relations

Japan shall be permitted eventually to resume normal trade relations with the rest of the world. During occupation and under suitable controls, Japan will be permitted to purchase from foreign countries raw materials and other goods that it may need for peaceful purposes, and to export goods to pay for approved imports.

Control is to be maintained over all imports and exports of goods, and foreign exchange and financial transactions. Both the policies followed in the exercise of these controls and their actual administration shall be subject to the approval and supervision of the Supreme Commander in order to make sure that they are not contrary to the policies of the occupying authorities, and in particular that all foreign purchasing power that Japan may acquire is utilized only for essential needs.

7. Japanese Property Located Abroad

Existing Japanese external assets and existing Japanese assets located in territories detached from Japan under the terms of surrender, including assets owned in whole or part by the Imperial Household and Government, shall be revealed to the occupying authorities and held for disposition according to the decision of the Allied authorities.

8. Equality of Opportunity for Foreign Enterprise within Japan

The Japanese authorities shall not give, or permit any Japanese business organization to give, exclusive or preferential opportunity or terms to the enterprise of any foreign country, or cede to such enterprise control of any important branch of economic activity.

9. Imperial Household Property

Imperial Household property shall not be exempted from any action necessary to carry out the objectives of the occupation.

APPENDIX G

Japanese Draft Constitution

(*April 22, 1946*[1])

CONSTITUTION OF JAPAN

(Simplified Version Submitted by Japanese, 22 April 1946)

We, the Japanese people, acting through our duly elected representatives in the National Diet, determined that we shall secure for ourselves and our posterity the fruits of peaceful cooperation with all nations and the blessings of liberty throughout this land, and resolved that never again shall we be visited with the horrors of war through the action of government, do proclaim the sovereignty of the people's will and do ordain and establish this Constitution, founded upon the universal principle that government is a sacred trust the authority for which is derived from the people, the powers of which are exercised by the representatives of the people, and the benefits of which are enjoyed by the people; and we reject and revoke all constitutions, laws, ordinances, and rescripts in conflict herewith.

Desiring peace for all time and fully conscious of the high ideals controlling human relationship now stirring mankind, we have determined to rely for our security and survival upon the justice and good faith of the peace-loving peoples of the world. We desire to occupy an honored place in an international society designed and dedicated to the preservation of peace, and the banishment of tyranny and slavery, oppression and intolerance, for all time from the earth. We recognize and acknowledge that all peoples have the right to live in peace, free from fear and want.

We hold that no people is responsible to itself alone, but that laws of political morality are universal; and that obedience to such laws is incumbent upon all peoples who would sustain their own sovereignty and justify their sovereign relationship with other peoples.

To these high principles and purposes we, the Japanese People, pledge our national honor, determined will and full resources.

[1] The first draft of the new Japanese Constitution was published on Mar. 6, 1946. A revised draft was submitted by the Japanese Government to SCAP on Apr. 22, 1946 and is the version which appears here.

CHAPTER 1

The Emperor

Article I. The Emperor shall be the symbol of the state and of the unity of the people, deriving his position from the sovereign will of the people.

Article II. The Imperial Throne shall be dynastic and succeeded to in accordance with the Imperial House Law passed by the Diet.

Article III. The advice and approval of the Cabinet shall be required for all acts of the Emperor in matters of state, and the Cabinet shall be responsible therefor.

Article IV. The Emperor shall perform only such state functions as are provided for in this constitution. Never shall he have powers related to government.

The Emperor may delegate his functions as may be provided by law.

Article V. When, in accordance with the Imperial House Law, a regency is established, the Regent shall exercise his functions in the Emperor's name. In this case, paragraph one of the preceding article will be applicable.

Article VI. The Emperor shall appoint the Prime Minister as designated by the Diet.

Article VII. The Emperor, with the advice and approval of the Cabinet, shall perform the following functions of state on behalf of the people:

Promulgation of amendments of the constitution, laws, cabinet orders and treaties.

Convocation of the Diet.

Dissolution of the House of Representatives.

Proclamation of general elections.

Attestation of the appointment and dismissal of Ministers of State and other officials as provided for by law, and of full powers and credentials of Ambassadors and Ministers.

Attestation of general and special amnesty, commutation of punishment, reprieve, and restoration of rights.

Awarding of honors.

Attestation of instruments of ratification and other diplomatic documents as provided for by law.

Receiving foreign ambassadors and ministers.

Performance of ceremonial functions.

Article VIII. No property can be given to, or received by, the Imperial House, and no gifts can be made thereby, without the authorization of the Diet.

CHAPTER 2

Renunciation of War

Article IX. War, as a sovereign right of the nation and the threat or use of force, is forever renounced as a means of settling disputes with other nations.

The maintenance of land, sea, and air forces, as well as other war potential, will never be authorized. The right of belligerency of the state will not be recognized.

CHAPTER 3

Rights and Duties of the People

Article X. The people shall not be prevented from enjoying any of the fundamental human rights. These fundamental human rights guaranteed to the people by this constitution shall be conferred upon the people of this and future generations as eternal and inviolate rights.

Article XI. The enjoyment of the freedoms and rights guaranteed to the people by this constitution shall be maintained by the eternal vigilance of the people, and the people shall refrain from any abuse of these freedoms and rights and shall always be responsible for utilizing them for the public welfare.

Article XII. All of the people shall be respected as individuals, and their right to life, liberty, and the pursuit of happiness shall, within the limits of the public welfare, be the supreme consideration in legislation and in governmental affairs.

Article XIII. All of the people are equal under the law and there shall be no discrimination in political, economic, or social relations because of race, creed, sex, social status, or family origin. No peerage shall be granted. No privilege shall accompany any award of honor, decoration or any distinction; nor shall any such award be valid beyond the lifetime of the individual who now holds or hereafter may receive it.

Article XIV. The people have the inalienable right to choose their public officials and to dismiss them.

All public officials are servants of the whole community and not of any special group.

In all elections, secrecy of the ballot shall be preserved inviolate, nor shall any voter be answerable, publicly or privately, for the choice he has made.

Article XV. Every person has the right of peaceful petition for the redress of damage and other matters, for the removal of public officials and for the enactment, repeal or amendment of laws, ordinances or regulations; nor shall any person be in any way discriminated against for sponsoring such a petition.

Article XVI. No person shall be held in bondage of any kind. Involuntary servitude, except as punishment for crime, is prohibited.

Article XVII. Freedom of thought and conscience shall be held inviolable.

Article XVIII. Freedom of religion is guaranteed to all. No religious organization shall receive any privilege from the State, nor exercise any political authority.

No person shall be compelled to take part in any religious act, celebration, rite, or practice.

The State and its organs shall refrain from religious education or any other religious activity.

Article XIX. Freedom of assembly, association, speech, and press and all other forms of expression are guaranteed. No censorship shall be maintained, nor shall the secrecy of any means of communication be violated.

Article XX. Every person shall have freedom to choose and change his residence and to choose his occupation to the extent that it does not interfere with the public welfare.

Freedom of all persons to move to a foreign country and to divest themselves of their nationality shall be inviolate.

Article XXI. Academic freedom is guaranteed.

Article XXII. Marriage shall be based only on the mutual consent of both sexes and it shall be maintained through mutual cooperation, with the equal rights of husband and wife as a basis. Laws shall be enacted considering choice of spouse, property rights, inheritance, choice of domicile, divorce and other matters pertaining to marriage and the family from the standpoint of individual dignity and the essential equality of the sexes.

Article XXIII. In all spheres of life, laws shall be designed for the promotion and extension of social welfare and security, and of public health.

Article XXIV. All people shall have the right to receive an equal education corresponding to his ability, as provided by law.

Every person shall be obligated to insure that all of the children under his protection receive elementary education. Such education shall be free.

Article XXV. All people have the right to work. Standards for working conditions, wages and hours shall be fixed by law. The exploitation of children shall be prohibited.

Article XXVI. The right of workers to organize and to bargain and act collectively is guaranteed.

Article XXVII. The right to own property is inviolable, but property rights shall be defined by law, in conformity with the public welfare. Private property may be taken for public use upon just compensation therefor.

Article XXVIII. No person shall be deprived of life or liberty, nor shall any other criminal penalty be imposed, except according to procedure established by law.

Article XXIX. No person shall be denied the right of access to the courts.

Article XXX. No person shall be apprehended except upon warrant issued by a competent judicial officer which specifies the offense with which the person is charged, unless he is apprehended while committing a crime.

Article XXXI. No person shall be arrested or detained without being at once informed of the charges against him or without the immediate privilege of counsel; he shall not be detained without adequate cause; and upon demand of any person such cause must be immediately shown in open court in his presence and the presence of his counsel.

Article XXXII. The right of the people to be secure in their homes, papers and effects against entries, searches and seizures shall not be impaired except upon warrant issued only for probable cause, and particularly describing the place to be searched and things to be seized, or except as provided by Article XXX.

Each search or seizure shall be made upon separate warrant issued for the purpose by a competent judicial officer.

Article XXXIII. The infliction of torture by any public officer and cruel punishments are absolutely forbidden.

Article XXXIV. In all criminal cases the accused shall enjoy the right to a speedy and public trial by an impartial tribunal.

He shall be permitted full opportunity to examine all witnesses, and he shall have the right of compulsory process for obtaining witnesses on his behalf at public expense.

At all times the accused shall have the assistance of competent counsel who shall, if the accused be unable to secure the same by his own efforts, be assigned to his use by the government.

Article XXXV. No person shall be compelled to testify against himself.

No confession shall be admitted in evidence if made under compulsion, torture or threat, or after prolonged arrest or detention.

No person shall be convicted or punished in cases where the only proof against him is his own confession.

Article XXXVI. No person shall be held criminally liable for an act which was lawful at the time it was committed, or of which he has been acquitted, nor shall he in any way be placed in double jeopardy.

CHAPTER 4

The Diet

Article XXXVII. The Diet shall be the highest organ of state power, and shall be the sole law-making authority of the State.

Article XXXVIII. The Diet shall consist of two houses, namely the House of Representatives and the House of Councillors.

Article XXXIX. Both Houses shall consist of elected members, representative of all the people.

The number of the members of each House shall be fixed by law.

Article XL. The qualifications of electors and members for both

Houses shall be fixed by law. However, there shall be no discrimination because of race, creed, sex, social status or family origin.

Article XLI. The term of office of members of the House of Representatives shall be 4 years. However, the term may be terminated before the full term is up, by dissolution of the House of Representatives.

Article XLII. The term of office of the members of the House of Councillors shall be six years. Election for half the members shall take place every three years.

Article XLIII. Matters pertaining to the method of election of members of both Houses, electoral districts, and method of voting, shall be fixed by law.

Article XLIV. No person shall be permitted to be a member of both Houses simultaneously.

Article XLV. Members of both Houses shall receive appropriate annual payment from the national treasury in accordance with the law.

Article XLVI. Except in cases provided by law, members of both Houses shall be exempt from arrest while the Diet is in session. Any member arrested before the opening of the session shall be freed during the term of the session upon demand of his House.

Article XLVII. Members of both Houses shall not be held liable outside the House for speeches, debates, or votes cast inside the House.

Article XLVIII. An ordinary session of the Diet shall be convoked once per year.

Article XLIX. The Cabinet may call extraordinary sessions of the Diet. When a quarter or more of the total members of either House makes the demand, the Diet must be called into session.

Article L. When the House of Representatives is ordered dissolved, there must be a general election of members of the House of Representatives within forty (40) days from the date of dissolution, and the Diet must be convoked within thirty (30) days from the date of the election. When the House of Representatives is ordered dissolved, the House of Councillors must, at the same time, be closed, except that the Cabinet may in time of national emergency convoke the House of Councillors in emergency session. Measures enacted at such session shall be provisional and shall become null and void, unless agreed to by the House of Representatives within a period of ten (10) days after the opening of the next session of the Diet.

Article LI. Each House shall judge disputes related to qualifications and elections of its members. However, in order to deny a seat to any member, it is necessary to pass a resolution by a majority of two-thirds or more of the members present.

Article LII. Business cannot be transacted in either House unless at least one-third of the total membership is present.

All matters shall be decided, in each House, by a majority of those present, except as elsewhere provided in the Constitution. In case of a tie, the presiding officer shall decide the issue.

Article LIII. Deliberation in each House shall be public. However, a secret meeting may be held where a majority of two-thirds or more of those members present passes a resolution therefor.

Each House shall keep a record of proceedings. This record shall be published and given general circulation, excepting such parts of proceedings of secret session as may be deemed to require secrecy.

Upon demand of one-fifth or more of the members present, votes of the members on any matter shall be recorded in the minutes.

Article LIV. Each House shall select its own president and other officials.

Each house shall establish its rules pertaining to meetings, proceedings and internal discipline, and may punish members for disorderly conduct. However, in order to expel a member, a majority of two-thirds or more of those members present must pass a resolution thereon.

Article LV. A bill becomes a law on passage by both Houses, except as otherwise provided by this Constitution.

A bill which is passed by the House of Representatives, and upon which the House of Councillors makes a decision different from that of the House of Representatives, becomes a law when passed a second time by the House of Representatives by a majority of two-thirds or more of the members present.

Failure by the House of Councillors to take final action within sixty (60) days after receipt of a bill passed by the House of Representatives, time in recess excepted, may be determined by the House of Representatives to constitute a rejection.

Article LVI. The budget must first be submitted to the House of Representatives.

Upon consideration of the budget, when the House of Councillors makes a decision different from that of the House of Representatives, and when a joint committee of both Houses, provided for by law, cannot come to an agreement, or in the case of failure by the House of Councillors to take final action within forty (40) days, the period of recess excluded, after the receipt of the budget passed by the House of Representatives, the decision of the House of Representatives will be considered the decision of the Diet.

Article LVII. The second paragraph of the preceding article applies also to Diet approval required for the conclusion of treaties.

Article LVIII. Each House may conduct investigations in relation to national affairs, and may compel the presence and testimony of witnesses, and the production of records.

Article LIX. The Prime Minister, and the Ministers of State, may, at any time, appear in either House for the purpose of debating on bills, regardless of whether they are members of the House or not. They must appear when their presence is required in order to give answers or explanations.

Article LX. The Diet shall set up an impeachment court from the members of both Houses for the purpose of trying those judges against whom removal proceedings have been instituted.

Matters relating to impeachment shall be provided by law.

CHAPTER 5

The Cabinet

Article LXI. Executive power shall be vested in the Cabinet.

Article LXII. The Cabinet shall consist of the Prime Minister, who shall be its head, and other Ministers of State as provided for by law.

The Cabinet, in the exercise of executive power, shall be collectively responsible to the Diet.

Article LXIII. The Prime Minister shall be designated by a resolution of the Diet. This designation shall precede all other business.

If the House of Representatives and the House of Councillors disagree and if a joint committee of both houses, provided for by law, cannot reach an agreement, or the House of Councillors fails to make designation within twenty (20) days, exclusive of the period of recess, after the House of Representatives has made designation, the decision of the House of Representatives shall be the decision of the Diet.

Article LXIV. The Prime Minister shall, with the approval of the Diet, appoint the Ministers of State. The second paragraph of the preceding article shall apply to this approval.

The Prime Minister may remove Ministers of State as he chooses.

Article LXV. If the House of Representatives passes a no-confidence resolution, or rejects a confidence resolution, the Cabinet shall resign en masse, unless the House of Representatives is dissolved within ten days.

Article LXVI. When there is a vacancy in the post of Prime Minister, or upon the convocation of the Diet after a general election, the Cabinet shall resign en masse.

Article LXVII. In the cases mentioned in the two preceding articles, the Cabinet shall continue its functions until the time when a new Prime Minister is appointed.

Article LXVIII. The Prime Minister, representing the Cabinet, submits bills, reports on general national affairs and foreign relations to the Diet, and exercises supervision and control over various administrative branches.

Article LXIX. The Cabinet, in addition to other general administrative functions, shall:

Administer the law faithfully; conduct affairs of State.

Manage foreign affairs.

Conclude treaties. However, it shall obtain prior or, depending on circumstances, subsequent approval of the Diet.

In accordance with standards established by law, administer the civil service.

Prepare the budget, and present it to the Diet.

Enact cabinet orders in order to carry out the provisions of this Constitution and of the law. However, it cannot include penal provisions in such cabinet orders unless authorized by such law.

Decide on general amnesty, special amnesty, commutation of punishment, reprieve, and restoration of rights.

Article LXX. All laws and cabinet orders shall be signed by the competent Minister of State, and countersigned by the Prime Minister.

Article LXXI. The Ministers of State, during their tenure of office, shall not be subject to legal action without the consent of the Prime Minister, but the right to take that action is not impaired hereby.

CHAPTER 6

Judiciary

Article LXXII. The whole judicial power is vested in a Supreme Court and in such inferior courts as are established by law.

No extraordinary tribunal shall be established, nor shall any organ or agency of the Executive be given final judicial power.

All judges shall be independent in the exercise of their conscience and shall be bound only by this Constitution and the laws enacted pursuant thereto.

Article LXXIII. The Supreme Court is vested with the rule-making power under which it determines the rules of procedure and of practice, and of matters relating to attorneys, the internal discipline of the courts and the administration of judicial affairs.

Public procurators shall be subject to the rule-making power of the Supreme Court.

The Supreme Court may delegate the power to make rules for inferior courts to such courts.

Article LXXIV. Removals of judges shall be accomplished by public impeachment only unless judicially declared mentally or physically incompetent. No disciplinary action shall be administered by any executive organ or agency.

Article LXXV. The Supreme Court shall consist of such number of judges as may be determined by law; all such judges shall be appointed by the Cabinet and shall be retired upon the attainment of the age as fixed by law.

The appointment of the judges of the Supreme Court shall be reviewed by the people at the first general election of the House of Representatives following their appointment, and shall be reviewed again at the first general election of the House of Representatives after a lapse of ten years, and in the same manner thereafter.

In cases mentioned in the foregoing paragraph, when the majority of the voters show that they favor the dismissal of a judge concerned, he shall be dismissed.

Matters pertaining to the review mentioned in the foregoing paragraphs shall be prescribed by law.

All such judges shall receive, at regular, stated intervals, adequate compensation which shall not be decreased during their terms of office.

Article LXXVI. The judges of the inferior courts shall be appointed by the Cabinet from a list of persons nominated by the Supreme Court. All such judges shall hold office for a term of ten years with privilege of reappointment, provided that they shall be retired upon the attainment of the age as fixed by law. The judges of the inferior courts shall receive, at regular, stated intervals, adequate compensation which shall not be decreased during their terms of office.

Article LXXVII. The Supreme Court is the court of last resort with power to determine the constitutionality of any law, order, regulation or official act.

Article LXXVIII. Trials shall be conducted and judgment declared publicly. Where, however, a court unanimously determines publicity to be dangerous to public order or morals, a trial may be conducted privately, but trials of political offenses, offenses involving the press, and cases wherein the rights of the people as reserved in Chapter 3 of this Constitution are in question, shall be conducted publicly without exception.

CHAPTER 7

Finance

Article LXXIX. The power to administer national finances shall be exercised as the Diet shall determine.

Article LXXX. No new taxes shall be imposed or existing ones modified except by law or under such conditions as law may prescribe.

Article LXXXI. No money shall be expended, nor shall the State obligate itself, except as authorized by the Diet.

Article LXXXII. The Cabinet shall prepare and submit to the Diet for its consideration and decision an annual budget for each fiscal year.

Article LXXXIII. In order to provide for unforeseen deficiencies in the budget a reserve fund may be authorized by the Diet to be expended upon the responsibility of the Cabinet.

The Cabinet shall be held accountable to the Diet for all payments from the reserve fund.

Article LXXXIV. All property of the Imperial Household, other than the hereditary estates, shall belong to the State. The income from all Imperial properties shall be paid into the national treasury, and allowances and expenses of the Imperial Household, as defined by law, shall be appropriated by the Diet in the annual budget.

Article LXXXV. No public money or property shall be appropriated for the use, benefit or support of any system of religion, or religious institution or association, or for any charitable, educational or benevolent purposes not under the control of public authority.

Article LXXXVI. A final audit of all expenditures and revenues of the State shall be made annually by a board of audit and submitted by the Cabinet to the Diet during the fiscal year immediately following the period covered.

The organization and competency of the board of audit shall be determined by law.

Article LXXXVII. At regular intervals and at least annually the Cabinet shall report to the Diet and the people on the state of national finances.

CHAPTER 8

Local Self Government

Article LXXXVIII. Regulations concerning organization and operations of local public entities shall be fixed by law in accordance with the principle of local autonomy.

Article LXXXIX. The local public entities shall establish assemblies as their deliberative organs, in accordance with law.

The chief executive officers of all local public entities, the members of their legislative assemblies, and such other local officials as may be determined by law shall be elected by direct popular vote within their several communities.

Article XC. Local public entities shall have the right to manage their property, affairs and government and to frame their own charters within such laws as the Diet may enact.

Article XCI. A special law, applicable only to one local public entity, cannot be enacted by the Diet without the consent of the majority of the voters of the local public entity concerned, obtained in accordance with law.

CHAPTER 9

Amendments

Article XCII. Amendments to this Constitution shall be initiated by the Diet, through a concurring vote of two-thirds of all the members of each House and shall thereupon be submitted to the people for ratification, which shall require the affirmative vote of a majority of all votes cast at a special referendum thereon or at such election as the Diet shall specify.

Amendments when so ratified shall immediately be proclaimed by the Emperor, in the name of the People, as an integral part of this Constitution.

CHAPTER 10

Supreme Law

Article XCIII. The fundamental human rights by this Constitution guaranteed to the people of Japan result from the age-old struggle of man to be free. They have survived the exacting test for durability in the crucible of time and experience, and are conferred upon this and future generations in sacred trust, to be held for all time inviolate.

Article XCIV. This Constitution and the laws and treaties made in pursuance hereof shall be the supreme law of the state and no public law or ordinance and no imperial rescript or other act of government, or part thereof, contrary to the provisions hereof, shall have legal force or validity.

Article XCV. The Emperor or the Regent, the Ministers of State, the members of the Diet, judges, and all other public officials have the obligation to respect and uphold this Constitution.

CHAPTER 11

Supplementary Provisions

Article XCVI. This Constitution shall be enforced as from the day when the period of six months will have elapsed counting from the day of its promulgation.

The enactment of laws necessary for the enforcement of this Constitution, the election of members of the House of Councillors and the procedure for the convocation of the Diet and other preparatory procedures necessary for the enforcement of this Constitution may be executed before the day prescribed in the preceding paragraph.

Article XCVII. As regards those who hold peerage on the effective date of this Constitution, their title shall remain valid for their lives, but no right of peerage shall from this time forth embody within itself any power of government.

Article XCVIII. If the House of Councillors is not constituted before the effective date of this Constitution, the House of Representatives shall sit as the Diet on that date and until such time as the House of Councillors shall be constituted.

Article XCIX. The term of office for half the members of the House of Councillors serving in the first term under this Constitution shall be three years. Members falling under this category shall be determined in accordance with law.

Article C. The Ministers of State, members of the House of Representatives and judges in office on the effective date of this Constitution, and all other public officials who occupy positions corresponding to such positions as are recognized by this Constitution shall not forfeit their positions automatically on the effective date of this Constitution unless otherwise specified by law. When, however, successors are elected or appointed under the provisions of this Constitution they shall forfeit their positions as a matter of course.

APPENDIX H

Text of Moscow Tripartite Communique

(December 28, 1945)

EXCERPT PERTAINING TO KOREA:

1. With a view to the re-establishment of Korea as an independent state, the creation of conditions for developing the country on democratic principles and the earliest possible liquidation of the disastrous results of the protracted Japanese domination in Korea, there shall be set up a provisional Korean democratic government which shall take all the necessary steps for developing the industry, transport and agriculture of Korea and the national culture of the Korean people.

2. In order to assist the formation of a provisional Korean government and with a view to the preliminary elaboration of the appropriate measures, there shall be established a joint commission consisting of representatives of the United States command in Southern Korea and the Soviet command in Northern Korea.

In preparing their proposals the commission shall consult with the Korean democratic parties and social organizations.

The recommendations worked out by the commission shall be presented for the consideration of the governments of the Union of Soviet Socialist Republics, China, the United Kingdom and the United States prior to final decision by the two governments represented on the joint commission.

3. It shall be the task of the joint commission, with the participation of the provisional Korean democratic government and of the Korean democratic organizations, to work out measures also for helping and assisting (trusteeship) the political, economic and social progress of the Korean people, the development of democratic self-government and the establishment of the national independence of Korea.

The proposals of the joint commission shall be submitted, following consultation with the provisional Korean government for the joint consideration of the governments of the United States, Union of Soviet Socialist Republics, United Kingdom and China for the working out of an agreement concerning a four-power trusteeship of Korea for a period up to five years.

4. For the consideration of urgent problems affecting both Southern and Northern Korea and for the elaboration of measures establishing

414

permanent coordination in administration-economic matters between the United States command in Southern Korea and the Soviet command in Northern Korea, a conference of the representatives of the United States and Soviet commands in Korea shall be convened within a period of two weeks.

APPENDIX I

U. S. Policy Toward China

Statement by President Harry S. Truman

(*December 15, 1945*)

The Government of the United States holds that peace and prosperity of the world in this new and unexplored era ahead depend upon the ability of the sovereign nations to combine for collective security in the United Nations Organization.

It is the firm belief of this Government that a strong, united and democratic China is of the utmost importance to the success of this United Nations Organization and for world peace. A China disorganized and divided either by foreign aggression, such as that undertaken by the Japanese, or by violent internal strife, is an undermining influence to world stability and peace, now and in the future.

The United States Government has long subscribed to the principle that the management of internal affairs is the responsibility of the people of the sovereign nations. Events of this century, however, would indicate that a breach of peace anywhere in the world threatens the peace of the entire world. It is thus in the most vital interest of the United States and all the United Nations that the people of China overlook no opportunity to adjust their internal differences promptly by methods of peaceful negotiation.

The Government of the United States believes it essential:

1.—That a cessation of hostilities be arranged between the armies of the National Government and the Chinese Communists and other dissident Chinese armed forces for the purpose of completing the return of all China to effective Chinese control, including the immediate evacuation of the Japanese forces.

2.—That a national conference of representatives of major political elements be arranged to develop an early solution to the present internal strife—a solution which will bring about the unification of China.

The United States and the other United Nations have recognized the present National Government of the Republic of China as the only legal Government in China. It is the proper instrument to achieve the objective of a unified China.

The United States and the United Kingdom by the Cairo Declaration in 1943, and the Union of Soviet Socialist Republics, by adhering to the Potsdam Declaration of last July and by the Sino-Soviet treaty and agreement of August 1945 are all committed to the liberation of China, including the return of Manchuria to Chinese control. These agreements were made with the National Government of the Republic of China.

In continuation of the constant and close collaboration with the National Government of the Republic of China in the prosecution of this war, in consonance with the Potsdam Declaration, and to remove possibility of Japanese influence remaining in China, the United States has assumed a definite obligation in the disarmament and evacuation of the Japanese troops.

Accordingly, the United States has been assisting and will continue to assist the National Government of the Republic of China in effecting the disarmament and evacuation of Japanese troops in the liberated areas. The United States Marines are in North China for that purpose.

The United States recognizes and will continue to recognize the National Government of China and cooperate with it in international affairs and specifically in eliminating Japanese influence from China. The United States is convinced that a prompt arrangement for a cessation of hostilities is essential to the effective achievement of this end.

United States support will not extend to United States military intervention to influence the course of any Chinese internal strife.

The United States has already been compelled to pay a great price to restore the peace which was first broken by Japanese aggression in Manchuria. The maintenance of peace in the Pacific may be jeopardized, if not frustrated, unless Japanese influence in China is wholly removed and unless China takes her place as a unified, democratic and peaceful nation. This is the purpose of the maintenance, for the time being, of United States military and naval forces in China.

The United States is cognizant that the present National Government of China is a one-party Government and believes that peace, unity and democratic reform in China will be furthered if the basis of this Government is broadened to include other political elements in the country. Hence, the United States strongly advocates that the national conference of representatives of major political elements in the country agree upon arrangements which would give those elements a fair and effective representation in the Chinese National Government. It is recognized that this would require modification of the one-party political tutelage established as an interim arrangement in the progress of the nation toward democracy by the Father of the Chinese Republic, Dr. Sun Yat-sen.

The existence of autonomous armies, such as that of the Communist army, is inconsistent with, and actually makes impossible, political unity in China. With the institution of a broadly representative government, autonomous armies should be eliminated as such and all armed forces in China integrated effectively into the Chinese National Army.

In line with its often expressed views regarding self-determination, the United States Government considers that the detailed steps necessary to the achievement of political unity in China must be worked out by the Chinese themselves and that intervention by any foreign government in these matters would be inappropriate.

The United States Government feels, however, that China has a clear responsibility to the other United Nations to eliminate armed conflict within its territory as constituting a threat to world stability and peace—a responsibility which is shared by the National Government and all Chinese political and military groups.

As China moves toward peace and unity along the lines described above, the United States would be prepared to assist the National Government in every reasonable way to rehabilitate the country, improve the agrarian and industrial economy, and establish a military organization capable of discharging China's national and international responsibilities for the maintenance of peace and order.

In furtherance of such assistance, it would be prepared to give favorable consideration to Chinese requests for credits and loans under reasonable conditions for projects which would contribute toward the development of a healthy economy throughout China and healthy trade relations between China and the United States.

APPENDIX J

Marshall's Report on China

(*Text of statement by General of the Army George C. Marshall, President Truman's Special Ambassador to China, on the situation in China, at Nanking, Jan. 7, 1947. The statement was made only a few hours before announcement of General Marshall's appointment as U. S. Secretary of State.*)

The President has recently given a summary of the developments in China during the past year and the position of the American Government toward China. Circumstances now dictate that I should supplement this with impressions gained at first hand.

In this intricate and confused situation, I shall merely endeavor here to touch on some of the more important considerations—as they appear to me—during my connection with the negotiations to bring about peace in China and a stable democratic form of government.

In the first place, the greatest obstacle to peace has been the complete, almost overwhelming suspicion with which the Chinese Communist Party and the Kuomintang regard each other.

On the one hand, the leaders of the Government are strongly opposed to a Communistic form of government. On the other, the Communists frankly state that they are Marxists and intend to work toward establishing a Communistic form of government in China, though first advancing through the medium of a democratic form of government of the American or British type.

The leaders of the Government are convinced in their minds that the Communist-expressed desire to participate in a government of the type endorsed by the Political Consultative Conference last January had for its purpose only a destructive intention. The Communists felt, I believe, that the Government was insincere in its apparent acceptance of the PCC resolution for the formation of the new government and intended by coercion of military force and the action of secret police to obliterate the Communist Party. Combined with this mutual deep distrust was the conspicuous error by both parties of ignoring the effect of the fears and suspicions of the other party in estimating the reason for proposals or opposition regarding the settlement of various matters under negotiation. They each sought only to take counsel of their own fears. They both, therefore, to that extent took a rather lopsided view of each situation and were susceptible to every evil suggestion or possibility. This compli-

419

cation was exaggerated to an explosive degree by the confused reports of fighting on the distant and tremendous fronts of hostile military contact. Patrol clashes were deliberately magnified into large offensive actions. The distortion of the facts was utilized by both sides to heap condemnation on the other. It was only through the reports of American officers in the field, teams from Executive Headquarters, that I could get even a partial idea of what was actually happening and the incidents were too numerous and the distances too great for the American personnel to cover all of the ground. I must comment here on the superb courage of the officers of our Army and Marines in struggling against almost insurmountable and maddening obstacles to bring some measure of peace to China.

I think the most important factors involved in the recent breakdown of negotiations are these: On the side of the National Government, which is in effect the Kuomintang Party, there is a dominant group of reactionaries who have been opposed, in my opinion, to almost every effort I have made to influence the formation of a genuine coalition government. This has usually been under the cover of political or party action, but since the party was the Government, this action, though subtle or indirect, has been devastating in its effect. They were quite frank in publicly stating their belief that co-operation by the Chinese Communist Party in the Government was inconceivable and that only a policy of force could definitely settle the issue. This group includes military as well as political leaders.

On the side of the Chinese Communist Party, there are, I believe, liberals as well as radicals, though this view is vigorously opposed by many who believe that the Chinese Communist Party discipline is too rigidly enforced to admit of such differences of viewpoint. Nevertheless, it has appeared to me that there is a definite liberal group among the Communists, especially of young men who have turned to the Communists in disgust at the corruption evident in the local governments —men who would put the interest of the Chinese people above ruthless measures to establish a Communist ideology in the immediate future. The dyed-in-the-wool Communists do not hesitate at the most drastic measures to gain their end as, for instance, the destruction of communications in order to wreck the economy of China and produce a situation that would facilitate the overthrow or collapse of the Government, without any regard to the immediate suffering of the people involved. They completely distrust the leaders of the Kuomintang Party and appear convinced that every Government proposal is designed to crush the Chinese Communist Party. I must say that the quite evidently inspired mob actions of last February and March, some within a few blocks of where I was then engaged in completing negotiations, gave the Communists good excuse for such suspicions.

However, a very harmful and immensely provocative phase of the Chinese Communist Party procedure has been in the character of its propaganda. I wish to state to the American people that, in the deliberate misrepresentation and abuse of the action, policies and purposes of our

Government, this propaganda has been without regard for the truth, without any regard whatsoever for the facts, and has given plain evidence of a determined purpose to mislead the Chinese people and the world and to arouse a bitter hatred of Americans. It has been difficult to remain silent in the midst of such public abuse and wholesale disregard of facts, but a denial would merely lead to the necessity of daily denials; an intolerable course of action for an American official. In the interest of fairness, I must state that the Nationalist Government publicity agency has made numerous misrepresentations, though not of the vicious nature of the Communist propaganda. Incidentally, the Communist statements regarding the Anping incident which resulted in the death of three marines and the wounding of 12 others were almost pure fabrication, deliberately representing a carefully arranged ambuscade of a marine convoy with supplies for the maintenance of Executive Headquarters and some UNRRA supplies, as a defense against a marine assault. The investigation of this incident was a tortuous procedure of delays and maneuvers to disguise the true and privately admitted facts of the case.

Sincere efforts to achieve settlement have been frustrated time and again by extremist elements of both sides. The agreements reached by the Political Consultative Conference a year ago were a liberal and forward-looking charter which then offered China a basis for peace and reconstruction. However, irreconcilable groups within the Kuomintang Party, interested in the preservation of their own feudal control of China, evidently had no real intention of implementing them. Though I speak as a soldier, I must here also deplore the dominating influence of the military. Their dominance accentuates the weakness of civil government in China. At the same time, in pondering the situation in China, one must have clearly in mind not the workings of small Communist groups or committees to which we are accustomed in America, but rather of millions of people and an army of more than 1,000,000 men.

I have never been in a position to be certain of the development of attitudes in the innermost Chinese Communist circles. Most certainly, the course which the Chinese Communist Party has pursued in recent months indicated an unwillingness to make a fair compromise. It has been impossible even to get them to sit down at a conference table with Government representatives to discuss given issues. Now the Communists have broken off negotiations by their last offer which demanded the dissolution of the National Assembly and a return to the military positions of January 13 which the Government could not be expected to accept.

Between this dominant reactionary group in the Government and the irreconcilable Communists who, I must state, did not so appear last February, lies the problem of how peace and well being are to be brought to the long-suffering and presently inarticulate mass of the people of China. The reactionaries in the Government have evidently counted on substantial American support regardless of their actions. The Communists by their unwillingness to compromise in the national interest are evidently counting on an economic collapse to bring about the fall of the Government, accelerated by extensive guerrilla action against the long lines of rail communications—regardless of the cost in suffering to the Chinese people.

The salvation of the situation, as I see it, would be the assumption of leadership by the liberals in the Government and in the minority parties, a splendid group of men, but who as yet lack the political power to exercise a controlling influence. Successful action on their part under the leadership of Generalissimo Chiang Kai-shek would, I believe, lead to unity through good government.

In fact, the National Assembly has adopted a democratic Constitution which in all major respects is in accordance with the principles laid down by the all-party Political Consultative Conference of last January. It is unfortunate that the Communists did not see fit to participate in the Assembly since the Constitution that has been adopted seems to include every major point that they wanted.

Soon the Government in China will undergo major reorganization pending the coming into force of the Constitution following elections to be completed before Christmas Day 1947. Now that the form for a democratic China has been laid down by the newly adopted Constitution, practical measures will be the test. It remains to be seen to what extent the Government will give substance to the form by a genuine welcome of all groups actively to share in the responsibility of Government.

The first step will be the reorganization of the State Council and the Executive Branch of Government to carry on administration pending the enforcement of the Constitution. The manner in which this is done and the amount of representation accorded to liberals and to non-Kuomintang members will be significant. It is also to be hoped that during this interim period the door will remain open for Communists or other groups to participate if they see fit to assume their share of responsibility for the future of China.

It has been stated officially and categorically that the period of political tutelage under the Kuomintang is at an end. If the termination of one-party rule is to be a reality, the Kuomintang should cease to receive financial support from the Government.

I have spoken very frankly because in no other way can I hope to bring the people of the U. S. to even a partial understanding of this complex problem. I have expressed all these views privately in the course of negotiations; they are well known, I think, to most of the individuals concerned. I express them now publicly, as it is my duty, to present my estimate of the situation and its possibilities to the American people who have a deep interest in the development of conditions in the Far East promising an enduring peace in the Pacific.

INDEX